50 YEARS RECEIVING VATICAN II

In gratitude to Brian and Pat and their incredible family who continue to help me stay in touch with the reality of everyday life.

Kevin T. Kelly

50 Years Receiving Vatican II

A Personal Odyssey

the columba press

First published in 2012 by
the columba press
55A Spruce Avenue, Stillorgan Industrial Park,
Blackrock, Co Dublin

Cover by Bill Bolger
Original artwork for the cover, *Orange Light*, by Deirdre Crowley
www.deirdrecrowleyart.ie

Origination by The Columba Press
Printed by SPRINT-print

ISBN 978 1 85607 7774

All royalties from the publication of this book will be donated equally
between CAFOD and Trócaire according to the author's wishes.

Contents

The Eucharist and Vatican II

Conclusion

KEY TO ABBREVIATIONS

Vatican II Documents

LG   *Lumen Gentium* Constitution on the Church

GS   *Gaudium et Spes* Pastoral Constitution on the Church in the
                    World of Today

SC   *Sacrosanctum Concilium* Constitution on the Sacred Liturgy

My own published books

NDMT   *New Directions in Moral Theology: The Challenge of Being
            Human*, London, Geoffrey Chapman, 1992

NDSE   *New Directions in Sexual Ethics: Moral Theology and the
            Challenge of AIDS*, London, Geoffrey Chapman, 1998

FPB   *From a Parish Base: Essays in Moral and Pastoral Theology*,
            London, Darton, Longman & Todd, 1999

Unfortunately, all the above are out-of-print. However, the respective publishers have kindly given me permission to make the texts available, free of charge, online. Courtesy of Liverpool Hope University, they can be accessed at the following address (alongside a comprehensive bibliography of my other writings):

http://www.hope.ac.uk/theology-religious-studies/kevin-t-kelly.html

Other Abbreviations

CDF   Congregation for the Doctrine of the Faith

UNI   Upholland Northern Institute

ICEL   International Commission for English in the Liturgy

CDW   Congregation for Divine Worship

EE   *Ecclesia de Eucharistia*   Encyclical on the Eucharist in its
                                           Relationship to the Church

FOREWORD

Vatican II opened on 11 October 1962. I had been ordained as a priest four years previously in 1958. Hence, 'receiving Vatican II' has been a major inspiration for most of my fifty-four years of service in the ministerial priesthood. Having experienced Catholic life prior to Vatican II, I am able to appreciate what a Spirit-inspired and transforming gift the Council has been to our life, liturgy and theological understanding in the Catholic Church. Moreover, 'receiving Vatican II' is an ongoing process. The challenge at present is to keep that process alive and on course and to resist any temptation to backtrack in any way on the fundamental vision and spirit of Vatican II. When I get the impression, as at present, that this seems to be what is happening, it pains me very deeply. It is like discarding or even burying a precious treasure that has been offered to us by the Spirit.

In the fifty years following Vatican II I have had the great privilege of being involved in pastoral work in a variety of challenging and very exciting parish settings. During those years I have also taught and written as a moral theologian. Whenever possible, I have tried to combine both these ministries at one and the same time. I hope that has added a special pastoral dimension to my talks and writings over the years. My hope has been that, in their various ways, these different facets of my ministry have all been inspired by the spirit and teaching of Vatican II. In fact, when I looked back at the end of five years involvement in Clergy In-Service Training and Adult Christian Education, it struck me very forcibly that the kind of work I had been doing was actually a form of remedial education, for myself as well as for others. It had been a case of trying to interiorise the spirit of Vatican II so that I could in turn share it with others. Because of my grass-roots pastoral involvement, many of my writings have dealt with practical issues affecting people's everyday lives, often touching neuralgic moral issues, including how people have struggled to cope with teaching which they feel is contrary to their own experience or pastorally unhelpful in the complexity of their lives.

After I finally retired from parish ministry, I had more time to trawl through my writings and unpublished papers to see if any of them might still be pastorally helpful to people even in our changed situation of the early twenty-first century. For a while I found it difficult to see how I could give any kind of coherence to the items which I thought might possibly still be helpful to readers today. A hotchpotch of disconnected writings would not make an attractive book. Hence, I struggled for some time with this project, finding it difficult to summon up any enthusiasm for it. Perhaps also the ageing process was affecting my concentration and creativity!

Then the light dawned, thanks to my good friend and former teacher, Ladislas Orsy SJ, an inspired and inspiring canon lawyer, now in his late 80s. In the Epilogue to his *Receiving the Council* (Collegeville, Liturgical Press, 2009), he reminds his readers of the resounding cry *Adsumus* – 'We are present and attentive to the Spirit' - of the Bishops at the beginning of each day's deliberations during the four years of Vatican II. He ends his book with the following proposal:

> Whereas the years from 2012 through 2015 will be the fiftieth anniversaries of the Council, they should be solemnly declared the years of the Council – when the entire people, 'from the bishops to the last of the faithful' (*Lumen Gentium*, 2, quoting St Augustine), recalls the memory of the 'Sacred Council', studies its determinations, and exposes itself to the transforming light and force of the Spirit – as the Council Fathers did. Over four years again, let the cry *Adsumus*, 'we are present and attentive, resound – not within the walls of St Peter's Basilica but throughout the face of the earth. The Spirit of God will not fail to respond' (p. 152).

It suddenly struck me that the link unifying all my writings and pastoral experience was the reception of Vatican II. It has been my burning conviction that God's Spirit was present and active within the Church and the world in a very special way in the Council; and that over the fifty years since then we have been given the privilege and responsibility of being channels of the Spirit enabling Vatican II to be made flesh in real life. That suggested to me an appropriate title for this book, *50 Years Receiving Vatican II*. This reception process is something all of us in the Church are involved in and share a responsibility for.

It is not a simple process. It involves struggle. Not all in the Church see Vatican II in the way I do. Tragically, some even look on Vatican II as a disaster. My own belief is that it is greatest gift of the Spirit to the Church in our age. I feel that deeply in my bones, in my heart and in my mind. I know I am not alone in that. In fact, it was also the overwhelming conviction of the vast majority of the bishops attending the Council. So, although my enthusiasm for Vatican II is deeply personal, it is not something purely individualistic and subjective. I feel it links me to the faith of the whole church. This realisation has given me a sense of purpose. Maybe, by sharing some of my writings and reflections over the years since Vatican II, I might be able to make a little contribution to a combined Golden Jubilee process of rekindling the Spirit of Vatican II and giving a new impetus to the reawakening of its vision in the church.

After a talk I gave on one occasion a woman said to me, 'Thank you for what you said. You put into words what I have always believed but have never been able to express.' I know I am not an original thinker. I do not come up with new insights or ideas. Nevertheless, in my extensive reading of the Vatican II texts and commentaries and later writings on the Council, I have 'received' a definite vision, spirit and meaning of Vatican II. When I have shared that with others whose views and spirituality I respect, they have responded very affirmatively. The fact that they share that same vision confirms me in my belief. If they disagree on certain points and help me to see that there might be more to an issue than I am aware of, that enables me to refine my position. We are a learning Church as well as a teaching Church. That has implications for the respect due to the Magisterium in the Church. However, that is a topic which will dealt with more thoroughly later in this collection.

In a number of my writings, I have asked readers to add the phrase 'I may be wrong but …' to every personal judgement I make. That is not just a 'get out' clause! But neither is it because I believe that my judgement might well be wrong! In fact, I believe, usually very profoundly, that what I say is true. Yet, I recognize my personal limitations. That is why I constantly pray to the Spirit for the gift of wisdom and for the healing of any blindness in me.

This book is not a systematic study of Vatican II. That would be beyond me, especially at this time in my life. All I am trying to do is share with readers some of what 'receiving Vatican II' has meant to me over the years. For much of the time I have been able to combine my teaching and research as a moral theologian with my pastoral ministry in a number of exciting and challenging placements in Liverpool Archdiocese. That has been a wonderful opportunity for what my good friend, Jack Mahoney SJ, has described as 'making faith-sense of experience and experience-sense of faith'. The pieces in this personal odyssey are largely the result of my trying to be faithful to Jack's advice. I have tried to listen to the stories of people's experiences in the light of the story of Jesus as told in the Gospels and at a time in the life of the Catholic Church when the inspired insights of Vatican II have opened our eyes to so much buried treasure in our Christian story down through the ages. Moreover, the experiences of people have been given an added depth as a result of the riches made available to us in our modern age through the explosion of human knowledge and the advances in scientific technology.

This amazing increase in human knowledge has thrown fresh light on who we are as human persons. Moreover, modern technology has changed the nature of human communication with the result that our understanding of our one world has opened up for us entirely new avenues of experience. Such new experience reveals to us entirely new ways of being true to our Christian vision. As the Gospel says, the wise man brings forth from his riches new things and old. A medieval writer makes the same point when he says 'we see further than our forebears – we are like dwarfs sitting on the shoulders of giants'. Dwarfs we may indeed be but we really do see further from our raised vantage point. New horizons have opened up for us.

It was this approach to faith and life that Vatican II opened up for us with its embracing fully the truth of historical consciousness. We are now much more aware of what has, in fact, always been true, namely, that we are makers of history. We do not just exist in history. We exist as history. That is true of ourselves as human persons and of the communities, societies and cultures in which we live. Darwin's 'Theory of Evolution' has opened our eyes to how far reaching is this truth. It is equally true of God's dealings with our human family and with the whole of creation. And it is certainly true of the Church and our Christian vision. I am further encouraged by the fact that my good friend, Jack Mahoney SJ, has just produced a challenging new book which explores the implications for our Christian faith of living in an evolutionary context: *Christianity in Evolution*, Georgetown UP, Washington DC, 2011. We can no longer close our eyes to the kind of human persons we are as historical beings. That is how God has made us – and our world. Our Christian faith in the Incarnation is simply recognising that God reveals Godself within history.

I have called this a 'personal' odyssey because most of the pieces that follow either give an account of some of my own experiences or those of people whom I have known and respect. Also included are some of my personal reflections on life and ministry in the Catholic Church during the years following Vatican II up to the present. Some are about the kind of pastoral practice I have followed or are examples of the pastoral advice I have offered over the past fifty years. Others are talks I have given to help fellow Catholics receive Vatican II in practice or understand the underlying spirit of the changes it was promoting in the life of the Church and its relationship with other Churches, faiths and the world in general.

I have called it an 'odyssey' because I have experienced all I am writing about as part of an ongoing journey. It has not been a journey in a straight line, all plain sailing. There have been plenty of storms on the way, detours and deviations, and the final destination, though assured, is hidden in the distant mists. It has certainly not been a boring, uneventful journey. And it has been an enjoyable journey.

Moreover, my odyssey is very much a shared journey – an ecumenical and inter-faith pilgrimage along with all other human beings. After all, as human beings we are essentially interdependent. The Africans have an expression for it – Ubuntu. And as Christians we are conscious of our interdependence in an even deeper sense. And in the age in which we are living, we are more aware how closely this interdependence links us to all living creatures and the whole of creation. Moreover, the Lord is with us all the way on this odyssey.

Many of the items in this collection have been published previously, as chapters in books, or as contributions to periodicals. On re-reading them, far from finding them 'past their sell-by date', I have actually found them rekindling my own commitment and enthusiasm for the spirit of Vatican II. To be perfectly honest, I have found some of them very exciting. I hope at least some readers will be touched in a similar way.

Receiving Vatican II is an ongoing process. It is a long road to take. It does not yet seem to have reached the stage of solving or eliminating most of the pastoral problems discussed. In fact, readers will notice that some of the practical issues keep coming up again and again en route. I was tempted to eliminate all such repetitions. However, on further reflection, I felt that would weaken the text. In the end, I have kept in the text repeated considerations of such neuralgic issues as same-sex relationships, remarriage after divorce, contraception and women priests.

When appropriate, I have taken the liberty of altering the original text, sometimes for the sake of clarity and sometimes because my thinking has developed further or the pastoral scenario had changed. Also, I have added short explanatory introductions to most of the items. I hope these will situate contributions in their original contexts and also point the reader to their wider ramifications.

There are four sections to the book. The first section is by way of an introduction. It is intended to set the tone of the whole work. This is not an abstract volume intended to grace the shelves of academia. It is motivated by a desire to further the process of 'receiving' Vatican II in the Church at large. That will not happen unless there is a deep appreciation that Vatican II is truly a personal 'gift' given to all of us by God's Spirit. In this overview I share how that gift has affected me personally. For me to have lived in the age of Vatican II and its aftermath has been an immense privilege.

The second section, 'Parish and Pastoral Ministry in the light of Vatican II', looks at some of the implications of Vatican II for parish life and pastoral ministry. As well as reminding readers of the high promise engendered by the 1980 National Pastoral Congress, it includes a thorough examination of the key issue of collaborative ministry and also a theological reflection on reports from various parishes drawn from a professional survey covering a number of dioceses. This section also includes an account and critique of my own very privileged ten-year experience as parish priest in a shared RC/Anglican Church in Widnes.

Since an important part of my personal odyssey has involved my role as a moral theologian, it is natural that there should be a distinct section entitled, 'Moral Theology after Vatican II'. This includes reflections on my own experience as a moral theologian as well as my appreciation of two of my fellow moral theologians. There are also items on some general and specific issues such as conscience, authority, collegiality, believing in a sinful Church, the divorced-remarried, clerical sex-abuse and HIV/AIDS prevention and condoms.

In the fourth section, 'The Eucharist and Vatican II', there are reflections on the role and impact of the Eucharist in the parish and in the wider Church community. It also covers some neuralgic issues linked to ministry and priest-hood and the new translation of the Missal and the core principles of person-centred liturgy.

Because experience has played such a major part in my personal odyssey, I decided to include in the concluding section a few examples of some formative experiences from earlier in my life. They are a few extracts from my diary of a two-month visit to India, the Philippines and Peru. The extracts are all taken from my time in the Philippines. I see them as symbolic of the amazing inter-dependence which lies at the heart our lives as Christians and human persons. Reflecting the fact that I am approaching my 80th birthday, the concluding section also looks at retirement and theology. It closes with a short chapter facing the important question, 'Are we ready for Vatican III?'

My fervent hope and prayer is that this book will offer something life-giving for the good of all and that it might reawaken enthusiasm for Vatican II in the hearts of those for whom it is but a distant memory or an item of ancient history.

In the course of my personal odyssey I have been fortunate to have had five books published. Sadly they are all now out of print. The first was my doctoral dissertation, written prior to Vatican II. All the others were attempts to express as clearly as I could where I felt the reception of Vatican II was taking the Church, especially in its moral theology and pastoral practice. Hence, they played an important role in my personal odyssey. Moreover, in addition to con-tributing chapters to various books, I have also had the privilege of having nu-merous articles published in the following journals and periodicals in the UK and Ireland, *The Tablet*, *The Furrow*, *The Clergy Review*, *The Month*, *Priest and Peo-ple*, *New Blackfriars*, *The Way*, and the supplement to *The Way*.

In my introduction to the various chapters, I acknowledge whenever the content is drawn from the above sources including my three most recently pub-lished books listed on the final page. I am most grateful to the publishers, T & T Clark (Continuum) and Darton Longman & Todd and the Porticus Trust for permission to include quotations or longer sections from my writings published by them. I am also very grateful for permission to include articles originally published in the journals and periodicals listed at the end of the previous para-graph.

I would also like to add a special word of thanks to Sister Mary McCallion SND who painstakingly read the whole script and alerted me not only to typos but, even more importantly, to places where my words have not done justice to the truth I was trying to convey. My thanks are also due to Philomena Harvey and Kitty Cannon for providing typing assistance when needed. A lot of very good friends have been very supportive and patient with me during the years I have been working on this project. I will not mention them by name but they know how grateful I am to them for their friendship and encouragement.

Last but not least I would like to thank Columba Press for welcoming this book so graciously and for publishing it at such short notice in time to celebrate the fiftieth anniversary of Vatican II, and to Donal O'Leary, for introducing me to them. I am particularly grateful to Michael Brennan for his initial welcome and especially to Patrick O' Donoghue and Fearghal O Boyle who have overseen the production process with immense care from beginning to end. Also, to Valerie Devitt and Shane McCoy I extend my thanks for all their help. To Bill Bolger who was responsible for designing the fantastic cover I extend my deepest gratitude.

The striking and very beautiful landscape painting on the front cover is the work of Deirdre Crowley, a well-known Cork artist. I am deeply grateful to Deirdre for accepting my invitation to contribute so significantly to the cover. Deirdre's uncle, the late Fr Pat Crowley, was a very close friend of mine. He played a key role in my post-Vatican II odyssey. Along with the other members of the Upholland Northern Institute, between 1975 and 1980 we shared in the experience of introducing the riches of Vatican II to priests and laity in the north of England, a steep learning curve for ourselves and all concerned – a truly inspirational experience. Deirdre's powerful painting captures very vividly the excitement and hopes of the new life generated in the Church through the Spirit-inspired Vatican II experience. It suggests the inextinguishable fire of the Holy Spirit blazing out anew from the inner depths of the Church after Vatican II, a fire bringing warmth and life to everything touched by its flame; also a purifying fire capable of melting the hearts of any resisting the reception of the Sprit-inspired post-Vatican II renewal.

Pat Crowley also gave me the precious gift of being welcomed as a close friend into the families of his brother, Flor and Sally (Deirdre's parents) and his sister, Kay and Pat Doyle. The love and friendship of both families has enriched me more than I can say. Through them and through my own very precious family and some very special friends, my life has been abundantly blessed. And when I think of all the other wonderful people who touched my life over the years, I am lost for words. Thankfully, the Spirit can cope with that! (Romans 8:26-27).

Kevin T. Kelly
March 2012

INTRODUCTION

My Personal Odyssey – An Overview

This essay was first published in a Festschrift edited to mark my retirement by three of my fellow moral theologians, Bernard Hoose, Julie Clague and Gerard Mannion, Moral Theology of the 21st Century, (T & T Clark, London, 2008). Until 2011 Publication was limited to a hardback edition costing £80. Hence, this piece was not easily accessible to most readers. In the course of 2011 a paperback edition was published. The original title of the piece was 'The Role of Personal Story in the Teaching of Moral Theology'. I have made some slight alterations to the text to accommodate it to its new context.

(1) Early years

I was blessed with a very happy childhood. I felt loved and secure at home. In my innocence little did I realise how my childhood was also 'deprived'. I had no sisters, an impoverishment which deepened still further when, at the age of fourteen, I moved to the all-male establishment of the seminary at Upholland College. Unconsciously I was being affected by an atmosphere of emotional deprivation and so did not receive the kind of well-integrated education in personal and sexual relationships which is now recognised as part of any young person's healthy development. This all-male environment encouraged a macho culture in the seminary. Discipline was strict. Feelings were not for public display. The image of a priest put before us was of a man, strong, independent, able to control himself and others, and totally obedient to the will of God which came through the voice of authority and the rules of the seminary. *Tintinabulum vox Dei est* ('the bell is the voice of God') was drilled into us. Later, the attitude to authority this had inculcated into me was bound to have a negative influence on me when I began studying moral theology – and, in fact, the whole of theology and spirituality. Moreover, this ethos of the seminary was itself a by-product of the kind of theological thinking which held sway in the Church in those days.

My initial theological education was in a pre-Vatican II seminary. I was ordained in 1958, four years before the council began. Yet it would be unfair to present my seminary education as all doom and gloom. While I could not say it did me no harm, I am still grateful for much of the seminary experience. The senior seminary staff at Upholland College in those days included two outstanding priest Biblical scholars, Alexander Jones and Tom Worden, both of whom played a major role in awakening the Catholic Church in the UK to the renewal in Biblical studies beginning to emerge in places like the École Biblique in Jerusalem. Moreover, their spirit of critical enquiry was infectious and was not restricted to biblical studies. It is worth mentioning one experience I have never forgotten and which, I suspect, had a long-term influence on my later theology. While I was in the Sixth Form we followed a course on St John's Gospel given by Alexander Jones. He went to a lot of trouble explaining to us his particular interpretation of a passage in chapter six of John's Gospel. When it came to the end-of-year exam, I had the nerve to reject his interpretation and offered my own alternative complete with my reasons why. That was totally against the ethos of seminary education. It was not just the bell which was the voice of God; the teacher was too. I was expecting to fail my exam because of my foolhardiness. Instead I was given top marks. Looking back, I feel sure that the case I argued was probably very flawed. I suspect that my high mark was for being prepared to approach the issue in a spirit of critical enquiry.

I had respect, even affection, for Paddy Hanrahan, the Irish priest who taught moral theology in the seminary. Yet much of his course was light years away from the approach to moral theology which emerged from Vatican II. The three-volume moral theology manual by Noldin was our text. Its subtitle was *'secundum mentem S Thomae'* ('according to the mind of St Thomas'). When, later, I studied moral theology in Switzerland from the actual text of Aquinas I discovered that Noldin was very far from the mind of Thomas. In addition, a great deal of the Upholland moral theology course was devoted to canon law – not unnaturally, since Noldin's treatment of the sacraments was largely based on canon law. The manual's coverage of sexual ethics was in a separate volume on the sixth and ninth commandments and said little, if anything, about sexual maturity and healthy relationships. Its main aim was to specify as accurately as possible all the kinds of sins against chastity and to offer guidance on determining what guilt was involved.

(2) Further studies

After my ordination in 1958, I was sent to Fribourg University in Switzerland in preparation for eventually returning to the Upholland Seminary to teach Moral Theology. My remit was to do a Licentiate in Theology there, and then go to Rome for a Doctorate in Canon Law. That was seen as giving the necessary competence to teach moral theology. Even at that early stage that struck me as putting the cart before the horse, so I managed to get approval to reverse the priorities. I was able to complete the two-year Licentiate in one year, which enabled me to spend the necessary time at Fribourg and elsewhere to complete my Doctorate in Moral Theology. So my Canon Law studies were reduced to a Licentiate. I have since enjoyed describing myself as a lapsed, non-practising canon lawyer!

My theological studies at Fribourg were truly a liberating experience. Although we studied from the actual text of St Thomas's *Summa Theologica*, that text was seen in its historical context, wrestling with the problems of its day.

Its very methodology encouraged a critical approach to theology. The *quaestiones* (questions) in the text presented key problems that the contemporaries of Aquinas were struggling with. They were far from Aunt Sallies, set up deliberately to be knocked down. They actually engaged one's personal faith. The teacher was the leader of the exploratory expedition, rather than an oracle whose teaching had to be taken on faith. I and my fellow students were engaged in a struggle for meaning, delighting in any insights into the truth we achieved, though always conscious that the truth was something much bigger than we would ever grasp or understand. This approach gave us a respect for tradition. It was also a reminder that it is a living tradition, to be further enriched and we all share responsibility to try to develop this living tradition.

My appreciation of the complexity of this living tradition deepened as a result of my doctoral work on conscience and the Caroline divines, a group of mainly Anglican theologians in seventeenth-century England who kept alive the very fertile insights of Aquinas on conscience and the virtue of prudence. This was at a time when the neo-Scholastics were sucking the lifeblood out of this tradition and reducing prudence to a fearful cautiousness instead of seeing it as a virtue of creative initiative in the face of the exigencies of real life with all its particularities. My interest in this field was stimulated by my tutor, Cornelius Williams OP, an Irish Dominican who became a close friend. Though not a brilliant lecturer, our paths crossed at just the right moment. He also introduced me to the writings of his predecessor, Thomas Deman, a French Dominican who died in his early forties, but not before producing some magnificent writing on prudence and conscience. Although I never met Deman, his writings have inspired much of my later writings and practice.

My two years of Canon Law at the Gregorianum University in Rome were far from inspirational. However, there were two redeeming features. The first was a course on the philosophy of law by the German Jesuit, Bertrams. Though the dullest of lecturers, he opened my eyes to the importance of having a sound philosophy of law. That frees moral theology from the shackles of legalism. Laws are no longer chains depriving us of our freedom. Rather they are tools enabling us to live together, respecting each other's freedom and life-commitments through a shared vision of the common good, while at the same time doing justice to the demands of the uniqueness of individual situations through the exercise of '*epikeia*', part of the more general virtue of justice.

The second redeeming feature was a seminar with Ladilas Orsy. The subject matter of the seminar was not the important thing – in fact, I cannot remember what it was. What has affected me ever since was the way Orsy personified 'the human face of canon law'. For him – as for Jesus himself – laws are made for people, not people for the law. The impact of Bertrams and Orsy on my moral theology can be seen in a whole variety of ways. It probably comes out most clearly in my short piece entitled, 'Mind the Gap': Person-centred Liturgy, later in this volume, where I describe '*epikeia*' as a 'gap virtue'.

(3) Initial parish experience and teaching in the Seminary

After completing my further studies, I spent two years as a curate in St Clare's, a very busy parish in Liverpool. Vatican II was in full spate at the time. I still remember my parish priest (also vicar general), Mgr Adamson, looking up from his breakfast table reading of *The Times* and saying to me with a note of puzzled excitement in his voice. 'What do you think of this? "The church is a community of churches".' The excitement in his voice told me that his heart was in the right place theologically. That moment has remained embedded in my mind. Somehow it was symbolic of an energy-releasing fusion of two very different mindsets.

From five to nine most weekday evenings all four priests in the parish engaged in house-to-house visiting. Having covered every Catholic home in my district about three times in my first six months in the parish, I was feeling pretty desperate. I rang a good friend of mine, Jimmy Collins, a very inspirational priest, and asked him: 'Jimmy, what the hell do you talk about when you visit people in their homes?' I have never forgotten his reply. It has deeply influenced my moral theology and pastoral practice ever since. 'You don't talk about anything', he said, 'you listen to people's lives.' I am not opposed to the academic dimension of moral theology. However, if that becomes the be-all and end-all of moral theology and if moral theologians lose touch with people's lives, I think moral theology will lose its soul.

After my two years in the parish, I returned to the seminary to teach moral theology. I was struck by the unreality of the situation on my first night back. As the senior students, all aged from eighteen to about thirty, processed out of chapel on that first evening, the thought came to me that in many of the homes I had visited in St Clare's parish, young men of this age were already married, fathers of young children and holding down a job. Whereas any responsibilities the seminarians carried were fairly minimal and artificial. To all intents and purposes they were treated as minors and subject to the rigid discipline of the institution. Such a situation had massive limitations in terms of personal maturation and also as forming future priests in an experience-based and pastorally sensitive moral theology.

Fr Tom Worden, whom I have mentioned above as one of the lights shining in the darkness, had returned from being a peritus at Vatican II. As Dean of Studies, he set about renewing the whole approach to the theological and biblical studies. Formal lectures were reduced to a minimum. Great emphasis was placed for the students on writing regular essays, which enabled them to give their personal and reflective response to reading usually suggested by the tutor. Each essay would be evaluated by and discussed with the tutor for that particular course. In addition, weekly seminars were held at which the students shared with each other the fruits of their research. This was designed to inculcate in students a kind of mindset in keeping with the spirit of Vatican II. It tried to equip the students to feel at home in a climate of radical change. In this way the seminary itself became a kind of laboratory of how changes occur. Staff and students had to cope with all the struggles and criticism which accompany any radical change. They had to learn how to live with ambiguity, recognising that in any process of change, despite all its benefits, some good things are inevitably lost and new weaknesses are taken on board. Nevertheless, feeling at home with change, though disconcerting, is a more appropriate preparation for a Vatican II-style moral theology.

(4) Early writings

While I was at the seminary I took my first tentative steps in writing on issues of moral theology for publication. Again, the personal element comes in here. I had first got to know Michael Richards while I was in Rome. We both lodged at the Beda College. It was Michael who made possible the publication of my doctoral dissertation, Conscience: Dictator or Guide? (1967) in a series he was editing for Geoffrey Chapman. When he became the Editor of The Clergy Review he began to encourage me to publish in that periodical and later invited me on to its Editorial Board. I have never forgotten my first piece. It was in two parts and entitled 'The Authority of the Church's Moral Teaching' (The Clergy Review, 1967, pp. 682-694 & pp. 938-949). I showed it to my predecessor and former moral theology teacher, Paddy Hanrahan, who was still on the staff. When he returned my manuscript, he had corrected any spelling or punctuation errors but offered no other comment. On reflection, I appreciated what he had done. He was implicitly saying to me: 'It's up to you to get on with it now. I have done my bit.' That tied in with the attitude of historical consciousness which I had imbibed in my time at Fribourg. He had been true to his times. It was up to me now to be true to my times. And the times they were a-changing!

An example of the best of his times was the regular feature in The Clergy Review entitled, 'Questions and Answers'. In each issue practical problems raised mainly by priests in parishes were discussed and answers provided. Canon E.J. Mahoney was the expert over many years, eventually succeeded by Mgr Lawrence McReavy. Many, though far from all, the problems raised had a canonical basis to them. Mahoney's two volumes of Questions and Answers were prominent on the shelves of most priests and were frequently consulted.

In the years leading up to Vatican II Karl Rahner had been writing on the importance of helping people in forming their own consciences so that they would be a position to discern what they should do in any situation which presented itself. This will ring bells with anyone familiar with the Ignatian Exercises. The weakness with the 'Questions and Answers' approach was that, for most of the moral questions raised, answers were traced back to some kind of authoritative Church teaching, often papal statements or declarations of the then Holy Office. In the absence of such authoritative statements, a search was made of 'the approved authors'. That was the title given to the more renowned authors of the many manuals of moral theology written over recent centuries and used as text books in seminary training. Although these 'approved authors' would discuss the arguments for and against a particular position, at least as much weight was given to the 'authority' of the author as to the strength of his arguments. Moreover, there was no suggestion that the views and personal experience of the present or future confessors reading these texts carried any weight. As for penitents, their opinions did not enter into the equation.

When Michael Richards asked me to take over the 'Questions and Answers' column, my reaction was that a totally different approach was needed for our post-Vatican II age. Consequently, I wrote an introductory article entitled, 'Do-it-yourself moral theology' (*The Clergy Review*, 1970, pp. 52-63 – reprinted in an abbreviated form in this volume) where I expressed the hope that the members of our recently formed 'Association of Teachers of Moral Theology' (ATMT) would be able to supply a series of articles which would give readers a grounding for tackling their own problems. I have to confess that no more than a trickle of such articles appeared for a couple of years and then the stream dried up. Whether my decision to abandon the 'Questions and Answers' format was a good thing or not, it is not easy to judge.

The ATMT was founded by Jack Mahoney and myself. We had never met each other and neither of us knew other moral theologians teaching in the seminaries. We both agreed that that was not a healthy situation. So we invited our colleagues to join us for an initial meeting in Manchester. Since then we have been meeting twice a year for residential weekends. It has proved to be a great source of inspiration and ongoing learning. At each meeting we discuss papers submitted and read in advance. This encourages a conversational methodology in which members are never out to score a point but are focussed on trying to help each other deepen our understanding of the topic under consideration. In such a non-threatening climate the ATMT has developed into a group of friends as well as professional colleagues. On a number of occasions we even had shared meetings with the bishops. The listening and learning approach was much in evidence in one such session held after the publication of John Paul II's encyclical, *Veritatis Splendor* which dealt with fundamental moral questions. The meeting, carefully prepared by a small joint planning group led by Bishop Jack Brewer, opened with bishops and moral theologians sharing how they felt on first reading the Pope's letter. Only after we listened to each other's feelings did we move on to discuss some of the actual issues raised by the encyclical. This was very much a listening and learning exercise, a good model for a Church committed to a collaborative model of teaching authority. A fuller history of the ATMT is found later in this volume.

(5) Humanae Vitae

The issue of conscience came up with a vengeance with the publication of Paul VI's encyclical, *Humanae Vitae*, in 1968. After outlining a very person-centred approach to marriage and sexuality, the Pope gave his decision on the very down-to-earth issue of birth control. He based it on a rationale which did not sit easily with the person-centred approach of the rest of the document. Moreover, his decision went against the advice of his so-called 'Birth Control Commission' which included moral theologians, social scientists and some extremely committed married people. Their final report carefully argued that a change in the Church's teaching would do justice to the heart of what is contained in the Church's living tradition and it even included a supplement proposing a way this change could be presented to the Church at large. Three moral theologians on the Commission privately submitted to the Pope their own document which argued that such a change would harm the credibility of the Church. Sadly, it was their unofficial advice which was heeded.

Extensive reading and research had convinced me that there would be a change in the Church's teaching. Hence, *Humanae Vitae* came as a great shock to me. I had actually supported Archbishop Beck in preparing the Liverpool clergy for such a change and in offering appropriate pastoral guidance to them. An inadequate grasp of ecclesiology and the role of authority in the Church led me to respond to the encyclical in a way which I can now see, with hindsight, was theologically inadequate and pastorally unhelpful. I feel I let people down on this point. Moral theologians like Charles Curran had foreseen such an eventuality and had anticipated and worked through the ecclesiological issues raised by it. Hence, they were able to disagree immediately and publicly with the Pope's teaching and supported people in their conscience decisions to continue using birth control. I argued rather feebly in long articles in *The Catholic Pictorial* and *The Clergy Review* (1972, pp. 108-120, pp. 174-186, pp. 261-275, pp. 330-349 & pp. 803-808) that *Humanae Vitae* presented the Church with something new and that we needed time to weigh up and wrestle with its teaching. I recognised that, though it was a word spoken by legitimate authority, it might not be the last word or even the best word. I felt we needed to reflect on it before we could responsibly disagree with it and reject its teaching. However, I did recognise that it was a matter with immediate and practical consequences for the lives of married couples. Hence, their conscious decisions needed to be respected during this time of reflection and that they not be coerced into conduct which they considered harmful to the good of themselves and their children.

A major learning experience for me in this matter occurred some months after the encyclical was published. I was asked to speak to a large group of married couples in Rockferry on the Wirral. They were very committed Catholics who used to meet regularly in cells to support each other in their married life. They asked me to explain the thinking of *Humanae Vitae* to them. Believing that the lived experience of such committed couples was an important source for theological reflection on marriage, I thought that my meeting with them could be a good learning experience for me. Hence, in addition to speaking to them about the encyclical, I asked them – a group of about two hundred – to write down for me how far the teaching of *Humanae Vitae* tied in with their lived experience. I was taken aback – and chastened – to find that pretty well all of them said that it did not fit in at all with their understanding and experience of marriage. Their response comes back to me every time I read that challenging passage in Jack Mahoney's magnificent book, *The Making of Moral Theology* (Oxford, Oxford University Press, 1987):

> In the case of *Humanae Vitae* ... Pope Paul may appear to imply that the reception of his teaching by the Church at large will have, through the complementary influence of the Spirit, at least a confirmatory value in establishing the truth of his teaching. The possibility cannot be ruled out, however, that in such non-infallible teaching on a matter which is not contained in revelation the response of the body of the faithful will be less than whole-hearted in agreeing with the papal teaching and the considerations underlying it. For the influence of the Holy Spirit in the hearts of the faithful, as described by Pope Paul, is envisaged purely as disposing them to be receptive, whereas it might be a more positive one of refining, qualifying, or even correcting the papal teaching (p. 295).

Cardinal Hume was surely right when, at the 1980 Rome Synod on Marriage, he said that the experience of married people can be 'an authentic source of theology from which we, the pastors, and indeed the whole Church can draw'.

(6) Upholland Northern Institute (UNI)

My appreciation of the importance of human experience deepened still further when I was appointed Director of the newly-formed Upholland Northern Institute after the Upholland College Senior Seminary moved to the North-East and was amalgamated with Ushaw College, Durham. UNI was set up as a centre for Adult Christian Education and In-Service Training (IST) for clergy. Actually, our very first course was an IST course for the Bishops of England and Wales on the theme, 'The Bishop as Teacher'. My own talk to the bishops was precisely on that topic. My input was deeply influenced by a course of Adult Learning our UNI team had recently undergone. That, combined with Brian Wicker's analysis of the 'seminar leader' model of teaching authority, led me to suggest that teaching authority in the Church is an exercise of collaborative ministry and we all have our part to play in it. The Church is both a learning community and a teaching community. A fuller version of the kind of approach I put forward is found in a later chapter of this book. Such an approach obviously has implications for an issue such as disagreeing with 'official' Church teaching. This is an issue which refuses to go away. I get the impression that the heavy-handed way many European bishops today are interpreting *Ex Corde Ecclesiae*, the Vatican document on Catholic Universities, is leading to a situation where the only form of moral theology seminarians will be exposed to is one of strict compliance with 'official' teaching. There will be no chance of their hearing the Spirit speaking through voices expressing loyal and responsible disagreement.

(7) My three-pronged sabbatical

After five very fruitful and stimulating years as Director of UNI, I was succeeded by Fr (now Archbishop) Vincent Nichols. That gave me the opportunity to enjoy the great privilege of a seven-month Sabbatical. Two separate blocks of two months were spent as a Fellow of St Edmund's House, Cambridge. To broaden the learning experience, I asked a scientist friend to recommend a non-theology book which might open my mind to new horizons. His suggestion, Thomas Kuhn's *The Structure of Scientific Revolutions* (University of Chicago Press, 1962), blew my mind. Kuhn's analysis of 'paradigms' of knowledge enabled me to make sense of the changed approach to the theology of marriage found in Vatican II. It gave a solid basis to my book, *Divorced and Second Marriage* (Collins, London, 1982). Though most of the writing was done at Cambridge, it was not finally completed until I became Leader of the Skelmersdale Team Ministry. The learning experience at Cambridge was intensified through many stimulating personal contact, most notably visiting fellows Ellen Leonard from St Michael's, Toronto, an expert on Modernism especially here in England, and Peter and Ann Pettifer Walshe who have managed to keep alive their enthusiasm in the hardly revolutionary setting of Notre Dame University, where Peter is Professor of Government and International Studies and Ann edits an alternative campus newsletter entitled *Common Sense*. Their continuing friendship has been a rich theological resource for me.

Two months of my sabbatical comprised visiting a number of developing countries, notably, India, the Philippines and Peru. I had the privilege of seeing liberation theology and inculturation put into practice in real life. It was an experience that has marked me for life. My sabbatical ended with a thirty-day Ignatian retreat at Dollymount in Dublin. One unforgettable insight from that retreat was to do with the will of God. I have always been attracted to the spirituality of Charles de Foucault and continue to recite daily his well-known 'Prayer of Abandonment'. It came home very powerfully to me during this retreat that to pray 'Father, I abandon myself into your hands' lacks any real credibility if, in fact, I am not prepared to exercise my will. It is to give God nothing. I had tended to accept too passively whatever happened as God's will. I now realise that it is only by fully accepting responsibility for whatever lies in my control that I am enabling God's will to be truly realised. In a sense, it is up to me to 'create' God's will.

(8) Skelmersdale Team Ministry and The Queens College, Birmingham

After my sabbatical I was appointed Leader of the Roman Catholic Team Ministry in Skelmersdale New Town. This was a steep learning curve for me since the Team Ministry had been in operation for a number of years. It was made up of priests, sisters and laity, well formed and experienced in the skills of collaborative ministry. It certainly taught me that any mission statement at any level of Church life has to be based on an analysis of the local situation in which the Church community in the area is called to live its life and exercise its ministry. (cf. chapter three of my FPB, 'Collaborative Ministry: a Pastoral Experience in Skelmersdale') I learnt that a mission statement which could apply to any Church community, regardless of time, place or culture, will never arouse people's enthusiasm and set them on fire.

At the end of five years in Skelmersdale I was becoming worried that there was very little writing taking place in the UK in the field of moral theology. Because of my training and experience I could not ignore such a lacuna. Although I had thoroughly enjoyed my years in the Team Ministry, I decided that I would make better use of my talents, such as they were, by re-engaging with teaching and writing in moral theology. To give myself time to catch up with developments, I applied for and was awarded a one-year Research Fellowship at The Queens College in Birmingham, an ecumenical establishment for training for the ministry. Although Skelmersdale had been a rich ecumenical experience, The Queen College offered me a much broader form of ecumenical life, especially in the field of liturgy. With Queens being an ecumenical foundation, free from the restraints of different denominational Churches, I had the opportunity to experience the Eucharist celebrated according to the rites of various Christian Churches, sometimes even under the presidency of ordained Methodist and German Lutheran women. This was prior to the Church of England accepting women's ordination. I was happy to find myself feeling completely at home with a woman presiding at the altar.

Moreover, my research project was itself ecumenical. It was an examination of the positions taken up by different Christian Churches on the ethics of in-vitro fertilisation (IVF) which was a new development at that time. My research was published by Collins in 1987 under the title, *Life and Love: Towards a Christian Dialogue on Bioethics*. My growing appreciation of the importance of women's contribution to the full life, ministry and teaching of the Church led me to include a specific chapter entitled, 'What some women are saying about IVF'. Later on when the rich contribution of women had had an ever great impact on me, I went much further than that. In my 1992 book, *New Directions in Moral Theology*, one of the major chapters was entitled, 'Moral theology – not truly human without the full participation of women.'

Arriving in Birmingham a few weeks after the Handsworth riots, I had the enriching experience of helping out each weekend in St Francis parish, Handsworth, courtesy of its amazing and inspiring parish priest, the late Fr Tom Fallon, very much a man of the people. My experience in Birmingham also introduced me to the inter-faith scene. I visited far more mosques than Catholic Churches during my year there and I made good friends with some delightful Muslims. Attending Muslim and Hindu prayer services never left me feeling that the God they were praying to was a foreign or alien God. Despite major doctrinal differences I could sense the truth in the expression, 'We all believe in the same God.' Looking back years later, I would add: 'And the same God believes in us.'

(9) Combining Parish and University: Eldon St, Liverpool and Heythrop College
After Birmingham I was determined to combine parish experience with teaching moral theology. My good friend, Jack Mahoney, offered me the opportunity to join him at Heythrop College in the University of London, while at the same time engaging in pastoral ministry in Our Lady's parish, Eldon St, in inner-city Liverpool. Although the original suggestion was that I should involve myself in Heythrop as much as I felt able, by the time I arrived there Jack had been appointed Professor of Christian Ethics at Kings College, London and I was left carrying the full teaching load in moral theology on a part-time basis. It was very hard work but I enjoyed every minute of it. I would catch a Sunday evening train from Liverpool Lime Street to London Euston so that I could start work at crack of dawn on Monday morning. Thursday afternoon would see me dashing with a heavy bag of books on my shoulder to Oxford Circus Tube station to get to Euston in time for my return train to Liverpool. I never once missed it, even though at times I had only minutes to spare! I found the twice-weekly three-and-a-half hour train journey a very valuable time to catch up with my theological reading.

Both sides of this 'double life' fed off each other. Eldon St was a very privileged pastoral setting. The Eldonians, an incredible community and housing group in this area of multiple deprivation in Liverpool, were still in their early days, though they had already weathered their battle with Derek Hatton and his militant tendency in Liverpool City Council. The ground work was solidly in place, due to the inspired leadership of former dock crane-operator, Tony McGann and the combined force of the local community, solidly supported by the two local priests, Jim Dunne and Michael Lane. To be dropped into such a situation was an immense privilege and one I will never forget. It would be impossible to attempt to summarise the theological richness of such an experience. I can only point readers to 'Struggling to Live the Gospel in Inner-city Liverpool: a Case Study', chapter two of my *From a Parish Base*. There I have tried, very inadequately, to capture some of the inspiration and excitement of those early days. My ten years in Eldon St parish offered me a theological 'source' which I was able to share in my theological teaching in Heythrop and which the students seemed to appreciate greatly. Heythrop possesses one of the best theological libraries in the UK. The Eldonians provided me with a library of a totally different kind. I was privileged to read the 'living Gospels' incarnated in their everyday lives. The remarkable thing is that the wonder of the Eldonians is just as much alive today as it was then.

(10) HIV/AIDS and CAFOD

During my early days at Heythrop College I was introduced to a second experiential theological 'source' which affected me deeply on my first encounter with it and which has continued to have a major influence on me as a moral theologian. In the early nineties HIV/AIDS was beginning to make its presence felt. Initially considered to be restricted to the gay community, people soon recognised that it was affecting heterosexual people on a far wider scale, especially in sub-Saharan Africa. The Roman Catholic Aid agency CAFOD quickly realised that HIV/AIDS, as well as being a terrible and terminal medical condition, was also a major development issue. CAFOD responded very quickly by setting up a HIV/AIDS section with its own advisory committee. A Medical Missionary of Mary sister, Dr Maura O'Donohue, headed the whole venture. Her medical expertise, combined with her extensive experience of Africa and her deep commitment to social justice and respect for the dignity of women, enabled her quickly to become a key figure in the Church's response to HIV/AIDS. She became an 'expert' in the fullest sense of the word. In other words, her knowledge and understanding of HIV/AIDS was based on grassroots personal experience of how people were being infected and affected by this pandemic. Maura invited me to join her advisory committee and my eyes began to be opened to the enormity of HIV/AIDS, a process of personal enlightenment which has continued to this day. Along with Dr Mary McHugh, chair of the advisory committee, and two CAFOD staff, Maura enabled me to have a three-week exposure experience of the grass-roots reality of HIV/AIDS in Uganda, a visit I shall never forget. I saw how poverty was a major factor in the spread of HIV/AIDS – and vice versa. I was also confronted with the feminisation of poverty, while being bowled over by the extraordinary resilience of the women involved in one way or another. The slogan, 'Living positively with AIDS', made a deep impact on me and I had to face the startling truth that 'The Body of Christ has AIDS.'

My contact with CAFOD also led to my being invited to share in theological reflection on the pandemic with moral theologians and people living with AIDS from the UK and Ireland, USA and Asia at conferences in New York, Dublin and Bangkok. After the Bangkok meeting, I stayed on for an additional two weeks to meet people working with and living with AIDS in Thailand and the Philippines.

This was to ensure that the book on AIDS I was working on was firmly grounded in real life. Unfortunately, the publishers would not accept a book exclusively devoted to HIV/AIDS. They insisted on my discussing some wider issues of sexual ethics. Nevertheless, my primary emphasis on HIV/AIDS comes through very clearly in the subtitle, *New Directions in Sexual Ethics: Moral Theology and the Challenge of AIDS* (Continuum, London & Washington, 1998).

Part of 'living positively with AIDS' for me has been the great privilege of meeting many inspiring people such as Noerine Kaleeba, Ursula Sharp MMM, Archbishop Pius Ncube, Sister Mary Courtney, Bob Vitillo, Julian Filokowski, Martin Pendergast, Ann Smith, Bishop Kevin Dowling and two very dedicated and multi-talented U.S. moral theologians, Jim Keenan and Jon Fuller. Although I am neither gay nor HIV-positive, HIV/AIDS is a key dimension of my personal story. In any teaching of moral theology I have been engaged in, it has certainly made its presence felt. 'AIDS is my gift'; I have never forgotten those words of a poor man in Thailand whose broken life was transformed and given new purpose when he was diagnosed as HIV-positive. He was sharing his experience at a meeting of Asian moral theologians in Bangkok.

I have kept detailed diaries of my three extensive exposure experiences in Uganda, Zimbabwe, Nairobi and Zambia. Perhaps publishing a collection of some excerpts from these diaries could be another positive task for me now I am retired. An awareness of HIV/AIDS can not only transform our own lives. It can also galvanise us to combat the many dehumanising factors which fuel injustice in our world and which also lie at the roots of the pandemic. It was not without reason that the last subtitle I use in the final chapter of NDSE is 'A Time of Grace: AIDS – a window of opportunity for our global society.' In the words of Enda McDonagh, we are living in 'a time of AIDS'. I finished my book on a challenging and hopeful note:

> Many individuals living with HIV/AIDS experience a conversion to living more fully and with more commitment to what life is all about. Our human family is now living with HIV/AIDS. Will that experience turn out to be a conversion experience for us? … Theologically, I would suggest, our world is faced with a redemptive moment. If that is not a challenge to Christians and Christian Churches, what is? (pp. 212-213).

(11) Ecumenism

For the next ten years of my personal odyssey I was parish priest of a shared Roman Catholic/Anglican Church in Hough Green, Widnes. A fuller account of that experience is given in a later chapter. This experience served to deepen my conviction that the future is ecumenical – and more than ecumenical. As a Hindu priest once said to me, 'Religion, though good, can also narrow our minds. God is not narrow. God is all-embracing.'

Almost from its inception nearly thirty-five years ago, the Association of Teachers of Moral Theology (ATMT) has been graced with a small, but highly influential ecumenical membership. In past years I remember people of the calibre of Professor Gordon Dunstan, Ann Loades and Oliver O'Donovan attending our meetings. Professor Ronald Preston, the eminent Manchester Anglican ethicist specialising the field of social ethics was a very faithful participant at our twice-yearly residential weekends until his death in 2001. He had a deep impact on all of us and we treasured him as a good friend and wise adviser.

Chapter two of my *New Directions in Christian Ethics* is entitled 'Graceful Disagreement'. In it I try to wrestle with the phenomenon of disagreement on moral issues between different Christian Churches. This is a far cry to those early days when authoritative papal or Vatican statements were regarded as the final word on most moral questions. When the English-language version of *The Catechism of the Catholic Church* was published in 1994, I highlighted still further the ecumenical context in which that document needed to be read, insisting that 'when there are particular issues of moral disagreement between the major Christian Churches, the Catechism's presentation of the current authoritative Catholic teaching should not be presumed to be the final and definitive Christian position on this topic,' and I also pointed out that, 'it would ecumenically harmful if such a presentation was understood to carry such authority that any other position must be rejected as unchristian' (*From a Parish Base*, p. 135).

Life in Christ, an Agreed Statement by the Second Anglican-Roman Catholic International Commission (ARCIC II), authored by a body co-chaired by Cardinal Cormac Murphy O'Connor, is a powerful witness to the fact that, even on specific moral issues where these two Churches disagree, they may still share the same vision and are committed to the same common values. Furthermore, sections 29 and 32 of *Life in Christ* offer a challenging comment on the formation of conscience and how a well-formed conscience actually contributes to the development of the Church's moral teaching:

29. The fidelity of the Church to the mind of Christ involves a continuing process of listening, learning, reflecting and teaching. In this process every member of the community has a part to play. Each person learns to reflect and act according to conscience. Conscience is informed by and informs, the tradition and teaching of the community. Learning and teaching are a shared discipline, in which the faithful seek to discover together what obedience to the gospel of grace and the law of love entails amidst the moral perplexities of the world.

32. Teaching developed in this way is an essential element in the process by which individuals and communities exercise their discernment on particular moral issues. Holding in the mind the teaching they have received,

drawing upon their own experience, and exploring the particularities of the issue that confronts them, they have then to decide what action to take in these circumstances and on this occasion. Such a decision is not only a matter of deduction. Nor can it be taken in isolation. It also calls for detailed and accurate assessment of the facts of the case, careful and consistent reflection and, above all, sensitivity of insight inspired by the Holy Spirit.

My personal story in the setting of our Shared Church of St Basil and All Saints has only made me more convinced of the truth and importance of the above quotations.

A new phase of my personal odyssey began after I retired at the end of June 2008. Austin Smith CP, a good friend of mine who died recently, used to describe retirement as 'disengaging to re-engage'. That could be a description of this whole volume, even though, in the concluding chapter I offer a few specific reflections on the theme of retirement as a theological experience.

Parish and Pastoral Ministry in the
Light of Vatican II

CHAPTER ONE

We, the People of God, are the Church

In May 2000 the Liverpool Archdiocesan Newspaper, the Catholic Pictorial asked me to sum up the changes in theology since Vatican II in eight hundred words … an impossible assignment! All I could do was high light a few ways in which its readers' lives had been changed by the theological renewal resulting from Vatican II. This piece appeared in the 21 May 2000 issue and was written for a readership of ordinary parishioners in Liverpool. The following abbreviated version might offer a helpful introduction to this section on Parish and Pastoral Ministry in the light of Vatican II.

The Church that emerged from Vatican II was a bit like the dignified figure of Nelson Mandela, walking free from captivity, eager to give his all to promote peace, unity and reconciliation in a sick and bleeding country. John XXIII, through Vatican II, freed the Church to repossess the dynamism of its living tradition. Surely that was the greatest exercise of Church authority this century.

Our Church
Theology today sees the Church as far more than an administrative structure, functioning along hierarchical lines. The bishops at Vatican II very deliberatively put the 'People of God' before the hierarchical structure of the Church. 'We are Church' sums up a fundamental theological truth which has within it the power to energise a movement for renewal in the Church which has far reaching implications. To take but one example, it moves us to go beyond any tendency to regard women as minor partners in that 'we'. It has moved many women among us to take their rightful place within the important work of theological reflection within the Church.

Our Eucharist
In the light of eucharistic theology today, no longer do we see ourselves as attending the priest's Mass. The ministry of the eucharistic celebrant is precisely to enable us all to share together in our community Mass. People-participation is a much higher priority than observing rubrics.

Our Parish
A parish is a community with a mission. People and priest, we all share responsibility for the life of the parish community and its mission. Such co-responsibility should flow naturally into collaborative ministry. A primary role of the priest should be to encourage and enable each of us to undertake our share in the work and mission of the parish. We are not just 'helping Father'! As a wise

priest once said: 'Collaboration is not a way of doing something more efficiently; it is a way of being Church more authentically.'

Our Bible

The Bible is no longer a closed book reserved to experts. God's Word is given to us all to inspire our lives. The aim of good Bible scholarship should be to help us to read the Bible for ourselves – intelligently and faithfully. Intelligently – recognising the text as written by believers in a specific historical context; faithfully – bridging the gap between that context and our own times. Making the text our own frees us from a fundamentalist slavery to a dead letter, devoid of any living context. In that way we can be enriched and challenged by the faith of our forebears while recognising that our world today and the problems we face are very different to theirs.

Our experience

Theology involves 'making faith-sense of experience, and experience-sense of faith' (Jack Mahoney SJ). That is why it takes human experience seriously, as the bishops did at Vatican II. Most of us are not professional theologians, but our experience is still theologically important. For instance, if very many Catholics today say that the Church's official teaching on contraception does not speak to their own experience, they are not being theologically ignorant. They may, in fact, be making an important theological statement that needs to be listened to.

Our teaching authority

The Church is not made up of teachers and learners. The Church as a whole is a learning Church and a teaching Church. Theologians are still exploring the implications of the Vatican II statement that the whole Church has a share in the charism of infallibility. The Pope and the bishops have the role of speaking authoritatively in the name of the Church, but the real author of such teaching is God. That is where the rest of us have a role to play. In receiving such teaching, we 'own' it as God's teaching. In some instances the Church as a whole may feel unable to 'own' a specific piece of teaching as presently promulgated. It fails to make experience-sense of their faith and faith-sense of their experience. At times God's spirit can be even more active in this process of non-reception than in the process of reception. In such instances, non-reception, sometimes misleadingly referred to as 'dissent', should be seen as loyal and faithful cooperation in the teaching ministry of the Church and needs to be listened to respectfully by the Pope and bishops in exercising their teaching authority.

Our ecumenical sisters and brothers

As Pope John Paul II pointed out in *Ut unum sint* (1995), we are not faithful Roman Catholics if we do not take ecumenism seriously. That means accepting that God's spirit is truly present and active in other Christian Churches. The full implications of this still need to be further explored, as the John Paul II admitted when he invited other Christian Churches to discern with him how best the role of primacy should be exercised to promote communion between all Christians. As Christians we all share in the one baptism which makes us members of the one body of Christ. International ecumenical commissions like ARCIC have laboured hard to produce agreed statements which have gone far beyond mere words. They are the fruit of a growing together in faith through the lived experience of their members. Moreover, the experience of growing together in faith has not been limited to the members of such commissions. For instance, the experience of many ordinary Church members has convinced them that the present ruling on intercommunion fails to make faith-sense of their experience or experience-sense of their faith. This was brought out very simply but powerfully in a very moving story related in the L'Arche communities' comment on One Bread, One Body. In an ecumenical community the response of one of the disabled non-Catholic residents when refused Communion by the priest was a simple 'Don't be silly, Jack!'. 'Out of the mouths ...!'

Our one World

Vatican II defined the Church as 'a kind of sacrament or sign of intimate union with God and of the unity of all humanity' (LG, 1). This means that we cannot claim to be Christians and opt out of responsibility for our world. In fact, the bishops went even further: 'The split between the faith they profess and the daily lives of many people is to be counted as among the more serious misconceptions of our day ... Christians who neglect their temporal duties are neglecting their duties to their neighbour and even to God and are endangering their eternal salvation' (GS, 43). At the 1971 post-Vatican II Synod on Justice, the bishops expressed the same truth in a more positive way. They said that working for justice and peace was an integral element of preaching the Gospel:

> Action on behalf of justice and participation in the transformation of the world fully appear to us as a constitutive dimension of the preaching of the Gospel, or, in other words, of the Church's mission for the redemption of the human race and its liberation from every oppressive situation.

Certainly, post-Vatican II theology rejects a purely 'churchy' Christianity. And now ecological and environmental issues are also accepted as an integral part of the redemptive and liberation agenda.

CHAPTER TWO

Listening to Parishioners and Priests

As part of the much wider Queen's Authority and Governance Project begun in 1996, 350 parish respondents, including twelve parish priests, from six dioceses in England, Scotland and Wales were interviewed in an exercise looking at 'parish reality on the ground, especially with regard to pastoral strategy, organisation and communication'. I was asked to write a theological reflection on the reports from twelve of the parishes interviewed. This appeared as Some Theological Reflections on the Parish Reports in the volume, Diocesan Dispositions and Parish Voices in the Roman Catholic Church, edited by Noel Timms and published in 2001 by Matthew James Publishing Ltd. This whole project offered a very valuable resource to help the Roman Catholic Church in this island to reflect on how it was responding at parish level to the challenges of Vatican II. When I originally wrote this piece I had the impression that the project did not receive the attention it deserved. There have been considerable changes in parish life and organisation since that time. I am not convinced that all these changes are for the better. Perhaps we still have lessons to learn from this project.

My own reflection, with some minor alterations, is republished with the permission of the Trust which supported the project. It helps to throw light on the process of receiving Vatican II at parish level.

Introduction

To offer an adequate theological appraisal of the rich and varied life of twelve parishes in the space of a short article is impossible. All I can do is offer a few theological reflections based on my reading these parish reports. Others reading the reports might react quite differently and their theological reflections might bear little resemblance to my own.

The experience of these twelve parishes, as living cells of the Church, provide a very rich theological resource for all of us. Listening to their lived experience as parish communities should stimulate us in our theological thinking. I am not suggesting that this will result in the solution of all or even any of our problems in the field of pastoral theology. However, it should help us to isolate and articulate some of the important questions which need to be faced.

The stories of these parishes are so rich and the issues they raise are so varied and thought-provoking, the temptation for any theological commentator is to go off in all sorts of directions. I will try to resist that temptation and restrict my attention to certain basic issues related to the implications of Vatican II for parish life.

- The major issue I will focus on is how these parish reports throw light on what is meant theologically by describing the parish as a community.

- A second issue to which only minor attention can be given is the theological significance of the feeling shared by many of the parishes that their mission and ministry is rendered less effective and even somewhat disorientated by the lack of any coherent diocesan policy.
- Finally, I shall conclude the chapter with a series of brief comments on other theological questions arising from the parish reports.

The Parish as a Community

The word 'community' occurs constantly in every one of the twelve parish reports. In their differing ways each of these parishes would claim to have grown and developed as a community, though some more strongly than others, over the years following Vatican II. Any Catholic reading these reports would, I am sure, be very struck by this development. In many cases it has been helped by the leadership of enlightened and inspirational parish priests; in some it has occurred even while the parish was experiencing extremely difficult problems with their parish priest.

However, their impressive community life raises a theological question. Although 'community' is the 'in' word to describe a Vatican II parish, it is not clear theologically what kind of community this should be. In the parishes under consideration, three different community dimensions, each having its foundation in Vatican II theology, are found. While evidence of all three of these dimensions can be found in each of the parishes, what makes an enormous difference between them is the emphasis given to one or other of these dimensions. That is where I see us facing a major theological question with regard to the nature and mission of the local Church.

The first of these 'community' dimensions is the *Belonging* dimension. The keywords here are welcome, affirmation, belonging and security. In the parishes where this dimension is given prime importance, a stranger attending the parish liturgy might comment, 'See how these Christians love one another.' Parishioners obviously care about each other. The general mood of the liturgy is to enable people to feel the warmth of God's love. There is an emphasis on participation, everyone feeling at home and playing their part in the life of the parish community. This is the main purpose behind most of the parish groups, whether they are involved with the various liturgical ministries, including visiting sick members of the community, or whether they look after such mundane matters as cleaning the Church or financial and administrative issues. Parish 'functions' are seen as important since they help to foster a sense of belonging. A warm and welcoming priest who believes in collaborative ministry is an important element in this belonging dimension, even though, paradoxically, the parish studies show that where 'belonging' is a lived reality a parish can carry a priest with very profound personal problems, whether at the level of an abusive relationship or alcohol-addiction. The wider Church, especially the diocese, is perceived as hardly affecting local life, though the Pope and even the local bishop, can function as an important symbol of belonging. Even when the diocese does impinge on the local community, its impact tends to be felt as interference (as when a priest is moved) or as lack of effective pastoral management and concern (as in the case of priests with problems).

The second 'community' dimension could be called the *Missionary Parish* dimension. Here the emphasis is on the Gospel as a challenge to the parish community as a whole and how it should respond collectively to this challenge. The belonging dimension is still there, but it is a belonging for mission. The liturgy, still participative, is understood and celebrated as an experience of God's love commissioning his followers to go forth as channels of his love. There is always a disturbing and uncomfortable side to it. The poor of this world, near and far, challenge the parish to a continuing conversion of their lifestyle and priorities. Justice and peace is the responsibility of the whole parish, not just a specific group. The priest's role is that of a missionary inspirer (through the liturgy) and he may even represent the parish on various social action and civic communities. The wider Church fits more easily into this 'missionary' mindset since it is able to facilitate cooperative collective action between parishes for a whole variety of social concerns, at home and abroad. There will still be a plethora of parish groups. Many, if not most, of them will continue to serve the 'belonging' dimension. However, some will have a distinctive concern for issues related to justice and peace, at home or abroad. Their aim will be to ensure that the whole parish see such issues as an essential part of their life as a community. They will resist any tendency for the parish to see itself exclusively as a haven of safety, welcoming people adrift in a hostile world and offering them security.

The *Christian in the World* is the third 'community' dimension which is discernable in the parishes under consideration, though admittedly fairly minimally in most of them. Here the main emphasis lies on the liturgical, transformative and educational role of the parish, helping the individual parishioners to be sufficiently inspired and formed as Christians to play their part in whatever sphere of life they are involved – somewhat along the lines of the YCW ethos. This also means being involved in whatever is happening to improve the quality of life in their own neighbourhood, especially in partnership with organisations working with the poor and marginalised. Consequently, the multiplicity of parish groups and participation in them is not the criterion for a healthy 'Christian in the world' parish. Nevertheless, the belonging and participation dimension is still extremely important. At the liturgical assembly parishioners are not just isolated individuals. They all gather as members of the body of Christ and the liturgy is their community action. Here too the gospel that is preached is both disturbing and inspiring. Parishioners are called to be lay missionaries, commissioned to challenge all forms of injustice or established disorder affecting their community. Some parish groups may also be needed to help individuals develop skills such as social analysis and to initiate the process of developing local leadership in a demoralised community. I tried to describe this 'Christian in the world' dimension when I was writing about the Eldonian community in Liverpool in chapter two of my book, *From a Parish Base*.

All three of these dimensions have their roots in the theology of Vatican II and they are found to a greater or lesser extent in all the parishes surveyed. The question posed by these parish reports concerns the 'mix' of these three dimensions. The 'belonging' dimension is the one which is found most strongly in many, if not most, of the parishes; and in some cases its predominance in the mix is such that the other two are a very minor ingredient. In fact, in some cases, the 'Christian in the world' ingredient is barely discernable. I would hazard the guess that this is a fairly accurate picture of many parishes in Britain. Does this mean that what was described in *Gaudium et Spes* as one of the gravest errors of our time still has a grip on our Catholic life: 'One of the gravest errors of our time is the dichotomy between the faith which many profess and their day-to-day conduct' (GS, 43).

Could this be linked to some other burning questions affecting the Catholic Church today? Could it be one reason why many young people feel that our Church does not speak to them and their concerns? Maybe they are not interested in belonging to a community whose main focus is on the security and welfare of its members? Could it have anything to do with the diminishing numbers of adults attending Church? Is the spirituality presented in the parishes too Church-centred and failing to support and challenge them in their everyday lives?

Parishes feeling the lack of any coherent diocesan policy

The Dutch theologian, Edward Schillebeeckx OP coined the expression 'contrast experience'. By that he meant a kind of collective cry of pain which erupts from people when they are faced by what is not in keeping with their deepest humanity. It is as though some very profound instinct within them is crying out: 'This should not be. This is not how life should be lived.' I get the impression that in many of the parishes interviewed the lack of any coherent pastoral policy on the part of the diocese is experienced as a kind of 'contrast experience'. It provokes the cry of collective pain which can be detected in many of the reports. If this is the case, such a cry of pain would be extremely important theologically. It could perhaps be interpreted as God's creative Spirit crying out from the grassroots of the Church and calling for renewal at local and diocesan level. It is as though people feel the ground is moving under their feet and know that something earth-shattering is happening all around them, not only in the Church but in society in general. They are deeply disturbed. Yet their faith enables them to cling on to the hope that in the midst of what could seem like the death throes of the Church as we know it, God's Spirit might be urging us to discern signs of new life breaking through.

This cry of pain does not seem to saying to the diocesan authorities: 'Tell us what to do.' Rather it seems to be saying: 'We are living in a situation of great upheaval and urgency. It is no good burying our heads in the sand or lamenting the times we live in. Let us seize this 'kairos' moment, this time of opportunity. We need to get together, all of us as local Church, to discern where we should be going and what we should be doing.' This cry of pain has the feel of a movement of the Spirit calling for greater participation, consultation and involvement. In other words, the coherent diocesan policy of which people feel a deep need should not be something to be owned by priests and laity, once it has been determined by the-powers-that-be. Rather, in the very process of its determination and formulation there should be the widest consultation that is humanly possible. In other words, as many of the People of God as possible should also be on board for this communal act of discernment. This will not be easy to achieve, though the 1980 National Pastoral Congress could offer some pointers towards a viable process. It might also be useful to seek advice from those most highly skilled in the field of participative processes.

Parishioners are aware that the world all round them is changing rapidly and radically. It pains them to feel part of a Church which seems to be floundering in the midst of all this change and gives the impression that it does not know how to cope. What makes it all the more exasperating is that many of them have experience of coping with change in their professional and home lives.

Priests are one of the presenting problems highlighting the need for change within the Church – the diminishing number of priests and their advancing age and declining health. The main response being given to this problem is perceived by many lay people as being purely short-term. In the absence of a resident parish priest alternative arrangements are made (e.g. clustering groups of parishes) for providing Mass for people. It cannot be denied that for most parishioners one of their major concerns is that they do not lose their Sunday community Mass and that they have a priest to look to in times of need. Nevertheless, as seen already, whichever dimension of community is to the fore in a parish, the availability of a priest for Sunday Mass is only one element among many contributing to making a parish a healthy community according to the mind of Vatican II. That is why many Catholics today feel that this so-called 'crisis situation' is actually a time of opportunity. It offers the chance to turn the spotlight away from the priest and forces us to restate the question in terms of how the laity, in keeping with their baptismal vocation, can be more fully involved in the life and mission of the local Church.

However, talk about more comprehensive lay involvement will not be credible to people unless they see that their diocese is embracing such a development positively and enthusiastically. And that means adequate resource allocation. To many, including myself, that means making the budget for the training of priests merely one item, and not necessarily the most important item, within the budget for ministerial formation in general. It also means situating the formation of priests within the wider human context of formation for all ministries, full-time or part-time, thereby reducing the danger of priests seeing themselves as 'men apart'. Instead they should be recognised as partners in collaborative ministry with the special responsibility of empowering their sisters and brothers to have confidence in their God-given gifts and in using them for the good of others and so for the glory of God.

BRIEF COMMENTS ON OTHER THEOLOGICAL QUESTIONS ARISING OUT OF THE PARISH REPORTS

*The non-reception by parishioners of certain elements
of official Church teaching.*

One by-product of the kind of participatively-discerned and coherent diocesan pastoral policy suggested above could be to help break the theologically unhealthy dichotomy between the parish (and individual parishioner) and the wider Church. If this is seen as a positive mutual relationship of correspondence, then the issue of widespread dissent on the part of faithful and committed Catholics (laity and priests) from official teaching could also be viewed more positively. No longer would it be dismissed by the powers-that-be as a dangerous instance of 'doing your own thing' leading to some kind of anarchic relativism. Rather it would be treated with the respect due to any seriously constructive critical stance of non-reception. In such instances of widespread non-reception, individual Christians, through sharing a common mind (*conscientia*) with others, would be contributing from their unique situations to the ongoing process in the Church of gradually appropriating the truth and how best to discern its application to complex life-situations. On this point Karl Rahner comments:

> On any true understanding there is, even in the Catholic Church, an open 'system' in which the most varied factors (the 'instinct' of the faithful, fresh insights on the part of individual Christians and theologians, fresh situations that arise in a particular age, the new questions to which these give rise and much else besides) work together to throw fresh light upon the Church's own awareness of her faith, and to produce a development of doctrine (*Theological Investigations*, London, Darton, Longman & Todd, 1974 vol xi, p. 286).

The non-accountability of priests

Although most of the priests mentioned in the parish reports are clearly trying to be faithful to a form of priestly life and ministry in keeping with Vatican II, here and there are found hints that the bottom line tells a different story. In other words, in the end it is the priest who controls the parish agenda and he can make decisions as he thinks fit in all areas of parish life, whether liturgy, finance, administration or pastoral policy. It is true that the language of 'co-responsibility' and 'collaborative ministry' features largely in most reports. Yet, despite this language and even in parishes where great efforts have been made to develop collaborative ministry, there is no getting away from the power of veto of the parish priest. He has the last word.

Such a situation leaves any parish at the mercy of the whim of an incoming new parish priest who may decide to reverse much of what has been achieved by the parish in its efforts to implement the vision of Vatican II. The fruits of years of hard work and pastoral imagination undertaken jointly by the former parish priest and the main body of the parish can be scuttled by a mere dictate of the incoming priest. Incidentally, this problem is not restricted to parishes. There have been some tragic instances of dioceses where the achievements of the inspired and collaborative leadership of a former bishop have been well-nigh destroyed by the appointment of a new Ordinary who is utterly opposed to the direction in which the diocese had been moving. The dismantling of the creative pastoral initiatives of Cardinal Arns and Archbishop Helder Camara are two tragic cases in point.

Coming back to the parish level this emphasises the importance of a Parish Mission Statement which has been decided upon and owned by the parish as a whole and which any incoming priest is obliged to honour. Obviously, such a parish mission statement needs to be consistent with any agreed diocesan pastoral policy and both should be in line with the overall mission of the Church and grounded on sound principles of pastoral theology. Such a diocesan mission statement should be agreed upon only after extensive consultation and collaborative decision-making throughout the whole diocese. Obviously, a parish or diocesan mission statement is not something static, engraved on stone. It will always be open to revision in the light of new situations to be faced, or deepening theological or pastoral insights, or even to enable the parish or diocese to incorporate the special gifts of some new individuals or groups who have come on the scene and who offer a rich pastoral resource for the parish or diocese.

There seems to be a growing awareness in the Church that, unless priests are open to some kind of accountability, the Vatican II notion of co-responsibility, consultation and collaborative ministry will ring very hollow. Even programmes of self or peer appraisal, though important and greatly to be encouraged, still leave something to be desired. An important part of the leadership role of a bishop is to support, encourage and inspire his priests. But that must not be to the detriment of his oversight of the pastoral care of the people. In some instances, hopefully rare, the bishop will need to take whatever action is needed to make sure that serious harm is not done to the faith of parishioners and their pastoral welfare by the gross insensitivity, pastoral ineptitude or sheer ignorance of a priest in their parish. This is delicate ground. However, the safe-guards against the professional misconduct of priests should not be any less rigorous than, for instance, in the teaching and medical professions.

The issue of democracy in the Church
In a number of the parish reports the phrase, 'of course, the Church is not a democracy', occurs in one form or another. Such a statement should not be al-lowed to pass without comment. It can be based on very questionable theolog-ical assumptions. Edward Schillebeeckx concludes the third and final volume of his magisterial work on Christology with a chapter entitled, 'Towards Dem-ocratic Rule of the Church as a Community of God'. He argues that the Church should reflect our highest level of human societal experience. That would imply that today the Church should reflect democratic ideals and practices much more than those of a monarchy, autocracy or oligarchy. He asks:

> Why in the past this Church government could with great assurance take over the civil forms of feudal government and later those of an absolute monarchy, while being completely closed to modern forms of govern-ment and rule, especially democrative forms of authority (*Church: The Human Story of God*, (SCM, London, 1990, p. 220).

The fact that authority in the Church community is different from authority in civil society does not automatically exclude its democratic exercise. Schille-beeckx writes:

> 'Not lording it over' does not exclude democracy! Why then should the Church not be able to democratize its model of government and rule without in so doing harming its subjection to the word of God? As if an authoritarian government went better with the subjection of the Church to God's word than a democratic government, in which the voice of the whole people of God is listened to more clearly and accurately! (p. 219).

He even argues that the democratic exercise of authority in the Church seems more in keeping with our understanding of the Church today than is the monarchical model we are currently living with. Similar thinking to this is ex-pressed in a teaching document from the bishops of Quebec, *Annoncer l'Evangile dans la culture actuelle au Quebec*, (Montreal, Fides, 1999):

> Our culture is profoundly marked by the spirit of democracy. Democratic society values the participation of all. The democratic spirit builds a new relationship to the truth. The Church is to proclaim the Gospel in a relevant

way. It is not sufficient to insist that the Church is not a democracy, even if that statement is correct. Integration into the Church in a democratic society leads to a new relation to authority and a different manner of proclaiming the Gospel. What is required is a certain degree of participation and a careful listening to all the voices that want to be heard. Nothing can be imposed simply by authority: there is no single word (from abridged English text in *The Ecumenist*, Winter 2000, pp. 1-3).

The assertion, 'the Church is not a democracy' can be used to justify the theologically untenable position that lay people (and priests too) do not have any right to have their views heard. This can lead to a very watered-down version of consultation and can suggest that there is no need to follow the best available advice and expertise on the processes of consultation. It can also produce a version of lay-involvement which is much more one of benevolence rather than empowerment. The Brazilian poet-bishop Pedro Casaldaliga once said: 'I don't want the Church to be a democracy. I want it to be something better than a democracy. I want it to be a community.' I understand Schillebeeckx to be saying that a community in which authority is exercised through democratic processes offers the 'best practice' of being community available to us today, unlike a community in which authority works more autocratically.

At present women are virtually excluded from the main corridors of power within the Church. Even in the rare instances in which they hold important positions of authority, they are still subject to the final word coming from parish priest or bishop or Vatican congregation. This is due to the link between orders and jurisdiction. Perhaps the way many women's groups, including women religious, go about their decision-making has a lesson for the Church. Their fidelity in following processes designed to help achieve consensus is reminiscent of the custom in some tribes in Africa and other cultures. It might even be preferable to Western democracy and could be a gift which Church authorities might receive from women's groups within and beyond the Church. Such a way of exercising authority might have even more compelling 'intrinsic theological reasons' in favour of its being followed within the Church.

The question – 'Are you in favour of married priests or women priests?'
This question can raise the hackles of many people. It can touch some very deep and unconscious prejudices within us. In some strange way, associating the priesthood with women and also with marriage seems to touch some unresolved problems regarding sexuality in some people. This is particularly the case with some Roman Catholics, but it also affects people in other Churches, as is clear from the resistance to the ordination of women well beyond the confines of the Roman Catholic Church. Nevertheless, it is surprising how much support for married priests and women priests comes out in the parish reports.

Yet I must confess that I feel slightly uneasy about the question as posed in the survey. I wonder whether it might have been more helpful pastorally to have approached the issue from a different angle. There is no doubt in virtually all the reports that the priest plays a key role in the parish community. The impression is given that the interviewees could not envisage a parish community without the involvement of a priest in some way or other. Given such a strong belief in the priestly ministry, perhaps a more open question from a pastoral point of view might have been: 'How are we to ensure that this ministry continues?' That offers the possibility of viewing married priests and women priests not as a problem or a threat but as a possible, even desirable, solution to a very real need.

The disaffection of young people from the parish

This certainly raises a major question for the Church. Given the disaffection of young people on such a wide scale, is the Church as we know it going to survive? However, here again, perhaps Church survival should not be starting point for our self-questioning as Church. The Church does not exist for itself. It is a servant-Church whose mission is to help others see a meaning to their lives through an encounter with the living Word of God. The first question posed to us by the disaffection of young people, therefore, should not be one about the survival of the Church. It should be more at the level of: Are we failing in our mission to serve young people? In other words, are we in danger of too readily assuming that the problem lies with the young people? Do we too easily assume that the basic problem lies in their having become slaves to the consumer society with its spotlight on instant gratification, whether through drugs, alcohol, sex or fashion, with the result that they have no time to stop and think about the deeper things in life?

Without denying that the modern world is a very enticing and distracting place for young people (and, at times, a very cruel place too), do we in the Church need to ask ourselves whether it could be the Church, not young people, that is the problem? Could it be that the Gospel we are presenting to them lacks the inspiration and attraction of the 'the mind of Christ' as specifically appealing to young people? Could it be that the liturgy we offer them says nothing to them? When they reject it as 'boring', are they being unspiritual, or are they saying that it is not in tune with the kind of spirituality they are searching for? Is this a problem just for young people? When they reject the Church's moral teaching as 'out of touch', are they simply flaunting their immorality or amorality, or might they be saying that they do not find that the Church whether in its teaching or its community-life, offers them a challenge which they find exciting and which gives them a dream and a vision of a life worth living? Perhaps what is needed is not a mission to young people to convert them, but rather putting more effort into listening to young people and into trying to learn from them about the meaning of the Gospel as they see it for today's world.

CHAPTER THREE

Vision of a Vatican II Parish

The following offers a possible blueprint for a Vatican II parish. It is an abbreviated version of a much longer article I wrote for The Month, 1996, April, pp. 129-136 under the title, Archbishop Worlock's Legacy to Liverpool. A shorter version of the original appeared as chapter one of my book, From a Parish Base, DLT, London, 1999. In each version I was trying to offer a blueprint for how a parish might look which has tried to be faithful to the Vatican II vision of the Church?

At the end of this piece I have added some reflections on ways in which, fifteen years later, I can see some major omissions in what I have written and I suggest some additions to the text.

A parish committed to furthering the coming of the Kingdom in society
Lumen Gentium defined the Church as 'a kind of sacrament or sign of intimate union with God, and of the unity of all human kind" and as "an instrument for the achievement of such union and unity.' (LG, 1) The 1971 Synod, Justice in the World put more flesh and blood on this definition when it proclaimed:

> Action on behalf of justice and participation in the transformation of the world fully appear to us as a constitutive dimension of the preaching of the Gospel, or, in other words, of the Church's mission for the redemption of the human race and its liberation from every oppressive situation (*Vatican Edition*, p. 6).

In other words, the Church is not a mutual assurance club to serve the interests of its members. Its very *raison d'être* lies in its mission to society and to the world. Vatican II's vision is not one of a 'churchy' Church but of a 'worldly' Church. The Church exists to serve the world. An essential part of its service lies in 'action on behalf of justice' and 'liberation from every oppressive situation'.

This would suggest a parish with the following characteristics:

- a parish organised according to the understanding that it is principally in the local neighbourhood and not in the Church and Church societies that the work of building God's Kingdom is, or is not, taking place;
- a parish which judges its fidelity to living the Gospel by the extent that its members are willing to play an active part in the local community rather than by whether they regularly attend Mass;
- a parish where the victims of oppression can feel at home and where the perpetrators of oppression feel disturbed and challenged;

- a parish in which the homily is not reduced to an other-worldly spiritual message but where it resonates with the nitty-gritty of people's everyday lives, raising up the down-hearted and overturning the mighty;
- a parish which is automatically involved in the social analysis of the causes of local injustices or other issues of community concern, whether in the field of housing, (un)employment, health care, welfare provision, education, drug addiction, nursery provision etc;
- a parish where women feel they belong, not because they are presumed to be naturally pious, but because they sense that their oppression and exploitation as women is recognised and is treated as a matter of serious concern;
- a parish where gays and lesbians can feel secure, because their dignity as human persons is fully accepted, their struggle to live out loving and faithful relationships is appreciated and celebrated, and the pain and injustice they have suffered through homophobia is acknowledged, even to the extent of guilt being confessed and forgiveness requested;
- a parish where the sale of Catholic papers is of much less concern than the manipulation of the media by powerful vested interests and the consequent distortion of vision unjustly foisted upon readers and viewers.

A sacramental parish

By 'sacramental' parish I mean one which recognizes that the whole of life is sacramental. In other words, a parish which believes that the presence and action of God is mediated to us through the daily humdrum of our everyday lives. A sacramental Church helps people to become aware of the presence of God in 'deep down things', as Gerard Manley Hopkins so succinctly expressed it.

Vatican II's choice metaphor for the Church was 'the people of God'. While that metaphor brings out very forcefully the truth that we are all the Church and that ministry is for service, it also evokes the immanence of God in the depths of all people. Hence, it is intimately bound up with the sacramentality of the Church as described above. This sacramentality is even more fundamental to the Church than its hierarchical character.

What would a parish be like which was sacramental in this sense? It might have the following characteristics:

- a parish in which the priest is not a cleric, confined within a functional role imposed on him by the institution (and perhaps by some strong-minded parishioners), but instead can feel free to help people discern what is going on deep in their lives and to follow where the Spirit is moving them, even if this does not easily fit into the usual institutional categories;

- a parish in which creativity and imagination (neither of which is syn-onymous with gimmickry) are used in a spirit of responsible freedom in the preparation and celebration of the liturgy so that it resonates with whatever is affecting people most profoundly in their lives or is of deep concern to the community as a whole;
- a parish with a genuine respect for the consciences of individuals, recognising the uniqueness of each person and his or her life and aware that each person's journey through life follows its own special route with all the ups and downs of the dying-and-rising process pe-culiar to the story of this unique individual;
- a parish which believes so strongly in the Holy Spirit that it has the courage to trust the movement of God's spirit in the lives of its mem-bers; and which also believes that this one Spirit we all share may, at times, lead us to challenge and be challenged by each other.

An inclusive parish

The Vatican II metaphor of the People of God contains the germ for the inclu-sive image of the Church. Inclusive here is a very rich concept. It implies the inclusion of people's giftedness in the ministry of the Church. This lies at the heart of collaborative ministry.

The following are a few indications of what a parish might be like if it tries to live out this vision of an inclusive Church:

- a parish totally committed to collaborative ministry. Therefore, a parish in which the parish priest sees himself and is seen by parish-ioners as a team leader and in which the team he leads is not a chosen few but represents all who are exercising any kind of ministry in the parish. In fact, the team members should themselves be team leaders in an ever-increasing series of concentric circles of shared ministry. Moreover, ministry here is interpreted in a very wide sense, includ-ing, for instance, parents, teachers, people caring for sick or aging rel-atives at home.
- a parish in which decision-making is not exclusively in the hands of the parish priest but is shared and spread through the concentric cir-cles of collaborative ministry, due account being taken of the principle of subsidiarity, the need for competence, cooperation, consistency, ac-countability and, when appropriate, specialised knowledge;
- a parish which has been able to work out its own Mission Statement which has been owned by all its members, so that there is a common vision and sense of purpose in the ministry in which people are col-laborating and so that the life and mission of the parish is not depend-ent on the whims or prejudices of any incoming priest;

- a parish in which those who often feel marginalised in Church and society are able to feel at home and have a sense of belonging; hence, a parish in which there is a welcoming forum where those who feel excluded are given a sympathetic hearing; which, in turn, means a parish which is not afraid of criticism, even self-criticism, and which is prepared to change anything in its lifestyle which tends to exclude rather than include people.
- a parish which has a problem with being asked to pray for vocations by a Church which, through its exclusion of women from the priesthood, refuses to believe that God might be calling them to this form of ministry.

An ecumenical parish

The post-Vatican II Church is called to be an ecumenical Church. This means that we need to use our imagination to envisage what sort of parish we should want if we are to be true to this dimension of the post-Vatican II vision of the Church. A few suggestions might stimulate us to think further about this:

- a parish in which the parish leaders have developed a good working relationship, a sense of mutual trust and friendship and a shared concern for the Church's mission in the neighbourhood with the leaders of the other local Christian Churches through meeting regularly to share in prayer, collaborative planning and to develop personal and denominational understanding and friendship;
- a parish which is fully committed to the principle that nothing should be done separately which can be done at least equally well together;
- a parish where ecumenical cooperation and friendship is not the sole preserve of the parish leaders but where all parishioners have the opportunity to meet their non-Catholic Christian sisters and brothers through shared worship in each other's Churches, through actively collaborating with each other in ministry and mission and through developing closer understanding and friendship by means of ecumenical house groups or joint social gatherings;
- a parish which is prepared to tackle the structural obstacles to ecumenical progress; making sure, for instance, that Church schools foster ecumenical understanding and association rather than consolidate disunity by keeping children separate; that inter-Church marriages are welcomed as exciting experiments in Christian unity already achieved;
- a parish which refuses to accept any implication that intercommunion is shocking and scandalous but which believes that it is actually called for by the very meaning of the Eucharist; hence, a parish which is unhappy with the teaching of One Bread One Body, believing that the

main thrust of eucharistic theology is not towards defining boundaries of exclusion but towards stretching inclusion to the furthest limits which are consonant with safeguarding the essentials of unity; a
parish, therefore, which is anxious that the possibilities of Eucharistic
intercommunion envisaged in no. 129 of the 1993 Ecumenical Directory be extended as widely as possible.

A catholic parish

'Catholic', as we have all been taught, means universal. In that sense it ties in
with what has been said above about a parish being 'inclusive'. 'Catholic'
should not be used as a term to define ourselves over against others. Our
Catholicity is a gift to be shared. Vatican II stressed the catholicity of the Church
in a whole variety of ways. For instance, its teaching on collegiality among the
bishops emphasised that the pastoral responsibility of bishops was not confined
within the boundaries of their own dioceses.

What are the implications for parish life of a Church which is truly catholic?
Again, I offer a few suggestions as to what a parish would be like which is trying to be true to that vision:

- a parish which is not too 'parochial' in its concerns; and hence...
- a parish which is prepared to accept that parish interests need not be
  the only or even the determining factor in some difficult decisions affecting it - for instance, amalgamating or even closing a parish school;
  losing one of its priests or even sharing its only priest with another
  parish; giving up its presbytery or even its Church; sharing the financial burdens of less well-off parishes; or even the extreme case of ceasing to exist as a parish in order to merge with another parish or to
  embark on a more experimental form of local Church community;
- a parish in which justice and peace issues, at home or abroad, are the
  concern of the whole parish and not just of the select few in the local
  J & P group and this being reflected in the liturgy, educational programmes and financial priorities of the parish;
- a parish which is well-informed about what is happening, positively
  and negatively, in the wider Church; and hence...
- a parish which instinctively networks with positive Church initiatives
  nationally and internationally
- and a parish in which concern is felt and expressed about injustice
  within the Church, as well as in society, and in which respect for the
  Pope and his ministry of communion among the Churches is not understood as meaning an uncritical response to everything emanating
  from the Vatican.

A praying and worshipping Church

Obviously, prayer and worship is an essential part of the life of every parish. Still, it is worth using our pastoral imagination to envisage additional ways in which a parish can be true to Vatican II's call to be a praying and worshipping community:

- a parish which puts more emphasis on prayer, than on prayers;
- a parish in which spending time in prayer is a natural expectation for anyone prepared to involve themselves in the more organised collaborative ministry in the parish;
- a parish in which the priest, in particular, is a good prayer, giving prayer a high priority in his daily *horarium*, feeding his prayer and preaching through scriptural and other nourishing reading and allowing himself sufficient space for solitude and retreat;
- a parish where the deep human events in the lives of individuals, families and the community are allowed sensitive and meaningful expression in the liturgy; and hence …
- a parish where it is recognised that the priest needs at least as much preparation for the celebration of a baptism, marriage or funeral as do the people themselves, a preparation which enables him to tune into the deeper human meaning of this event in their lives; hence …
- a parish where families experience the funeral liturgy as an authentic and very personal celebration of the life of whoever has died, as well as a faith-filled support and comfort for them in their grief;
- a parish where the language used in the baptism of a child, as well as expressing its deep theological significance, also enables the parents and family to celebrate the birth of their child, to thank God for entrusting this precious gift to their care and to commit themselves as parents and family to its human and Christian upbringing;
- a parish where the preparation for and celebration of a marriage clearly recognises that this is a key moment in the growth of a couple's love for each other, enabling them to pledge and celebrate that love publicly and affirming them in their faith and courage to continue on their exciting but difficult journey together; hence …
- a preparation and celebration which feels no need to express any condemnation of the couple if they have been cohabiting up to this point but which is able to rejoice with them in the goodness they have experienced in their shared love and which is also able to feel at ease with the active participation in the wedding of any children who may already be the fruit of that love;
- a parish in which the full and active participation of the people, as demanded by Vatican II, is the top priority in liturgical celebration and in which more detailed liturgical regulations are kept subservient to this top priority; hence …

- a parish which feels not only free but even obliged to bend the letter of the liturgical law in order to achieve its authentic spirit, even when this involves such practices as general absolution and the careful adaptation or even composition of eucharistic prayers for particular occasions.

Meeting the unpredictable future 'with hope in our hearts'

It would be presumptuous to be too specific about the kind of Church God is calling us to be. Throughout this chapter I have consistently taken for granted the ongoing existence of the parish. Though it is hard to envisage any Christian alternative to the gathered community of people in a locality, whether we call it parish or not, God's spirit could possibly be demanding a depths of dying and rising in the Church which is beyond our present understanding.

On further reflection ... fifteen years later!

Fifteen years after the original article was written, I am very aware of some major omissions. The most obvious is my not highlighting the Eucharist at the heart of the life of a Vatican II parish. It is implicit throughout but should have been given a more central place. The same is true of the parish as a community. While also implicit, it should have featured much more prominently. I hope Part III of this collection, 'The Eucharist and Vatican II', goes some way to making up for the first omission. Likewise, what I have written about community in the previous chapter might help to supply for the second omission. Rather like the little fish who asked the big fish where the ocean was only to be told 'You are in the middle of it', I think my own parish life and ministry was so immersed in both Eucharist and community that I took them too much for granted in what I wrote!

Under the bullet heading 'An inclusive parish' it might help to add the following: - a parish which lays great emphasis on lay leadership and on the careful selection and training of lay-leaders. A pool of lay-leaders with thorough pastoral formation who would provide a rich source from which suitable married or single men or women could be put forward for ordination, if and when this becomes accepted practice in the Church, as, for instance, when needed to prevent the community from being deprived of the Eucharist.

What I have written under the second bullet point, 'Catholic', needs to be modified lest it be understood as implying Vatican II approval for totalitarianism in the Church. Maybe a better formulation might be – 'Parish interests need to be balanced against the interests of the Church in the wider locality. While a wholesale amalgamation of parishes to cope with a shortage of clergy would be contrary to the person-centred and community nature of a parish in the vision of Vatican II, that same vision could mean that in some extreme situations it has to be recognised that a parish or school has become unviable due to lack of sufficient numbers due to demographic changes.'

CHAPTER FOUR

Spirituality of a Vatican II Parish

This is a slightly modified version of Spirituality and the Parish which originally appeared in The Way Supplement, 2001, pp. 129-137

Spirituality: a dimension of being human

We sometimes look on spirituality as something esoteric, reserved for people of a religious disposition. Nothing could be further from the truth. The spiritual is simply a dimension of our being human persons. It is something we all share. It is our ability to see beneath the surface of life, to discern deeper meaning under the veneer of everyday experience. Gerard Manley Hopkins spoke of seeing 'deep down things'. The spiritual is as much part of us as all the other dimensions of our being human.

It is true, of course, that we may not always be in touch with our spiritual dimension. That is not surprising, since the same is true of the other dimensions of our being. We are bodily persons and yet can be blind to much of the richness of bodily presence and touch. We are also social persons and yet, in our highly individualist society, we may not recognize just how interdependent we are and how crucial the social realm is in our everyday lives.

Similarly cultural factors can drown our spiritual dimension too – the speed and noise of modern living, the emphasis on instant gratification purveyed by advertising in our consumer society, the tendency to see ourselves atomistically as individuals among other disconnected individuals, the post-modern rejection of any meaning and purpose common to human life.

Yet the spiritual in us is so deep-rooted it does not drown that easily. Paradoxically, the very factors which threaten it also cause it to struggle to the surface and fight for survival. In fact, these days spirituality seems to be making a strong come-back. This is in marked contrast to the diminishing popularity of institutional religion, especially those Churches with more formal and highly organised structures of worship and rules for living.

Key question: Is our spiritual hunger fed by parish life and worship?

The main question I would like to face here is this: Is there a mismatch between our spiritual dimension and the life and worship experienced in most parishes today? In other words, even when we are in touch with our deepest spiritual hunger, do we find that hunger being fed by our parish life today or do we find ourselves searching elsewhere for sustenance?

I suspect that often there is such a mismatch. Many people do not find their spiritual hunger satisfied by what they experience in their parishes each week.

Admittedly, that is a vast generalisation and is not based on any formal analysis of research data. Nor am I suggesting that it is true of every parish and certainly not of everything going on within each of our parishes. Nevertheless, my suspicion is that for many people for much of the time their spiritual hunger is not being satisfied by much of what they experience in their parishes. If this is true, it could make us look at the drift away from regular Church-going in a different light. Such a drift might not be indicative of a weakening faith on the part of many parishioners.

In raising these questions I am aware that there is a danger of confusing the popular with the truly spiritual or genuinely religious. We are not in the game of fighting for audience ratings. The answer to diminishing congregations is not full Churches, however attractive that prospect might be to many church people.

Dwindling congregations, fewer and aging priests are only a symptom of a much deeper problem. I do not believe that the problem is that the Gospel has lost its appeal. It might be that the appeal of the Gospel is not being heard. And that might be because it is not being communicated.

So it is the priests who are to blame! They are not doing their job! No! That is not at all what I am trying to say, even though most of us priests would probably acknowledge some truth in this – while adding that why we are not doing our job as well as we might is because we are confused and unsure about the meaning of priestly ministry today. We are unsure as to what our role is. Maybe it is healthy to admit that. At least it is better than complacency or burying our heads in the sand. A problem acknowledged and explored can actually become an opportunity for new growth.

A dichotomy between spirituality and religion

Perhaps the real underlying problem has something to do with a dichotomy between spirituality and religion in today's world. The spiritual dimension is woven into the very texture of people's everyday lives. It is not an extra ingredient, an add-on factor. In the liturgy we should feel that the down-to-earth integrity of our everyday lives is being acknowledged and celebrated. Down-to-earth gives the clue. What is celebrated is not just some esoteric, quasi-mystical dimension of our lives. It is much more down-to-earth than that. It involves all the ambiguity and glory that makes up our multi-dimensional everyday lives. The spiritual, the deep-downness referred to by Gerard Manley Hopkins, is only a dimension of this richness.

Could a major part of the problem be that many people imagine religion to be something other-worldly. They feel they are doing something 'extra' when they come to Church? It is something over and above their everyday lives, the 'religious bit'. Admittedly, they do not see this extra bit as totally divorced from the rest of life. In fact, they see it as sanctifying the rest of life, a kind of religious 'value-added' blessing.

Encountering God in everyday life

In reality, perhaps the exact opposite is the case. It is primarily in our day-to-day lives that we encounter God, more often than not quite unconsciously. This is brought out by Margaret Rogers in a *Catholic Pictorial* article (4 February 2001). She writes about a young woman, Jenny, in her mid-twenties with three children under the age of six whom she looks after on her own. Her partner prefers to go out with his mates for a drink. She gets virtually no help from the rest of the family, seeing little of her brothers, and having to attend to her mother who has some form of mental illness. One of her children has a chronic medical condition needing frequent hospital visits. So Jenny has to cope with awkward bus journeys, made more difficult by having the other toddler in tow and by long waits at the clinic. Money is very short and future prospects are poor.

> Each day she got the little ones ready, walked them to school, returned home, out again to take the middle child to toddler group, shopped or returned home with the baby. Before she had time to think she was back again to collect him. Often one or more of the children would be fractious, one might be ill, or the weather might be bad. Time spent with the children and the constant demands that little ones make, the whole gamut of household chores and seeing to her mother filled her days, week in week out, month in month out. Some days she ached just for a bit of time and space for herself, for a bit of variety and a chance to do something different.
>
> Jenny is not a Church-goer and knows little about the gospels or creeds ('I'm not into that kind of thing.'). She would certainly not look on herself as a 'holy' person. She simply accepts the hardship of her life and gets on with it with real faithfulness and commitment. She has no 'head' knowledge of God and only names him as an expletive. What an apparently dismal life!'

Margaret Rogers fully appreciates its hardness and drudgery. But she also sees the 'deep down' wonder of Jenny's life. Her words make this point much more convincingly than any words of mine:

> If we substitute the word 'Love' for God ('God is Love and anyone who dwells in love dwells in God and God dwells in him/her') then it looks a very different picture. Jenny had plenty of knowledge of Love (God) but it was a knowledge gained through the heart and through her life experience. Each day, as she 'denied herself and took up her cross daily', she entered ever deeper into the life and mystery of Love (God). Jenny's story is that of so many people in our society, who in hidden ways, behind

closed doors, live out a life of love, commitment and dedication. A wise woman friend of mine once said: 'Parenthood is the way we ordinary people find out what Love (God) is all about.' It can take us to the sharp edge of self-sacrifice and self-denial in a way that little else in life can.

Margaret is suggesting that the stuff of really profound spirituality is there in abundance in Jenny's life. The tragedy is that she is being given no help in recognising the miracle of her tremendous self-sacrifice or in being able to see that in this self-sacrifice God's love is in her and she in God.

It should be part of the Church's role to give her this help. It is tragic when the Church seems unable to respond to her need. If only the words and actions of its liturgy were sufficiently in tune with the nitty gritty of her ordinary, every-day life, they would enable Jenny to recognise that her daily round is, in fact, 'holy ground' and the deep presence of God is there. Sadly, that is rarely the case at present. So people like Jenny are being deprived of that sense of their own dignity and goodness. (Sadly the new translation of the Missal is likely to aggravate this problem with its special 'sacral vernacular' language!)

Bridging the chasm

Jenny's story, typical of so many, brings out just how wide can be the chasm between spirituality and religion. How can that massive chasm be bridged?

Margaret has given voice to the profound spiritual dimension in Jenny's life. In the light of the Gospel she has interpreted the 'deep down' profundity of Jenny's apparently dismal and hopeless life. In so doing Margaret has probably helped many like Jenny to find meaning and dignity in all the hardship of their lives.

What about Jenny's parish – and the parishes of the many other Jenny's in our world? In an ideal world, Jenny should be able to find in her parish the en-couragement and inspiration she has received from Margaret. At present that rarely seems to be the case. Could Margaret's article help to change that situa-tion? No and yes! No, if it is simply read as an interesting piece and then laid aside. Yes, if it helps to initiate a process in a parish whereby the everyday lives of people are listened to as 'holy ground' where God is encountered. To be lis-tened to in this way, people need to be empowered to give voice to the experi-ence of their everyday lives 'in the assembly of the faithful'. That, in itself, is no easy thing to achieve. And those listening to their voice need to listen with antennae finely tuned to recognising the presence of God 'deep down' within the life experiences they are privileged to hear. Such discernment may be a rare gift in a parish and one that needs to be fostered and made available for the benefit of the parish as a whole.

Parish liturgy and everyday life

Even if this process is going on within a parish, how can the spiritual profundity of everyday life accessed in this way find its way into the celebration of the parish liturgy? After all, it is from the celebration of the liturgy that parishioners should hope to draw inspiration, encouragement and hope for their lives. How can the rich vein of spirituality latent in Jenny's life come to be celebrated in the liturgy of her parish. Unless that can be achieved the Vatican II ideal of 'full and active participation' in the liturgy will be meaningless for Jenny and the many like her.

The problem with our liturgy is that it tends to be celebrated as though it was taking place on a higher plane to everyday life, certainly not the plane on which Jenny is living her life. OK, the bidding prayers are more down-to-earth, though even they tend to be focused on issues of more general and even international concern. The homily provides an opportunity to flesh out the meaning of God's words in terms of everyday life. Yet, sadly it is an opportunity we priests rarely make the most of – our words are often up in the air and rarely connect with the 'down-to-earth' lives of people like Jenny. Perhaps this is partly due to the fact that a combination of celibacy and clerical culture leaves us largely out-of-touch with the nitty-gritty of most people's everyday lives.

I have no secret formulae for making our liturgies the life-celebrating and liberating experiences they should be for people like Jenny. We priests tend to blame the intransigence of liturgical law. Maybe that is an excuse we hide behind. After all, the Vatican II Constitution on the Sacred Liturgy states very clearly:

> The Church very much wants all believers to be led to take a full, conscious and active part in liturgical celebration. This is demanded by the nature of the liturgy itself … This full and active sharing on the part of the whole people is of paramount concern in the process of renewing the liturgy and helping it to grow, because such sharing is the first, and necessary, source from which believers can imbibe the true Christian spirit (no. 14 – Translation from Norman Tanner, Ed., *Decrees of the Ecumenical Councils*, London, Sheed & Ward, 1990, II, p. 824).

That provides the over-riding principle for our interpretation of more specific liturgical laws in parish life. In other words, how we interpret every other liturgical law in parish situations is to be judged on whether it helps or hinders 'a full, conscious and active sharing' in the situation we are dealing with.

And 'sharing' here means more than being given a specific function in the liturgy. Even more importantly it is about whether our everyday lives are named, celebrated and inspired in the liturgy. A liturgy could be rubrically perfect and yet in gross violation of this basic principle. If sharing at this profound level is impeded by the legal inflexibility of liturgical texts, then such inflexibility must take second place. Likewise, if "full, conscious and active sharing" is impeded by laws forbidding someone like Margaret to feed the congregation by her inspired insights into the word of God and its impact on every day life, then the respect we owe to these laws must give way before our respect for the congregation's need for the word of God to satisfy their spiritual hunger. Respect for the homily as applying God's word to the realities of everyday life demands competence in being able to understand and interpret God's revealed word. That is why a priest is given professional training at this level. But what about competence in the humdrum experience of everyday living and being able to discern this as a sacred place for encountering God. Most of us priests lack proper competence at this level, whereas some lay people are particularly gifted in this way. Does not the principle of "full, conscious and active sharing" in the liturgy demand that parishioners are not denied the rich interpretation of their lives in the light of God's word that such gifted lay people are able to give?

As an example of such a homily, let me instance the following passage taken from a letter I received a few years ago from a close friend of mind, Paula, at whose wedding I had officiated. She was writing from Australia, describing the wonder of their first child, Simon, and how he had revealed so much to her and her husband, Ian, about the presence of God in their lives:

> The miracle is that a small, dependent baby has the power to teach us what love is all about. All of this he does without words, simply by looks, gazes and touches. The first thing he learnt to do was smile. That struck me as saying something about our need to communicate - our need to feel related to each other. Among the many gifts a baby brings is the gift of joy. It's infectious and wonderful.
>
> They have the gift of revelation. They reveal both the human and the eternal. I watch Ian with Simon and in that process Ian's tenderness, gentleness, strength and vulnerability is revealed. It is as if a baby allows us to be more truly ourselves. They accept and give unconditionally from the word 'go'. That is liberating for those who are privileged to have them in their lives and share their journey with them.
>
> So babies reveal something of the human in men and women. And our great God is in all this, calling us to grow, give and receive graciously.
>
> I am continually confronted with this thought: If we, with all our limitations and petty insecurities, can love so much, and simply ache with tenderness and be driven with a desire to nurture, how great is our God's love. That's mind-blowing, wonderful and freeing. So perhaps for the first time in my life I feel this deep and powerful sense of being connected to our creator God. I have begun to comprehend the unconditional love our God lavishes on us.

We know that through the gift that is Simon, our God is calling us to love and not to count the cost, to be dependent and to know no fear, to accept ourselves and one another, to bask in our God's love and know the peace that brings. Parenthood is a gifted, wonderful and challenging experience - and an incredibly humbling one.

I read that letter out as my homily on one occasion. I suspect that the parishioners listened as they had never listened before – or since! I have received two further letters (potential homilies) from my friend, a beautiful one on the continuing revelation involved in parenting (they now have two children) and a very challenging one on married priests (three of the last four priests in her parish have married). They are both written with enormous wisdom and love.

I am not advocating liturgical anarchy in our parishes, I am simply suggesting that observance of liturgical law should be faithful to the fundamental liturgical principle of 'full, conscious and active sharing'. Liturgical inflexibility can dehumanise parish liturgy and so can be in serious violation of that basic principle. Such inflexibility only widens the chasm between the spiritual and the religious. In the previous chapter I suggested that the blueprint of a Vatican II parish should include the following two items:

> ... a parish in which creativity and imagination (neither of which is synonymous with gimmickry) are used in a spirit of responsible freedom in the preparation and celebration of the liturgy so that it resonates with whatever is affecting people most profoundly in their lives or is of deep concern to the community as a whole;

> ... a parish which feels not only free but even obliged to bend the letter of the liturgical law in order to achieve its authentic spirit, even when this involves such practices as general absolution and the careful adaptation or even composition of eucharistic prayers for particular occasions.

I return to this point later in my essay, '"Mind the Gap": Person-centred Liturgy' in Section II, 'The Eucharist and Vatican II' where I also offer a few samples of possible Eucharistic Prayers.

Spirituality, parish and local context

Some years ago my own Archdiocese of Liverpool launched a consultative process to discern its key priorities as well as those of each parish and deanery. To kick-start this process all parishioners were given a leaflet listing twenty-four pastoral priorities (resulting from two earlier clergy meetings!) and asked to select their top three, adding others if they so wish. The heading on the leaflet gave the first draft of a mission statement for the Archdiocese:

The mission of the Roman Catholic Archdiocese of Liverpool: To be faithful to the mandate of the Lord Jesus to evangelise: 'Go into the world and proclaim the good news to the whole creation' (Mk 16,15).

At an earlier clergy meeting this draft mission statement was criticised as too general and rather anodyne. Despite its Gospel language, there was nothing in it to arouse enthusiasm. It could apply equally well to any diocese in the whole world. It was totally a-cultural. It did not speak specifically to that part of the God's world embraced by the boundaries of the Liverpool Archdiocese. Sadly the Mission Statement finally adopted, though briefer, remains equally non-contextual and uninspiring: 'Taking to heart the last words of the Lord Jesus, we will go into the world to proclaim the Good News to the whole of creation.'

This brings out very clearly the need for the spirituality of a parish to be contextualised. It has to be tuned into life, if it is to be alert to the call of God coming from the midst of life. This is not something that can be done easily. It requires a lot of listening, especially listening to those who experience this particular culture/society or even the Church itself in this specific locality as oppressive and dehumanising – and often these voices are stifled and not easily heard. It also requires a positive attitude of appreciation and celebration, recognising human goodness wherever it is found, even sometimes in the most surprising places, and seeing the grace of God present and at work there. One of the most beautiful things I read in a collection of parish reports from various dioceses was written by the priest in an area where the numbers of Catholics had dwindled dramatically and yet the parish as a liturgical centre had burst into new life through being open to celebrate the 'spiritual' in the lives of the people in the neighbourhood:

> Increasingly, our parish ritualises the important events in the lives of individuals and in the life of the whole community, is a refuge for those of any religion or none who are in need, a place where celebrations of all kinds take place to which all are invited. It is becoming an agent for toleration, integration and love with the whole community and a pointer to the wider world outside. It has ceased to be a 'chaplaincy for Roman Catholics'.

CHAPTER FIVE

Being the Catholic Parish Priest of the shared Roman Catholic/Anglican Church of St Basil & All Saints, Widnes

The final ten years of my parish ministry gave me a rare and very privilege ecumenical experience. It was a most wonderful and thoroughly enjoyable experience. This chapter with its two supplements tells that unforgettable story. Towards the end of this account I share with the reader my growing awareness of some serious errors of judgement I made towards the end of my time in the parish. I also express criticism of decisions made by my own Archbishop, Patrick Kelly, at that time. I felt I owed it to Archbishop Kelly to show him the text of what I had written. I was deeply impressed by his very generous reply (30 January 2009): 'I think it is best if I simply leave it entirely to your judgment what you print since obviously it is very likely I would tell the story in a rather different way.' This article is also due to appear in the ecumenical periodical, One In Christ.

The Gift and Challenge of Ecumenism

There had been no Roman Catholic priest at the shared Church of St Basil and All Saints, Widnes for over three months when I was appointed in 1998, after having been interviewed by the Joint Church Council (JCC) to assess my suitability. At the very same time the Anglican congregation were just ending an inter-regnum with the appointment of Guy Elsmore as vicar – also following a similar JCC interview. As well as giving the two of us a very valuable experience of receptive learning through our growing together into the shared life of the parish, it also meant that we were able to arrange a joint Induction by both area bishops. The planning of this joint Induction service was itself a rich experience of receptive learning for both congregations, as well as for Guy and myself, as was the shared Induction Service itself.

The two of us soon realised what a rich experience of ecumenical sharing we were being offered through different forms of liturgy, prayer, Church life and social involvement. Early in our programme of weekly planning meetings Guy and I made a commitment to exchange pulpits four or five times a year. It was a great blessing for both of us to be able to listen to how each of us interpreted the Sunday readings from the agreed Common Lectionary. It was also a great privilege to be able to break the Word of God with each other's congregation and to experience how they responded to our preaching. This gave both of us and our congregations a further opportunity for receptive learning since we were sharing the privilege of experiencing and learning from the faith of each other's congregation as it expressed itself in the liturgy. When Archbishop

Kelly conducted his parish visitation in January 2007, I was due to preach at the Anglican Eucharist. The Archbishop was happy to preach instead of me, much to the delight of the Anglican congregation.

When I attended the 2006 First Durham International Ecumenical Consultation on Receptive Learning, Mary Tanner reminded us all of the key role of 'grass-roots ecumenism'. Her very moving words made me even more aware that this was precisely what had been going on in St Basil and All Saints for nearly twenty-four years. Mary's words made me much more conscious of how privileged I was to be serving as parish priest in this unique and graced situation. On the next occasion I preached to our shared community, I told them how deeply I had been affected by Mary Tanner's words and went on to challenge them with the following words:

> Do we really appreciate how gifted we are in our Shared Church? Do we cherish this gift – every single one of us here in our community? Or do some of us just put up with it and even hope that it might go away and we can get back to being like an ordinary 'Roman Catholic' or 'Anglican' parish? We hold this precious gift on trust. We have a shared responsibility for it. We cannot feel complacent about it or hide it away like buried treasure. Our prime responsibility is to let it live and grow in us. It is not for nothing that God's Spirit, the driving force of Christian unity, the giver of all gifts and the life-principle of the Church, is often portrayed as a strong wind or burning fire. Jesus did not promise an easy life to those to whom he gave the gift of his Spirit.

Going back to the Beginning

The Shared Roman Catholic/Anglican Church of St Basil and All Saints, Hough Green, was formally opened by Archbishop Derek Worlock and Bishop David Sheppard on 22 March 1983. Although these two Liverpool bishops were internationally renowned for their deep ecumenical commitment and gave the shared Church their full and enthusiastic support, this far-seeing new venture was due to the initiative of the two local clergy, Pat Conefrey and Bill Broad, with the full support of both congregations. St Basil & All Saints was built on what was originally a green-field site. In the early eighties Hough Green was beginning to be developed to house people who were being moved out from the inner-city area of the Dingle in Liverpool and from parts of Widnes devastated by the chemical industry. The development plans had clearly marked sites for two separate Churches on opposite sides of the road. Fr Pat Conefrey was disturbed at such a prospect and went to see his Anglican opposite number, Revd Bill Broad. Bill's response was an immediate 'Pat, you are an answer to prayer!' Both of them were convinced that to build two separate Churches facing each other would be completely contrary to the Gospel message of unity, especially as it was being understood in the developing ecumenical climate of the time. They initiated a consultation of the people and held several public meetings. By far the overwhelming majority were in favour of a shared Church. In fact, those attending the public meetings gave it unanimous support, while only thirty-two of the four hundred and thirty-two written replies were against it.

Over the years parishioners of the shared Church have enjoyed the privilege of being able to share together in exploring their Faith, caring for the sick and housebound, remembering their dead (both at funerals and also at a major full-to-capacity non-Eucharist shared service in November), showing commitment to their brothers and sisters in the developing world (support for CAFOD, Christian Aid and especially for the Home-Care HIV/AIDS project in Living-stone, Zambia, which is so dear to all their hearts), jointly caring for their beau-tiful Church building and their inspirational Garden of Hope, and in celebrating socially all the major human events of life (weddings, birthdays, anniversaries for example). On top of that they have helped care for the young people of the area through the usual uniformed and other groups (Guides, Brownies, Boys Brigade and 'Ignite') and through their involvement in and support for their local Church schools, especially St Basil's and All Saints Pri-mary Schools and Sts Peter & Paul's Roman Catholic High School (cf. Appendix for full list of areas of shared life, worship, ministry and service). Sadly the sep-arate primary schools were built prior to the shared Church but every effort has been made to draw them closer together.

St Basil & All Saints Shared Church celebrated its 25th Birthday in 2008. The parishioners decided to extend the celebration over the full twelve months in the form of a 25th Anniversary Year, thus focussing attention on the ecumenical dimension which they see as a treasure entrusted to the Church today.

On the base of the shared baptismal font in St Basil and All Saints are in-scribed the words of the well-known text from Ephesians 4:5, 'One Lord, One Faith, One Baptism.' This is surely saying that 'communicating Faith ecumeni-cally' is not a pastime for a few ecumenical enthusiasts. It is about a passionate commitment, implanted by the Spirit deep in the heart of every Christian. It is an essential dimension of our very being.

Cardinal Kasper made this point very forcefully in his address to the open-ing session of the 3rd European Ecumenical Assembly (5 September 2007) held in Sibiu Romania:

For us, ecumenism is a task given us by Jesus Christ, who prayed 'that all might be one'. It is set in motion by the Holy Spirit and answers a need of our time. We have stretched out our hands to each other and do not want to let them go again.

We ought not to take the divisions between us as something normal, get used to them or gloss over them. They go against the will of Jesus and as such are an expression of sin.

There is no responsible alternative to ecumenism. Anything else would contradict our responsibility to God and the world. The question of unity ought to disturb us; it needs to burn within us.

Despite their commitment to the shared Church ethos, parishioners in St Basil's and All Saints' communities retain their specific identities with their wider Anglican and Roman Catholic Church communities. Nevertheless, their distinctiveness becomes a much richer reality through being coloured by their shared life. In addition to their daily weekday Mass, each weekend, St Basil's parishioners have their own 6.00 pm Saturday vigil Mass and 11.15 am Sunday morning Mass. All Saints have their Sunday Eucharist at 9.45 am and also a Tuesday evening Eucharist at 7.30 pm. There is a Parish Council for each congregation and a Joint Church Council, consisting of the membership of both Parish Councils. Each meets alternately about four times a year.

Simultaneous Eucharist – an early development
One challenge they had to face early in their shared story was how the two communities celebrate the Eucharist on the occasion of the Church's major feasts when both needed to use the shared Church at the same time, especially at Christmas, Holy Week and Easter. For the first couple of years both communities attended each other's Eucharists which were held back to back. This did not lend itself to good liturgy and was experienced as very uninspiring.

It was soon realised that there was no problem about fully sharing in the Liturgy of the Word –which, on occasions like Holy Week, is very extensive. The actual celebration of the Eucharist presented much more of a problem since ecumenical concelebration is forbidden in Roman Catholic Church law. Paul Crowe, a former Parish Priest of St Basil's, tells how they were supported by Archbishop Worlock and Bishop Sheppard in working out an acceptable form of simultaneous celebration of the Eucharist, quite distinct from concelebration.

The following pattern of simultaneous celebration was used on shared major feasts. The Liturgy of the Word is shared completely in common. The prayers for the celebrant are shared between both ministers. The readings likewise are shared between readers from both Churches. This is facilitated by the fact that both Anglicans and Roman Catholics now share the same cycle of Readings over the Church's Liturgical Year. The homily would be preached by one other celebrant and the Prayers of Intercession were shared between readers of both communities.

The Offerings are brought up by members of both congregations and are received by their own Minister. Both celebrants then stand side by side at the altar, each with their respective offerings of bread and wine in front of them. Parts of the Preface and certain sections of the Eucharistic Prayer are shared between the two celebrants. The Epiclesis and the Words of Institution are said by both celebrants in unison, but quite explicitly with reference only to their respective bread and wine.

For the distribution of Holy Communion, the two congregations come up to receive from their own Ministers. Out of respect for the discipline of the Roman Catholic Church, parishioners have always adhered faithfully to this practice. This experience of 'divided communion' is obviously an occasion for shared pain which is felt very deeply by the members of both congregations. Nevertheless, such ecumenical pain can be healthy and even healing. This is true in a special way when parishioners experience it together at the same time and in the course of the same liturgy.

These simultaneous celebrations on major feasts of the Church's year (especially Holy Week and Christmas) have been a very important experience of receptive learning , helping parishioners of both St Basil's and All Saints to see each other not simply as Catholics and Anglicans sharing the one Church building but also as one united, though still divided, community of Christian disciples.

A few years ago Guy Elsmore and I gave the Archdiocesan Ecumenism Commission a presentation on all aspects of life at St Basil & All Saints. We included a full account of our practice of simultaneous celebration of the Eucharist on key festivals. Subsequent to this, the Commission named St Basil & All Saints as a 'sample of good practice' in its 'Ecumenical Review 2005-06' sent out to all parishes with the approval and support of Archbishop Patrick Kelly. Presumably this was meant to give the message to other parishes in the Archdiocese that the vision and dedication of the pioneers of St Basil and All Saints shared Church should be an inspiration to help them grow in faithfulness to the movement of the Spirit today, especially as found in the ecumenical thrust of Vatican II and given momentum in so many ways since then. Certainly, the people of St Basil and All Saints see their shared Church as a symbol of their desire and commitment to live and share their faith as closely as possible while respecting the disciplines of their two Churches.

The ongoing story – an unhappy conclusion to its present chapter
The story of St Basil and All Saints continues – and, please God, will continue for many years to come. However, what follows describes how the current chapter ends on an unhappy note.

Eventually, the Anglican vicar, Guy Elsmore, moved on to be Team Vican of a group of parishes in central Liverpool. He was succeeded by Peter Dawkin, appointed after the usual process of being interviewed and approved by the JCC. Meanwhile, I was due for retirement at the end of May, 2008, when I reached the age of seventy-five. Because Vatican II had instilled in me the importance of collaborative ministry, I had told parishioners in 2003 that I would be retiring in five years time and so they would need to prepare for that event by taking on even more parish responsibility. As the time approached for my retirement, I wrote a number of letters to the Archbishop stressing the importance of someone suitable being made available to succeed me.

The selection of my successor had been made more complicated by the fact that in recent years Liverpool Archdiocese had been (and still is) going through a process called 'Leaving Safe Harbours'. This is about developing a stronger base for being a truly missionary Church in the modern-day world. Some of the process involves rethinking the way individual parishes relate to each other within the one deanery (now renamed 'pastoral areas'). Many neighbouring parishes are having to share their resources – and their priest – and are even merging into one new community.

There is one major weakness in the whole 'Leaving Safe Harbours' process. It has been an exclusively Roman Catholic process within the Liverpool Archdiocese. This seems alien to any commitment to receptive ecumenism. Perhaps part of the learning experience provided by St Basil and All Saints could have been to alert our two dioceses – and the wider Church – to the fact that renewal processes like 'Leaving Safe Harbours', if they are initiated and implemented in isolation without shared consultation and planning between the Churches, might be contrary to the basic principles of ecumenism and so risk running counter to the flow of the movement of the Spirit.

Obviously, when it comes to the selection of a new parish priest for a shared Church like St Basil and All Saints, the 'Leaving Safe Harbours' process presents some problems. One temptation would be to abandon its almost unique ecumenical experience. I felt deeply that that would be a sin against the Spirit. It would be rejecting the special gift the parish has been given, a gift to be treasured and shared, not discarded as though dead and lifeless. The other temptation would be to ring-fence what is going on in the shared Church, as though it was a kind of museum piece or an oddity which has no relevance for the wider Church. In the light of my ten years ministry there, I had come to believe that the presence of St Basil and All Saints in the local Pastoral Area and in the Archdiocese could be a kind of two-way 'receptive learning experience'. The parish as a shared Church could learn from their changed situation; and the Pastoral Area and Archdiocese, in their turn, could learn from the gift of St Basil and All Saints' experience of being a shared Church. If both could be receptive to each other and truly open to learning, together they could both grow in pastoral experience by accepting the mutual gifts they have to share.

As the time for my retirement approached and no names for a possible successor were forthcoming, I wrote a number of letters to the Archbishop stressing the need for urgent action. Early in 2008 the Auxiliary Bishop, Vincent Malone, called a meeting with the clergy of the Pastoral Area at which we were told that a concrete suggestion would be made. After outlining the various administrative issues confronting the Pastoral Area, the bishop came up with a suggestion that the Roman Catholic pastoral oversight of St Basil & All Saints be taken over by the St Bede's team ministry of three young priests, under the leadership of Fr Matthew Nunes. Already, over the previous year or so this team had taken on shared responsibility for three of the parishes in Widnes, St Bede, St Pius X and St Raphael, all in the process of forming one overall community. Moreover, in January 2008 this team had also accepted pastoral responsibility for the parish of Holy Family, Cronton, which is a close neighbour of St Basil & All Saints.

Bishop Malone's suggestion was a possibility that had never entered my mind. Clearly, the addition of St Basil & All Saints to their pastoral care would present the team with an additional challenge of how to integrate a shared RC-Anglican Church into a Roman Catholic team ministry serving a number of other Churches. In particular, how could the Vicar of All Saints, Revd Peter Dawkin, be fully involved in the Roman Catholic team ministry set-up. A top priority would need to be making sure that he was not left feeling on his own and isolated from the team.

While being taken aback by Bishop Malone's suggestion, at the same time I found myself being attracted by it. I could see how it might offer some creative possibilities for the ecumenical future in Widnes. For instance, it could provide an opportunity to bring the ecumenical experience of St Basil & All Saints more into the mainstream of Church life in Widnes. The parishioners of St Basil & All Saints had always wanted their shared Church life to be more integrated into Widnes as a whole. If the priests making up the team ministry were really fired by the flame of a true ecumenical spirit, they would be able to bring the ecumenical dimension into the whole of their ministry. The positive and negative aspects of the suggestion was discussed.

It was this point that I made the first of a series of mistakes which I can see now, with hindsight, were to have serious negative repercussions for the shared Church.

My first mistake was in asking the St Bede's team for an ecumenical commitment there and then at the meeting. That was very unwise, since what such an ecumenical commitment involved was completely vague and I did not spell out all the implications of being the RC priests serving the shared Church of SBAS. Moreover, it was unfair on the St Bede's team since it put them on the spot and did not give them time to look into all the implications involved in undertaking pastoral care of a shared Church in coalition with the Vicar. I should have asked Vin Malone to put his proposal on hold until I had had time to explore in depth how the St Bede's team felt about the Simultaneous Eucharist and the overall shared Church arrangement at SBAS and whether they would be committed to maintaining it and enabling it to have a wider impact on the Pastoral Area.

My second mistake lay in not consulting Fr Bill Redmond, the Pastoral Area Leader, after the meeting. It was only much later that I learned that Bill had very strong reservations about the proposed arrangement. Since I respected Bill's judgement, if I had realised that at the time, I might have been less positive myself.

In the course of the team meeting mentioned above, I told Bishop Malone that the appointment of the St Bede's team would need to be approved by the Joint Church Council (JCC) at St Basil & All Saints. That meant that the team would need to be interviewed by the JCC and their approval given. The Bishop agreed to this, though he insisted that this should be done as quickly as possible since the appointment of my successor had been dragging on for too long.

Soon after this meeting, at all three SBAS Eucharists (RC and Anglican) one weekend, I explained the proposal and spoke in favour of it. My third mistake lay in expressing publicly in this way my personal support for this proposal on the grounds that it would widen out the ecumenical impact of SBAS. I should have simply put forward the pros and cons of this arrangement, leaving it up to the parishioners to discuss among themselves and draw their own conclusions as to how far such an arrangement would be in keeping with their life and worship as a shared Church.

Soon after this, on 3 March Fr Matthew Nunes rang to tell me that the Archbishop had asked him not to continue the Simultaneous Eucharist at SBAS. I was appalled at this news and I insisted that Matthew and I should meet as soon as possible with the vicar, Peter Dawkin, to discuss this development. I felt that if this news was made public in the parish it would provoke a massive negative reaction among the parishioners of both communities. So I suggested to Peter and Matthew that, for the time being, we should hold it in confidence between ourselves to give us time to put as much pressure as we could on the Archbishop to rescind this decision. My thinking was that the parishioners might launch a public protest and that this would almost certainly strengthen the Archbishop in his resolve to stop the Simultaneous Eucharist. I thought there was more chance of getting him to rethink through quiet diplomacy behind the scenes.

This was my fourth mistake. The parishioners had every right to know what was going on. Moreover, I am sure they would quickly have pointed out to me something I only adverted to a couple of years later. The Archbishop was jumping the gun since Matthew and the team and not yet been interviewed by the JCC and so no appointment had yet been agreed.

I had originally intended not to interfere in what would happen in St Basil & All Saints after my retirement. However, the Archbishop's 3 March request to Matthew Nunes not to continue the Simultaneous Eucharist made it impossible for me not to get involved. So I wrote a series of very long letters and memoranda to the Archbishop, expressing very strongly my conviction that his decision was theologically unjustified, pastorally misguided, based on an unnecessarily rigid canonical interpretation of Church law and running counter to the direction in which the Spirit seemed to have leading the parish over the past twenty-five years. I was careful to run each of these letters and memoranda through Peter Dawkin and Matthew Nunes before sending them to the Archbishop. If the three of us had not agreed to keep the Archbishop's request confidential, my natural instinct would have been to have shared with parishioners, or at least with the JCC, all the points I was making to the Archbishop. That would have been a good learning experience for all of us. The same would have been true of the excellent and very supportive letters written to the Archbishop by Paul Crowe and Ray Bridson, respectively former Parish priest and Vicar at SBAS.

Looking back now, I can see how my suggesting to Peter and Matthew that we keep the Archbishop's request secret for the moment was a blatant instance of my collusion with the Church's inbuilt lack of openness and accountability – its habit of making key decisions behind closed doors. I cannot speak for Matthew and Peter, but I feel it was a serious mistake and was responsible for much of the terrible pain experienced later in the process – and which is still felt by many.

The meeting between the JCC and the St Bede's Team Ministry on 16 April went very badly. My fifth mistake was in failing to ensure that this meeting was properly thought out and planned by the JCC Chair and Steering Committee (myself and Peter included). At the meeting itself, because no one knew about what the Archbishop had said apart from Matthew, Peter and myself, Matthew (who spoke most on behalf of the St Bede's team) was unable to give any clear answer to JCC's urgent desire to know whether the team would be willing to continue with the Simultaneous Eucharist. As a result, people picked up the impression that the St Bede's team were not in favour of Simultaneous Eucharist. That made it a very difficult meeting for everyone involved.

When the meeting ended, I felt sorry for the St Bede's team since they had been under a lot of pressure and clearly did not feel able to speak freely to the JCC. So I brought them into the Presbytery for a drink to give them time to recover. That was my sixth mistake – and an extremely serious mistake. If the meeting had been properly planned, what should have happened at the end of the meeting was that the St Bede's team should have retired to the Presbytery and the whole JCC (myself included) should have discussed (and even voted on) whether we were happy to accept their appointment. When I had undergone a similar interview by the JCC prior to my own appointment, I had made it clear to the JCC that, if they did not think I was suitable, I would not accept the appointment. That discussion and vote did not take place in the case of the St Bede's Tam. I can honestly say that it was only a couple of years later that this terrible omission dawned on me. I fail to understand how it was overlooked at the time. My feeling for the St Bede's priests must have distracted me. I think I have to accept most of the responsibility for this serious omission.

In June 2008 the Archbishop met with Matthew Nunes, Peter Dawkin and myself. His starting point was strongly against simultaneous Eucharist. However, as we talked he seemed to modify his opposition somewhat, so much so that it was finally agreed that he would come to the parish on the evening of 24 September 2008 to continue the conversation with the JCC and Matthew and Peter. Since I would be retired by then I felt confident enough to leave the on-going conversation in the capable hands of the JCC and the two clergymen.

The Archbishop began the September meeting by stating categorically that he had decided to call a halt to the simultaneous Eucharist celebrations in the parish. This announcement came as a shock and caused considerable hurt and distress among all parishioners present. They had understood that the meeting was to continue the conversation. They had even held a series of meetings to prepare for this. They had come in a 'receptive listening' frame of mind and were expecting the same from the Archbishop. They were totally dismayed by his decision, even though they had known it was a possible outcome of the meeting. It seemed to call into question the integrity of their experience of simultaneous Eucharist over the years. What they found especially disconcerting was the fact that he announced it at the very beginning of a meeting which they were expecting to have a consultative flavour and at which they were hoping to be able to present their views for consideration. It is possible, of course, that in the time since June, with so many other important issues on his mind, the Archbishop had overlooked the fact that he agreed to a 'continuing the conversation' meeting.

There is one final mistake, my seventh, which I need to highlight. At no stage did I suggest or even entertain the possibility of having recourse to any of the Liverpool Ecumenical bodies which exercise oversight over the various ecumenical projects in Liverpool. Again, I can now see that as a symptom of the clerical culture I had absorbed and not yet been fully liberated from. In other words, I considered that the Archbishop had the last word and there was no point in appealing to a higher level. If the parishioners, Anglican and Catholic, had known what was happening from the beginning, they might well have decided to make an appeal against the Archbishop's decision to some alternative or even higher seat of authority, whether Anglican or Roman Catholic or ecumenical.

There are probably other mistakes I have made over this whole sad saga and of which I am unaware, though others may be very conscious of them. I realise that I have to accept personal responsibility for all the mistakes I made. I am not proud of them. I apologise for my share in causing so much pain to parishioners and for mishandling the affair so badly. However, life is a learning process and I hope others in ecumenical tension points might be able to learn from my mistakes. I realise, too, that I was not the only person involved in the events mentioned above. The others involved may see things very differently. Clearly, I can only speak about my own personal mistakes and misjudgements.

Though we need to learn from our mistakes, there is no point in crying over spilt milk. The clock cannot be turned back. The important thing now is for the people of SBAS to continue move forward with faith in God's Spirit at work in them as a shared (Pilgrim) Church. As I said in my retirement Mass homily (text in Appendix Three), 'We cannot tie the hands of God's Spirit. Our God of Surprises may well have other and even better tricks up his sleeve!'

Conclusion: Keeping hope and commitment alive

Despite the demoralising impact of no longer being able to enjoy simultaneous celebration of the Eucharist at key times in the Church's year, there is a great determination among most of the parishioners to continue sharing everything they can together. That means that all the activities in the list given in Appendix One will continue, apart from the Simultaneous Eucharists marked with *. I am consoled by the fact that, among a very committed core group there seems to be a deep commitment to grow even more closely together ecumenically as a shared Church community. Readers with a special interest in ecumenical theology and practice might be interested in Appendix Two which brings together some of the points I submitted to Archbishop Kelly in my memoranda to him.

APPENDIX ONE

Shared Services & Simultaneous Eucharist Services during the Year

Advent & Christmas
1.   Each Sunday evening (6.00 p.m.): Advent reflections (Thirty mins)
2.   Pre-Christmas: Distribute Christmas cards with service times to every
         house in area
3.   Sunday before Christmas (4.30 p.m.): Carols by Candlelight
4.   Christmas Eve (3 p.m.): 'A Christmas Surprise'
         (under 5's, stories & songs around crib)
5.   * Christmas Midnight Eucharist (12 midnight)
6.   * Christmas Morning Eucharist (10.00 a.m.)
7.   * First Sunday of Year/Epiphany: 10.30 a.m. Eucharist
         (instead of two separate Eucharists at 9.45 a.m. & 11.15 a.m.)

Lent
1.   * Ash Wednesday (7.30 p.m.): Distribution of Ashes & Eucharist
2.   Weekly Ecumenical House Groups
3.   Pre-Easter: Distribute Easter cards with Holy Week Service times to
     every house in area
4.   Fridays in Lent (7.30 p.m.): Stations of the Cross
5.   Tuesday of Holy Week (7.30 p.m.): Reconciliation Service
6.   * Maundy Thursday (8. p.m.): Liturgy of the Last Supper
7.   Good Friday (3 p.m.): Commemoration of the Lord's Passion
8.   Holy Saturday (11 a.m.): 'Easter Bunny's Craft Club & Café'
         (for under 11's)
9.   * Holy Saturday (8 p.m.): Easter Vigil & First Eucharist of Easter

Rest of Year
1.   * Pentecost Eucharist: 10.30 a.m. Eucharist
         (instead of two separate Eucharists at 9.45 a.m. & 11.15 a.m.)
2.   A Sunday afternoon in October (2.30 p.m.): 'Healing' Service
3.   A Sunday afternoon in November (4.30 p.m.): 'Remembering Our
         Dead' Service.
4.   Full morning event: Joint School Y5 Project with shared service.
5.   Weekdays after 8.30 a.m. or midday Mass: Morning (or Midday) Prayer
6.   Occasional - involvement in Baptisms, marriages or funerals.
7.   Special Occasions: Joint Induction of Kevin & Guy by both bishops,
         20th Birthday of Church; Opening of Garden of Hope,
         Opening Service for 25th Anniversary Year of Shared Church.
8.   Swapping pulpits – by Kevin and Guy (and later, Peter) about four
         weekends per year.

Shared Groups and Activities

1.   Joint Church Council (meets quarterly)
2.   Weekly Newsletter (*Sunday Joint*)
3.   Joint Premises Committee
4.   Adult Education Group – plans joint sessions for each term
5.   Parish Priest/Vicar – Working lunches, coffee meetings and Away days
6.   Working lunches between Heads of both primary schools and Vicar & Parish Priest
7.   Uniformed Groups – (Guides, Brownies, Rainbows) – monthly Parade Service at Anglican Eucharist
8.   Garden of Hope Project (Community Garden, including plot for ashes) – opened September 2004
9.   Life for Zambia Group (fund-raising for AIDS/HIV Home Care Team in Livingstone – also involves many social activities) – Sept 2004, two-week visit to Livingstone by four group members plus Kevin
10. Hough Green Millennium Arts Projects Group – Zambia group with a different hat! ('prominent speakers')
11. Shared ecumenical presentations(Cologne group, Manchester/ Toulouse group, Burnley joint Church project, LOM weekend, Hope Ecumenical Course, Hope Mission Advisory Group)
12. For two years Guy and Kevin jointly ran a module on ecumenism at Liverpool Diocese Local Ordained Ministers training weekend
13. Annual Pantomime (soon developed its independent highly successful existence)

Asterisk (*) denotes simultaneous Eucharist which can no longer be continued.

APPENDIX TWO

Canonical and Theological Reflections on the
Decision to discontinue the Simultaneous Eucharist.

One objection raised by the Archbishop to simultaneous Eucharist was that it is forbidden by canon 908 of the Code of Canon Law which states: 'It is forbidden for Catholic priests to concelebrate the Eucharist with priests or ministers of Churches or ecclesial communities which are not in full communion with the Catholic Church.' This ruling is repeated in the 1993 Ecumenical Directory, no. 104, (e).

However, a very important principle of canonical interpretation which has been accepted over many centuries is *Odiosa restringenda sunt*. That means that restrictions and prohibitions should be interpreted as narrowly as possible.

Consequently, canon 908 should not be interpreted as forbidding the kind of simultaneous celebration practised in St Basil and All Saints. That is essentially different to concelebration. As one who has been involved in this practice for the last ten years never once did I understand what I was doing to be concelebrating with my Anglican confrere. The elements over which I had prayed the *epikesis* and spoken the words of Institution were the bread and wine presented to me by the members of the Roman Catholic community. In no way did I see myself as praying these words over the bread and wine of the Anglican Eucharist. Any objection raised to the practice cannot be on the grounds that it is concelebration. It most certainly is not. To maintain that it is runs counter to a hallowed principle of canonical interpretation.

The Archbishop argued very strongly that he really believed in the decision he had made. In conscience, he could not let simultaneous Eucharist continue. He was not just hiding behind the law. He was convinced that it was not in line with sound Eucharistic theology. For him the words of the approved Eucharistic Prayers are sacrosanct, a sign that the Eucharist is being celebrated in union with the Pope and the whole Catholic Church. Hence, he could not accept any inclusion of praying for the Archbishop of Canterbury or the Anglican Bishop of Liverpool within the Canon nor could he countenance any shared 'Amen' at the end of the Eucharistic Prayer. In my final 30 September 2008 letter to the Archbishop I wrote: 'I find the theology of the Eucharist on which you seem to be basing your decision does not do full justice to my own Eucharistic faith and that of many people I know and respect.'

The Archbishop also insisted that simultaneous Eucharist was contrary to the mind of the Church. He said that the Vatican had urged bishops, though not in writing, to put a halt to it. In the case of St Basil and All Saints, people have always believed that the evolution of this practice took place with the implicit approval of the former Archbishop of Liverpool, Derek Worlock, whose credibility as an ecumenical witness along with his Anglican counterpart, Bishop David Sheppard, is renowned in the city of Liverpool and far beyond.

Archbishop Kelly in an earlier letter to me had quoted from two letters of Archbishop Worlock (to Paul Crowe) which seem to suggest something very different to 'implicit approval':

> I have no power to give you authority to celebrate a joint Eucharist. Even a shared simultaneous Eucharist does not have the approval of the Holy See. Even though it may occur in certain places, to judge by Bishop Cormac's assertion, it is not with a 'doctrinal' Eucharistic prayer and should never be for a normal parish celebration. I have had to make it plain that had you sought my permission for this before Christmas, I would have declined to grant permission, just as by agreement with Bishop David, we have withheld permission for a simultaneous Eucharist or joint

Eucharist in other places. You will know our views that there is no way
forward through breaking rules (29 January 1988).

As a matter of principle I must now discuss your request with Bishop
David as our stand with regard to the simultaneous Eucharist is a position mutually agreed and upheld (28 March 1991).

Though seeming to be the last word on the issue, these letters need to be read
in the light of the wider context. Paul Crowe, then Parish Priest at St Basil and
All Saints, explains that the 1988 letter was written after the Papal Nuncio had
contacted Archbishop Worlock following some complaints made to Rome.
These complaints were based on misinformation as became clear when Paul
Crowe and his Anglican counterpart, Ray Bridson, met with the Archbishop
and were able to explain exactly what they had been doing and why. Thereafter
they were able to go ahead with an agreed format of simultaneous Eucharist,
knowing they had the support, rather than permission, of both Archbishop
Worlock and Bishop Sheppard.

Three years after the 1991 letter, when he succeeded Paul Crowe as Parish
Priest, Fr Peter McGrail tells how Archbishop Worlock invited him to Archbishop's House to discuss his appointment and asked him to continue the practice of simultaneous Eucharist within the established liturgical parameters
which he explained. Dr McGrail, now an eminent priest-theologian at Liverpool
Hope University, is quite clear about this. Furthermore, Claire Davidson, Chair
of Liverpool's Archdiocesan Ecumenism Commission, assures me that a simultaneous Eucharist was certainly celebrated at the Grail Centre in Pinner by
Archbishop Worlock and Bishop Sheppard.

How do we explain such an apparent discrepancy? It could be that, through
his personal experience of receptive ecumenism, Archbishop Worlock came to
appreciate that in certain particular situations some form of simultaneous Eucharist was liturgically appropriate and pastorally acceptable. After all, his
unique ecumenical relationship with his Anglican colleague, Bishop Sheppard,
was itself an ongoing experience of receptive ecumenism. It should also be
noted that Archbishop Worlock was renowned for being very careful about
anything he committed to writing. In his 1988 letter it is noteworthy that he insists that he "has no power to give you authority to celebrate a 'joint Eucharist'.
That need not be interpreted as his prohibiting simultaneous celebration since
there is no actual law explicitly forbidding it although he admits that 'shared
simultaneous Eucharist does not have the approval of the Holy See'. In his later
1991 letter, Archbishop Worlock speaks of 'discussing' the request for 'simultaneous eucharist' with Bishop David. Worlock's very precise use of words
could be interpreted as his taking care to put nothing in writing that could disturb the Vatican, while leaving the then parish priest free to exercise his own
responsible pastoral judgement.

The 2007 International Anglican/RC Agreed Statement, Growing Together in Unity and Mission, in its practical second section, challenges all Christians, but especially bishops, to develop 'strategies' for the appropriate expression of our shared faith. To my mind that is exactly what has happened in St Basil and All Saints. Over the years, there has never been the slightest suggestion that what the clergy were involved in was any kind of surreptitious concelebration. If anything, the pain of separation came out even more strikingly in the simultaneous consecration of separate bread and wine and in the scrupulous way the parishioners always received Communion from their own clergy.

The practice that has evolved at St Basil & All Saints has been a natural growth in that particular situation rather than a model for other parishes to follow. It is difficult to imagine any other solution which, on major feasts in the liturgical calendar, would satisfactorily hold in creative tension the integrity of sharing one Church for worship while still acknowledging the fact of the community's dividedness. It has managed to express at one and the same time both unity and dividedness. The feelings of the parishioners of St Basil and All Saints are aptly expressed in the words of Cardinal Kasper quoted earlier: "We have stretched out our hands to each other and do not want to let them go again."

To my mind our ecumenical responsibility demands that we value such a precious gift and do everything possible to bring it to the attention of others to stimulate them to consider what might be appropriate in their particular situation. That is why, in my letter to Archbishop Kelly following his September meeting with parishioners, I wrote: 'I am convinced that eventually something like our practice of simultaneous celebration of the Eucharist will be rediscovered by our two Churches and embraced as a gift enabling us to hold together both the grace of partial unity and the pain of partial disunity.'

APPENDIX THREE

My Retirement Homily preached at final simultaneous Eucharist
Sunday 29 June 2008

The 'Sister Mary' referred to at the beginning and end of this homily is Sister Mary Courtney. She is the Director of the St Francis HIV/AIDS Home Care Project in Livingstone, Zambia. To celebrate the Millennium a group from St Basil & All Saints set up a project to help support the wonderful work being done by Sister Mary and her volunteers. In September 2004 four of the group, Chris Lappine, Sue Shellien and Angela and Graham Kaye, representing both communities, went out for a two-week visit to the project. This had a massive impact on them and, through them, on the whole Shared Church Community. Sadly, Graham died totally unexpectedly in 2009. Since 2000 the parish 'Gift of Life for Zambia' team have sent out to them a total of nearly £135,000. Sister Mary Courtney was present for my retirement homily, since at the

time she was visiting the parish en route to Ireland for her three-yearly break. She and
her team of nearly one hundred carers, many of them living with HIV themselves, are
an inspiration to the whole parish.

A preacher needs to be alert to the mood of his congregation – how they are
feeling. I get the impression from what many have been saying or writing to
me that they are feeling sad, anxious and fearful about the future of St Basil &
All Saints. That is why the focus of this homily will not be on saying welcome
to Sr Mary. We have all done that already and we will continue do that during
her stay here. Nor do I intend to use this homily as an opportunity to say 'good
bye'. I don't even want to wrestle with some of the problems which will un-
doubtedly lie ahead when St Basil's will no longer have a resident parish priest
and the Vicar of All Saints is living in the next parish.

What I feel will be most helpful to us all to focus on this morning is our
shared belief that God's Holy Spirit is present and active in our own parish
community here.

The week before I first came here, I made a retreat in Chester. It was this
same time of year, 22-27 June 1998. Let me read you part of my Retreat notes:-

> With reference to my move to St Basil's, what came into my mind was a
> kind of infra-red image showing the heaving mass of movement going
> on beneath the surface. That is like God's activity in the situation into
> which I am moving. I am not going in as God's agent into a lifeless, pas-
> sive situation. God's action is vibrant there already. I feel excited at the
> prospect of witnessing it, listening to and observing its signs, feeling
> wonderment at it and helping to be part of celebrating it in Eucharist
> and worship.
>
> I am not going in principally to fill a management role. Rather it will
> much more a matter of enabling people to be aware of God's presence
> and action in their everyday lives. What is of primary importance is what
> God is doing there - in the lives of individuals and families - and in the
> community as a whole. I am being invited to be part of that. But I will
> only be part of it, if I am open to it and am prepared to spend time lis-
> tening to what is going on.

At the end of ten years, I am still just as convinced – in fact, even more so – that
God's Spirit is present and active in our shared parish community. It has been
a great privilege to share life here over the past ten years, while recognising the
shadow side of my own failures and also the shadow side of our shared failures
in responding to God's spirit. The life-principle of our shared Church is not the
clergy but the Holy Spirit. And the Holy Spirit dwells principally in the Community rather than in the clergy. Or rather, the Holy Spirit dwells in all of us
together – as the Third Eucharistic Prayer says, 'one body, one spirit in Christ'.

I have often heard people here saying "What is happening here is too important to be dependent on the clergy whoever they may be at any particular time". We are a Spirit-led community, not a clergy-dominated Church. If we truly believe this in our heart of hearts, it should lead us to feel a great sense of confidence. If our shared Church community really is Spirit-inspired, it will not fail. In fact, it cannot fail, whatever difficulties and problems it might encounter. If we truly believe this, it should make us hopeful and confident in ourselves and our community. It should lead us to a deeper commitment and to greater mutual encouragement.

It is because I deeply believe this that I can feel peaceful – even happy – to retire. I know it won't be easy for you. And I suspect it won't be easy for me either. My leaving is no more a threat to our shared Church than would it be if I dropped dead tomorrow. Fr Conefrey's sudden death was a terrible shock to everyone. You must all have felt utterly devastated. But in no way did it put a halt to the presence and action of God's Spirit working in and through you all and in the community.

I've not mentioned Saints Peter and Paul, the feast we celebrate today. A good friend of mine, Fr Hugh Lavery, a most inspiring lecturer, had a great gift of looking into the deeper meaning of words. I once heard him do that with the word 'polarisation'. To produce light and energy, he said, we need both poles – positive and negative. Without that there is no life, just apathy. One pole is not enough. Maybe that gives a clue to why Christians celebrate these two saints on the same day. On one of the few occasions when they met, the sparks were flying. Paul confronted Peter to his face – just as Jesus himself did, 'Get behind me, Satan. The way you think is man's way, not God's.' Both these confrontations turned out to be growth moments in the life of the Christian community.

Maybe, celebrating these two saints together reminds us of the need for tension in the Church – tension that gives off energy and new life, creative tension, which can even fuse divisions into unity. There are plenty of tensions at a wider level in both our Churches at present. It is hard to see how some of these can be creative and life-giving. There is also plenty of tension being felt in our own shared Church community – especially over the future of our simultaneous Eucharist. Some fear this might be our last one.

Who can tell what the future holds. Most certainly over the years we have experienced the presence and action of the Holy Spirit in our simultaneous Eucharistic celebrations. We are all grateful for that gift – I certainly am. Yet we cannot tie the hands of God's Spirit. Our God of Surprises may well have other and even better tricks up his sleeve.

Maybe the in-built tension of today's bi-polar feast of Sts Peter & Paul is a reminder to us that the Spirit is too big to be possessed by one side of a conversation. Last year I attended a remarkable ecumenical conference in Durham on 'receptive learning'. Its basic theme was this. In any conversation where views are divided and opposed, it is not enough for both sides to shout louder. We need to think inside each other. We need to try to get inside the other person's skin. For tension to be truly creative and life-producing, we need to listen deeply to each other. A closed mind and a closed heart prevents tension from being truly creative.

The presence of Sister Mary among us helps to put our problems and worries in perspective. She and her wonderful team of volunteers face massive life and death problems in their AIDS-related work of caring for the poor, the orphaned children and the sick and dying. Our parish project is called 'Gift of Life to Zambia'. Maybe, Sister Mary's visit is bringing the Gift of Life from Zambia to Hough Green, reminding us what our Christian Faith is all about.

The prophet Amos issued a dire warning against making religious practice the ultimate value rather than justice and integrity. Our simultaneous Eucharist has been a tremendous blessing to us over the years and we thank God for it. God's Spirit has truly been in that experience. But if we make our simultaneous Eucharist the 'be-all and end-all' of our shared Church, we might run the risk of hearing a word from the Lord similar to that spoken by Amos (5:21), 'I hate your simultaneous Eucharists'.

We are most truly a shared Church, when the heart of what we are lies not in our sharing one building, and not even in our sharing in one Eucharist, but in our sharing with those in need.

Perhaps that is the Gift of Life from Zambia that Sister Mary brings to us.

CHAPTER SIX

The National Pastoral Congress 1980
and Collaborative Ministry

This is a slightly abridged version of a talk I gave to the 2005 Quest Annual Conference held in Liverpool. The theme of the Quest Conference was 'Our Place as Equals'. Quest is a group for lesbian and gay Catholics. It has a network of local groups across the country which meet regularly for Mass, discussion and social events. Quest believes that the Church could do more to provide welcome and support to lesbian and gay Catholics, both nationally and within parishes. I was impressed by the fact that Quest was one of the few Catholic organisations which marked the 25th Anniversary of the National Pastoral Congress (NPC). Liverpool was a natural venue since the NPC took place there. No doubt my having been a participant influenced their inviting me to be one of their speakers. Because Quest members felt somewhat on the margins of the Church, collaborative ministry was a very appropriate theme, especially since it had been such a major topic at the NCP. Because Quest is a group for lesbian and gay Catholics, it is appropriate to add as an Appendix the text of a short letter on the spirituality of gay and lesbian relationships which I wrote to the Tablet (13 February 2010). That letter gives a brief account of where I now stand on the issue of gay and lesbian relationships. A much fuller treatment is found in my book, NDSE, especially chapter four, 'Sexual Ethics – Denying the Good News to Gay Men and Lesbian Women.'

Introduction
Let me begin with a few words about the National Pastoral Congress – as seen by one who was there. It took place over the long Bank Holiday weekend in May 1980. 2115 Catholics came from all over the country, including forty-two bishops, 255 clergy and 150 religious. That meant, in fact, that the vast majority attending were lay men and women – 1568 in all. I have a memory of Archbishop Worlock preaching at a preparatory Mass for the Liverpool delegates a few months beforehand and stating very bluntly: 'People have often said to me, "Aren't you nervous at inviting so many lay people together to express their views openly and honestly?" and I always reply: "Don't you believe in the Holy Spirit in the Church?"'

Enormous efforts were put into the preparation for the Congress at diocesan, deanery and parish level in all the dioceses. In each parish meetings were held, giving people the chance to raise whatever topics they wished and express their frank and honest views on them. Over 20,000 replies were received and more than 100,000 people took part in this preparatory process. This process provided the agenda for the Congress. Participants came as delegates, not just nominal representatives, of their parishes and dioceses.

A fascinating summary of the diocesan reports drawn from these parish discussions fills nearly fifty pages of the volume, *Liverpool 1980: Official Report of the National Pastoral Congress* (St Paul Publications, Slough, 1981), which gives the proceedings of the whole Congress. The full text of this summary was given to each of the more than 2000 delegates before Congress. The Congress itself met in seven sectors, each devoted to one of the main themes coming from the grass-roots consultation – 1. Co-responsibility and relationships; 2. Ordained ministries; 3. Family and society; 4. Evangelisation; 5. Christian education and formation; 6. Witness; and 7. Justice.

A precious seam of gold in the Liverpool 1980 volume is the very full report of the group discussions in each of the seven sectors and the final report which was voted on and approved by everyone in each sector. In the course of the whole Congress only twice did the whole entire group of delegates meet together. The first occasion was on the opening Friday evening for a solemn Liturgy of Renewal and Reconciliation in the Metropolitan Cathedral. The second was for the closing session which began in the Philharmonic Hall with the whole assembly listening to the Seven Sector Reports and ended with the closing Eucharist in the Metropolitan Cathedral.

A word about the documentation available on the Congress. The volume, Liverpool 1980 is of immense value and contains most of the key preparatory and final documents. The Liverpool Archdiocesan weekly newspaper prepared a daily broadsheet for all the delegates informing them of the previous day's proceedings. A few months after the Congress there appeared a major document, *The Easter People* – prepared by Derek Worlock and a team of helpers with the full approval of the whole Bishops' Conference and billed as their reflection 'in the light of the Congress'. Its text is also printed in *Liverpool 1980*. There are many good things in *The Easter People*. For instance, its very first heading is 'The Sharing Church' and it opens with a sub-heading, 'Initiative in shared responsibility' in which the opening sentence speaks of the Congress as 'an extraordinary experience of what the Church is and a foretaste of what it can grow to be'.

The title, *The Easter People*, was chosen because of its obvious reference to the Resurrection. Ironically, *The Easter People* effectively buried the Congress. This was not due to any deliberate intention on the part of those composing it. In fact, some excellent people were involved. The basic problem was that this written document took the place of any effective vehicle for keeping alive the fire which had blazed in the hearts and minds of the participants. What was needed in the wake of the Congress was some kind of collaborative group, involving laity and clergy, to keep the fire alive and help it spread throughout the whole Church in England and Wales. Sadly, the only follow up was this written text. Effectively, the initiative for any further action was left in the hands of the Bishops' Conference. It would be churlish to lay all the blame for this on the bishops. Those of us who shared in the Congress must bear our share of responsibility for not creating any effective structure to carry forward the exciting impetus given by the Congress.

I would not want to suggest that the Congress failed to achieve anything. One important impact was the fact that the views of the Congress delegates calling for a deeper listening to the experience of married couples and greater compassion for those who had suffered the tragedy of marriage breakdown was clearly heard in the halls of the Vatican when Basil Hume & Derek Worlock both made impassioned interventions at the 1980 Synod on the Family. Another very positive result was the major impact it had on the minds and hearts of most of the delegates. I am told on good authority that that impact still influences many of them twenty-five years later.

In 1995, fifteen years after the Congress, a remarkable document, The Sign We Give, from a Working Party of the Bishops' Conference of England and Wales, was published by the bishops. It is a report on Collaborative Ministry and, to my mind at least, is a fruit of the kind of thinking and experience that took place at the Congress. It is almost as though the seed needed to lie in the ground for fifteen years before germinating. The Chair of the Working Party was Pat Jones, who had been one of the group which produced The Easter People. Amazingly, the Congress is not mentioned anywhere in the text! I would recommend The Sign We Give very highly. It is essential and inspirational reading for all committed to genuine 'collaborative ministry'.

'Collaborative ministry' is not the most attractive term. For the older among us it evokes memories of the war against Hitler when 'collaboration' was a bad word. It meant helping the enemy. Whereas in the Church of today – at least in theory – it touches on what we are all about as Church. All the baptized share the mission given by Christ to the Church. We are all co-workers (co-labourers – collaborators) under the one Lord.

When I celebrated my seventieth birthday I told the parish that I was starting to retire on that very day. My retirement would be a long process and they were all involved in it. It was not a disaster but a God-given opportunity for them to grow still further in shared responsibility for the parish and its life and mission. I was anxious to make the point that collaborative ministry is not some kind of stop-gap, temporary measure to cope with the present shortage of priests 'until normal service was resumed later'. Rather it is a key part of our self-understanding as Church which the Spirit seems to bringing to the fore in our age.

There are three sections to this paper:

1. The Theology of Collaborative Ministry
2. Collaboration in the Church's Teaching Ministry
3. Quest and the Teaching Ministry in the Church

1. The Theology of Collaborative Ministry

When *The Sign We Give* was published in 1995, the Editor of *The Tablet* praised it very highly and remarked that 'Vatican II remains an event in the future waiting to happen rather than one which ended 30 years ago'. His point was that 'the post-Vatican II understanding of the primacy of baptism has not yet worked through into ordinary Catholic life'. For that to happen there needs to be a "complete overhaul of the culture of clergy-laity relationships". Such a relationship change needs to be worked out in terms of 'partnership, equality, mutuality, cooperation and collaboration'. I would add two other relationship qualities to the Editor's list, co-responsibility and collegiality. These are all Vatican II markers for relationships within the community of the Church.

The following are some key quotations from what *The Sign We Give* says about collaborative ministry. I have prefaced each quotation with a heading of my own and have added a short comment in italics after each.

Life of the Trinity is the theological basis of collaborative ministry

The central mystery of faith is the Trinity; the belief that God's very being is relationship. God is Father, Son and Spirit, a communion of persons. In God's own life, there is communion and relationship, distinction and diversity. Our faith in the Trinity is not just about who God is as God, but also about who God is for us. Trinitarian life is also our life, as we have been included as partners in God's own life. As human persons, we are made in the image of a God who is Trinity … We will reflect God's life if we live in the spirit of communion and collaboration and if our relationships are characterised by equality, mutuality and reciprocity (pp. 19-20).

To understand the theology of collaborative ministry, we need to go the very heart of our Christian faith. Collaborative is not just a passing fad – and certainly not a merely temporary measure.

Priesthood of all believers

(Vatican II) re-discovered the scriptural insight that all the baptised share in the one priesthood of Christ, that it is the whole Church that is a priesthood (p. 18).

Hence, there can be no such thing as a 'priest-less parish'!

Theology of communion, collaborative ministry, inclusion and diversity

The theology of communion, especially when expressed in today's cultural context, has an important message about inclusiveness. Communion means that unity can be found within diversity and that differences can be respected and accepted as enriching and not divisive. In an important sense, to be inclusive is what it means to be catholic ... As many kinds of difference as possible should be represented in some way as a sign of the inclusiveness or catholicity of Church communion. Collaborative ministry is the most obvious and effective way of doing this (p. 26).

This has profound and very obvious implications for Quest members – and all gay and lesbian Christians.

Equal Terms and equal valuing

The theology of communion implies a radical and true equality among all those who share in that relationship. This equality is based on what it means to be human persons and the dignity and integrity which follow. It incorporates diversity of vocation, role and activity... In collaborative ministry there is a genuine need and desire to work together on equal terms... The theology of communion implies equal valuing based on personhood and gift (pp. 24-25).

This is a very relevant passage in the light of the QUEST Conference subtitle i.e. 'Our Place as Equals'.

The role of the ordained priest in collaborative ministry

If the priest's primary task is to enable communion to grow, rather than to 'run the parish', the quality of relationships he develops will be central to his ministry. It is through the quality of relationships that he will most effectively invite people to make full use of their gifts and energy in ministries and other activities (p. 23).

Leadership is about empowerment, serving others through enabling their gifts to be recognised and allowed to grow and flourish.

Collaborative ministry involves (p. 17):

- recognising that we all have a shared but differentiated responsibility for the life and mission of the Church;
- working together on equal terms;
- seeing our different vocations and gifts as complementary and mutually enriching – 'recognition and use of people's expertise and energies' (Sign, p. 32).
- agreeing that we are accountable to each other for the way we fulfil our ministry;
- accountability and acknowledging the need for our ongoing formation if we are to continue as competent ministers.

Collaborative ministry is essentially an attitude of mind even though it needs to be translated into practical ways of acting and appropriate structures.

The following are some other important points made in *The Sign We Give*. They do not need any further comment from me.

Implications for formation of ordained priests –

Formation for the priestly ministry must be a preparation for the exercise of this collaborative ministry … It should be clear before ordination that each student is capable of the relationships of mutual trust, recognition and collaboration with both men and women which will be expected of him in today's parishes (p. 37 & 39).

Relational skills needed for collaborative ministry:

… evaluation, self-appraisal, listening, consulting, discerning, consensus decision-making, planning, group facilitation and handling conflict (p. 30).

Collaborative ministry as an attitude of mind, more than cooperation or lay-involvement

There may be parishes with strong lay involvement but little genuine collaboration … Collaborative ministry does not happen just because people work together or cooperate in some way. It is a gradual and mutual evolution of new patterns, new attitudes and new self-understanding … The decision to make a parish more collaborative needs to be made by priests and laypeople together; both have to be willing to change themselves, rather than anxious to change each other (p. 28 & 36).

Spirituality of collaborative ministry

Collaborative ministry draws deeply upon faith in the Trinity. It is not simply a way of re-organising work or structures. It is a way of expressing …what God is like in the ways we live and work together (p. 35).

Some additional comments of my own regarding what collaborative ministry should mean in practice.

The task ('labour') of the Church in a particular parish is the shared task ('co-labour') of the whole parish, not just of the clergy. All members of the parish have a shared responsibility for this task. They are all co-labourers i.e. involved in collaborative ministry. Hence, it is vital that everyone feels a shared 'ownership' of the parish, its life and mission

This is because we are all fully and equally members of the Church through the sacraments of baptism, confirmation and eucharist. These are the basic sacraments of membership. There cannot be a membership fuller than full membership. Even the Pope himself or our own local bishop are not fuller members of the Church than we are. The sacrament of orders is secondary to baptism, confirmation and eucharist and is meant to be at their service. The ministries of lay people are not delegated by the priest because he cannot manage to do it all himself. They flow from their full membership of the Church.

When Bishop Gray came as Auxiliary Bishop to Liverpool, he remarked at the reception following his Episcopal Ordination: 'When I was ordained priest, I thought it was the greatest day of my life, to share in the priesthood of Christ. Now I see that this is the greatest day of my life, when I share in the fullness of Christ's priesthood.' A short time afterwards Archbishop Beck was introducing him to members of the Southport Deanery and mentioned this remark of Bishop Gray. The Archbishop commented: 'He left out the most important day of his life – when he was baptised.' I warmed to that comment, even though a bit of me felt that the most important day of his life was when he was born, loved into existence by God.

It is not the laity who are there to help the hierarchy be the Church; it is more the other way round. The hierarchy helps the rest of the People of God exercise their ministry and mission. Priests enable parishioners to become community, to become a living and loving parish. By virtue of their baptism, lay people are the Church, the parish, the diocese. Ministry is not a privilege. It flows from our baptism. When I was Leader of the Team Ministry in Skelmersdale New Town, some of the parishioners used to say: 'You priests come and go. It is we the lay people who really are the Church here in Skelmersdale. This is our Church. We are not just passing through.'

There is always a danger of 'Churchifying' collaborative ministry i.e. reducing it to liturgical ministry or Church administration. The ministry of the Church is to the world, outgoing, sharing people's joys and sorrows. The last parish where I served as parish priest helps to support a HIV/AIDS Home Care project in Livingstone, Zambia. I have been out there twice – on the second occasion along with four parishioners. The project is spearheaded by a little group of nuns with much of the work being done by about one hundred volunteers. It seems to be completely independent of the local clergy. I have never seen any priest involved in the work. CAFOD is another example of 'out-going' ministry with a strong basis of lay-leadership and responsibility. This dimension is underlined in *The Sign We Give*:

> Ministry overlaps with, and flows into, mission. It is the forms of life and activity through which the baptised express their discipleship in the various areas of their life; home and family; neighbourhood and wider society; parish and diocese … these activities are indeed mission (p. 18).

It is also brought out forcefully and very beautifully by Denys Turner in his Summary of Sector B, Topic Four of the National Pastoral Congress ('The Apostolate of the Laity'), cf. *Liverpool 1980*, pp. 146-150. A few quotations to whet readers' appetites:

Though the Gospels and the Council are unequivocal about this calling (i.e. to be apostles in our daily lives), we do not in practice see the Church calling us in a manner which makes such clear-cut demands on us ... far too often the clergy would rather have us as willing sheep in the administration of our parishes – if that – rather than as apostolic leaders in the world (p. 147).

It is important that the voice of the laity is listened to far more attentively within th Church than it is at present ... too many clergy are dragging their feet over consultation within the parishes. We urge the hierarchy to listen to and trust our own distinctive insights and experience when they are drawing up statements and directives on the many social and moral issues which form so central a part of our apostolic programme ... the value of our apostolate in the Church derives from our unique experience of being the Church in the world. This experience must not be lost to the Church (p. 147).

We must emphasise, we are not the people in the Church who have no vocation. Ours is the basic vocation of service and love in the world. The ordained ministers are servants of that service ... there is no reason why lay people should not be asked to preach more often and good reasons why they should (p. 149).

An important dimension of the leadership role of the priest in the faith community consists in drawing out, drawing upon and drawing together the gifts, talents and leadership qualities in the parish. Even the specific 'leadership of the faith community' role of the priest should be exercised collaboratively. To lead is to empower, not to replace (cf. *Sign*, p. 19).

In the final analysis, collaborative ministry is not a way of doing something more efficiently. It is a way of being Church more authentically.

2. Collaboration in the Church's Teaching Ministry

The Church's mission of teaching and evangelization is essentially a collaborative mission. Often when we talk about 'teaching', we think of someone called the 'teacher' passing on knowledge, information or skills to other people called the 'pupils' or 'learners'. The word 'teaching' focuses on what the teacher is doing. It makes his/her activity the major ingredient in what is happening. If I as the teacher know my material and put it over clearly, then the responsibility rests with the pupils if they fail to learn. For much of my time teaching moral theology in the seminary that is how I thought of teaching. I taught; my pupils were taught. However, some years ago, as a result of a course on the processes of adult learning, I underwent a kind of Copernican revolution in my understanding of my role as a teacher. I came to realize that I was working within the wrong frame of reference.

The principal frame of reference is not 'teaching', but 'learning'. Our main concentration must be on the learning process. If no learning occurs, no real teaching is taking place, however well a teacher might think he or she is teaching and however excellent their material might be, objectively speaking.

As Church we are not a community divided into two groups,
1) The teachers (the pope and the bishops).
2) Those who are taught (the rest of us).

That kind of presentation was a nineteenth-century innovation and went very much against the more traditional and biblical notion which saw 'learning' and 'teaching' as two activities involving the whole Church. As Christians we are all learners and as Christians we are also all teachers. Unpacking the two halves of that statement might help us to appreciate the collaborative nature of Christian teaching.

'As Christians we are all learners'. We remember the words of Jesus: 'You must not allow yourselves to be called teachers, for you have only one teacher, the Christ' (Mt 23, 10). In fact, the word 'disciple' means 'learner'. Moreover, we are all equally dependent on the Lord for the gift of faith, be we pope or peasant. We are all believers. At this level we are all equal. At this level, strange though it might sound, we all share equally in the charism of infallibility. This is the infallibility of the Church in believing (cf. LG, 12).

In any group gathered together to share a learning experience there is always a certain dynamic element at work. In the Church it is the Holy Spirit who is the dynamic element in the learning process. (cf. Karl Rahner, *The Dynamic Element in the Church, passim*) That is why the Church needs to have a basic trust and confidence in its internal learning process and should allow it to take its natural course. Archbishop Worlock voiced that trust in his 'Don't you believe in the Holy Spirit' comment to the assembled Liverpool delegates for the National Pastoral Congress quoted earlier

The heart of this learning process in the Church does not lie in the passing on of correct teaching from one generation to the next. Revelation, or Tradition, is not a block of objective knowledge committed to the apostles by Jesus and passed down from age to age. In his book, *The Theology of Vatican II* (London, 1967), Bishop Butler states that 'a revelation is not fully given until it is received'. In other words revelation is a living reality which occurs in every generation, in the sense that the process of self-discovery in Christ has to be worked through by the Church in every age and in each culture. The Word of God being received and appropriated in each generation is the living process of revelation. That is the heart of Christian tradition.

'As Christians we are all teachers'. This is true within the learning community of the Church. We all share our faith with each other and thus help on the growth process in the body of the Church – parents, teachers and catechists

88

doing this in a very crucial way. By virtue of our baptism we also share in the missionary function of the Church. 'Go and teach all nations' is a word of the Lord spoken to all of us. This is put forward very forcefully by Paul VI in his Apostolic Letter, Evangelization in the modern world, following the 1974 Synod of Bishops. In this letter the pope seems to opt for the learning frame of reference rather than the teaching one when he says: 'In fact, the proclamation only reaches full development when it is listened to, accepted and assimilated, and when it arouses a genuine adherence in the one who has thus received it' (23). In other words, the heart of evangelization does not lie in what we do but rather in what happens in the hearts and minds of those with whom we are trying to share the gospel. This links in with one of the insights of modern literary theory. There is a dynamic interaction between the text and the reader, between the word and the listener. The reader or listener brings his or her own experience into their interpretation of the text or their reception of the spoken word. It is amazing how often the same homily conveys a different message for different people! Yet this should not be surprising. The gospel is being shared by people who, within their unique situations in life, are hungry for the word of God.

What about the teaching authority of the pope and the bishops?
Again it depends on whether one adopts the teaching frame of reference or the learning one. If we go for a rigid teaching model, the pope and the bishops are in an impossible position. They would need to be one-person universities – experts in the bible, theology, philosophy, ethics, pastoral care, and Church history. Obviously that is humanly impossible. If a learning model is accepted as the prime process, the leadership role of the pope and bishops lies within rather than outside the learning process. They remain one hundred per cent members of the learning community. Their particular function is to facilitate the learning process within the community. It is worth exploring what this role means within the Church.

First
Ultimately Holy Spirit is the one teacher in the Christian community – the life-giving spirit of truth which Christ has breathed into his Church.

This Spirit permeates the whole Church and so those exercising 'teaching authority', whether pope, bishop or the CDF, should not see themselves as the repository of all wisdom and knowledge or as having some kind of 'hotline' to God. Gerard Hughes SJ offers a timely warning on this point:

We cannot confidently lay claim to the guidance of the Spirit, whether as individuals or as a Church, unless we take the normal human means to try to arrive at the truth (cf. 'Natural law ethics and moral theology', in *The Month*, 1987, p. 103).

They will see themselves very much as listeners, trying to discern all the riches of the Spirit's wisdom coming through different members of the community. When they discern the voice of the Spirit, coming from whatever quarter, they will see it as part of their role to enable that voice to be heard as widely as possible in the Church.

Second

Vatican II has made us more aware that the Spirit-guided learning community must not be restricted to the Roman Catholic Church. Even outside the gathering of Christian believers, the learning process is going on and the Spirit of God is active. Only if the Church is true to the listening and learning dimension of its teaching role in each age and culture will the heart of revelation be clothed in the best riches of the world's true self-understanding (Cf. GS, 58 & 44).

Third

Dialogue is an essential part of teaching according to the learning model. In his very first homily as Pope as his Mass with the Cardinals, Benedict XVI laid great emphasis on dialogue, mentioning it no less than four times in the course of a very brief sermon. Listening and speaking lie at the heart of genuine dialogue which is directed partly towards listening and learning and partly towards sharing one's own beliefs and convictions. Cardinal Walter Kasper has recently stressed the ecumenical importance of dialogue – it helps us to become truly 'Catholic':

> The truth is always bigger than our formulas. None of us has the truth, but the truth has us. Through dialogue, with its exchange of gifts, we don't reach a new truth, but we come to a fuller understanding of the truth, which we believe we have in Jesus Christ. This is the dynamic dimension which helps us discover our full 'catholicity'.

The late Jacques Dupuis remarks on the importance of dialogue in the field of inter-faith relations: 'The same God is present and acting in both dialogue partners.' It involves 'getting inside the skin of the other, walking in the other's shoes, seeing the world as the other sees it, asking the other's questions.' Dialogue is something sacred: 'The same God speaks in the heart of both partners, the same Spirit is at work in both.'

Fourth

Dialogue can offer an interesting model for 'teaching statements'. Roman Catholic authorities can be open to the temptation of thinking that all Church statements should be infallible or at least one hundred per cent certain. In fact, such an expectation is normally virtually impossible. So a different temptation raises its head – either the Church is silent when some kind of tentative statement could be helpful to the debate or else it claims a level of' authority for its statements which they will not bear.

In the dialogue model, Church statements can be seen as contributions to an ongoing conversation – 'I may be wrong, but …'. In my book, *New Directions in Sexual Ethics*, I explore statements from various Churches on sexual issues in the light of that 'ongoing dialogue' model (cf. chapter five, especially pp. 96-99).

The way the US bishops went about the writing of their two pastoral letters on peace and the economy are good examples of this dialogue process in action. Draft versions were made public and comments were invited from all and sundry. The reason why the document on the Common Good published by the Bishops Conference of England and Wales had such a major impact, apart from the richness of its content and its accessibility, may have been because it was presented not as a dogmatic statement but as a serious contribution to the thinking of the nation prior to an important General Election.

Fifth

The role of articulating the community's grasp of the truth when it reaches sufficient clarity and agreement clearly demands attentive listening and careful discernment. It includes listening to earlier teaching, as is witnessed to by the wise saying of a medieval theologian: 'We see further than our forebears. We are like dwarfs sitting on shoulders of giants.'

Yet it also includes accepting the possibility of a development of doctrine or even of a change of teaching when a growth in moral sensitivity in the human family makes us aware that certain things we held as true in the past are now seen to be erroneous or at least in need of a radical restatement. This has occurred with regard to slavery and certain aspects of our self-understanding in the area of sexuality. It is an ongoing refining and reforming process that we can expect to continue in the future. If teaching develops or changes, this must be acknowledged and the reasons for it understood.

Christian tradition is something alive and active. Healthy development and change is not a betrayal of our forebears. It is being faithful to the living tradition they handed on to us.

Sixth

Prophecy is not linked necessarily to the role of the teacher, though some teachers in the Church have also been prophets. However, part of the teacher's role is to listen out for the voice of the prophet and then enable that voice to be heard as widely as possible.

In that sense, it could be argued that the most important exercise of teaching authority last century was the calling of Vatican II by Pope John XXIII. He enabled the prophetic voices in the community to be heard by the whole Church.

What about dissent from authoritative teaching in the Church?

Provided it is not tantamount to the denial of the heart of our Christian faith, within the learning frame of reference there is room for dissent in the Church. Personally, I prefer the term 'disagreement' to 'dissent' since it is more in keeping with the conversational model. Within the teaching model dissent usually involves confrontation, since it is virtually saying to the 'teaching authority', 'You, the teacher, are wrong. You are in error.' Despite that, it is still allowed for in exceptional circumstances even in the traditional manuals of theology.

In the learning model, disagreement need not involve any confrontation with teaching authority, since it is simply suggesting that the articulation of the teaching put forward by the teacher does not do justice to the full riches of what the Church really believes. Hence, rather than being seen as a negative confrontation, it presents itself as an attempt to collaborate in the Church's teaching ministry. A helpful indicator of its value may be found in the reaction of the rest of the community, especially those most intimately involved through their own experience in that specific issue. That is why the 'non-reception' of some of the Church's teaching on sexual and marital issues cannot be dismissed too easily. It has even been suggested that such 'non-reception' is actually the dynamic action of the Holy Spirit in the minds and hearts of those who know the truth of the matter in the light of their own experience. After all, it was Cardinal Hume who reminded the Rome Synod on the Family in 1980 that the experience of Christian married couples is a genuine source for the Church's understanding of the theology of marriage.

Collaboration in the Church's mission of teaching and evangelization is a privilege and responsibility of us all. The Church will be truly honouring collaboration in this aspect of its mission when the voice of the Spirit is heard and listened to, through whomsoever it speaks and from whatever unlikely quarter it might come.

3. QUEST AND THE TEACHING MINISTRY IN THE CHURCH

'Arising from your experience, what would you say to the Pope if you had the chance to speak to him?' 'I could put my message into one word: Listen. Listen to people's stories so that we can discover the sacred in them. The difficulty I have with the Church and the hierarchy is a positive inability to listen to people's stories, so they're not dealing with a movement I believe to be of God's spirit.'

This was the answer given by a US Catholic priest who had been ministering to gay men in the US living with HIV / AIDS (cf. NDSE, p. 70).

Another person commented:

AIDS has opened a door between gay people and the Church. It has been an agent prompting reflection on sexuality ... they see heroism and selfless activity in the gay community. They come to ask: How could this be bad? How could this be what the Church is telling us it is? (NDSE, p. 94).

The word 'Listen' has cropped up frequently in this reflection on collaborative ministry and the Church's teaching ministry – seen from a learning/teaching perspective. In 2004 the Bishops of England and Wales launched a LISTENING 2004 project. Like many such things, it seemed to go off half-cock. However, one fruit of it was an Assembly here in Liverpool which I attended and which I found quite remarkable. From morning until teatime one Saturday over 100 people, including our bishops, listened to what people throughout the diocese had been saying on the theme, 'My Family, My Church'.

One of the presentations was entitled 'Joe's Story':

Our son's name is Joe. He was thirty-three last week. Joe was a lovely child, the happiest baby going, full of life as a toddler and buzzing with energy and love of life. As he got older he always seemed to be involved in things and had lots of hobbies and interests. But as he got into his mid-teens, he became quiet and subdued. He stopped mixing and would withdraw from many social situations. He became moody and irritable. We put this down to the teenage blues and were concerned but felt it would all pass in time. It didn't. He started to be skitted at school and had episodes of real misery, not wanting to go out any more. We were at our wits end –what had happened to our lovely young son? We talked with him, tried to get him to talk to us, we shared our anxieties with some of our closest friends, talked with our doctor. Nothing seemed to help. One night we came home to find he had swallowed a lot of tablets and was unconscious. A rush to hospital followed and … well, I won't go on. But to cut a long story short, what emerged was that Joe had started to realise that he was gay.

Although we accepted him completely and continued to give him all our love, Joe despised himself, felt different, as if there were something wrong with him. There followed many years of unhappiness and he attempted suicide on two more occasions. He found it difficult to accept himself. His self-esteem was at rock bottom and there was little joy in his life. His sense of being different dominated his existence and ours.

And then, when he was about twenty-six or twenty-seven, he met Brian, a lovely fellow. They had such a lot in common. They started to meet up regularly and then had a holiday, something Joe hadn't done for years. He started to pick up hobbies and interests again instead of drowning himself in work and TV.

That was six years ago. They have been living as partners for the last five years and these days Joe is much more like a grown up version of the lively youngster we knew. He is happy, fulfilled, enjoys life and is involved in all sorts of worthwhile activity. He is a fantastic uncle to his nieces and nephews. My wife and I are so delighted to see him happy again and thank God daily that he has come through those terrible times. I know this is another of the stories, where things aren't right by the book but to us it feels as if salvation has come to our son.

What I found remarkable on that Saturday was the complete and unquestioning acceptance by all present of how Joe's parents feel at the end of the story. Remember their closing words in the story: – 'Salvation has come to our son' – a perfect example of Mahoney's 'making faith-sense of experience and making experience-sense of faith'. Margaret Rogers, one of the organisers of that Saturday's listening session, finished her presentation in this way:

> What has been highlighted is how much love and energy go into creating and supporting the family, whatever shape or structure it may have. It is an awesome task, truly worthy of the name vocation. It is what occupies most of our time. This daily working and reworking of relationship embodies the mystery of life – of creation, growth and resurrection.
>
> How can we, as Church, find ways of giving due emphasis to this business of living and relating that people are finding so challenging? Because when it goes wrong, people really do perish.
>
> Families (relationships) can be places of love, support, warmth, tenderness, fun & joy (Creation). They can also be places of bitterness, hurt, harshness, cruelty, abuse & domination (The Fall). It is through the daily struggle (Redemptive Love) that families (relationships) become communities of love (Salvation).

The other organiser of the Liverpool Listening assembly, Fr Tony Slingo, began his final summary with a very challenging statement: 'When it works, Church is massively important for people. When it doesn't work, it is massively wounding. The voice of the families challenge me about making room at the table.' He pointed out that the Church can be rigid, judgemental, excluding, rejecting and cruel when people do not come up to the Church's norm. And this is made all the worse when it is a norm to do with personal relationships and one which does not seem to fit with the reality of people's lives. The result is legalised exclusion or people withdrawing and hiding away. Tony closed his reflection by saying: 'There seems to be a call for our Catholic culture to continue broadening out to value much more visibly what is good human living in itself and not only what is fully paid-up, card-carrying officially Catholic.'

What has all this to do with collaborative ministry. Collaborative ministry is based on the theology of communion. In other words, it goes in the opposite direction to exclusion. It is about having a place at the table – not by invitation of the priest or bishop, but by invitation of the Host who is notorious for his open hospitality. All kinds are welcome at the table. It is a gathering of wounded people – and that means all of us. It involves the patience needed for the seed to grow, even in the midst of choking weeds, as the parable of the darnel reminds us. Disputes and conflicts have their place around the table. They should not covered over or hidden away, as in a dysfunctional family. *The Sign We Give* makes that point very strongly in its section, 'Learning to deal with conflict' (p. 30-31): 'If collaboration is to grow, conflict must be brought into the open. It can be paralysing when it remains hidden. The courage to face and work through conflict … are not weaknesses, but signs of maturity and commitment.'

What does the teaching on collaborative ministry say to QUEST members in terms of your involvement in the learning/teaching ministry of the Church?
Most of all, value your place at the table. You are a gift to the other guests, as they are to you. Often cruel and rigid opposition to gays and lesbians is due to people never having had the healing, grace-filled experience of personal contact with gay or lesbians, whether individuals or couples. You in QUEST are uniquely qualified to remedy this. It is only people like yourselves who can help the Church find the appropriate language for making 'faith-sense' and 'experience-sense' of the lives of gay and lesbian members of the Church.

When Christians in general first began to be challenged by the 'grace-filled' experience of gay partners living lives which carried all the marks of a 'loving relationship' – and so revelatory of God - the initial reaction of theologians like myself was that this experience must be listened to. However, that initial reaction presumed that heterosexual theologians like myself would do the listening. We would examine the experience presented to us and then evaluate whether we needed to reformulate our sexual theology to take account of what we had learnt in this process. In this reaction we were missing the point. The language about homosexuality which we had all been brought up on was not adequate for expressing the positive experience of gays and lesbians. Hence, new ways of speaking about gay and lesbian experience had to be found. Initially, this could only be done by gay people like yourselves since it was your experience as persons which was being expressed. Gay theology can only be done by gay people. James Allison is an outstanding example of this.

Moreover, what theologians like myself were failing to appreciate was that gay Christians seeking to articulate their experience are actually 'doing theology'. Finding the right language is actually part of the theological process. This kind of work needs to be accepted gratefully by the Church as a rich contribution to its ongoing commitment to the truth. Without this kind of theological reflection and its public expression, there is no possibility of real dialogue on this issue in the Church. And without dialogue there is no collaborative ministry in searching the truth.

Of course, to present the Gospel positively as genuine 'good news' for gay men and lesbians does not mean that the Gospel does not challenge them to eradicate from their lives whatever violates the dignity of persons or is destructive of personal and social relationships. Part of a more open dialogue towards a positive spirituality for homosexual persons will surely need to have on its agenda how to discern which kinds of gay and lesbian relationship are expressive of genuine love and which are abusive of persons? And also which kinds can develop the capacity to sustain faithful loving commitments and which prevent growth in personal and emotional maturity? These same questions apply equally to heterosexual relationships. I have never forgotten the comment of my US Jesuit friend, Jon Fuller, an expert in integrated HIV / AIDS care: 'There is nothing so similar to heterosexuality as homosexuality. They are both about loving persons precisely as persons.'

Sexuality is a dimension to our being human persons which we all share, whatever our sexual orientation. As a Christian, I believe that this sexual dimension is an important aspect of our being made persons in the image of a relational, loving and life-giving God. We are most true to ourselves as sexual human persons, therefore, to the extent that we realise the potentiality of our sexuality by going out to each other in love, by joyfully expressing that love in a way which is appropriate to the character and depth of our relationships and by contributing to the life-giving enterprise of receiving our human existence as gift and accepting our responsibility to prepare a future worth passing on to future generations.

A Christian sexual ethics which is able to embrace and express the positive goodness to be found in loving gay and lesbian relationships should be all the richer – and Christian – since it is now based on a more comprehensive appreciation of the giftedness of the human person. Such a positive evaluation would help gays and lesbians to feel that 'it is wonderful for us to be here'. I am suggesting that QUEST members have the privilege – and responsibility – of making their own unique contribution to that positive evaluation. It is a task which, in today's climate, will often be painful and which, sadly and tragically, will sometimes be met with rejection.

I cannot resist quoting my favourite text from Timothy Radcliffe, words spoken to the 2002 National Conference of Priests:

When Jesus ate and drank with tax collectors and prostitutes,
it was not a duty.
It was utter delight in their company,
in their very being.
When he touched the untouchable,
it was not a clinical gesture,
but a hug of joy.

So it belongs to us as Christians
that we rejoice in the very existence of people,
with all their fumbling attempts to live and love,
whether they are married or divorced or single,
whether they are straight or gay,
whether their lives are lived
in accordance with Church teaching or not …

The Church should be a community in which
people discover God's delight in them.

I have never ceased to wonder at the semi-mystical experience Thomas Merton
had in a shopping mall in Louisville when he was suddenly overwhelmed by
his oneness in God with the vast throng of people all around even though all
total strangers. He was inspired to write:

How can you tell people that they are all walking around shining like
the sun... If only we could see ourselves and each other through the eyes
of God. I suppose the big problem would be that we would fall down
and worship each other (*Conjectures of a Guilty Bystander*, London, Sheldon Press, 1977 edit, pp. 155).

God's Kingdom will come a stage nearer for our Catholic community when we
are prepared to fall down and 'worship' our gay and lesbian brothers and sisters as the persons they really are in the eyes of God!

APPENDIX

Letter to The Tablet (13 February 2010) on Homosexual Relationships

Dear Editor,
As a moral theologian, my view on same-sex relationships has changed radically over the years. I now believe that God's call to lesbians and gays is to accept themselves as they are as a gift from God; to accept their homosexual
orientation as the way God has gifted them to live their lives as loving persons.

Consequently, provided their loving tries to be self-giving, faithful, life-enhancing, just, mutually respectful and not self-centred nor exploitative (all demands applying equally to heterosexual loving), then their relationship and
their loving can truly be experienced as a sharing of God's love in their lives –
and, in that sense, sacramental.

Although what I have written above is not the approved teaching of the
Catholic Church, I believe that it expresses more adequately the richness of a
Catholic sexual ethic based on the person-centred theology of Vatican II. For
me to say anything else would be to betray my vocation as a moral theologian.

Moral Theology after Vatican II

CHAPTER SEVEN

Receiving Vatican II:
An Ongoing Challenge for Moral Theologians

This unpublished text of a 2007 talk I gave at Trinity and All Saints University, Leeds, was also discussed by my peers at a meeting of our Association of Teachers of Moral Theology.

Ordained in 1958, I am old enough to remember the excitement of Vatican II. Following further studies in Switzerland and Rome, I returned to Liverpool in 1963. Vatican II was just beginning. I still treasure the privilege of helping the girls at our local high school enjoy full and active participation in the liturgy for the first time. Later there was the refreshing experience of exploring crucial issues of ethics and social life, especially the burning topic of contraception, with highly articulate lay people whose lives were touched very intimately by the topics being talked about. Those were certainly heady days. Vatican II was having a massive impact on me at every level, but especially as a priest and moral theologian.

The initial excitement continued for many years. However, the situation we are all living in has changed dramatically as has the Church itself. There are different signs of the times today from those faced by the bishops at the Council. We are living in what people call a post-modern age and globalisation is in the air we breathe. This has affected people's approach to all institutions including the Church. Authority is not given automatic respect. It needs to prove itself. The spread of scientific knowledge has changed the way we think about ourselves, our world and the whole of creation. These advances in knowledge pose new questions to believers, questions which come to us not just from other people but from our own hearts and minds. How do we experience God in this new world and what is the role of organised religion, Church membership, liturgy and prayer? Vatican II opened our eyes to the reality that we are already in the world and there is nowhere else we can be. These are questions for us just as much as for non-believers or agnostics.

Vatican II excites me as much today as it did in the 1960s. That is because I believe it is about a process, a way of being human and Christian, a style of thinking, relating, living and a way of being Church in the world. Although the Church has changed enormously over the years since Vatican II, sadly some of the more recent changes have not always been in line with the Council's spirit and style.

A couple of years ago I was invited to write a chapter for a Festschrift on the theme of 'Towards Vatican III'. I replied that I could not accept that title since I did not believe that we had fully taken on board the radical spirit of Vatican II. My piece eventually appeared under the title, 'Do we need a Vatican III?' and appears later in this volume.

I gave myself a Vatican II treat in the Summer of 2006. I went for a quiet reading holiday and brought with me the five volumes of Giuseppe Alberigo's *History of Vatican II*, plus some other less voluminous though extremely helpful reading on the Council. I found it an immensely rewarding experience. Besides bringing back many happy memories, it opened my eyes to fresh riches in the Vatican II treasure chest. It also made me much more aware of the great struggle of minds and hearts that took place behind the scenes during the Council. I appreciated even more the tremendously hard work and suffering of those who felt inspired by the Holy Spirit to enrich the Church with the life-giving spirit of Vatican II. At the same time this sustained reading made me face the human limitations of the Church and how the strength of some passages in the Conciliar texts was weakened as a result of unhealthy intrigues and stratagems at the very heart of the Council process. It was a warning to me that I should never assume naively that the Holy Spirit bypasses the vagaries and ambiguities of ordinary human behaviour.

Although Vatican II ended on 8 December 1965, that was just the beginning of a process which is still going on today. This process can be called the reception of Vatican II. Reception means much more than all members of the Church saying 'Yes' or 'No' to the documents of the Council. It is a much more active and creative process. It certainly includes interpreting the clear wishes of the Council within the widely differing cultural settings of the many local Churches throughout the world. But even more than that is involved by reception. It means being infused by the spirit of Vatican II so that our way of being Church internally and in relation to the world grows more and more in conformity with that spirit. The implications of that will be discussed later. Furthermore, part of the genius of Vatican II was its ability to give opposing views a place within the same document rather than settling for the lowest common denominator between them. Reception also involves continuing the word of the Council by striving creatively to resolve these tensions.

To understand the process of reception of Vatican II and its impact on the field of moral theology, it might help to look first at the spirit or style of Vatican II and then explore the implications of that for the role of a moral theologian post-Vatican II.

1) The Spirit or Style of Vatican II

The US Church historian, John O'Malley SJ, sees the heart of Vatican II as consisting in a call to be Church in a new way. For him Vatican II has been a radical event in the life of the Church. It is the Church going back to its roots and seeing itself, its mission and its relationship to the world through new eyes. This new vision is deeply influenced by our encounter with all that is good, enriching and authentically inspiring in our world today. It comes from our deeper self-understanding arising from how we are better able to understand ourselves in all our complexity as embodied human subjects, part of the material world, who are relational, sexual, independent social beings, each of us unique, yet sharing a common humanity, and capable to being open to the transcendent. While human persons have experienced themselves in these core dimensions down through the ages, never before has there been such an immense and far-reaching expansion in personal and social self-understanding as there is today. For instance, globalisation, despite its bad press and the way it can be misused, has made us aware as never before that we are one human family, whose lives are intertwined as in some massive tapestry and whose future survival lies in all our hands – a World Wide Web with a difference. Our increased knowledge in such fields as evolution, quantum physics, genetics, biology, sociology, psychology and socio-biology has enabled us to see ourselves and our world with new eyes. The growth in our historical consciousness has made us appreciate the massive impact of culture, context and time in our lives and the lives of our fellow humans today and down the ages. Likewise, advances in gender studies have enabled us to see ourselves and the story of our human family through new and critical eyes.

The eyes through which we see ourselves and our world today are radically different from those of previous ages. It is with these same eyes that we interpret the Bible and the God-revealing story of Jesus. To be a Christian today is very different to being a Christian at the time of the early Church. It is also true to say that being a Christian today is very different to being a Christian prior to Vatican II. What might be more difficult to take on board is to recognise that the world in which we are living today is itself very different to the world at the time of Vatican II.

What John O'Malley has highlighted is that the sea-change brought about by Vatican II in our way of being Church enables us to feel at home in such a constantly changing world. The incarnation was God being born into human history in the person of Jesus. Christianity is essentially a historical faith. It does not have an a-historical existence outside of history. It is historical through and through. Therefore the Gospel needs to be constantly incarnated and inculturated in all the vicissitudes of human history and in a vast array of human cultures.

In an article entitled, 'Shape of Vatican II', in *America*, 24 February 2003 pp. 12-15, John O'Malley describes what he sees to be the five essential components of the new style of being Church to which the bishops at Vatican II committed the whole Church. Because of the importance of the point O'Malley is making, I have taken the liberty of quoting a very long passage from him. There is no way I could improve on the way he has put it:

First, the council called the Church from what had been an almost ex-clusively vertical, top-down style of behaviour to one that took more ac-count of the horizontal traditions in Catholicism. This is most palpably manifested in the recurring use of horizontal words like 'cooperation', 'partnership' and 'collaboration', which are true novelties in ecclesiastical documents. It receives its most potent expressions in the word 'collegial-ity'. The partnership and collaboration extend to relations between pope and bishops, bishops and priests, priests and parishioner – bishops and laity. In repeatedly describing the Church as 'the people of God' we see clearly the intrinsic relationship between style and content – between the 'what' questions and the 'how' questions.

Second, the council called the Church to a style and mentality more consonant with serving than with controlling. One of the most amazing features of Vatican II is the redefinition it consistently interjects into the words 'ruler' and 'king', equating them with 'servant'. The pastoral im-plications are immense. To serve effectively means to be in touch with the needs of those being served, not supplying them with prefabricated solutions.

Third, nothing is perhaps more striking in the vocabulary of the coun-cil, nothing perhaps so much sets it off from previous councils as words like 'development', 'progress' and even 'evolution'. This is a sign of a break with the static framework of understanding doctrine, discipline and style of being characteristic of all previous councils. Vatican II never uses the word 'change', but that is precisely what it is talking about re-garding the Church. What this implies, of course, is further change in the future. It suggests that its own provisions are somewhat open-ended. Whatever the interpretation and implementation of the council mean, they cannot mean taking the council's decisions as if they said, 'thus far and not a step further'. The council's style is thus oriented to the future and open to it.

Fourth, the council substituted for the traditional vocabulary of ex-clusion a vocabulary of inclusion. Instead of anathemas and excommu-nications, it is filled with friendship words like 'sisters and brothers', and 'men and women of good will'. In this regard the handshake of friend-ship was extended not just to other Christians but to anybody wanting to work for a better world.

Fifth, the council moved from a vocabulary suggestive of passive ac-ceptance to one that indicates active participation and engagement. The active participation of the whole congregation in the Mass was the fun-damental and explicit aim of the reform of the liturgy. If the way we pray is a norm for the way we believe, may it not also be a norm for the way we behave? That is, may it be constitutive of our style as Church?

For O'Malley Vatican II is the kind of Church we need to be today if we are to operate effectively in today's world as disciples of Christ. He insists that 'Vatican II had a big agenda' and 'cannot be interpreted in a minimal sense'. He argues that the 'greatest achievement' of the Council lies in a 'redefinition of the way the Church operates'. He even goes so far as to state that 'Vatican II has never been more relevant than it is at this moment in the history of the Church.'

2) Being a moral theologian in the spirit or style of Vatican II

How do O'Malley's five essential components impact on the life and teaching of a moral theologian who is committed to what Vatican II is all about? Taking each of the five components individually – though recognising how closely they interact with each other – I would offer the following comments.

a) Horizontal

Moral theologians have sometimes been accused of living in ivory towers, out of touch with the real-life problems of people. If this was ever true, it is certainly completely contrary to the spirit of Vatican II. Moral theologians are not an isolated 'experts'. They should be much more people deeply in touch with the spirit of the age, including the major cultural and social influences affecting people's lives. Hence, moral theologians need to be a listeners, observers, conversationalists and dialogue partners. The 'texts' they need to be conversant with are everything which touches deeply the human condition, whether in the genre of novels, poetry, drama, films, art or music, as well as culture, history and social trends. Without being a polymath, a moral theologian needs to be conscious of the impact of all these major influences on the human condition. In a sense, it is not the responsibility of a moral theologian to provide moral 'answers', but to ensure that the moral dimension has its place and is properly integrated in any conversation which will have a determining influence on human affairs. By 'the moral dimension' I mean 'what is truly human, all things considered'.

The qualities 'cooperation', 'partnership', 'collaboration' and 'collegiality' which O'Malley highlights all have a direct application to the role of the moral theologian. This would suggest a list of ground rules, perhaps including the following:

1. No thorough-going discussion of particular moral issues should be conducted by moral theologians on their own. Those most experienced and knowledgeable about the issues concerned should be part of the dialogue.
2. It is unwise, counterproductive and a misuse of resources for separate Churches to set up committees or hold meetings to consider moral issues in isolation from their sister Churches.

3. The modus operandi of the CDF investigating the allegedly question-able views of particular moral theologians should take the form of a peer-evaluation process. The person under consideration should be fully involved in the process from the very beginning and the validity of the questions raised about his or her writings should be submitted to critical peer evaluation. Since the theologians whose works are under investigation are frequently people who have made major con-tributions at the cutting edge of theological investigation, the im-mense benefits their theological writings have brought to the Church should be clearly celebrated, even if it is felt necessary to voice one or two critical questions. At present, the Vatican II style pin-pointed by O'Malley's is far from the current procedure of the CDF, despite some minor improvements.

4. Perhaps in an even deeper sense, the qualities of 'cooperation', 'part-nership', 'collaboration' and 'collegiality' do not seem to be much in evidence in the preparation and publication of the various documents and statements on moral issues emanating from the Pope and various Vatican congregations and other bodies. The same seems to be also true of moral statements and documents from some Bishops' conferences.

b) Serving

Needs are generally associated with a local situation even though a wider con-nection cannot be ignored. It is usually the local Church which sees these needs most clearly, whether on its own or in conversation with its concerned neigh-bours. The Council's teaching on collegiality is crucial here. Collegiality is very different from centralisation. In a communion of Churches the role of the centre of unity is not to dictate, nor even authorize, local solutions. It is to encourage local Churches to have the vision and courage to respond positively and cre-atively to local needs and to foster an awareness of how local Churches can learn from each other in this respect and be similarly creative. Sometimes it may be through alerting a neighbouring Church to the impact, positive or neg-ative, their initiative may be having beyond their own locality. In such instances the centre of unity can encourage dialogue between the Churches so affected. The recent process of holding a series of continental synods was, in theory, an appropriate exercise of such a ministry by the centre of unity. Unfortunately, in practice this process seems to have been vitiated by the strong controlling influence of the Vatican prior to, during and after each Synod. Moreover, al-though originally envisaged by Vatican II as continuing the living experience of collegiality, the constitution drawn up in Rome for such synods made this virtually impossible. At Vatican II the bishops were in 'decision-making' mode. In a synod their role is purely 'consultative'. Peter Phan's book, *The Asian Synod: Texts and Commentaries*, New York, Orbis, 2002, clearly shows how frustrated the Asian bishops were by this whole process in the 1998 Asian Synod.

It is here that the actual event of Vatican II was so important – perhaps even more than all the documents emanating from it. Despite its limitations, Vatican II gave the bishops an experience of genuine collegiality. They were not being 'consulted' by the Pope. They were meeting in 'decision-making mode' with him in the Council. Though very tiring, and at times very frustrating, they found this experience so inspiring they came to the decision: 'this is what being Church is all about. This is the way we should live Church at every level.' Vatican II was a call to the whole Church to become collegial in its life and decision-making. Sadly, this call has not yet really been heeded. There seems to have been a lack of courage and determination to carry it through. Although authority is spoken of as 'service', in the final analysis the power to decide remains almost entirely in the hands of 'authority' (i.e. bishops and parish priests). Any preliminary sounding out of views is purely consultative. This hierarchical mode affects moral theologians and their teaching in a whole variety of ways.

c) Change

The Pope's decision to ring-fence discussion of contraception and exclude it from the agenda of Vatican II not only ran counter to what the council was about as a collegial experience. It also proved disastrous in that those who found 'change' impossible to contemplate were given the time and opportunity needed to gain access to the ear of Paul VI. The final and only official Report of the Birth Control Commission had come down firmly in favour of a change in teaching. It had even prepared a draft pastoral statement to help Catholics understand how this change would enable the Church to be true to a deeper level of continuity in its understanding of marriage and sexuality. Four members of the Commission, without any authorisation of the general body, used their influence in the Vatican to get a personal text of their own to the Pope. Its central argument was that the Church cannot possibly change its teaching. Otherwise, people would conclude that, if the Church had misled them on this issue, its whole authority would be thrown into question.

What these opponents of change failed to grasp was that it is precisely through changing its teaching in the light of a deeper knowledge and understanding of ourselves as sexual human persons that the Church is able to maintain a much deeper level of continuity in its teaching. By deepening our understanding of what is involved in being a human person in the world, we are able to enrich our previous teaching and thus change and correct it when it no longer does justice to our self-understanding.

The implications of this understanding of change are enormous for all involved in theological teaching and research. The theologians who most threaten the 'traditional' teaching of the Church are those who fail to recognise that it is a 'living tradition'. A living tradition is the action of God's Spirit leading us into all truth. It cannot be set in stone once and for all in any ultimate formulation. As new knowledge and understanding come our way, as cultures develop and change, this living tradition is calling constantly to be kept 'alive ' through translation and interpretation so that its powerful vision can inspire men and women of each generation and every culture. Theologians have an important role to play in this interpretation and translation. To repeat unthinkingly yesterday's formulas is to dishonour Christian tradition rather than conserve it.

d) Inclusion

As part of an analysis of the moral section of the *Catechism of the Catholic Church*, some years ago I wrote the following:

> Since Vatican II, any presentation of Catholic faith must have an ecumenical dimension to it. This entails more than a longing for the unity for which Christ prayed. It also involves a recognition that God's Spirit is at work in other Christian Churches. It is in this spirit that the moral section of the Catechism needs to be read. This implies that, when there are particular issues of moral disagreement between the major Christian Churches, the Catechism's presentation of the current authoritative Catholic teaching should not be presumed to be the final and definitive Christian position on this topic. The Catechism offers a helpful ecumenical service in presenting an authoritative Catholic position. However, it would be ecumenically harmful if such a presentation was understood to carry such authority that any other position must be rejected as unchristian. The importance of this point was brought out all the more through the publication in 1994 of *Life in Christ*, an Agreed Statement by the Second Anglican-Roman Catholic International Commission (ARCIC II). This agreed statement is a powerful witness to the fact that, even on those specific moral issues where these two Churches disagree, they still share the same vision and are committed to the same common values ...
>
> Something similar to the point made in the previous section needs to be said with regard to those occasions when the Catholic Church's moral teaching is in conflict with the deeply-held moral convictions of most ordinary good-living men and women, be they Christian or not. This is not suggesting that moral truth can be reduced to a majority vote. Rather, it is based on a fundamental insight of Vatican II, which is reflected in the Catechism's title of Part III, Part I, The Human Vocation: Life in the Spirit. This makes us aware that every human person who is open to the call of the transcendent in life and who responds respectfully and unselfishly to the other, and his or her needs as encountered in life, is being moved by God's Spirit. As Schillebeeckx says, 'a Church attentive to the prompting of God's Spirit will listen to "foreign prophecy" coming from outside its own ranks' (*From a Parish Base*, pp. 135-136).

Acceptance of this foundational principle at this point in history obliges us to recognize that one of the major signs of our times is the crying need to accept totally and work out at all levels of life the full and equal humanity of both men and women. Because the full human dignity of women is not, in fact, accepted in practice (and sometimes even in principle) in various ways in our world today, we can appreciate why the US moral theologian, Margaret Farley, feels obliged to suggest that a litmus test for our commitment to the dignity of every human person lies in the authenticity of our acceptance of the full human dignity of women. Hence, she expresses this principle in the following dramatic sentence:

> Whatever diminishes or denies the full humanity of women must be presumed not to reflect the divine or an authentic relation to the divine, or to reflect the authentic nature of things, or to be the message or work of an authentic redeemer or a community of redemption.

e) Active participation and engagement

In my earlier essay on the National Pastoral Congress, I have already emphasised the importance of collaborative ministry at all levels of Church life and decision making. I tried to spell out all the practical implications of that and the skills and safeguards needed to ensure that it is fully respected. In that same essay I also wrote about the implications of collaborative ministry for the teaching role of the Church. Rather than repeat what I wrote at length in that essay. I encourage readers to refer back to that essay, especially pp. 85-90 on 'Collaboration in the Church's Teaching Ministry". Readers may also be interested in the examples of collaboration between the ATMT and the Bishops' Conference of England and Wales described in a later essay (cf. *infra*, pp. 124-125).

CHAPTER EIGHT

The Changing Face of Moral Theology after Vatican II

This essay is a weaving together and expansion of material from some of my writings on the impact of Vatican II on moral theology. Its two main sources are Being a Moral Theologian Today, which appeared in Priests and People, 1996, 318-323; and Confessions of an Ageing Moral Theologian, a talk originally given to the Theology Department at Leuven University (16 May 2007) and subsequently published in The Furrow, 2004, pp. 82-91.

The title of one of Richard Niebuhr's sermons is 'The Shaking of the Foundations'. That could be an apt description of what has been happening in moral theology since Vatican II. I have had the good fortune to have lived through that 'moving' experience. Some readers might not like the image of the shaking of the foundations. They might find it too unsettling. I warm to it. To me it suggests an upheaval which can itself be stabilising insofar as it shows up where the weaknesses lie and hence enables the foundations to settle once again in their new and consolidated realignment. It also reminds us that living with God's spirit is like living on a seismic fault-line. We can expect many more shakings of the foundations in the future.

The medieval saying, 'We see further than our forebears; we are like dwarfs sitting on the shoulders of giants', offers wise guidance for moral theologians following the shaking of the foundations at Vatican II. It reminds us that we are not wiser or more learned than our predecessors. When I look at the writings of my forebears in moral theology, I certainly feel like a dwarf in comparison with some of them. However, thanks to Vatican II and the age in which we are living, moral theologians today can see in a way which was humanly impossible in earlier ages. However, we will only be able to benefit from this new field of vision if we are true to where we are now in history. That means recognising that we are inheritors of the tradition that our predecessors have passed on to us but recognising, too, that this is a living tradition. God's spirit is active within it and, in our own day, for Roman Catholics most notably in the spirit-inspired gift of Vatican II. Through the continuing inspiration of the Spirit, we are offered the gift of discernment enabling us to be appreciative of the strengths and richness of the tradition we have inherited while also being critically aware of its weaknesses.

This shaking of the foundations through Vatican II and its aftermath has obviously had a major impact on moral theology and the thinking of moral theologians. It is true that there is only one direct reference to moral theology in the documents of Vatican II. That is in the decree on Priestly Formation

(*Optatam Totius*) where it insists that 'special attention needs to be given to the development of moral theology', and goes on to say that 'its scientific exposition should be more thoroughly nourished by scriptural teaching' and that 'it should show the nobility of the Christian vocation of the faithful, and their obligation to bring forth fruit in charity for the life of the world' (no. 16). Though these are very general statements, they get over the message that the Council Fathers want moral theology to be nourished by the solid findings of modern scientific biblical scholarship and also that they want it to be a positive encouragement, inspiration and challenge to the lives of lay people living in the world. No longer should it be confined by the narrow, and narrowing, focus of training priests for their work as confessors, a focus which tended to concentrate too much on the sin-dimension of life.

This article will look at nine influential factors operative over recent years which have radically renewed moral theology from how I and my contemporaries first experienced it in the 1950s. I believe that the changes resulting from this radical renewal, as well as being faithful to the spirit of the living tradition we have inherited, have made moral theology more accessible and practically helpful to those working in pastoral ministry. Moral theology today is more in tune with the everyday concerns of people in general, both within and beyond the Church. Sadly, however, this renewal in moral theology has met some strong resistance within the Church and has not always been fully embraced at all levels of Church life.

(1) The basic criterion of the good of the human person, integrally and adequately considered.

Although moral theologians like myself recognise that moral theology has been challenged and enriched by the Second Vatican Council, we can still forget how fortunate we are. We constantly need to remind ourselves that we are living in a very privileged time in the history of moral theology. Many of the other headings elaborated below are linked in some way to Vatican II. However, to my mind, one point stands out above all others with regard to the impact of Vatican II on moral theology. That is its insistence that the primary criterion for moral evaluation is the good of the human person. Its focus, therefore, is on persons. This is not a rejection of objective morality. Far from it. It is opposed to the kind of subjective morality which would claim that the human subject alone can arbitrarily decide what constitutes moral rightness or moral goodness. For Vatican II morality is not subjective in the sense that, as subjects, we are free to create our own morality to suit our own convenience. That would be succumbing to a reductionist approach to the human person, seeing the person purely as subject, while totally ignoring all the other dimensions of human personhood, material, corporeal, relational, social, historic/cultural, unique and transcendental. Vatican II insists that morality must be objective in a way which views the human person holistically. In other words, the criterion of objective morality is the nature of human person 'integrally and adequately considered'. Following the eight-dimension analysis of Professor Louis Janssens of Louvain, I tried to fill out what this means in chapter three of my *New Directions in Moral Theology: The Challenge of Being Human*, London, Geoffrey Chapman, 1992.

As a moral theologian I was delighted and excited that Vatican II was saying loud and clear that human persons are far more important in the eyes of God than man-made laws and human institutions. In this the bishops were voicing for today's world the subversive words of Jesus, 'The sabbath was made for humankind and not humankind for the sabbath' (Mk 2:27). Prior to Vatican II, many Catholics did not feel encouraged to behave as free, thinking and responsible adults in the Church and found some aspects of the Church's teaching, especially on issues of sexual morality, did not ring true to their own personal experience. Many felt a sense of liberation at the simple words of Pope John XXIII that the Council would open the windows and let much-needed fresh air into the Church.

That God's self-revelation in Christ is the ultimate source of the dignity of the human person is highlighted by Vatican II: 'It is only in the mystery of the Word incarnate that light is shed on the mystery of humankind … It is Christ … who fully discloses humankind to itself and unfolds its noble calling by revealing the mystery of the Father and the Father's love' (*The Church in the World of Today*, no. 22).

This person-centred 'good news' of Jesus is at the heart of Vatican's vision of human and Christian morality. It is emphasized in a variety of council documents. Chapter one of the Pastoral Constitution, *The Church in the World of Today*, is entitled, 'The Dignity of the Human Person'. Its opening sentence states: 'Believers and unbelievers are almost at one in considering that everything on earth is to be referred to humanity as its centre and culmination.' (no. 12) Later the bishops go on to speak of 'the exceptional dignity which belongs to the human person' and even appeal to Jesus' words about the Sabbath as they highlight the social dimension of the human person:

> The social order and its progress ought then continually to favour the good of people since the order of things should be subordinated to the order of persons, and not the other way round, as the Lord indicated in saying the Sabbath was made for us and not we for the Sabbath (no. 26).

The very title of the Declaration on Religious Liberty is The Dignity of the Human Person (*Dignitatis Humanae*). It opens with the powerful statement:

> The dignity of the human person is a concern of which people of our time are becoming increasingly more aware. In growing numbers they

demand that they should enjoy the use of their own responsible judgment and freedom, and decide on their actions on grounds of duty and
conscience, without external pressure or coercion (no. 1).

Vatican II's person-centred criterion of morality has challenged and enriched
the work of moral theologians in many other ways, including:

- its teaching on the dignity of conscience and its freedom;
- the right and even responsibility of individual lay people and priests
  to offer their own contribution to the Church's ongoing work of moral
  understanding and evaluation;
- its insistence that individuals have to shoulder responsibility for their
  own decisions and must not always expect detailed moral guidance
  from their bishops or priests;
- its recognition that the agenda for moral reflection and action comes
  mainly from the world (its joys and hopes, its sorrows and fears)
  rather than from the Church;
- its person-centred approach to marriage with its consequent emphasis
  on the paradigm of covenant/relationship rather than that of contract;
- its embracing of a Christian-humanist approach to life and its rejection of any approach based on a radical dichotomy between this life
  and the next;
- its rejection of an individualist approach to morality that overlooks
  the social dimension of the human person and so is blind to the evil
  of structural sin.

(2) The experience and reflection of women
When I first began teaching moral theology, to my shame it never entered my
head that women might have any special contribution to make to the field of
moral theology, let alone that they should actually become moral theologians.
Thankfully, a rich collection of women friends, parishioners and colleagues
have helped to change my thinking on this matter. Consequently, in my book
referred to above, NDMT, chapter five is entitled 'Moral theology – not truly
human without the full participation of women'. At the beginning of that chapter I argue that Christian theology – and therefore moral theology too – is:

substantially flawed because it has been constructed predominately by
men and in the light of men's experience of a world in which women
were second-rate citizens and in which women's experience was not considered to be theologically important (p. 86).

I firmly believe that women's experience must be firmly in place on the agenda of moral theology. Moreover, it must not be there simply for male moral theologians to consider. Women must be fully – not just tokenly – represented within the field of moral theology. That is beginning to happen. There are some outstanding women Roman Catholic moral theologians in the United States, to name but two from among many, Lisa Sowle Cahill and Margaret Farley. On this side of the Atlantic Linda Hogan and Julie Clague both have an international reputation as moral theologians. Throughout the world it is remarkable how women moral theologians have played an increasingly key role in the World Conference of Catholic Ethicists, inaugurated in 2006 by the visionary US moral theologian, James Keenan SJ. If the net were extended to include women moral theologians from other Christian Churches, the picture would be even more encouraging.

When the Association of Teachers of Moral Theology (ATMT) was founded in 1968 there were no women teaching moral theology in Roman Catholic institutions in the UK. At the time I saw nothing untoward about that. I failed to recognise that the ATMT was the poorer for the fact that the voice, experience, reflection and insights of women were not offering their specific contribution to our discussions. Now, thank God, there are good grounds for thinking that our women members will probably produce some of the most influential writing in moral theology in the UK in the years ahead.

Women moral theologians have also made us all more aware that a positive acceptance of our essential interdependence changes the whole focus of the power relationship. A truly human exercise of power lies in the direction of empowerment. This even has implications for the handling of disagreement on moral issues. The power syndrome would approach disagreement in terms of an argument to be won. Some moral theology manuals, following an earlier tradition, used to call those who disagreed with their position '*adversarii*'. The mutuality and empowerment approach see disagreement as an opportunity for mutual enrichment. Conversation comes from the same root as conversion. It is an important theological tool. It implies a willingness, if need be, to be converted to the truth the other might be sharing with us.

(3) The ethical thinking and teaching found in other Christian Churches
The ethical writings of theologians outside the Roman Catholic Church were hardly mentioned in the moral theology I studied in the seminary. That was despite the fact that, when I pursued my post-graduate work at Fribourg University, I discovered a very rich vein of moral theology in the Anglican Caroline divines of the seventeenth century. In fact, I found that they were more faithful to the authentic teaching of Aquinas than were many of the Catholic manuals of moral theology (cf. my *Conscience: Dictator or Guide? A Study in 17th century Protestant Moral Theology*, London, Geoffrey Chapman, 1967).

Today the ecumenical dimension of moral theology is taken for granted. As a Catholic moral theologian, I can honestly say that my appreciation of Christian morality has been greatly enriched by the writings of numerous theologians from other Churches writing in the field of Christian ethics and also by personal contact and friendship with many of them in this country.

1994 saw the publication of an Agreed Statement on moral issues by the Second Anglican-Roman Catholic International Commission, *Life in Christ: Morals, Communion and the Church*. This is a new theological resource, both challenging and enriching, which moral theologians have to take account of. It is an attempt by two Churches to try to think inside each other's approach to moral issues, both at a general level and with regard to some particular issues which might seem to put these Churches on a collision course. There is no attempt on either side to claim that their approach is the only valid one or that their teaching on this particular issue has a monopoly of the truth. This is a long way from 'the truth, the whole truth and nothing but the truth' of the moral theology I learnt in the seminary. A couple of quotations might help to illustrate the point I am making. They discuss two specific issues on which the two Churches disagree. The first deals with divorce and remarriage, the second with contraception:

> Roman Catholic teaching and law uphold the indissolubility of the marriage covenant, even when the human relationship of love and trust has ceased to exist and there is no practical possibility of recreating it. The Anglican position, though equally concerned with the sacramentality of marriage and the common good of the community, does not necessarily understand these in the same way. Some Anglicans attend more closely to the actual character of the relationship between husband and wife. Where a relationship of mutual love and trust has clearly ceased to exist, and there is no practical possibility of remaking it, the bond itself, they argue, has also ceased to exist. When the past has been forgiven and healed, a new covenant and bond may in good faith be made (no. 75).
>
> Anglicans understand the good of procreation to be a norm governing the married relationship as a whole. Roman Catholic teaching, on the other hand, requires that each and every act of intercourse should be 'open to procreation' … (no. 81). The immediate point at issue in this controversy would seem to concern the moral integrity of the act of marital intercourse. Both our traditions agree that this involves the two basic 'goods' of marriage, love union and procreation. Moral integrity requires that husband and wife respect both these goods together. For Anglicans, it is sufficient that this respect should characterise the married relationship as a whole; whereas for Roman Catholics, it must characterise each act of sexual intercourse (no. 82). The Roman Catholic doctrine is not simply an authoritative statement on the nature of the integrity of the marital

act … The definition of integrity is founded upon a number of considerations: a way of understanding human persons; the meaning of marital love; the unique dignity of an act which can engender new life; the relationship between human fruitfulness and divine creativity; the special vocation of the married couple; and the requirements of the virtue of marital chastity. Anglicans accept all of these considerations as relevant to determining the integrity of the marital relationship and act. Thus they share the same spectrum of moral and theological considerations (no. 80).

Both these statements seem to be saying something much more significant than that they agree to differ. Before agreeing to differ, they are agreeing that they both hold to the same Christian vision and the same fundamental values which lie at the heart of the issues under discussion. They also seem to be agreeing that the position with which they disagree should be respected as an honest and conscientious attempt to be true to this vision and these values. If that is an accurate reading of these statements, it would seem to suggest that a similar respect should be shown to those within each Church who disagree conscientiously with their own Church's position on these issues.

(4) The explosion of our empirical knowledge and consequent advances in human technology
It is commonplace to say that we have far more knowledge about ourselves as human persons than people in previous ages. We know far more about ourselves as sexual beings at both relational and reproductive levels. We understand much more about the subconscious and the enormous impact experiences in early childhood can have on the human psyche. We are more aware of the many ways in which our human freedom is limited. We have much deeper understanding of the animal dimension to us and also the purely biological and chemical side of our bodies and how this can interact with our minds and emotions. Our understanding of social processes has also increased, even though in economics we still do not seem to know how to control what is happening at a global level. We have also developed complex technologies, especially in the field of communications. All this new knowledge does not necessarily make us wiser people. That depends on how we use this knowledge.

This is the world in which moral theologians today have to ply their trade. Gone are the days when the moral theologian was able to speak with presumed authority on any and every subject. The kind of knowledge needed for informed comment on many specific issues is so specialised that many moral theologians are concentrating on very specific fields. In the field of medical ethics, some moral theologians are specialising in particular areas of medicine such as life and death issues, reproductive medicine or genetics. Some moral theologians are even beginning to specialise in the ethics of advertising or tourism.

Other moral theologians are going in the opposite direction and are focussing their attention on that part of the discipline which used to be called
fundamental moral theology. In other words, they are concentrating more on
what are called meta-ethical questions. These are issues which have a bearing
right across the board in all areas of life. How do we go about moral decision-
making? What is the role of conscience? Where does authoritative Church
teaching come in and what are the legitimate parameters of legitimate response
to it? How do we handle our moral beliefs in a pluralist society? Can a civilised
society exist without some kind of agreed common morality? What are the basic
principles or values of such a common morality and how are they grounded?
The list of such questions is endless. However, moral theologians are not re-in-
venting the wheel. Our human family has been wrestling with these or similar
questions down through the ages. As mentioned earlier, we are like dwarfs
standing on the shoulders of giants. Perhaps one important role for moral theology today is to make sure that the wisdom of the giants is fed into the contemporary debate.

(5) Historical consciousness

Formerly history tended to be looked on as the study of the past. Today it is
seen as a dimension of the present. We are essentially historical persons. We
are shaped by our past. The kind of person we become is greatly influenced by
our personal, family, neighbourhood, ethnic, cultural and national histories.
The same is true at Church level. Vatican II was not a rejection of our history
and tradition. It was a rediscovery of the vitality and dynamism of our living
tradition through recovering a sense of historical consciousness. There is a paradox about a living tradition, as Newman pointed out. It needs to change if it
is to maintain its true identity. Kevin Nichols puts it well: 'If it fails to do this
(i.e. 'change in order to remain the same'), its formulations turn into relics, fixed
and dead, like flies elegantly preserved in amber' (Kevin Nichols, *Refracting the
Truth: Learning the Languages of Faith, Dublin*, Lindisfarne Books, 1997, p. 39).

Historical consciousness also challenges the notion of 'the truth, the whole
truth, and nothing but the truth'. Without going down the blind alley of relativism, moral theologians today need to be conscious that any formulation of
moral truth is historically conditioned. It will have been crafted and refined in
the course of historical debates, often arising from a consideration of particular
moral problems that have arisen at a certain point in time. In a sense, down
through the ages, within its own particular historical context, it is always struggling with the same question – what is the meaning of being human in the light
of the best self-understanding of our age and what are the implications of this in
real life. Sometimes the process of struggling with that question works in reverse.
Practical ethical decisions have to be made, often without time for long and pro-
tracted reflection. That comes later. If a decision has had to be made 'on the hoof',

as it were, our conviction that this was the right decision leads us to reflect later about what this says about how we understand ourselves as human persons.

The basic structures of human life and social relations, marriage, even gender and sexual orientation, have not dropped down fully formed from heaven. They are human artefacts in the sense that human beings have found these patterns of living and relating as necessary if they are to do justice to themselves as human persons. These basic institutions are natural in the sense that human beings have discovered them by looking at themselves as human persons. Yet that same process of self-discovery continues to be ongoing throughout history. Moreover, it always takes place in a cultural context. Though basic human institutions such as these may be fundamental to human living, that does not mean that their present form is carved on stone and completely unalterable. They have been shaped by our forebears in the light of their best self-understanding. We have the responsibility to be faithful to this continuing task they have passed on to us. Therefore, if new knowledge or experience teaches us that aspects of these basic institutions need to be reformed in any way, we would be failing in our God-given responsibility if we refused to accept this challenge. Such a position is fully in keeping with a dynamic interpretation of natural law thinking since it is the only way we can be true to the God-given gift of ourselves as human persons.

A few years ago I was speaking to the priests of the Bray Deanery in Dublin, along with their bishop, and this historical dimension was an aspect of my talk that they found particularly helpful – and supportive of their own pastoral practice. Some warmed to my using the parable of the wheat and the darnel to highlight this growth dimension:

> Normative ethics helps us recognise both wheat and darnel. However, the owner of the field … has faith in the healthy growth of his wheat, despite all the darnel mixed in with it. His principal concern is to protect his wheat from the misguided zeal of those intent on destroying the darnel without any regard for the harm this might do to the wheat …
>
> Part of the pastoral role of moral theology is to help the seed to grow, despite soil deficiency, adverse weather, surrounding weeds and lots of other threatening dangers. It would be tragically ironic if moral theology itself became yet another danger by threatening to uproot the growing plant by turning over the soil and pulling up the weeds. Moral theology is not meant to condemn the plant emerging from the seed simply because it does not live up to the promise of the idealised picture on the packet. Rather it appreciates the growth that occurs. Sometimes what might look like a puny and undeveloped plant might, in fact, be a miracle of growth, given the adverse conditions under which it has had to struggle (FPB, pp. 107-108).

Under the subheading 'Messy & dirty' (hardly theological categories), I went on:

> For the most part, the 'normative ethics' role of moral theology neces-
> sarily has to be very exact and precise. Clarity of analysis is very impor-
> tant. However, in practice the role of promoting growth in adverse
> conditions can sometimes be a much more messy procedure. At times it
> can involve getting one's hands dirty, cutting corners, adopting a flexible
> approach to Church rules and so on. It also needs faith and a sense of
> humour in the face of accusations that one is compromising the truth, or
> falling into the error of relativism or situation ethics (FPB, p. 109).

In a recent book, *Embracing Sexuality*, edited by Joseph Selling, in a chapter headed 'Bodiliness and Sacramentality' I was delighted to read the comment: 'everyday life is messy, it is a kind of "orderly chaos" … it is ambivalent and ambiguous.' That is the mess within which pastoral theology has to operate and celebrate all the goodness found there.

The Leuven moral theologian, Robert Burggraeve, draws out the implications of the historical dimension especially in the case of young people. He actually speaks of 'an interim or growth ethics'. I have drawn on his thinking not
just in my writings but, even more so, in the pastoral theology I have shared
with others, priests, teachers and lay people in general, and in my own pastoral
practice. Burggraeve has further refined and developed his thinking on growth-
ethics in his chapter on HIV / AIDS in the book edited by James Keenan & others,
Catholic Ethicists on HIV/AIDS Prevention, New York / London, Continuum, 2000.
I am sure people working at the grass roots level in the AIDS scene will draw
great practical help and positive encouragement from what he has written.

(6) Human experience

Certainly, my own thinking was changed radically through being exposed to
the first-hand experience of others. This is particularly true with regard to marriage and sexual ethics. Consequently I was delighted when, at the 1983 Synod
in Rome, Cardinal Hume made the point that the experience of married people
is 'an authentic source of theology from which we, the pastors, and indeed the
whole Church can draw'.

A few years before *Humanae Vitae* a fairly traditional French Catholic magazine sent a questionnaire out to its readers about their experience of birth reg-
ulation. Their replies were published in a little book entitled *3000 Couples Speak*.
One thing stands out in my mind from reading it: *Cauchemar*, a French word
which I was not familiar with, was used repeatedly and always in the same
context – a woman describing how she experienced sexual intercourse when
she was fearful of becoming pregnant again. I soon discovered that it meant

'nightmare'. That spoke volumes to me. If anything was grossly immoral, it was ethical teaching which resulted in many women experiencing the act of love-making as a nightmare. I think this experience gave me confidence in drawing up pre-*Humanae Vitae* guidelines for Archbishop Beck to give to our Liverpool priests to help them support couples using some form of contraception as the best or only way of safeguarding or promoting the basic values of their marriage. Of course, in suggesting these guidelines I also drew on the important historical research and philosophical thinking of people like Louis Janssens, John Noonen and many others.

When *Humanae Vitae* was published in 1968, I wrote a four-part article for *The Clergy Review*, entitled 'A Positive Approach to Humane Vitae'. I wrote it believing that *Humanae Vitae* was a new theological datum on which the Church needed time to reflect. With the benefit of hindsight I can recognise my defective ecclesiology which led me to write this piece. I was still teaching in the seminary when I wrote it, so had little contact with the experience of married couples. Soon after, I was asked to share my thinking with a group of about two hundred married couples, all deeply committed Catholics, who met regularly in little house groups to reflect on their experience of marriage in the light of the gospel. I decided to use this opportunity to tap into their experience. So, as well as listening to their reactions to my talk, I also gave them a questionnaire, asking them to say how far the teaching of *Humanae Vitae* on contraception spoke to them and whether they felt inspired or alienated by it. To my surprise, their answer came back loud and clear. It did not speak to their experience. In no way was it in tune with the message of the Gospel from which they drew inspiration at their regular meetings. I confess that these couples helped to heal my defective ecclesiology and began to make me more aware that the Church's teaching on contraception in particular – and on sexual ethics in general – is in need of a radical overhaul.

(7) Dialogue

The need for dialogue flows from our renewed self-understanding as Church. We have to be a learning Church as well as a teaching Church. If we are to learn, we have to share in dialogue with those who see life somewhat differently from ourselves. Such conversation is not focused on convincing them that they are wrong. It starts from the belief that we have riches to share with them and that, almost certainly, they too have riches to share with us. Hence, dialogue is not just about speaking. Listening is an essential ingredient to dialogue.

For moral theologians today dialogue must be part of our trade. We have to dialogue with other disciplines so that we can better understand ourselves and the world we are living in. We have to dialogue with other Churches so that we can mutually enrich each other about the moral implications of the faith we share. We have to dialogue with other faiths since we believe that the wisdom and action of God's spirit is not locked up within the confines of the Christian faith. Moreover, without this kind of respectful dialogue we cannot expect to get an attentive hearing for the riches we believe we can contribute to our partners in conversation.

Dialogue is also necessary within our own Catholic community. It is interesting how we are prepared to engage in dialogue and even expect some measure of disagreement on issues of social ethics, for instance. An outstanding example of this is the fine pastoral letter on the economy published by the United States bishops after an exemplary dialogue process, including the publication of preparatory drafts followed by public hearings and linked to an open invitation for comment. In the final version, the bishops explicitly recognise that, apart from their basic Gospel-rooted fundamental principles, people should feel free to disagree with their more specific teachings, provided they are willing to give them a serious hearing:

> 134. In focusing on some of the central economic issues and choices in American life in the light of moral principles, we are aware that the movement from principle to policy is complex and difficult and that although moral values are essential in determining public policies, they do not dictate specific solutions. They must interact with empirical data, with historical, social and political realities, and with competing demands on limited resources. The soundness of our prudential judgements depends not only on the moral force of our principles, but also on the accuracy of our information and the validity of our assumptions.

> 135. Our judgements and recommendations on specific economic issues, therefore, do not carry the same moral authority as our statements of universal moral principles and formal Church teaching; the former are related to circumstances which can change or which can be interpreted differently be people of good will. We expect and welcome debate on our specific policy recommendations. Nevertheless, we want our statements on these matters to be given serious consideration by Catholics as they determine whether their own moral judgements are consistent with the Gospel and with Catholic social teaching (Economic Justice for All: Catholic Social Teaching and the U.S. Economy, full text in *Origins*, 27 November 1986, pp. 408-455).

The strange thing is that such a warm invitation to dialogue and openness to the possibility of disagreement is not deemed acceptable in matters of sexual ethics or bioethics. Sadly, it is here that dialogue is sometimes most difficult. Our Catholic community seems to have a curious blind spot in this regard. This anomaly makes life particularly difficult for moral theologians since many of the issues which crop up in public debate are precisely in those two areas of ethics.

(8) Listening to the Pastoral Situation

The demands of pastoral practice must always come first if we are to minister pastorally after the model of Christ himself. An appropriate translation of *salus animarum suprema lex*, could read 'where there is a gap between the Church regulations and the needs of pastoral practice, the latter must always take priority'. Of course, obedience has a place in pastoral ministry. Pastoral ministers are not commissioned 'to do their own thing'. But obedience (*ob-audire*) is about listening; listening and responding to the pastoral needs of people is one of the main ways a pastoral minister is obedient to the call of God.

In 1995 the National Conference of Priests of England and Wales expressed concern about 'the growing gap between the official regulations of the Church and the demands of pastoral practice'. They asked me to write two sides of an A4 sheet as a background paper for their discussion of this topic. This paper was also offered in response to a similar request from the bishops' conference.

I suggested to them that some sort of gap is unavoidable. Down through the centuries the Church has always acknowledged that laws, because of their universality, have at best only general validity (*ut in pluribus*, as Aquinas puts it, following Aristotle). Priests and other pastoral ministers have to be able to discern when the good pursued by any law would be vitiated in a particular instance by insisting on the strict letter of the law. This gift of discernment is traditionally called '*epikeia*'. For Aquinas it is part of the general virtue of justice. Far from being an anarchic way of evading the law, it aims to make sure that the law achieves its prime aim. This will always be the pastoral good of persons in some form or other. '*Epikeia*' is an essential virtue for all engaged in pastoral ministry, especially in recent years when there is an increasing gap between the Church regulations and the demands of pastoral practice. In Joseph's Selling's book, *Embracing Sexuality* referred to above, Anna Roper, a university chaplain, relates this to her experience of young people: 'There is clearly a widening gap between the received teaching of the Church and the pastoral experience of this teaching in the lives of young people.'

CHAPTER NINE

The Responsibility of Moral Theology to Church and Modern Society

This is the unpublished text of a talk originally given to the Catholic Theological Association of Great Britain meeting at Trinity and All Saints, Leeds, in September, 1999.

Introduction

Moral theology does not stand between Church and society. It is a discipline which has its life and activity within the Church. By the same token, as well as being within the Church, moral theology is also within society.

If moral theology stands within the Church and within modern society, it has to avoid the danger of sundering its allegiance to one or the other. If it sees itself as responsible only to the Church, or only to modern society, it is really being untrue to itself. It is refusing to own part of its identity. It is deserting one of the twin bases for being truly human.

Despite what I have written above, for the Christian moral theologian, the primary location of moral theology is within the Church. That follows from its being theology which, for Christians at least, involves reflecting, exploring and searching within the community of the Church, past and present. In his 1999 Marquette lecture, 'Moral Theology at the End of the Century', Charles Curran insists that 'moral theology exists in the service of the Church and this aspect can never be forgotten' (p. 41).

Yet that 'reflecting, exploring and searching' which is at the heart of moral theology can only take place within the society in which we are living (i.e. modern society), using all the cultural inheritance of language and symbols of our society and wrestling with the challenging human questions and decisions facing us today.

It would seem to follow, therefore, that perhaps the major element in moral theology's responsibility to the Church lies in its being faithful to its responsibility to modern society. If moral theology evades its responsibility to modern society, it is in fact failing the Church. This point was made very strongly by a US bishop, James Malone, way back in 1986:

A democracy lives by open, public debate where all parties are both free to speak and accountable for the implications of their positions... Catholicism is not a democracy; but that truism does not touch the question of how Catholicism lives in a democratic culture ... Bishops and theologians must preserve the faith and share the faith in a culture which values the courage of convictions openly stated, openly criticized and openly defended ... (There is need for) a teaching style which fosters within the Church and with the wider society what Father Murray called 'civilized conversation' ... The cultivation of such civil discourse between bishops and theologians should be a model for extending the same dialogue into Church and society ('How Bishops and Theologians Relate', June 1986 address at Marquette University, full text in *Origins*, 31 July 1986, pp. 169-174 at p. 174).

A consequence of this would seem to be that moral theologians are conscience-bound to resist any attempt on the part of the Church to prevent their exercising this responsibility to the world.

I would suggest, therefore, that there are a number of unacceptable interpretations of the responsibility of moral theology to the Church and to society which need to be firmly rejected.

For instance, unacceptable interpretations of moral theology's responsibility to the Church are implicit in the following, often-heard statements:

- 'a moral theologian must always show loyalty to the Holy Father and his teaching and to all who teach in his name.'
- 'moral theologians must be careful not to disturb the simple faithful.'
- 'moral theologians should respect the nature of the Church as a communion in faith and so should do nothing to shake the boat.'
- 'the Pope should insist that moral theologians toe the line and submit their human judgements to his divine authority.'
- 'moral theology should be less concerned about the things of this world and should focus much more on spiritual issues.'

With regard to moral theology's responsibility to modern society, equally unacceptable interpretations are found when a moral theologian sees his or her role as one of:

- Claiming that the Church has all the knowledge and wisdom needed to give modern society all the answers it is searching for;
- accepting uncritically the agenda of modern society;
- accepting uncritically the role which modern society tries to impose on the Church, whether it be one of a purely sacristy Church or one of enforcing whatever moral standards modern society chooses to promote;
- offering a tame, compromised moral theology, which provides moral respectability to some ethical committees while keeping clear of the sharp cutting edge of critical moral reasoning;

There is a further question arising from our title, The Responsibility of Moral Theology to the Church and Modern Society.

Can moral theology as such be responsible for anything? In any organisation, questions about responsibility ultimately have to get down to named persons. If we are discussing the responsibility of moral theology to the Church and modern society, we need to pin down who carries this responsibility. Is it a responsibility which all moral theologians have to carry either individually or collectively, as for instance through the Association of Teachers of Moral Theology? Or is it a responsibility of the Church as a whole, and so particularly of its leaders, the bishops, including the Pope and the Vatican Congregations? Or, in these days of co-responsibility, is it a responsibility of all Church members, both individually and jointly?

I would suggest that a 'yes' answer can be given to all those questions. In other words, the task of ensuring that moral theology is faithful to its responsibility to the Church and society is shared by all the people I have mentioned above, though with different degrees of accountability.

If this is accepted, it raises some very interesting possibilities.

For instance, what about a papal encyclical addressed to moral theologians, insisting that they face their responsibility and get involved in the public debates on all issues of moral concern and warning them that they will have to answer before God if they merely repeat uncritically the party line and fail to exercise their own critical judgements on these issues, even when this results in disagreement with current Church teaching?

Or what about a letter from the Pope sent to all the bishops reminding them that they should make sure that their local Church is served by moral theologians of independent mind and sound critical judgement – and even urging the bishops to do all in their power to make sure that women are given the chance to serve the local Church as moral theologians? Perhaps even a local bishops' conference or bishop might challenge their moral theologians for not getting sufficiently involved in the cut and thrust of local moral debate.

What about promoting a climate within the Church built on sufficient trust and confidence that people could feel it worthwhile to write letters of complaint about moral theologians who too readily accept official teaching and who seem out of touch with the real human problems of the day?

A few months ago, in connection with a Chapter entitled, 'The Mission of the Bishop', in a preparatory Synod document, my own Archbishop wrote to me asking me for a 'one-side of A4' response to the question:

Describe the relationship between the bishops and theologians; one of mutual respect? of collaboration in proclaiming the Gospel? of mistrust? of disagreement? In what areas?

In my answer, I outlined the various joint meetings between the bishops and the ATMT and noted that 'disagreements have been faced honestly and aspects of current Church teaching have been criticised, when appropriate'. I then went on to add the following final paragraph:

The disagreements faced collaboratively together suggest that It would help the above healthy relationship between bishops and moral theologians if:

1.   It was more evident that the views of different schools of moral theology were better represented in moral statements from the CDF;

2.   The text of forthcoming moral statements were made available to moral theologians prior to being released to the media;

3.   Bishops did not work on the presumption that the proclamation of the Gospel is best served by their publicly agreeing with every moral statement from the Vatican. Their ministry to the truth and their credibility as Gospel-inspired moral teachers might be enhanced if they were prepared, when theologically appropriate, to respond to a document with positive criticism;

4.   It was presumed that moral theologians, who, for solid theological reasons, disagree with some aspect of current moral teaching, are being true to their particular role of collaboration in proclaiming the Gospel and are in no way being disloyal to the Church;

5.   The theological grounding of both the Final Report of the Birth Control Commission and *Humanae Vitae* were subjected to a reappraisal in the light of the Vatican II teaching on marriage and the family as found in *Gaudium et Spes*; and this reappraisal be undertaken by a study commission whose make-up respects the truth, emphasised in the Synodal Preparation paper no. 11, that 'all Christians – as individuals or as a group – have the duty and the right to collaborate in the mission of the Church, in keeping with their vocation and their gifts of the Spirit.' Consequently, such a study commission should be ecumenical, include married people and give a voice to the particular concerns of women, as well as representing different schools of moral theology.

I am still wondering what kind of reaction there was to that paragraph both on the part of my own Archbishop and the committee compiling the response of our Bishops' conference.

CHAPTER TEN

Receiving Vatican II: The Contribution of the Association of Teachers of Moral Theology

In May 1968 a group of teachers of moral theology from some of the seminaries in the UK held a meeting in the Cenacle convent in Manchester. This meeting gave rise to what is now known as the Association of Teachers of Moral Theology (ATMT). Its original purpose was to provide mutual support to help teachers of moral theology to develop their discipline in the light of Vatican II. After meeting twice-yearly on a residential basis, a special 30th Anniversary Conference was organised by Professor Jack Mahoney SJ, one of the founding members, at UNI. Jack also arranged for the papers presented to be published in a special edition of The Month (August 1999). As one of the original members, I contributed the following piece to ensure that the early history of the ATMT was duly recorded. Forty-three years after its inception, the ATMT continues to meet twice yearly at Hinsley Hall, Leeds. Though the numbers are small, almost invariably members from Holland, Belgium and Germany attend and make very valuable contributions to the meetings.

When I began teaching moral theology at Upholland Senior Seminary in 1965, apart from Fr. Pius OFM Cap, I did not know any other person teaching moral theology in the UK or Ireland. At that time, there were four other major seminaries in addition to Upholland – Ushaw, Oscott, Wonersh and Allen Hall. A number of male religious congregations also had their own theologates – the Jesuits had Heythrop College (then in the countryside outside Oxford) the Redemptorists, Hawkstone Hall, the Sacred Heart Fathers, Malpas and the Capuchins, Crawley. The Missionary Institute was still in its early days, staffed mainly by the Mill Hill and White Fathers. There were also two major seminaries in Scotland, at Drygrange and Cardross.

A full four year course in moral theology was being taught in all these twelve establishments. Since the teaching of moral theology had been thrown into the melting pot by the movement of theological renewal which, in the wake of Vatican II, achieved respectability and authorisation and gained increasing momentum, those of us who were beginning to teach moral theology at that time felt as though we were moving into waters which were largely uncharted. I, for one, felt very alone and needed help and support from other moral theologians who were in the same boat. I shared this feeling with Jack Mahoney who had also just begun teaching moral theology and felt much the same as myself. So a letter was sent out to our fellow teachers of moral theology in Britain, suggesting that it might be helpful if we were to meet and pool our experiences. A first meeting was held in May, 1968, an overnight session at the Cenacle Retreat House in Manchester.

All nine attending were priests. The whole meeting was devoted to our sharing how each of us went about teaching moral theology. The first meeting of which I have any written record was held at Upholland College on 13-15 November, 1970.

The written report indicates that this meeting was a defining moment in the developments of the ATMT's methodology:

> It was thought that the system of having the Respondent as Chairman of the meeting had worked well and it was decided to follow the same procedure at the next meeting. The distribution of the papers before the meeting had also proved successful and it was suggested that in future the papers should be distributed as early as possible beforehand and at the meeting the paper writer should give a very brief resume of his paper and then the Chairman-Respondent should open the discussion and continue to guide it.

The format of that 1970 meeting is virtually identical to the one still followed over forty years later. Ronald Preston, our first Anglican member, came to the third meeting and has been a most valued and faithful member ever since. The 1970 written report also notes that those present decided to restrict membership to 'those professionally engaged in teaching moral theology and allied subjects', though it was agreed that 'members may use their discretion in inviting other interested and competent persons after consultation with the Secretary'. It also states that 'the continued participation of Canon Preston was welcomed, but again no policy decision was made with regard to throwing membership open to experts from other Churches.

It is clear that the initial purpose of the Association was already developing far beyond that of the 'how' of teaching moral theology. There is agreement among members that their purpose in coming together is now being seen as 'joint creative study of the basic problems of Christian morality'. Very significantly, the word 'joint' is used in the report to describe the 'creative study' involved. This denotes an early recognition that the sessions are seen as 'working' sessions. Members attend not principally to update themselves by listening to papers given by 'experts' but to participate in wrestling with the issues raised in the preparatory papers. Over the thirty years of its history the Association has remained remarkably faithful to this aim.

The ATMT has consistently resisted any move to adopt a formal constitution. This was mainly because the members did not want to be labelled as the semi-official voice of moral theology in the UK. They felt that any such move would inhibit their freedom to engage in an honest and critical discussion of moral issues, including so-called traditional teaching or official Church statements. They were also wary of being regarded as a kind of answering service for any and every Church body which was looking for guidance on ethical issues. Nevertheless, members were conscious of their responsibility as moral theologians to be of service to the Church in its engagement with the modern world. They were also anxious to be as helpful to the bishops as they could, within the limits of their personal integrity as professional moral theologians. This last concern led to a relationship with the Hierarchy of England and Wales which has, to date, been consistently both constructive and positively critical.

Relationships with the Hierarchy of England and Wales
There have been four meetings between the bishops and members of the Association.The first came from an initiative by the ATMT who requested an informal meeting between Cardinal Hume and a couple of our members. We wanted to express some of our concerns to the Cardinal, while stressing that, as an Association, we would be very happy to be of service to the bishops, provided this did not compromise the informal nature of our Association. As a result of this conversation with the Cardinal, an overnight meeting between the ATMT and the bishops was held in 1979 at the Upholland Northern Institute. It looked at the theological and pastoral questions linked to the issue of remarriage after divorce. The preparation of this meeting was largely left to the ATMT. The overall theme of divorce and second marriage was broken down into a number of key issues and various ATMT members were assigned the task of preparing short inputs (no longer than an A4 sheet) on each of these topics.

The second meeting, held at the express request of Cardinal Hume, was also an overnight meeting, this time at Loyola Hall, Rainhill on 30 June-1 July 1987. The purpose of the session was partly to give the bishops an opportunity to share with ATMT members some of their concerns about the current method and content of moral theology teaching.

The third meeting on 19-20 February 1993 was again at Upholland and was part of the consultation process leading up to the publication of the new Catechism. Some ATMT members were asked to present short papers on various issues linked to the Catechism and moral teaching.

The fourth meeting was again the brain-child of Cardinal Hume and was designed to help the bishops and moral theologians look together at the encyclical, *Veritatis Splendor*, and how it had affected their different ministries. An overnight session at London Colney, 4-5 February 1994, was attended by the Cardinal and twelve bishops, as well as by fifteen ATMT members, including four women members, five members of the Bishops' Secretariate, including the Secretary of the Irish Bishops' Conference, and James Keenan SJ, a US moral theologian on sabbatical in the UK. Like the previous meetings, this session was carefully planned in advance, this time by a joint committee headed by Bishop Brewer, Chair of the Bishops' Theology Committee. The programme was arranged in such a way that the bishops were able to share with the moral theologians the way they had experienced the impact of the encyclical on their pastoral ministry as bishops. Similarly, the moral theologians were able to share how the encyclical had affected them and their teaching ministry. In the light of that sharing, the group were able to look together at a number of specific questions arising from *Veritatis Splendor*.

The consistent and continuing support of Bishop Brewer, Chair of Bishops' Theology Committee, is worthy of mention in this brief history. Bishop Brewer has made sure that the Secretary of the Theology Committee, Father Michael Campbell, OSA, attends each ATMT meeting as an explicit sign of his encouragement and also to keep channels of communication open between the ATMT and the bishops.

Links with moral theologians abroad
From its earliest days the ATMT has close links with moral theologians in Ireland. Membership has always been open to Irish moral theologians, and, more often than not, meetings have been enriched by the presence of one or more Irish members.

Joint meetings between the ATMT and its Irish equivalent have also been held on three occasions. All these joint sessions have been held in Ireland and the Irish members, through their respective colleges and religious congregations, have been more than generous in offering hospitality to ATMT members from England and Scotland.

The first joint meeting was held at Marianella Pastoral Centre in Dublin, 9-11 November 1990. The second took the form of a Theological Consultation on HIV/AIDS which was arranged and hosted by Caritas Internationalis. It was held at Marianella Pastoral Centre, 6-9 January 1994. The objectives proposed for this theological consultation were:

- To inform theologians about the pandemic of HIV/AIDS with special emphasis on the impact of this pandemic on individuals/families, development and social structure, and on pastoral/spiritual life.
- To stimulate discussion among theologians and those involved in HIV/AIDS education and service programmes on needs, concerns and issues raised by the pandemic.
- To encourage further theological reflection on the pandemic, with special emphasis on responding to pastoral and spiritual needs.
- To encourage further theological reflection on the ethical and moral questions raised by the pandemic

The third joint meeting was held at Maynooth College, 10-12 November 1995. Among items discussed in the Open Forum was the potential impact of the Internet on the study and teaching of moral theology.

When ATMT meetings have coincided with visits to the UK by moral theologians from overseas, they have been invited to our meetings. Such visitors have included Charles Curran and James Keenan from the USA, Bruno Schuller from Germany, Bill Daniels, Larry McNamara and Damien Heath from Australia, and Richard Greco (now bishop) from Ontario, Canada.

In the early years ATMT meetings were given added breadth of vision by the participation of moral theologians from the Missionary Institute who had spent time in Africa and Asia. They often forced us to look at moral issues from quite a different perspective as they brought in radically different cultural practices and expectations. In this way, we were already being prepared for the inculturation and inter-faith debates of more recent years.

The Ecumenical Dimension

While it has always been accepted that the ATMT is primarily an association of Roman Catholic teachers of moral theology, from the earliest days there has been an openness towards those from other traditions who are professionally involved in the equivalent field of Christian Ethics. Professor Canon Ronald Preston has been a most valuable, and extraordinarily faithful, member from the very earliest days. He has also been extremely sensitive to the ecumenical ambiguity linked to ATMT being a professedly Roman Catholic association which welcomes members from other Churches. Due to his influence and encouragement, over the years there has been a regular membership from outside the Roman Catholic Church, even though, sadly, this has mainly been from the Church of England. Over the years our membership list has also included Professors Gordon Dunstan, Peter Baelz, Oliver O'Donovan, Anthony Dyson, Duncan Forrester and Ian Markham as well as John Elford, Stephen Platten (now Bishop of Wakefield), Linda Woodhead and Anne Loades.

Although most Roman Catholic ATMT members are actually operating in ecumenical settings of one kind or another, there is always the danger that our focus narrows somewhat when we come together for our ATMT meetings. The presence of members from outside the Roman Catholic tradition has helped us avoid that pitfall. Hence, even when issues of a more specifically Roman Catholic nature are under discussion, it has invariably been refreshing and enlightening to be helped to see these issues from a somewhat different perspective. Such is the nature of moral theology, or Christian ethics, however, that for most of our discussions an outside observer would find it difficult to guess which Church tradition contributors belong to. Our disagreements about ethical matters usually have little or nothing to do with our particular Church allegiance.

Women and ATMT Membership

When the ATMT was founded in 1968 there were no women teaching moral theology in Roman Catholic institutions in the UK. Consequently, there were no women ATMT members in the early days. It is probably true to say that the ATMT members in those days saw nothing unusual about this. The study of moral theology at that time was largely the sole preserve of students preparing for the Roman Catholic Priesthood. It was taught by priests to future priests. I can only speak for myself but to my shame I saw nothing untoward about that. Hence, I failed to recognise that the ATMT was the poorer for the fact that the voice, experience, reflection and insights of women were not offering their specific contributions to our discussions.

Before too long, as ATMT members our eyes began to be opened. Not only did we become more aware that the vision of moral theology was seriously impaired through the absence of the feminine dimensions, we were also forced to recognise that women were beginning to play an increasingly important role in theology in general, and that this was starting to impact on the field of moral theology. We knew we needed to open ourselves to this important 'sign of the times' in the life of society in general and of the Churches in particular. Consequently, we contacted Daphne Hampson, who was probably the leading and most challenging feminist theologian in the UK at the time and asked her to join us for a whole weekend in order to help us understand the specificity of feminist theology. She presented two papers to us, one entitled 'Feminist Ethics', the other, 'On Power and Gender'. She also played a full part in all our sessions and discussions over the weekend. It must have been a very difficult experience for her and there were a few rather hurtful reactions. However, the overall consensus was that it was a most valuable weekend. In hindsight, it probably marked a milestone in the life of the ATMT.

What is also becoming more evident is that the contribution of women moral theologians, who are increasingly active members in the ATMT, will figure increasingly prominently in Roman Catholic writing in the field of moral theology in Britain,

Concluding Reflections

A quick glance through the list of papers and their authors confirms a regrettable fact that has often been commented upon in ATMT meetings. On the whole, the active ATMT membership is drawn almost entirely from what might be described as the more liberal school of moral theology in the UK today. That is regrettable. Sadly, the original close link between the ATMT and those teaching moral theology in the seminaries and religious theologates is becoming more and more tenuous.

I am left wondering, therefore, about the appropriateness of continuing to call ourselves the Association of Teachers of Moral Theology. For many years our meetings have paid little or no attention to issues related to the actual 'teaching' of moral theology. We have focused far more on the substance of moral theology itself – how we arrive at our moral knowledge as human persons,

Christians and members of a specific Church with its particular teaching claims; what kind of certainty we can have about moral truths; the meaning of moral goodness and virtue and their opposites; how we go about making our moral judgements in a sin-infected world and allowing for our unique history of moral woundedness and/or growth; also specific issues relating to social, personal, sexual, medical and environmental ethics. Clearly, all these questions have far-reaching implications for the way moral theology is actually taught. Nevertheless, the actual 'how' of teaching moral theology would seem to be an additional skill and one which has never been a matter of great concern in our ATMT meetings.

We are constantly being told that information technology is bringing about a major revolution in the way we live our lives. If that is true, then it has implications for moral theology – and for an association of teachers of moral theology or moral theologians. Even though there is no substitute for us as moral theologians to make personal face-to-face contact with each other, once we have got to 'know' each other as persons, contact through e-mail or other forms of IT becomes much more three-dimensional and value-added. As the ATMT faces the future it might we worthwhile exercising our imagination to explore how new developments in information technology might open completely new possibilities for us, not just as individual moral theologians but as an association.

CHAPTER ELEVEN

Towards an Adult Conscience

A revised version of an article first published in 'The Way', October 1985, pp. 282-293. An abbreviated version, entitled 'Conscious Formation and Conscious-raising in the Parish', appeared as chapter two of my book, From A Parish Base: Essays in Moral and Pastoral Theology (DLT, London, 1999).

I used to be puzzled by the French having only one word, 'conscience' to cover our two English concepts, 'conscience' and 'consciousness'. Now I can see more point to their running the two together. I am becoming more and more convinced that 'consciousness' catches the fullest flavour of what we really mean by conscience.

Genuine spirituality recognizes a close link between our deepest desires and the will of God. This is to be expected when we accept that 'the love of God has been poured into our hearts by the Holy Spirit which has been given us' (Rom 5:5). If we can really get in touch with our deepest selves, we are at the contact point between ourselves and the Spirit of God. This is what GS means when it speaks of conscience as 'the most secret core and sanctuary of a person where we are alone with God, whose voice echoes in our depths' (no. 16).

A legalist approach to conscience is de-personalizing. It takes away our individual input into any decision we make; but, even worse, it leaves no room for the Holy Spirit to touch us as persons. The 'will of God' is objectified in laws, principles and the directives of Church authorities. And even the laws and principles lose their soul by being removed from the sphere of ongoing questioning, searching and probing. God's will becomes equated with an objective law, whereas it should be the driving force and inspiration in our decision-making process. As St Thomas puts it so beautifully, 'The New Law in its essence is the gift of the Holy Spirit' (*Summa Theologiae*, I-II, 106:1).

In a legalist approach to God's will, we can feel safe as long as we are doing what authority tells us to do. A deeper understanding of God's will means that if we are listening to the Spirit in the depths of our being, we will constantly be disturbed out of our comfortable security.

Whether true or not, legalism is certainly what many older Catholics believe was taught to them and it is what many still believe and live by today. What authority says, goes. Obedience is the important attitude. Our conscience is clear if we do what the Church says. And conversely, we feel guilty if, for whatever reason, we have not fulfilled the objective requirements of one of the Church's laws. For instance, it is disturbing how many Catholics still feel a need for absolution if they have missed Mass on Sunday, even if they were quite ill at the time. This is nothing less than an extreme oppression of conscience. A person who operates on this level has a seriously immature conscience.

There can be no liberation from this oppression until a person comes to believe that our Christian God is a loving God and that there is nothing God wants more deeply than our personal and communal good and happiness. Once we see God in that light we are able to see that sin has no other meaning than what is person-injuring. God is affected by sin only because human persons are precious to him and the last thing he wants is for persons to be harmed. To paraphrase St Thomas, we offend God only to the extent that we harm ourselves and others (cf. *Contra Gentiles*, III, no. 122).

It follows from all this that we only come to understand what is sinful by gradually discovering what ways of acting are against the true good of human persons. What is good and evil does not flow from some arbitrary 'will of God'. It flows from the very nature of the human person in community. Therefore, if we want to use the phrase 'law of God' or 'God's will', we must remember that we are not referring to divine edicts handed down from on high. Rather we are talking about a growing awareness among humankind as to what really serves the good of human persons and what contradicts that good. Developing this awareness is a momentous task shared by all men and women down through the ages. Each period of history has to face the fresh questions raised by changes in culture, new breakthroughs in human understanding, and a whole variety of scientific and technological developments.

In facing these questions, the Church has no hotline to God. God's will does not arrive from heaven in diplomatic bags carried by some angelic courier. The Church has to join in the common search, confident that its belief in the human person as loved by God in Jesus, will give it something precious and unique to offer in this human quest for truth in personal and communal living.

Following the urging of GS, the Church has to engage in a dialogue with the world; and that is a dialogue from within. The Church does not look in on the modern world from the outside. The men and women who make up the Church today belong to the modem world, they share the same hopes and fears, sorrows and joys.

Dialogue involves listening and speaking. As Church we must listen to and be up-to-date with the best of scientific knowledge and the most recent technological developments. We must also listen to our own instincts through which we can plug into the common-sense of humankind. We must listen to other people of good will – and obviously 'good will' is not the exclusive preserve of Catholics or Christians. We must listen to our catholic and Christian tradition.

Real sharing in dialogue also involves speaking. Some of that speaking can be checking out whether we have listened correctly. The opening paragraphs of GS are virtually the Church saying to the world, 'This is what I hear you saying: have I got you right?' Some speaking involves moving the dialogue on a stage further. And some speaking expresses our judgments or decisions. This kind of speaking is very crucial, especially in matters of urgency where decisions need to be made and acted upon.

Urgent and pressing decisions face our modern world. Therefore, our dialogue has to come to practical conclusions. Judgments have to be made. They must be the best we can do at the time but very often they can only be provisional, open to further refinement and perhaps even revision. To be practical they need to be definite but that does not mean they have to be definitive. A moral theologian whom I respect highly once said that he would love to read an encyclical letter which began 'I may be wrong but ...!' We need to have the courage of our convictions. An open mind does not mean a blank mind devoid of any convictions. But we do need to see ourselves involved in an ongoing search for truth. That does not mean jettisoning the truth as we currently see it but it might mean re-examining and re-thinking that truth so that we can appreciate its richness even more fully in the light of where we stand today in the ongoing story of human culture and civilization. The whole of *Gaudium et Spes* is written in this spirit but nowhere is it more clearly expressed than in no. 44 of that Constitution. After speaking about this whole process of dialogue, it then states: 'In this way, revealed truth can always be more deeply penetrated, better understood, and set forth to greater advantage.'

This dialogue process in the Church's involvement in the search for truth throws light on how the individual Christian moves towards a conscience-decision. I use the phrase 'conscience-decision' deliberately. Conscience is not some inner voice telling me what I should do, a kind of hotline to God. Neither is it a negative alarm signal which goes off when I am about to do something wrong. Put very simply, conscience is myself deciding what I should do if I am to respond fully to God in this situation facing me. And responding fully to God implies responding fully to life and to my own deepest level of being.

If we view conscience in this way, it is clear why our understanding of what is meant by 'the will of God' is so important and why we need to be freed from voluntaristic and de-personalizing interpretations of God's will. In a sense we create God's will; or better, God's will takes shape through our decisions. We are not puppets with the whole of our lives and everything we do already preprogrammed by God, the puppet-master. As each major decision looms before us in life, God's will is not already determined and filed away in some kind of divine computer programme. Discovering God's will is not a matter of discovering what God has already decided that we should do. Rather, discovering God's will lies in ourselves deciding what is the most loving and responsible thing for us to do. We discover God's will by actually bringing it into being.

I have always been fond of Charles de Foucauld's prayer of abandonment. Not so long ago I was thrilled to discover just how similar that prayer is to the famous 'Take, Lord, and receive' act of self-offering in the Fourth Week of St Ignatius' Spiritual Exercises. For many years, God forgive me, I had tended to interpret abandonment to God's will in a kind of fatalistic sense, God's will came to me mainly from the outside in the events of life and in the directives and instructions of my bishop and other legitimate authorities. I did not naturally link abandonment to God's will with what my deepest self really wanted to do.

Bit by bit I came to realize that it was meaningless to say to the Lord 'I offer you my mind and will' and then not use these precious faculties. That was not giving God my mind and will at all; it was simply ceasing to use them. That path leads to fatalism or grooms us to becoming victims of totalitarianism. So it gradually dawned on me that abandonment to God's will was very closely linked with having the faith and courage to respond actively, not passively, to the situations in life. It meant being prepared to make decisions myself and accepting responsibility for my own decisions.

Naturally I am not suggesting that at every moment of the day we are always engaged in important conscience-decisions. Most of the time we are living out of decisions previously made and any intermediate decisions are not of such major import. Sadly, sometimes we are living without any sense of direction at all and so we experience much of what we are doing as pointless i.e. lacking point or direction.

All this points to the importance of a traditional catholic practice which is often misunderstood and in its mistaken form becomes oppressive rather than liberating. I refer to the 'examination of conscience'. That has often been presented as a looking back over the day to see in what ways we have sinned. A truer version of it, and one more in keeping with its Ignatian inspiration, would see it as a time for deepening awareness in the busy and humdrum turmoil of daily life – almost an examination of consciousness. It is not a time when we make momentous new conscience decisions. It is more a time for sharpening our awareness of how the ordinary happenings of our day can have a deeper layer to them. They are not pointless. They fit into (or contradict) the purpose of our life as we have determined it to be through our deeper conscience-decisions. We encounter God in our everyday life.

Conscience understood in this way is light-years away from conscience reduced to guilt-feelings. The latter is an impoverishment of conscience and fails to take God's commitment to this life seriously. It breeds an attitude which I can only call 'irresponsibility towards life'. It fails to see how much this life matters in the eyes of God. It almost reduces our present life to being a kind of waiting-room for eternity, a supporting feature before the main film. The emphasis is on my personal immunity from guilt, my integrity. As long as my conscience is clear, I do not need to worry.

This life matters enormously to God. And above all, how human persons are treated is of paramount importance to God. Strangely enough, God seems well able to cope with guilt especially when it is good, healthy guilt arising from very real evil perpetrated and acknowledged. The acceptance of guilt is a major stepping-stone to forgiveness and real forgiveness is a deep experience of love. 'Her sins, her many sins, must have been forgiven her, or she would not have shown such great love' (Lk 7:47).

It is not guilt that poses a problem to God but blindness, It was the blindness of his people that caused Jesus to weep over Jerusalem. It was the blindness of the Pharisees that infuriated Jesus and caused him to use such strong language in an attempt to break down their resistance.

The problem with a guilt-centred conscience is that it focuses on itself and is blind to the real needs of other people and God's world. By being turned in on itself it becomes purely individualistic. *Gaudium et Spes* challenged Christians to leave that kind of conscience behind them.

> Profound and rapid changes make it particularly urgent that no-one, ignoring the trend of events or drugged by laziness, content himself with a merely individualistic morality … Let everyone consider it his sacred obligation to count social necessities among the primary duties of modern men, and to pay heed to them (no. 30).

If God really loves people and wants them to love and respect each other, it matters enormously to God how we treat each other and how we manage the world that we share as our communal home. God is not an impartial and uninvolved judge passing guilty or not-guilty verdicts on people. God is a committed and deeply involved lover to whom the dignity and happiness of each of us is of crucial importance.

A lover is a very vulnerable person since he or she suffers in and through the sufferings of the beloved. In freely creating humankind out of love, God has made himself completely vulnerable. Sometimes we speak of God as the unmoved mover, the changeless one. Though these expressions have a core of truth in them, we can so easily misunderstand and misinterpret them. They can give the impression that God is not really affected by what happens on earth and invulnerable to the sufferings of humankind. The stoic philosophers called this 'apathy' (painlessness, non-suffering). For them it was a state of perfection. For people today it is totally unattractive and inhuman.

A greater distortion of the God of the Bible and the God of Jesus could hardly be imagined. The Bible is full of feeling words applied to God – love, jealousy, anger, longing, desire and wrath, to name but a few. To apply the word 'apathy' to the God of the Old Testament could hardly be wider of the mark.

The same is true of Jesus – only more so. Jesus hanging on the cross gives the lie to any notion of God being invulnerable. The crucifixion could be called the vulnerability of God.

At the heart of Christian revelation lies the mystery of God's sharing his pain with us. By that I do not mean God inflicting his pain on us. I simply mean God letting us know how much he loves us by actually letting us know how much he suffers because of us. In his mysterious decision to love us into existence God has made himself totally vulnerable. This is what the figure of Jesus on the cross is saying to us.

The cross is the symbol of the pain of God. But the voice of the pain of God in every age – and therefore in our own age also – is the voice of the poor, the oppressed, the weak, the sick, those who are pushed to the margins of society. That is what the parable of the Good Samaritan (Lk 10:29-37) is saying to us. We hear the call of God in the cry of the person in need. It is the same message we find in the tableau of the Last Judgment in Matthew 25:31-46.

The voice of the pain of God in our world today is still the voice of the poor, the oppressed, those who are discriminated against, those who are pushed to the edges of our society, those who are always at the back of the queue, The Vatican Council gives voice to the cry of some of these when it denounces all forms of discrimination 'whether based on sex, race, colour, social condition, language or religion'. The voice of the pain of God can be heard at a global level-but the same voice is also to be heard in our neighbourhood, on our street, at work with us – or, more probably, not at work with us. In fact, the more we become sensitive to it, the more it becomes a deafening chorus, so much so that we can feel overwhelmed by it.

But we do not and must not hear it alone. As a family, whether in the Church or in society, we must listen to it together. And if we hear it in that context of our shared strength in the Church or in society, then far from overwhelming us, this cry of pain can become a challenge and an invitation.

Being a cry for a fully more human life, it is God's voice calling us into his future, inviting us to take up the challenge to continue creating a more human world. Becoming attuned to this voice is a vital factor in the formation of conscience. 'Consciousness-raising' is a very apt description of this process. If the listening process involved in this is really operative in us, then we are talking of an activity which can also be described as prayer.

There is always the temptation to close our cars to that cry of pain. To the extent that we are not sharers in that pain, to the extent that we want to keep our distance from it and not be disturbed by it, to that extent we want to stay where we are. And we try to justify 'where we are' by describing it as order, standing over against disruption, disturbance, any change that can let that pain infiltrate into our tidy corner of the world.

But to opt for order in that sense is really to love what is dead. It is like a death wish. It is to deny that human history is alive and that an essential part of its life is this cry for increasing emancipation. To be deaf to that cry is to be deaf to the voice of the living God. Through this cry God is calling us constantly into a more human future.

Of course, we need to be aware that what happens in reality is that often the cry of pain comes to us disguised as an outburst of anger, or resentment, or rebellion. Our natural reaction as individuals, and especially as a Church or as society, is to respond in the same language – anger for anger, rejection for rejection and so on – or else it is to try to muffle the cry by means of directing attention elsewhere or by tackling the superficial symptoms which are only the tip of the iceberg. We will never receive the gift of sharing another's pain unless we approach the other in love with a real desire to listen and a total absence of judgment and condemnation. A perfectionist, moralistic, over-demanding Church will find it difficult to share the pain of the weak and 'sinful' because such a Church will not give them that sense of security and trust which is needed for them really to reveal their pain.

One often hears an appeal today for the Church to give firm moral teaching on something or other. 'Why doesn't the Church take a clear stand on the issue?' people say. To my mind, there are far more people looking to the Church, not for clear moral principles, but for compassion and understanding and the assurance that they are not alone in their pain and in their suffering and that there are grounds for real hope for them.

Jesus went to the heart of the matter, he went down to the roots. That is because he was so concerned. If we are to share his concern, his outraged anger, we must not rest satisfied with living on the surface. We too must try to go to the roots of the evils causing pain in our society today.

In revising and abbreviating this article for the present volume, I cannot resist adding a completely new final section. I feel it flows naturally from the final section of this article.

In September 2004 I had the privilege of being present at a meeting of Medical Missionary of Mary Sisters in Nairobi. It was a gathering of all their sisters from across the world who had been serving people (mainly women and children) who were living with HIV/AIDS. The meeting was an opportunity to share their experience at the end of ten years working in this ministry. It was also an occasion when they could draw inspiration together from their common faith in a God of love, despite the horrendous sufferings they encountered in their heroic ministry. What follows is the account in my diary of the opening service which began their meeting.

We began our conference with a beautiful liturgy prepared and led by Kay Lawlor. It was on the theme of 'The Tears of God'. She had placed two tables in the middle of the room covered with very colourful African cloths. On each table were two glass bowls, two jugs of water and two floating candles. The big altar on the platform behind was also covered by a beautiful African cloth, a photo of their foundress, Mother Mary Martin, and some tasteful flower arrangements as well as a globe of the world.

The opening call to prayer read:

> We come to gather the tears of the women and children of the world, the tears witnessed and wiped by our Sisters throughout the world, the tears of God; to bring to our minds, hearts, prayer and discussions the pain of our world and the Compassion of God.

After that one of the sisters read Lk 23:27-30,

> And there followed Jesus a great multitude of the people, and of women who bewailed and lamented him. But Jesus turning to them said, 'Daughters of Jerusalem, do not weep for me, but weep for yourselves and for your children. For behold, the days are coming when they will say, "Blessed are the barren, and the wombs that never bore, and the breasts that never gave suck".'

The sisters were then invited to go to the jug and water corresponding to their zone and pour water from the jug into the bowls – representing the tears of women and children – and the tears of God. Quiet music was played in the background. Then a sister went up to each table and poured the two bowls of tears together into one bowl. These were then brought up to the altar and all poured together into one big bowl – beside the globe. The four floating candles were lit and floated in the one big bowl.

After this all the sisters said together the very powerful words of their Mission Statement as Medical Missionaries of Mary:

> As Medical Missionaries of Mary
> in a world deeply and violently divided,
> we are women on fire
> with the healing love of God.
> Engaging our own pain and vulnerability,
> we go to peoples of different cultures,
> where human needs are greatest.
> Our belief in the inter-relatedness of God's creation
> urges us to embrace holistic healing
> and to work for reconciliation, justice and peace.

Then we all listened to a most haunting song, *The Tears of God*, taken from Carey Landry's CD, *I will not forget you*, vol 2.

I saw a woman with her children, standing near the shelter door,
Hoping there would be a room,
A bed for one night more.
Then I saw a million people, poor and homeless 'round the world,
And I thought I saw a tear fall upon each one.

I thought I saw the tears of God.
I thought I saw the tears of God.
I thought I saw the tears of God.
Falling like the rain.

I heard a young child crying,
And when I turned to comfort her,
I saw a look upon her face, a hollow frightened stare.
Then I saw a million children,
Cold and hungry 'round the world
And I thought I saw a tear fall upon each one.

I thought I saw the tears of God.
I thought I saw the tears of God.
I thought I saw the tears of God.
Falling like the rain.

Nation fighting nation;
Hatreds settled with a gun;
Neighbour fighting neighbour;
Father against son.

Who will dry the tears of God?
Who will dry the tears of God?
Who will dry the tears of God
And help to heal the pain?

Blessed are the ones who suffer persecution for justice' sake.
Blessed are the sorrowing: they shall be consoled.
Blessed are the poor in spirit:
They shall know the reign of God.
Blessed are the pure of heart: they shall see their God.

Shall we dry the tears of God?
Shall we dry the tears of God?
Shall we dry the tears of God?
And help to heal the pain?

Shall we dry the tears of God?
And help to heal the pain?

I found this liturgy utterly powerful and deeply moving. It moved us all to tears.

With our finite minds, we cannot grasp the full meaning of what this care of God really means. But in the person of Jesus it comes to us translated into the human language of love. The love of Jesus embodies the truth that God really cares about us.

God's care extends to all – to every man, woman and child; and the proof of that lies precisely in his avowed love for those who in human terms are regarded as unlovable – the poor, the oppressed, the outcasts. God's so-called 'preferential love' for them is in fact the verification of his love for everyone.

And the genuineness of God's love is seen in the pain of God over the pain of those whom he loves – the sympathy of God (suffering with – diametrically opposed to 'apathy') incarnate in the person of Jesus and most clearly seen on the cross.

Paradoxically it is this pain of God, this outraged anger, which is the source of our confidence as Christians. If God shares our pain, there is no need for us to worry about the final outcome? This comes through very strongly in Paul's tremendous shout of trust and confidence at the end of chapter eight of Romans.

As Christians, we are empowered by sharing the outraged anger of God's love. More than that, if we believe that God's spirit is active in the depths of every man and woman, then in truth everyone is offered the gift of being empowered by the outraged anger of God's love. Surely we can say that this lies at the root of all human restlessness about what is wrong and out of gear and inhuman in our world. Pope Paul said something similar in 1971 when he wrote: 'Beneath an outward appearance of indifference, in the heart of every man there is a will to live in brotherhood and a thirst for justice and peace which is to be expanded' (*Octogesima Adveniens*, 1971). In 2008 Benedict XVI opened his major social encyclical, *Caritas in Veritate*, with a very similar message.

CHAPTER TWELVE

'Do it Yourself' Moral Theology

This is a modified version of an article which appeared in January 1970 edition of The Clergy Review' pp.52-63. As I have already mentioned in the Introduction to this volume, it was written to prepare the readers (mainly clergy) for the demise of the 'Questions and Answers' feature in the periodical. It was intended as a move to implement the vision of Vatican II with its emphasis on the role of conscience and personal responsibility and also to encourage priests (and moral theologians) to help people grow in the skills of discernment and decision-making needed if they are to benefit from this development in pastoral practice.

Introduction

Some time ago, after giving a talk to a group of Catholic doctors, I was asked for an answer to a very complicated case in the field of Medical Ethics. I admitted quite frankly that far from being able to give a clear answer I could not even understand all the medical data in the case. I suggested that it was not the role of moral theologians to provide ready-made answers but that their task was to help people made their own responsible decisions, taking into account all the factors which are morally relevant in any situation. In the case in question, I insisted, it is the doctor who must decide, not the moral theologian, since only a doctor could fully understand all that is involved in a complicated medical problem.

Later in the evening a lady came up to me and said very sympathetically, 'I was sorry for you this evening, Father, when you were unable to answer that question. It just goes to show that moral theologians ought really to be trained as doctors too.' No doubt she was trying to console me. In fact, she merely confirmed me in my basic position. What she was forgetting was that moral theology concerns every area of life – education, marriage, politics, law, economics, war, penal affairs, industry, social work and race relations. If her suggestion was taken seriously, a moral theologian would need to qualify as a teacher, lawyer, social worker, criminologist and economist, as well as getting married, engaging in politics, joining the armed forces and perhaps serving a prison sentence for good measure.

There has been a tendency to regard the moral theologian as 'the one with all the answers' and moral theologians themselves have not exactly discouraged this attitude. In fact, if one looks at the moral theology section of a seminary library, one will find a number of books with 'Questions and Answers' style titles. To be fair, many of the questions posed concerned issues of canon law and asked for a precise interpretation of some difficult point in law. Even one of Bernard Häring's books was entitled, *Bernard Häring Replies: Answers to 50 Moral and Religious Questions*.

Hearing the Call of God in the Historical Situation

The role of moral theologians today is more one of being 'people with questions'. I do not mean that their heads are full of unanswered questions (though there is some truth in that), rather, they are people who help others to question their own way of acting – not in any morbid introspective sense – but through a growing realisation that human living is simply a lived-out answer to God's question, 'Do you love me?'. The role of moral theologians is to highlight the connection between this question and human living. In this way, they will help individual Christians hear this question as it come to them in the demands of every life, so that they in turn can question the response they are making to these demands in their own unique personal situation.

A basic truth that we moral theologians must constantly draw attention to is that God's living call to people only has reality in the present to be lived and in the future to be realised. It is precisely in the situations of the present day itself that God's challenge to us is to be found, not in any body of universal principles or laws. Edward Schillebeeckx expresses this truth very powerfully:

> There is only one source of ethical norms, namely, the historical reality of the value of the inviolable human person with all its bodily and social implications. That is why we cannot attribute validity to abstract norms as such. Moreover, no abstract statement can produce a call or invitation … Therefore, these abstract, generally valid norms are an inadequate yet real pointer to the one real concrete ethical norm, namely, this concrete human person living historically in this concrete society. Ethical norms are requirements made by reality, and the so-called abstract general norms are but the essentially inadequate expression of this. Therefore, it is not the inadequate expression which, by itself, constitutes the ethical norm, but it is a pointer to the one and only norm: these persons who must be approached in a love that demands justice for all. (*God, the Future of Man*, Sheed & Ward, London, 1969, pp. 151-2)

Moral theologians who are not open to the demands of present-day situations might be called 'historians of moral theology' but certainly cannot be called moral theologians in the full sense of the word.

It is precisely in the face of the present-day situation that the distinct role of moral theologians is most clearly to be seen. They are indeed the ones with the questions but their questions must be realistic; they must be relevant to contemporary living. This is not just a question of adaptation of language. It is more a matter of discerning where the enduring demands of Christian living become incarnate in life today. Moral theologians do not make them incarnate. As demands they are already present. The man lying wounded on the Jericho road is incarnate in far too many forms in our world today. It is the role of moral theologians to help to locate the Jericho roads of today (i.e. where the unanswered needs of persons are to be found in our age) and to make Christians travelling on these roads (i.e. in industry, city-dwelling and immigration) aware of their responsibility. Moral theologians cannot produce blueprints for making the Jericho roads of today safe places for travellers; but they can and should insist on and explain the values to be promoted and the aims to be kept in mind. Moreover, moral theologians can sometimes draw on the wealth of Christian experience and offer more specific guidance, although they should avoid the temptation of thinking that Christians are the only ones who have anything to contribute in this way.

Towards a Wider Moral Outlook

Does this mean that moral theologians are going out on strike – no more answers to questions asked? Not at all! It is simply that moral theologians are keen to play their true role in the Church. If asked concrete questions, moral theologians will attempt to answer them – but the chances are that their answers will simply pose further questions. For instance, if moral theologians are asked whether it is right for a family to take squatters' rights in an unoccupied house if they cannot find accommodation anywhere, it is likely that they will refuse to answer that question in isolation but will link it with other questions which cannot be separated from it. For example, is it right for multiple house-owners to refuse entry to homeless families when one of their houses is lying unoccupied; is it right for those in local government housing departments to tolerate a situation in which families are homeless, especially when local property is lying empty; is it right for the citizens in a locality to remain silent if such a situation is tolerated. These and similar questions all find their origin in a basic Christian truth which goes back to the times of the early Church and which has often been quoted in recent Church statements, most notably by Paul VI in his Encyclical, *Populorum Progressio*:

> No one is justified in keeping for his exclusive use what he does not need, when others lack necessities. In a word, 'According to the traditional doctrine found in the Fathers of the Church and the great theologians, the right to property must never be exercised to the detriment of the common good'. (no. 23)

Moral theologians will refuse to be hemmed in by the questions put to them since they will consider their main task to be to bring to light the question that Christ is asking in any situation. This is the moral theologian's principal concern. It is not up to moral theologians to praise or condemn; theirs is not a judgemental science. Theology, as its name implies, concerns God; it is trying to know and understand God as he reveals himself. Moral theology in particular is trying to know and understand God as he speaks to us and challenges our love for him in the demands of ordinary everyday human life. The way a specific question is posed might very well hide God, since its formulation might be based on a view of God which is itself questionable to the modern mind. For instance, how is a moral theologian to answer the question, 'Is it a serious sin to miss Mass on Sunday?' Underlying such a question there might be a host of misconceptions about sin, Church law, liturgy and the Mass itself.

No one is denying that questions need to be asked. Every question is a request for help and cannot be ignored. However, the help needed may not be obvious. Often what may be needed is a change of outlook regarding the answer expected. There is a world of difference between, 'Tell me what is God's will for me in this situation' and 'Help me to be able to discern what is God's will for me in this situation.' If moral theologians can help at this second level, they are en route to making themselves redundant from the questioner's point of view. That cannot but be a good thing. Pius XII himself said:

> All sound education aims at rendering the one educated independent, within proper limits. This is also true of the education of the conscience by God and the Church. Its aim is someone who is of age and who also has the courage which goes hand in hand with responsibility (18 April 1952, cf. *Catholic Documents*, VII, p. 19).

This idea of a joint search for God's will is even true of the Church herself in her relationship with the world. Schillebeeckx writes:

> The Church does not simply have something to communicate. In order to communicate, she must also receive from and listen to what comes to her from the world as 'foreign prophecy' but in which she nonetheless recognises the well-known voice of her Lord. The relationship between the Church and the world is thus no longer the relationship of a 'teaching' Church to a 'learning' world, but the interrelationship of dialogue in which both make a mutual contribution and listen sincerely to each other (*God, the Future of Man*, Sheed & Ward, London, 1969, p. 126).

One of the basic values insisted on in Vatican II was personal responsibility. This obviously includes the idea that the consciences of Christians must be better educated so that they are not constantly asking questions of moral theologians or their local clergy. Rahner makes an interesting comment on this point:

Catholics are therefore inevitably left by the Church's teaching and pastoral authority more than formerly to their own conscience, to form the concrete decision independently on their own responsibility. The confessional in particular will therefore be concerned more than formerly with fundamental formation of the conscience which will then be committed to its own responsibility for the actual decision (*The Christian of the Future*, Herder-Burns Oates, London, 1966, pp. 43-44).

Christians can no longer see themselves as living in a kind of extra-territorial colony in the world. They are very much of the world precisely because they have been given the mission of being a sign of God's action in the world. This is clearly expressed in Council's Constitutions on the Church (LG), no. 1, 9 & 48 and on the Liturgy (SC) no. 5. Moreover, the whole of the Constitution on the Church in Modern World (GS) spells out the implications of this notion. It has also influenced many of the other Council documents, notably, the Decrees on the Church's Missionary Activity and on the Laity.

Because of this change of approach to the world and also because of the complexity of the problems of human living today, moral theologians cannot go far along the road to personal decision with individual Christians. Again Rahner expresses this truth very clearly:

The Church cannot overlook the fact that the road from universal principle to concrete prescription is even longer than it ever was, and that in practice the Church by official teaching and guidance, can accompany the individual to the end of this road much less often than formerly. Instead, however, and as the best substitute, the Church would need to give the individual Christian three things: a more living ardour of Christian inspiration as a basis of individual life; an absolute conviction that the moral responsibility of the individual is not at an end because he does not come in conflict with any concrete instruction of the official Church; an initiation into the holy art of finding the concrete prescription for his own decision in the personal call of God, in other words, the logic of concrete particular decision which of course does justice to universal regulative principles but which cannot wholly be deduced from them solely by explicit casuistry (op. cit., pp. 46-47).

What Rahner is saying here is very similar to GS. no. 43:

Lay people should also know that it is generally the function of their well-formed Christian conscience to see that the divine law is inscribed in the life of the earthly city. From priests they may look for spiritual light and nourishment. Let the laity not imagine that their pastors are always such experts, that to every problem which arises, however complicated, they can readily give them a concrete solution, or even that such is their mission. Rather, enlightened by Christian wisdom and giving close attention to the teaching authority of the Church, let the laity take on their own distinctive role.

However, Vatican II has called us away from a too individualistic morality and has laid great stress on the importance of social justice. The message of GS is particularly strong:

Profound and rapid changes make it particularly urgent that no one, ignoring the trend of events or drugged by laziness, rests content with a merely individualistic morality. It grows increasingly true that the obligations of justice and love are fulfilled only if everyone, contributing to the common good, according to their own abilities and the needs of others, also promote and assist the public and private institutions dedicated to bettering the conditions of human life ... Let all consider it their sacred obligation to count social necessities among the primary duties of the modern age and play heed to them (no. 30).

If moral theologians are to be faithful to their task as outlined in the Vatican II documents, they will have to widen their own horizon of moral questions and will have make a sustained effort to make such a wider outlook something which is taken for granted among Catholics. That such a widening is urgently needed is clearly exemplified by comparing the very slight reaction to *Populorum Progressio* and the massive protest and upheaval which followed *Humanae Vitae*. If the former were taken seriously its effects would be far more revolutionary.

In the light of the above comment, I am very conscious that this volume does not contain many items dealing with specific issues of social justice. Yet issues of social justice have occupied a major place in my personal odyssey of receiving Vatican II. In my formal teaching, at both Heythrop College and Liverpool Hope University, a large part of the syllabus I followed dealt with general and specific issues of social justice. Two months of my sabbatical in 1980 were taken up experiencing liberation theology in practice especially in the Philippines and in other parts of the developing world. As a member of CAFOD's HIV / AIDS advisory committee for nearly twenty years I was given the opportunity to visit Zambia, Zimbabwe, Kenya, Thailand and the Philippines and was able to see for myself how HIV / AIDS was a major development issues in many developing countries and how poverty, rooted in injustice, played a major part in the spread of the pandemic. Much of my writing in this area took the form of my personal diaries written during those visits and highlighting how some of the major root causes could be traced back to the roots of this injustice located in the developed world. I brought that out strongly throughout my book, NDSE. In fact, my final summing up in the concluding section (pp. 210-213) carries the heading, 'A Time of Grace: AIDS – A Window of Opportunity for our Global Society'.

At a more general level, most of my pieces about social justice have taken the form of homilies. In this volume the first two items in the section, 'The Eucharist and Vatican II', are examples of such homilies. The item immediately following this one is also a piece concerned with social justice. I wrote it at the request of CAFOD for their resource book, *Livesimply* for their 2008 campaign under that title.

I am very aware that this volume has little to contribute to what is probably the most far-reaching moral issue of the present day i.e. the global financial crisis. Quite honestly, I am left baffled by the complexities of modern global economics. The evils of the system seem to be staring us all in the face:

- The domination of 'the markets' which seem answerable to no one but themselves and which seem to have the power to destroy whole nations;
- The lack of any overall authority which can call the world's wealth-holders to account and force them to face their responsibilities.

How these evils can be overcome is another matter. I have often commented on the fact that I am often referred to as an emeritus moral theologian and have remarked that a literal translation of the term emeritus is 'past it'. In the present economic crisis I am very conscious just how true that description of my competence is.

CHAPTER THIRTEEN

Live Simply: Being True to Our Togetherness

As mentioned at the end of the previous item, this is a piece written at the request of CAFOD for their 2008 Resource Book, Livesimply. The chapter's title in that book is 'Togetherness'.

'Livesimply' is not just a strategy thought up by CAFOD and other AID agencies, a temporary measure to respond to a crisis situation. It is not a utilitarian game plan, a means to an end. 'Livesimply' is about being true to who we are. It is not something we do; it is what we are. It is mindset, a way of being.

Its starting point lies in the very heart of God, the God who lies at the heart of all existence and gives meaning to all that is. That God is not a loner God, a God living in isolation. God has revealed God's self as a 'together' God, a God of communion. Togetherness lies at the heart of God. God is oneness in togetherness, with the Holy Spirit as the love binding the Father and Son together. This blows our minds. It is mystery – but not in the sense of a puzzle. It is mystery in the religious sense of being so rich in meaning that there is no way in which we can fully understand it.

But we can experience that mystery. We experience it in the longing for togetherness which lies at the very heart of our being, our deep desire to love and to be loved. That longing is a movement of the Holy Spirit poured into our hearts, what one writer calls the 'in-between Spirit', a spirit which fills the space between us with a dynamic force attracting us together.

We are made 'in the image of God', as such, we are 'together-people', not loners. Kumi Naidoo quoted a beautiful African saying at the G8 Rally in London: 'I am because you are.' When I spoke at a HIV / AIDS conference of Asian moral theologians in Bangkok some years ago, I started from the notion of the dignity of the human person. One Filipino theologian challenged me: 'We do not start from the individual person', he said. 'We start from the community.' In fact, both are really the same starting point. Human persons, as well as being unique individuals, are essentially relational, interdependent, community and social beings. Not surprising, since we are images of God in communion.

Globalisation has brought this home to us even more vividly. It makes us much more aware of the togetherness of the whole human family. We really are mutually dependent. We are all in it together. In an even more dramatic way, the scare about climate change and environmental pollution has made us aware in a completely new way of just how mutually dependent we all are. In fact, this awakening to a new environmental awareness has opened out eyes to yet another level of who we are as 'together people'. As 'together people' we are not just bound together with other human persons. We are also bound together with all living creatures and the whole of creation. Clearly, there is far more to being 'together people' than meets the eye.

God becoming flesh in Jesus opens our eyes still further to the wonder of who we are. Vatican II's inspiring GS, no. 22, stresses that the Incarnation is not so much about revealing to us who God is, but much more about revealing who we are – the utter dignity of being human persons in one human family, all loved into being by God and held in being by God's love. Benedict XVI, in his recent Post-Synodal Exhortation on the Eucharist, *Sacramentum Caritatis* ('The Sacrament of Love') reminds us that a kind of 'nuclear fission' takes place in the Eucharist, setting off a chain reaction, 'leading ultimately to the transfiguration of the entire world, to the point where God will be all in all' (no. 11). The mystery deepens. At the other end of this process, it is not outlandish to suggest that, in a sense, the whole incarnation process began with the Big Bang.

'Livesimply', therefore, is very far from being a strategy to encourage commitment. It is nothing less than facing up to the wonder of who we are as human persons and how that impacts on our relationship with our sisters and brothers and the rest of creation.

'Livesimply' might sound simple. It is actually deeply radical. It is profoundly counter-cultural. That does not mean it is anti-human. It is not pushing a 'killjoy' attitude. There is nothing life-denying about it.

As deeply radical, it goes to the deepest roots ('radices') of who we are. Hence it touches our most profound human desires. Far from being 'killjoy', it is actually liberating. It frees us to be truly ourselves as 'together people'. It sets us free from our enslaving addictions and idols.

These addictions and idols are fed by some of the present-day trends. Some of these trends deny our togetherness and push a form of extreme individualism, encouraging an 'I'm alright, Jack' mentality. Some turn us into consumers, creating an artificial desire to have more, so that I can be more – a favourite ploy of advertising. In fact, the mindset it encourages really means 'having more than you' so that I can be 'more than you'. The unacceptable face of competitiveness. 'Branding' too comes in here as a trivialising of personal identity. Other trends enslave us to the false idol of celebrity status, blinding us to the inner dignity and worth of each person and valuing wealth, fame and achievement more than such basic human qualities as love, forgiveness and integrity.

'Livesimply' really is deeply radical. It is about 'turning the world upside down', to quote a popular hymn. Albert Nolan puts this even better when he speaks of turning an upside-down world the right way up (cf. his recent book, *Jesus Today: A Spirituality of Radical Freedom*, Orbis, 2006, p. 61).

Paul VI saw this clearly when he made his first visit to the developing world. He was struck by just how upside-down the world really is. This experience led him to write his epoch-making encyclical, *Populorum Progressio*, in which he made his own kind of 'The World Can't Wait' plea when he said: 'The World is Sick' (no. 66). Its sickness lies in its sinful structures. Yet that sickness infects us all, since our lives are lived within those sinful structures. Hence, while struggling to change the structures themselves, we also need to break free from the infectious, dehumanizing influence of those structures.

The 'Livesimply' prayer brings this out very powerfully. As well as being an amazing summary of who we are, it also includes a threefold prayer that we might become much more truly who we are – and be healed from being what we are not. Its threefold prayer: 'Create in us a desire to live 1. simply; 2. sustainably; 3. in solidarity …' is really praying that we may be true to who we are in ourselves, as related to other people, and as related to the whole of creation (The full text of this prayer composed by Linda Jones is given at the end of this piece).

The keyword in the prayer is the word 'desire'. It is repeated three times. And we pray that this desire be 'created' in us. We are asking for something new. We are not asking initially for knowledge, or bright ideas, or imaginative suggestions. Those are all helpful, but we are asking for something much deeper. We are asking God to create this threefold desire in us. We are asking for a new enkindling of the fire of the Spirit in us. The Medical Missionaries of Mary use the phrase 'fire in our bellies'. We are not asking to become fanatics, but people burning with deep desire.

This is not an impossible request. In fact, it is really asking God to put us in touch with our deepest selves, to help tune into our really real desires, as 'together persons' made in the image of a 'together God'. The alternative collect for Trinity Sunday brings this out very beautifully: 'You reveal yourself in the depths of our being, drawing us to share in your life and your love … Be near to the people formed in your image, close to the world your love brings to life'

Livesimply

Compassionate and loving God,
you created the world for us all to share,
a world of beauty and plenty.
Create in us a desire to live simply,
so that our lives may reflect your generosity.

Creator God,
you gave us responsibility for the earth,
a world of riches and delight.
Create in us a desire to live sustainably,
so that those who follow after us
may enjoy the fruits of your creation.

God of peace and justice,
you give us the capacity to change,
to bring about a world that mirrors your wisdom.
Create in us a desire to act in solidarity,
so that the pillars of injustice crumble
and those now crushed are set free.

Amen.

CHAPTER FOURTEEN

Two-Minute Talk at a Liverpool Public Rally, Protesting against Government Cuts

This is the text of a talk I was invited to give from the platform in front of St George's Hall, Liverpool at a Public Rally on 20 March 2011 protesting against the Government Cuts. As the opening remarks suggest, the Arab Spring was in its early days. Two minutes means extreme brevity, so I have left the text exactly as given.

We were all gripped by what happened in Cairo last Friday week.

- Mubarak's resignation.
- victory for peaceful People Power.
- and for freedom and democracy.

Some words of Pope Benedict helped me to see more deeply what was going on. He said:

Love is an extraordinary force which leads people into
courageous and generous work for justice and peace...
This force lies deep in every person
And has its origin in God (*Caritas in Veritate*, no. 1)

What I was seeing in Cairo was God's spirit present and active in those people in Tahrir square.

They were mainly Muslims, plus some non-believers and Christians.
Yet what the Pope called an 'Extraordinary Force' bound them together in their courageous and generous protest for justice.
God was truly present and active among them.

I feel the same today.
Whether we are people of faith or no faith.
God is truly present and active among us.
God lives in people more than in buildings.
For today at least, Liverpool has two Cathedrals to spare!

That same 'Extraordinary Force' makes Liverpool One here today.
One in our demand that, whatever cuts are made,
the needs of the poor and most vulnerable must come first.

One in our belief that
the good things of this world are gifts,
given to us in trust, to be shared fairly by all,
for the common good of all
not just for the rich.

One for justice here this afternoon
Together we give a new and deeper meaning to the term, LIVERPOOL ONE!

CHAPTER FIFTEEN

Saints or Sinners?
Towards a Spirituality of Growth out of Sin

This is an abbreviated version of chapter eleven of my book, 'From a Parish Base: Essays in Moral and Pastoral Theology'. That in turn was based on two much longer pieces, Sin, Spirituality and the Secular, (The Way, 1992, pp. 13-22) and The Changing Paradigms of Sin, (New Blackfriars, 1989, pp. 489-497). Another attempt to grapple with the topic of sin in a way which might be pastorally helpful at a practical level is found in The inhumanity of sin and the humanity of forgiveness, chapter seven in my New Directions in Moral Theology: The Challenge of Being Human (London, Geoffrey Chapman, 1992). Some of the thinking which I develop in section three below owes much to Gabriel Daly's book, Creation and Redemption (Gill and Macmillan, Dublin, 1988). Jack Mahoney has developed the same line much further in his book, Christianity in Evolution (Georgetown University Press, Washington, 2011). My review of Mahoney's book follows this essay.

Christian spirituality is about answering the call of Jesus. However, Jesus has said very categorically: 'I have come to call not the just but sinners'. Therefore, it looks as though, in some way or other, there is an essential linkage between spirituality and our being sinners.

Sometimes spirituality is presented as though it had nothing whatsoever to do with sin. At our Baptism we have renounced sin and so it is presumed that sin should play no further part in our lives. Sin is viewed as a regression. It is something we 'fall into'. This suggests that we are falling below what is seen as an acceptable standard for Christian and human life. It is hard to reconcile this perfectionist approach with Jesus saying that he has come to call sinners. Calling sinners suggests our being called out from our sinfulness, rather than our attempting to live some kind of perfect life free from sin. This would seem to imply that our sinfulness is actually the starting point for our spirituality. In this piece I look at the link between Christian spirituality and our sinfulness from three converging directions: first, spirituality being a life-long growth-process out of our being 'victims of sin'; second, its being a life-long growth process out of our being 'agents of sin'; thirdly, grappling with the objection that 'growth out of sin' seems too negative a starting point for Christian spirituality. Finally, I look at the social and ecological implications of such a spirituality.

(1) Christian spirituality as a person's lifelong process of growth out of being a 'victim of sin'.

If spirituality is to be viewed as a lifelong process of growth out of being a 'victim of sin', the question immediately arises: where does each person find his or her particular agenda for this growth? In other words, how am I to discern what Christ is asking of me, victim of sin that I am?

There is a tendency to answer that question along very individualist lines. Each of us is unique. We are not mass-produced on an assembly-line. Consequently, Christ calls each of us as unique persons. Each of us has his or her unique personal vocation. Following out this approach, we try to discern in what special ways each of us is a victim of sin, since it is there that we will discover our own personal woundedness and so our own unique need for healing.

That is fine as far as it goes. However, it does not go nearly far enough. To focus on what is unique about me is to take a very partial and impoverished view of myself as a human person. An absolutely essential dimension of my being a human person is the fact that I am, always have been and always will be bound up in a whole series of relationships of interdependence with other human beings. This has enormous implications for me if I am to arrive at a full diagnosis of where my personal woundedness lies. It means, for instance, that my personal woundedness will be connected to the woundedness of other people. Obviously, this does not mean that we are all wounded in exactly the same way. Nevertheless, it does mean that my personal woundedness will be linked to the woundedness of all the significant others in my life.

Moreover, these significant others in my life will be found within an ever-widening series of concentric circles – my parents, family, educators, friends and neighbours. Their woundedness is likely to have an impact on me in the various dimensions of my being a human person. For example, how I develop as a sexual and relational being will be affected by the woundedness of the people who are close to me as I am passing through the key developmental stages of my life. A United States theologian, Beverly Hildung Harrison, has brought this out very powerfully in speaking of what she calls the 'formidable power' of nurturing:

> We have the power through acts of love or lovelessness literally to create one another … because we do not understand love as the power to act-each-other-into-well-being, we also do not understand the depth of our power to thwart life and to maim each other. That fateful choice is ours, either to set free the power of God's love in the world or to deprive each other of the very basis of personhood and community … it is within the power of human love to build up dignity and self-respect in each other or to tear each other down … through acts of love directed to us, we

become self-respecting and other-regarding persons, and we cannot be
one without the other ('The Power of Anger in the Work of Love', in
Carol Robb (edit), *Making the Connections:Essays in Feminist Social Ethics*,
Boston, Beacon Press, 1985, p. 11-12).

My woundedness will also be influenced by the woundedness of the institutions which form part of my social existence – including the Church. Furthermore, it will also be marked, to a greater or lesser extent, by various forms of
social woundedness, such as patriarchy, racial prejudice, national and cultural
deficiencies, homophobia, ecological insensitivity and my belonging to a developed world whose affluence seems to be irretrievably linked to structures
of exploitation.

If some or all of these factors go to make up the way I, as a human person,
am a victim of sin, by that same token they should also feature on my personal
agenda for 'growth out of being a victim of sin'. In other words, they will constitute the complex medium through which the sinner that I am hears the call
of Christ. This means that they will form an essential part of the agenda for my
personal spirituality in my ordinary, everyday life.

If all this is true, it means that my growth out of sin cannot be something
that I can achieve on my own. Nor, in fact, can it be a growth that takes place
in me alone. For instance, where my woundedness is relational, the growth in
healing must necessarily be relational too. Likewise, where my woundedness
goes back to structural roots, growth towards healing may well demand of me
some kind of personal involvement in working for structural reform. Theologically, this is a strong argument in favour of the communal celebration of reconciliation. It does not argue from convenience – lack of opportunity for
individual confession due to excessive numbers or paucity of confessors. It is
based on the essential social dimension of our being sinners and the corresponding social dimension of our healing and reconciliation.

Moreover, as human persons we are 'historical' beings. We are the product
of history, we live in the midst of history and we ourselves play our own unique
part in fashioning history. History is full of ambiguity. Some opportunities are
seized, other are lost. Nevertheless, although Christians do not believe in inevitable progress, they do believe that God's Spirit is present and active wherever true human progress occurs in history (cf. *The Church in the World of Today*,
no. 26). This belief in the Spirit active within history should make us sensitive
to 'the signs of the times'. These signs of the times constitute part of the call of
Christ to the historical sinful persons that we are. Through them we discern
some of the growth out of sin that we are called to be part of in our contemporary world. It is significant that, when Council Fathers at Vatican II turned their
attention to what was implied in being a Christian in the world of today, the very
first thing they did was to try to interpret the signs of the times (cf. GS, nn. 4-10).

I am convinced that a spirituality cannot be truly Christian today if, for instance, it turns a deaf ear to what the Spirit seems to be saying to us through the voices of so many committed women who are articulating the deep sufferings and injustices inflicted on their sisters by patriarchal institutions, including the Church. The same would seem to be true of the voices of those calling us to a greater ecological awareness and responsibility.

(2) Christian spirituality seen as a lifelong growth process out of our being an 'agent of sin'.
The way we human beings bring about evil is not just to do with the consequences of our actions. It also has to do with ourselves as the agents of these actions. We cannot repeatedly act in an unloving way without becoming unloving persons. This would seem to be where the tragic link between being victims and agents of sin is located. If our capacity to act lovingly and justly has been seriously wounded, then that is likely to show in the way we behave towards others. In fact, experience seems to indicate that it is a very short step from being a victim of sin to becoming an agent of sin. This is very understandable. After all, part of the evil of sin in this sense is that it can injure and deform us as persons. That is why healing is such an urgent priority and this healing involves some sort of growth out of the woundedness inflicted on us by sin.

It would seem, therefore, that our growth out of being an 'agent of sin' is necessarily linked to our growth out of being a 'victim of sin'. That is a truth which has far-reaching implications for pastoral practice. For instance, it implies that Christian spirituality needs to lay much more emphasis on the root causes of why we cause some of the harm that we do. It need to recognize the inadequacy and unreality of demanding a massive act of naked willpower ('a firm purpose of amendment') through which we are immediately expected to be able to cease from the wrong-doing we are involved in. Because we are so interdependent, it may well be that, for the present and while other factors remain as they are, it is morally impossible for a person to break free completely from the wrong-doing he or she is involved in. In reality, this is a fact of human life which has always been acknowledged and allowed for by wise confessors, even though they did not have the benefit of our current understanding of just how multi-dimensional and far-reaching our interdependence on each other actually is.

Commenting on the fact that many Christians are experiencing a 'shift to an awareness of collective responsibility for individual sins, and individual responsibility for the collective sin', Monika Hellwig notes:

Sin and conversion for these Christians are seen in a new light. The question of imputing guilt, calculating the degrees of culpability of freedom and knowledge, simply does not arise in the consciousness of such

Christians. They are concerned with discerning patterns of disorienta-
tion in their society and in their own lives, without reference to the question of whom to blame. Instead their focus is on who can make a
difference in the sinful situation, how, why, when and where.

They feel a certain impatience ... with a spirituality much preoccu-
pied with the quest for perfection in an introspective fashion. They have
an urgent sense that the real agenda of continuing redemption is written
on a far larger canvas, and that endless preoccupation with perfecting
oneself and eliminating personal faults is petty and irresponsible in face
of the terrible and unnecessary sufferings of vast masses of our times
('Theological Trends: Sin and Sacramental Reconciliation, I. Contemporary Reflection on Sin', in *The Way*, 1984, pp. 221-222).

I would interpret Hellwig as saying that it is not for us to judge the culpability
or otherwise of people who are involved in what we consider to be wrong-
doing. We do not know how minimal may be the personal resources individual
people have for coping with the extreme pressures they may be under. Hence,
it is not for us to set ourselves up as 'sinless' and demand that these 'sinners'
overcome these pressures by an act of will which, for all we know, might be
completely outside their personal capacity. Rather, the credibility of our opposition to the wrong-doing these people are involved in will depend, to a large
extent, on how far we are committed to identifying and combatting the social
pressures which might be part of the 'sin' of which these people are 'victims'.
Moreover, recognizing ourselves to be linked in interdependence with these
fellow 'victims of sin', we should perhaps be on the lookout for ways in which
our own interests might be bound up with the maintenance of these social pressures which result in these people 'sinning' in this way. Any such complicity
on our part would reveal our shared 'agency' in their sinning. Maybe the words
of Jesus to the accusers of the woman taken in adultery are relevant here: 'Let
the one who is without sin cast the first stone.'

An example of a pastoral strategy which would seem contrary to this sober-
ing pastoral principle might be the aggressive targetting by some sections of
the pro-life movement in the United States of women entering abortion clinics.
It is significant that many of the women who attended Archbishop Weakland's
'listening sessions' on abortion focussed on a wide variety of social factors
which resulted in many women experiencing enormous pressures to resort to
abortion. Among these pressures the Archbishop's report instanced 'economic
pressures, increased violence, feminization of poverty, consumerism, a continued male dominated society' and it noted that these pressures weigh most
heavily on the increasing numbers of women caught in the poverty trap (Full
report in the *Milwaukee Catholic Herald*, 24 May 1990).

(3) Does 'growth out of sin' imply too negative a starting point for Christian spirituality?

We have seen how we can only hear Christ's call to us to the extent that we accept ourselves as 'sinners'. This means acknowledging that we are both 'victims of sin' and 'agents of sin'. We have also looked at how these two ways in which we are 'sinners' play an important part in setting the agenda for our personal 'spirituality'. This agenda is about our lifelong process of growth out of sin.

Growth is a term frequently used in discussions about human development. However, to talk of 'growth out of sin' might jar on some ears. It seems to assume a negative starting-point. That hardly seems in tune with how we envisage the normal processes of human growth. However, if we go back to the etymology of the Greek word for 'sin', 'hamartia', which means 'missing the mark or the target', we might be able to interpret 'growth out of sin' in a way which is more in keeping with the normal processes of human growth. The word 'hamartia' suggests that sin involves missing the point of life. It might help to explore that idea further.

Religious people are often tempted to think in terms of an original paradise from which we are expelled through our sin. That goes back to an interpretation of the 'Garden of Eden' story in Genesis chapter three, which would see this as a real, though picturesque, description, telling how sin entered into the world through our first parents. This overlooks the fact that this story is a myth which deals not with the past but with the present. The origin of sin, as people experience today and in every age, is not to be found in God but in ourselves as God's creatures. However, Christianity does not look to the Book of Genesis for the heart of its belief. Christianity is essentially a faith centred on the person of Christ in whom the fullness of God's unfolding revelation to us is made flesh. This means that the 'point of life' has only been fully revealed to us in and through Christ.

Christ reveals to us that the 'point of life' is the Kingdom of God. What this Kingdom means is a 'mystery' in the fullest sense of the word. In other words, it is something with such a rich abundance of meaning that we will never exhaust this meaning, either in the present age or in the age to come. The Kingdom is something we can have some experience of but which we can never fully comprehend. At times we may be able to say 'This is what the Kingdom of God is like'; but we will never be able to say 'Now I know what the Kingdom of God is all about'. The Good News of the Kingdom challenges us with the promise that being human has within it the potential for living a life far richer than we would ever have imagined possible. Jesus speaks of this abundance of life in the language of knowing and loving, our highest and most personal modes of human experience. In fact, the Bible often uses these two modes of human experience interchangeably. Put in simple Gospel terms, the point of human life is found in being known and loved by God and each other and in knowing and loving God and each other.

That is not the original state from which our first ancestors fell. Rather, it is a dream of which our earliest ancestors seem to have some inkling. However, the struggle to survive and gradually come to terms with the emergence of communal and social living meant that this dream was little more than a backcloth of hope in the midst of the harsh realities of everyday survival. Yet it was a dream that would not die. The process of evolution into humanness entailed this process of opening out to the transcendent. In God's providence this gave humankind a growing capacity to be open to God's self-revelation. Without such a capacity we would not have been 'human', we would not have been able to grasp the 'point of life' and the Word and Love of God could not have been made flesh among us.

I have been fumbling for words in the above paragraph. That is what happens when one tries to express the inexpressible. Nevertheless, if what I have been trying to say is basically true, however inadequately it is expressed, it throws a totally different light on the expression 'growth out of sin'. No longer does it imply that the starting point of this growth is some God-forsaken place, some kind of morass of evil into which humankind has regressed. It suggests, rather, that the 'point of life' is something towards which humankind as a whole is growing in a lifelong process of interdependence in love – and the expression 'lifelong' here refers to the life of the whole human family, not just to the life of single individuals.

Of course, this is not meant to imply a deterministic view of human history. An essential factor in being human is that we are persons with the capacity to make free decisions. Consequently, part of the 'mystery' which constitutes the 'point of human life' is that God's providential designs are and can only be achieved through the instrumentality of human freedom. However much people may believe in God, it pales into insignificance compared to the belief God has in people! In a recent theological discussion about how we should respond to the Millennium event, the Irish theologian, Enda McDonagh, spoke of the 'risk of God'. His use of that phrase was pregnant with meaning. Part of it was touching on the risk taken by God in the whole process of creation and incarnation and on how that risk follows through into our human and ecclesial task of building the Kingdom of God here on earth and not simply postponing its coming to the end of time.

The 'mystery' which is the 'point of human life' operates at both the macro and the micro level. The macro level is the total history of humankind. The micro level consists in the stories of our own unique personal lives. Here too this 'mystery' perspective enables us to see our 'growth out of sin' in a much more positive perspective. The 'sin' out of which we are growing need not be seen as a mass of unredeemed evil which we have inherited. It is rather the shadow side of our human family's fluctuating struggle to make the dream of the Kingdom a reality in our world.

This struggle is a story of partial success and partial failure, a mixture of heroic self-sacrificing love and narrow-minded self-seeking. It is full of the necessary human conflict involved in trying to make allowance for the conflicting claims of different individuals or groups. Each of us comes on the scene at a particular point in this ongoing story which is so full of ambivalence. Such is the complexity of our interdependence, each of us is affected by both the ebb and flow movements in the different dimensions of our being human persons. In some of these dimensions we may be predominantly 'inheritors of grace'; in others, 'victims of sin' might be a more accurate description of our situation.

This admixture provides the raw material out of which we have to construct our lives. Christ calls us as 'sinners' to receive the gift of this raw material and to live our lives as fully as possible out of this bundle of light and shade. Growth out of sin is merely another way of describing our lifelong task of playing our minor but necessary and unique part in the ongoing story of humankind as it continues its struggle to give living shape and substance to the 'point of life' revealed to us in Christ.

This interpretation of spirituality has no room for a perfectionist ethic. It is too solidly based in the God-given reality of the everyday world. There is no perfect human being which we are all called to be. In a sense, morality for each of us is a personal affair. That does not mean that it is individualistic, or relative, or something we make up to suit our own convenience. Rather it is personal in the sense that it flows from the person each of us is, 'integrally and adequately considered'. Christ's call to me is myself, the person I am, considered in all the different dimensions of human personhood. Whether my response to this invitation is one of acceptance or rejection will be revealed in my life. The way I live my life constitutes my faith-response to God. That is true of every person who has ever lived.

This spirituality takes on board the fact that, as we gradually come to self-awareness, we discover that the person we are growing into, due to the influence of others and our own reaction to their influence, is not as fully human as we might like. The dawning of this self-understanding can offer us the opportunity for entering into the lifelong process of personal healing. Accepting as gift the wounded person we discover ourselves to be, we can try to live as fully as we can within our limitations. In trying, however haltingly, to live positively in this way we are casting our vote in favour of life. The conversion process is beginning to take shape in us. This is beginning to believe in myself, the person God has given me to become.

God wants us to be as fully human as we can. I was almost going to add 'within our own personal and unique limitations' but that would merely be stating the obvious. There is no other way any of us can be fully human except within our own personal and unique limitations. Some women theologians these days are helping us become more conscious that our limitations are actually our opportunities. They provide the raw material with which, in God's providence, each of us has to work. This even implies that the precise way I am a 'victim of sin' will affect the way in which I grow into being more human. For instance, it should give me a sensitivity and compassion for those who are victims of sin in a similar way to myself and it should also make me appreciate the suffering caused by the inhumanity of sin in this particular dimension of human living.

Dorothy Sölle once made the comment: 'I have noticed that people with faith all walk around with a limp!' In other words, the scars of our healed woundedness will show. Each of us will bear our own unique scars. Like the glorious wounds of Jesus they will enhance our individual humanity. There is a kind of paradox at play here. The very experience of my woundedness and the inhumanity it brings into my life and that of others is the very stuff out of which repentance and healing is fashioned. It is a classic example of 'felix culpa'. To experience my need for healing and forgiveness is an inescapable stage in the process of being healed and forgiven. Jesus said he did not come to call the just but sinners. He insisted that it was the sick, not the healthy, who need a doctor. Remembering that the word, saviour, means 'healer', if we are to believe in a Saviour (Healer), we need to experience our own need of salvation (healing). I recently came across a lovely story which fits in beautifully with this theme.

A woman used to draw water daily from a well some distance away. She would carry two large pots to be filled. One pot was cracked and so would be half empty by the time she got back home. After some months the cracked pot plucked up the courage to speak to the woman. 'I feel ashamed! Each day you fill both of us pots with water. But since I am cracked, I am only half full by the time you get home. Isn't that a waste of effort for you?' 'No' replied the woman. 'If you look back along the path I follow, you will see lots of beautiful flowers growing on your side. I planted flower seeds all along your side of the path. Thanks to the water leaking from you, those seeds have been able to grow into a rich variety of beautiful flowers with which I am able to decorate my home. That gives me great pleasure and is a joy to all who come to visit me.'

Maybe God has made us all cracked pots – to his greater honour and glory! As a popular song puts it, 'It's through the cracks that the light shines through'.

(4) The social and ecological implications of a spirituality of growth out of sin
I noted earlier how Aquinas, writing about sin in his *Summa contra Gentiles*, makes the thought-provoking comment: 'God is not offended by us except in so far as we harm ourselves and others' (III, c. 133 - my own paraphrase). Not surprisingly, a similar understanding of sin is found centuries later in his fellow Dominican, Albert Nolan. He writes: 'Sin is an offence against God precisely because it is an offence against people … There is no such thing as a sin that

does not do any harm to anyone … In the last analysis sin is not a transgression of law but a transgression of love' (*God in South Africa*, London, Catholic Institute for International Relations, 1988, p. 38).

This approach to sin leads Nolan to make a statement which is at the heart of his whole presentation: 'Sin becomes visible in suffering' (pp. 38). After repeating this statement a few pages further on, he writes:

> If one were to try to discern the new starting point for modern theology and spirituality in most of the Christian world today, one would have to say that it is suffering. The sufferings of so many millions of people on this planet are one of the most fundamental signs of our times (p. 49).

In other words, Nolan is saying that if we want to know where to find sin in today's world, we need to look at where suffering is to be found. Although he is speaking of suffering brought about by human agency, he is not excluding suffering caused by structural or institutional factors or even, in some cases, suffering caused by so-called accidents and natural disasters. Very often such tragedies have a strong ingredient of human agency in them.

In exploring where God is to be met in today's world, Nolan concludes that the voice of God can be heard in the suffering of the oppressed. Their suffering reveals where the need for salvation is most evident in today's world. Following through all the causal links to the very roots of their suffering reveals to us where conversion is called for. This conversion will bring with it salvation through a changing of the oppressive relationships causing these sufferings. Radical conversion alone suffices and that entails a disowning of the oppressive system and appropriate participation in the processes needed to dismantle the system. Applying this more specifically to the apartheid situation in South Africa in 1988 (the era in which his book was published), Nolan writes: "… unless we, both white and black, face the monstrous reality of evil and suffering in South Africa, we shall not find God and we shall not hear his good news of salvation from sin (p. 57).

P.T. McCormick, in his article, 'Human Sinfulness: Models for a Developing Moral Theology', in *Studia Moralia*, 1988, pp. 61-100, writes in a similar mode to Nolan when he explores the notion of 'cooperative' or 'social' sin. Recognising that we are interdependent social beings, McCormick argues that we need to develop 'an anthropology which transcends the limits of individualism and incorporates the insights of a growing body of evidence about the social character of the human person' (p. 92).

Some structures which are found in the social dimension of human life can with justification be labelled 'sinful' – and this for two reasons. First of all, they are person-injuring. They destroy relationships based on justice and freedom and replace them by 'oppressive political and economic systems, developing pervasive social attitudes or voices of greed, hostility, indifference and narcissism' (p. 93). The result is what McCormick calls 'anti-communities antithetical to the Kingdom of God'. Secondly, these structures do not exist outside of human persons willing to accept and maintain them and working cooperatively within them. It is the actual cooperative effort of the individual members of the group or society which makes up the structure itself. As McCormick writes:

> Cooperation may take a number of forms and the degree of participation or responsibility may differ widely from member to member. However, systemic injustice and oppression depend upon a broad base of diverse sorts of cooperative effort (p. 93).

Moreover, part of their person-injuring character lies in the fact that they can even affect a person's 'core experiences of freedom and dignity'. Consequently, these sinful structures can be self-generating to the extent that people allow themselves to be conditioned into accepting them as either normal or at least inevitable and unavoidable. 'That's life', as the fatalistic saying goes. McCormick puts this point well:

> Members ... respond to their weakened and contextualized freedom with learned patterns of behaviour which support the ongoing relationships of injustice and/or contribute to the progressive disintegration of the group. Such cycles are ongoing, incorporating new members and generations in structures of oppressive and alienating injustice (p. 94).

It could even be argued that social sin is the prime analogue of sin. If this is true, then, as mentioned earlier, the communal celebration of the Sacrament of Reconciliation should be seen as the most fundamental form of the sacrament because it most clearly expresses this social nature of sin and our co-responsibility for it. The liturgical directive that the fully communal Rite 3 can only be used in an emergency when there is a shortage of confessors completely misses the point of communal celebration. Because sin is primarily communal, our owning or confession of sin should normally be communal, and likewise we should recognise that it needs cooperative effort to undo or heal the harmful consequences of our sin. Such communal commitment to the forgiveness of reality is a prerequisite for our forgiveness. So our hope for and belief in forgiveness also needs to be signified and accepted communally rather than individually.

McCormick would go even further and suggest that clinging on to an individualist interpretation of sin itself constitutes a form of 'social sinfulness' and can be compared to the corporate blindness that Jesus challenged in the pharisees (p. 88). Moreover, an individualist interpretation of sin can even be used by groups to 'blind themselves from a sense of sin and responsibility for the structures of injustice which they support'(p. 96). Social sin, on the other hand,

> instead of positing the origin of evil in anonymous and impersonal struc-
> tures, reveals how groups of persons cooperate in projecting their re-
> sponsibility for and participation in systems of injustice on to such
> invisible and anonymous structures of violence and oppression (p. 96).

Jon Sobrino lays great stress on what he calls 'forgiveness of sinful reality' ('Latin America: Place of Sin and Place of Forgiveness', in *Concilium* no. 184 – Special Issue on Forgiveness pp. 45-56 at p. 46). By this he means the eradication of the structures of oppression and violence and the building of new structures of jus-tice (p. 48). He even puts this forgiveness of reality before forgiveness of the sin-ner, though he should not be accused of thinking that a change of structures alone can 'forgive reality'. As he puts it: 'the forgiveness of reality is also a matter of spirituality ... Forgiving reality means loving, loving very much' (pp. 48-49).

Finally, creation theology has been slowly bringing home to the Church that there is another dimension of sin that we need to grow out of. This is sometimes called ecological sin. In fact, it opens our eyes to the disturbing truth that there is an ecological dimension in all sin. Humanity is bound up in an intrinsic and essential relationship of inter-dependence with the rest of creation. There are not two separate and independent ethical criteria op-erating in ecological issues – what is good for humanity and what is good for creation as a whole. To consider creation as a whole is to consider it as including humanity. It is to recognize humanity as creation reaching a higher level of existence, the level of personal and social consciousness. This level of existence does not constitute a breaking away from the rest of creation. Creational health remains an integral element of the good of humanity, just as does bodily health. And vice-versa. In other words, the health of the rest of creation is now dependent on humanity conducting itself in a way which befits its place and responsibility within the whole of creation. Humanity can be a cancerous growth within creation – and some 'deep ecologists' be-lieve it is such already. Or it can be creation reaching out to a yet higher level of life in which it can articulate its hymn of praise and thanksgiving to its creator and reflect in its very way of living the deeply personal and holistic life of its creator. For humanity to distance itself from the rest of cre-ation and lord it over it would be a form of alienation from an integral part of ourselves. At the moment, I believe that we are struggling to find the right language in which to articulate this ecological dimension of sin. It does not seem adequate to say that humanity is nothing more than one part among many within creation, even primus inter pares. Yet to say that is not to deny the fact that most of our ethical discourse tends to be too exclusively anthropocentric. It fails to do justice to the oneness of the whole of creation which is being revealed to us through the most recent discoveries in a whole range of scientific disciplines.

(5) Conclusion

The words of Jesus, 'I have come to call not the just but sinners' go hand in hand with his other words, 'I have come that you might have life, and have it more abundantly'. The title of this chapter is 'Saints or sinners? Towards a spirituality of growth out of sin'. I hope that what I have written above has been faithful to the Christian belief that we are both saints and sinners and that a Christian spirituality needs to do justice to both these dimensions. I have tried to show that the notion of 'growth out of sin' can be very helpful at a pastoral level.

Today people are fond of quoting the words of St Irenaeus, 'The glory of God is the human person fully alive'. Perhaps, that truth might be even better expressed through the language of growth, 'The glory of God is the human person becoming more fully alive'. A similar adaptation might even be made to the traditional phrase 'everlasting life'. A spirituality of growth might prefer to speak of 'becoming everlastingly more alive'.

Jack Mahoney SJ, 'Christianity in Evolution'
An online book review

This is the original text of my review of Jack Mahoney SJ, Christianity in Evolution (Washington DC, Georgetown University Press, 2011). The review appeared in a modified form in the Jesuit online website, ThinkingFaith.

I have been a fan of Jack Mahoney's writings over many years. His *The Making of Moral Theology* is acknowledged as a masterpiece by moral theologians worldwide. However, the book which had the deepest impact on me was his Bioethics and Belief. In it he describes theology as 'making faith-sense of experience and experience-sense of faith'. That has been an inspiration to me ever since. As he notes himself in the Introduction to his *Christianity in Evolution*, it was that insight which motivated him to undertake this major work:

> Because our common human experience is being faced with a major advance in our scientific understanding of human origins, intellectual integrity invites us to place that experience alongside our past and present

religious beliefs, and in the process to hope to cast light on both ... the dialectical activity of submitting experience to the bar of belief and of submitting belief to the bar of experience is today a requirement of every believer on pain of leaving their experience unanchored and their belief unsubstantiated (p. xiii).

Attempting to do theology with integrity in an evolutionary context leads Mahoney to a number of conclusions which many readers may find disturbing, to put it mildly! Yet he does not pull his punches:

I further argue that trying to preserve the traditional beliefs in original sin, the fall of humanity, and the death of Jesus as an expiatory sacrifice to appease an offended God, whether these beliefs are maintained in their traditional form or are subjected to various modernizing attempts to make them more acceptable, serves only to strain the belief of believers and the credulity of nonbelievers (p.xii).

Nevertheless, Mahoney is not trying to disturb but to strengthen people's faith. In fact, it could be argued that the line of thought he is exploring could open out completely new vistas to whatever is meant by 'the new evangelisation'. If we believe, as Benedict XVI clearly does, that at the heart of every person is a deep yearning to discover the full meaning of who we are as human persons, Mahoney is suggesting that the only thing that will satisfy that hunger is an understanding of the truths of our faith which is able to feel at home with the truths of evolution. He stresses this with regard to the riches evolution can bring to our understanding of the central doctrine of the Incarnation.

In the evolutionary approach, the creative energy of divine being is viewed as entirely immanent within all nondivine being, welling up within it like a spring of water in the process impelling noncreated being to transcend itself progressively in a variety of ways in the course of the onward evolutionary march of God's creative purpose. So much so that it is possible to consider that in one instance the divine presence and immanence in creative being reached such a peak of intensity that God actually became a human being, Jesus of Nazareth (p. 117).

This helps us to see Jesus as the summit of creation. I am writing this review on the Vigil of the Feast of Christ the King. The New Translation of the Missal has changed the title of this feast to Christ, King of the Universe. What an inspired choice!

Mahoney's book is remarkable for the extensive reading and research needed to give substance to his line of argument and for the courage he displays in challenging us, in the light of evolutionary truths, to look again at some of the ways our faith has been expressed. Some more specific comments:

I found the introduction and first chapter immensely attractive and enjoyable reading. I struggled with chapter two. It made heavy reading – for me at least. I warmed very much to what he was saying about sharing in the life of the Trinity. That has come home to me more and more in the last ten years or so. No mystical experiences or anything like that, just a deep conviction. However, I am not happy with Mahoney's use of the word 'altruism' for that inner life of the Trinity. It is far too bland and abstract. There is no life in it. It fails to move me with wonder and passion. It sounds like a philosophical theory rather than the red hot centre of the whole of creation, let alone the inner life of the Trinity. I'm sure the 'love' family of vocabulary could offer a richer and more appropriate word. The alternative Collect for Trinity Sunday puts it beautifully: 'You reveal yourself in the depths of our being, drawing us to share in your life and your love'. The omission of that prayer from the new Missal is a sad loss.

Death and Resurrection – Mahoney suggests that an evolutionary theology:

> proposes that the motive for the Word becoming flesh was not to save humanity from any inherited congenital sinfulness; it was for Christ to lead and conduct the human species through the common evolutionary fate of individual extinction to a new level of living with God. Nor was this done by the offering of Christ as an expiatory sacrifice to placate an injured God; it was achieved by Christ's freely confronting death and winning through to a new phase of existence to be imparted to his fellow humans in their evolutionary destiny to share fully in the life of God (pp. 14-15).

Sacrifice – I have always felt very uncomfortable with referring to the Mass as a sacrifice. Sadly, I note that the term is used even more in the new translation! Nevertheless, I suspect that what Mahoney is saying on this issue will raise loads of objections.

I feel comfortable with Mahoney's position on Original Sin, the Fall, Atonement, Justification and similar concepts which he suggests no longer sit comfortably in an evolutionary context. His description of sin in an evolutionary context is very helpful: 'Sin emerges as humanity's yielding to evolutionary selfishness and declining to accept the invitation to self-transcendence: it is a refusal to transcend oneself in the interests of others' (p. 43). Put like that, it makes sense of Paul VI's claim that 'the world is sick' (*Populorum Progressio*, no. 66) and his diagnosis of its sickness as 'the lack of brotherhood among individuals and peoples'. I also liked Mahoney's comment: 'What people in today's culture need most is not the recovery of a sense of sin but the acquiring of a sense of purpose in their lives' (p. 66).

The New Translation of the Missal does not sit easily with much of what Mahoney is proposing. Its more frequent description of the Eucharist as a 'sacrifice', is a case in point, especially when coupled with such words as expiatory or propitiation. Some might object – what about the ancient piece of Christian wisdom, 'Lex orandi, lex credendi'? I presume Mahoney would argue that our 'prayers' also have to make sense in an evolutionary age. Otherwise, we are just 'babbling as the pagans do!'

There is another issue also linked to the new missal and the principles of translation on which it is based. To be consistent with Mahoney's approach, rather than going back to an archaic, tired 'more sacred' form of words for the liturgy, perhaps a wiser criterion for translation would have been to use a form of language which combines beauty to the ear, simplicity for the tongue, richness in symbolism, while at the same time doing full justice to our understanding of the wonders of God's ongoing creation in our evolutionary age. That would be more in keeping with the 'new evangelisation'.

Though I can see where Mahoney is coming from, I feel uneasy about his suggesting:

> The possibility that belief in hell need not continue to be maintained in an evolutionary theology if those who are not destined to enter with Christ into the new phase of rise existence will not be condemned to everlasting suffering but rather will be allowed to cease to exist at death (p. 147-148).

Finding an eternal hell of punishment impossible to reconcile with a loving God, I can see the attractiveness of Mahoney's suggestion. However, I find Julian of Norwich's, 'All will be well and all manner of things will be well', more in tune with a God of love and compassion!

I have the bad habit of highlighting passages I find particularly memorable. In Mahoney's book, the biggest concentration of highlighting appears from p. 62 onwards, especially pp. 89-94, 115-122, 127-138, and the whole of chapter seven which is outstanding.

This book will certainly arouse a lot of discussion and there will be plenty of questions raised by some of the positions he adopts. Despite that, I believe that it is a very important contribution to the development of theology in our evolutionary age. Benedict XVI is not the only one who is showing amazing resilience in his advancing years.

CHAPTER SIXTEEN

I Believe in a Sinful Church

Chapter six of my book, 'From a Parish Base', bore the title, 'Co-responsibility and Accountability in a Sinful Church'. In line with my 'personal odyssey' theme, I think the title of this piece brings out much more clearly that it is within the Catholic Church, warped and sinful though it is, that I have received the gift of faith. The original version of this article was first published in The Way, 1993, pp. 106-116, under the title, 'Do we believe in a Church of Sinners?' I have since revised the text. Some readers may feel that this text could do with a further revision to take account of the clergy sex abuse scandal and its mishandling by some Church authorities. Rather than embark on such a revision of a revision, I treat that horrendous issue separately in an unpublished new essay later in this section, 'Is there a link between Sex Abuse and Systemic God Abuse in the Church?'

Raphael Gallagher, writing with the Irish scene in mind, takes a very interesting stance on the issue of the sinfulness of the Church in his article, In the Noise of War the Word Got Lost, in The Furrow, 1997, pp. 391-398.

Each time we assemble as Church to celebrate eucharist we begin by acknowledging our need for forgiveness; and we go on to prepare to share in holy communion by making a common declaration: 'Lord, I am not worthy …'. Since Vatican II tells us that 'the real nature of the true Church' is revealed in the liturgy (cf. SC, no. 2), it is clear that we are committed to a belief that we are a Church of sinners.

To say that we believe in a Church of sinners can be understood in a very weak sense i.e. it is within a Church of sinners that we believe. This would be saying no more than that the Church, though holy in itself, is made up of members who individually are more or less sinful. This would imply that the holiness of the Church is not affected by the sinfulness of its members. It exists on a higher plane beyond the reach of our personal sinfulness. In his two essays, The Church of Sinners and The Sinful Church in the Decrees of Vatican II (*Theological Investigations*, London, Darton, Longman & Todd, 1969, vol six, chapters seventeen and eighteen), Rahner reminds us that such a view is contrary to Catholic belief. There is no metaphysical Church which has an existence of its own, separate from the flesh and blood men and women who are its members. We, the members of the Church, actually are the Church. Our sins are sins of the Church. They do not merely weaken the Church's witness to God's call to universal holiness. Through us, the Church is actually the subject of sin.

Some Christians might feel uneasy with such a stark attribution of sinfulness to the Church and might be tempted to tone it down a little. After all, the creed professes belief in a Church which is 'holy', not 'sinful'. Would it not be sufficient to admit that this "holy" Church is, in its historical existence, defiled by the sins of its members but that, when the overall picture is seen, it is the holiness of the Church that predominates, not the sinfulness of its members?

Such a position is too complacent about the sins of the members of the Church. Christians who sin, sin as Christians. If, to use Paul's metaphor, Christians are members of the body of Christ, Christians who sin make the body of Christ the subject of sin. If that is so, surely it is horrendous. For Paul the horror of it is vividly expressed in the question he poses to the Church in Corinth: 'Do you think I can take parts of Christ's body and join them to the body of a prostitute?' (1 Cor 6:15).

In the course of history some Christians have tried to evade this whole issue by claiming that sinners do not really belong to the Church. They are only nominal Christians. In reality, their sin has either put them outside the Church or else has shown them up as never really belonging to the true Church. Movements for Church reform down through the centuries have often been tempted to adopt this position. In its wisdom the Church has always recognised that it is contrary to our Gospel-based faith to say that sinners do not belong to the Church.

This is a very salutary reaction. It means that the Church cannot be excused from tackling its own sinfulness. The sinfulness of the Church is a reality that cannot be denied. It is also a tragedy. The question every Christian has to face, if he or she really believes in the Church, is 'how am I to respond to the sinfulness of the Church I believe in? What am I going to do about it?' An obvious answer to that question is 'Physician, heal yourself'. In other words, each of us has to face up to his or her own sinfulness, since that is my own personal contribution to the sinfulness of the Church. Nevertheless, our concern for the sinfulness of the Church must look beyond our own sinfulness. The Church is more than a collection of individual Christians.

Sinner – an ambiguous term

Our usage of the word 'sinner' tends to be ambiguous. Perhaps it might help to make a distinction between the positive and negative ways Christians use the word.

For Christians 'sin' is fundamentally a positive word. Its Christian meaning is inextricably bound up with our belief in a God of healing and forgiveness. Hence, the very 'owning' of one's sinfulness (and sin) before God is a transformative act. It is the first step on the road to conversion. To acknowledge that I am a sinner and to 'own' my sin before God is to confess my need for forgiveness and healing. The Gospel parable assures us that the person who, with the tax-collector, sincerely prays: 'Lord, be merciful to me a sinner' returns home 'at rights with God'.

'Sinner' used in this positive way should not be taken to mean 'someone who used to be a sinner but is so no longer'. That is not what the tax-collector means when he prays, 'Lord, be merciful to me, a sinner.' He really is a sinner and he recognises himself as such. That is precisely why he recognises his need for the compassion and forgiveness of God. Even the words of Jesus to the woman taken in adultery, 'Go, and sin no more', are not an indication that she is no longer a sinner. She leaves Jesus a sinner, but a forgiven sinner, as do the many others who hear his life-giving words 'Go, your sins are forgiven.

However, the word 'sinner' can be used by Christians also in a negative way. A striking example of a sinner in this negative sense is the Pharisee in the parable who prided himself on his righteous life and who thanked God that he was not like the rest of humankind. The Gospel tells us that he did not return home at rights with God. There is no indication in the parable that there is any major ethical misconduct in his life. His sin is at a deeper level than ethical mis-conduct. He personifies the people to whom Jesus is addressing this parable – 'people who prided themselves on being virtuous and despised everyone else.' (Lk 18:9) It is this group of people who come under this negative use of the word 'sinner'. It is as though the only sin that ties the hands of God's forgive-ness is the sin of grounding one's self-worth on a belief in the non-worth of everyone else.

Sinners, in the positive sense mentioned earlier, clearly belong to the Church. No one would have any problem with that. What about Christians who are sinners in the negative sense outlined above? Do they belong to the Church?

Fidelity to the Gospel must surely make us recognise that they do. Yet at the same time the Gospels portray Jesus as being radically opposed to this group of sinners. What are we to make of this? Perhaps it highlights the paradox in their situation. They belong to the Church and yet they are a living contradic-tion to the faith of the Church. Maybe the pastoral approach to these sinners has to reflect this paradox. At one and the same time, the Church has to both 'own' and 'disown' them and their sinfulness.

This is consistent with the process of conversion in the case of 'sinners' in the positive Christian sense. Sinners in that sense, when they 'own' their sin-fulness and their sins, are both 'owning' and 'disowning' them at the same time. They are acknowledging that these sins truly are theirs. In owning their sins, they are recognising that these sins belong to them, they are part of their reality. Yet they are also acknowledging that, as disciples of Christ, they must also 'dis-own' these sins since they contradict what Christ stands for. That is why they want to 'die' to sin and be liberated from this side of their lives. Admittedly, the healing process might take a life-time – and beyond! Yet the initial act of both 'owning' and 'disowning' their sin is indispensable. Without that first step the healing process cannot begin.

This conversion process is short-circuited in the case of 'sinners' in the negative sense? As long as they remain enclosed within their self-inflicted blindness, there is no possibility that they will 'disown' their sin since they refuse even to 'own' it. This is where the Church has to step in. As well as 'owning' their sin, the Church must also 'disown' it, precisely because it is also the Church's sin. In the case of conduct which, though wrong, does not involve any major violation of the dignity of human persons, it is probably sufficient for such 'disowning' to be implicit in the ordinary run-of-the-mill moral teaching of the Church as commonly recognised by people. However, where more gross violations of human dignity are involved, the Church might feel obliged to 'own' the sin by a very explicit act of 'naming' it (and even the sinner, in some instances) and at the same time 'disowning' it by declaring it to be contradictory to Christian life and witness.

A very striking instance of such 'owning' and 'disowning' by the Church is found in a sermon preached in 1511 on the island of Hispaniola (the modern-day Dominican Republic). The preacher, Fray Antonio de Montesinos, a Dominican friar, was addressing a congregation made up of the Governor of the island and all the Christian notables who were making themselves rich by their exploitation of the native Indians. Taking as his text 'I am the voice of one crying in the desert', he began:

> I am the voice of Christ crying in the desert of this island. It is essential that you listen ... with your entire heart and your entire being ... the message of Christ to you is this: you are all in a state of mortal sin. You are living in mortal sin and will die in it, because of your cruelty and your tyrannical attitude towards innocent people ... are they, too, not human beings? ... are you not obliged to love them as yourselves? (*Catholic International*, vol 3, no. 19, p. 936).

It would be hard to imagine a more forthright condemnation of a group of people. The language is blunt, the judgement is clear and unconditional. Nevertheless, when this sermon is read in our own day when there is more readiness to acknowledge the collusion and even support of the Church for the appalling injustice committed against the Indians, it stands out like a beacon in the darkness. Fray Antonio had the integrity and courage to name the horrendous sin which was being committed against the Indians. And the context of his naming was the gathering of the community to celebrate the Eucharist. The Governor and the Christian nobility of the island had gathered to thank God for all the blessings they had received. I suspect that there would have been no Indians present at that gathering. The Christian invaders would have considered them 'not our kind'. No doubt, too, they would have thought of them as 'not God's kind' either, since they were sunk in idolatry and outside the grace of God.

These Christian nobles, like the Pharisee in the parable, would have thanked God that they were not 'like the rest of mankind' and particularly that they were not like these Indians.

To gather in eucharist in such a frame of mind is a horrendous sacrilege. Such people, in the words of the parable, would not go home again 'at rights with God'. Fray Antonio says the same thing in different language when he tells them they will go home 'in a state of mortal sin'.

What so outraged Fray Antonio was that this eucharistic gathering of Christians refused to own their blatantly obvious sin. As long as they refused to take that step, they were not en route for conversion. They were facing in the opposite direction. They were in a state of mortal sin. No doubt, the pastoral intention behind his sermon was salvific. By naming their sin with such candour (and he was 'one of them'), he was hoping that they might be stirred into recognising the inhumanity they were involved in. His naming their sin was an invitation to them to own it themselves.

It could probably be argued that some papal encyclicals, particularly in the social field, fit into this process of 'owning' and 'disowning' gross sins of violating the dignity of human persons. So too do prophetic statements of local hierarchies and Church groups when they speak out against violations of human dignity in their own countries. Such 'owning' and 'disowning' is clearly seen as an integral element in proclaiming the Gospel of God's love for all women and men. This is part of the Church's public witness. Of course, whether it has any credibility will largely depend on how faithful the Church is to the Gospel it is proclaiming. Paul VI made this point very clearly in his Apostolic Letter on Evangelisation: 'People today listen more willingly to witnesses than to teachers, and if they do listen to teachers, it is because they are witnesses' (no. 41). This salutary warning leads us to look at the credibility of the Church's own life and conduct. Granted that it is a Church of sinners, does the 'owning' and 'disowning' of sin by the Church in its own life and conduct give a credible witness to those outside the Church to whom it is proclaiming the gospel?

Difficulties with the credibility of the Church's public witness
In the eyes of many outside the Church, including those sympathetically disposed towards it, there is a major problem about the credibility of the Church's public witness. This is due to the fact that the current categorisation of certain groups of people in the Church as 'sinners' seems to run counter to our present-day perception of what constitutes inhumanity. Many who come into these categories are not perceived by people today as involved in any gross violation of the dignity of the human person. In fact, in many instances they are seen more as 'victims of sin' since it is their own dignity as human persons which has been violated.

Among such people are women and men who have had to face the shattering experience of recognising that the marriage on which they have staked their lives has failed and whose painful pilgrimage through a kind of death towards resurrection has eventually led them into a second marriage; or, again, gay men and lesbian women who have struggled with their sexual identity in the face of incomprehension, disapproval and even outright hostility from many in society (perhaps their own family in some cases), who, in their loneliness and hopelessness, may have sought some kind of passing relief in a series of transient relationships and who have eventually found peace, a positive direction in life and genuine love in a more permanent gay or lesbian relationship which, in turn, is sustained and deepened by the sexual expression of their love; or married couples who have found that methods of contraception condemned by the Church have helped them deepen their love for each other and their children by giving them the opportunity to make love when appropriate without being haunted by the fear of another pregnancy.

In their different ways, all these people have been made to feel that they are not fully accepted in the Church they regard as their home. They even experience this condemnation as a form of being 'disowned' by the Church.

For instance, those who are living in a second marriage, unless they are widowed or their first marriage has been annulled, are officially barred from receiving communion. Gay couples in faithful relationships are 'disowned' by official Church teaching in very strong terms. In fact, the recent letter of the CDF to the US bishops even justifies discrimination against them in the area of housing and certain forms of employment. The implication clearly is that they constitute a danger to society and are likely to corrupt the morals of the young. Those who cannot accept the teaching of *Humanae Vitae* and who find the practice of contraception beneficial to their marriage are told by the pope: 'What is called into question by the rejection of this teaching is the very idea of the holiness of God' (quoted in Bernard Häring, *My Witness for the Church*, New York, Paulist Press, p. 227).

Of course, the point will be made that there is no problem for any of these people provided they are prepared to both 'own' and 'disown' their sin. If those in a second marriage are prepared to live as 'brother and sister', they can receive communion. If gays and lesbians renounce their lifestyle and practise celibacy, they will be fully accepted. If couples practising contraception would only take advantage of the enormous advances in the reliability and availability of natural family planning, the Church would have no moral objection to their deliberately avoiding having any further children.

However, the problem is not as simple as this solution seems to suggest. For the most part, these people have really tried to 'own' and 'disown' whatever sin may perhaps have been involved in the tragic situations they have lived through. In no way are they denying that they are sinners. Many of them feel their sinfulness very profoundly – but in the positive sense mentioned earlier. They can identify very deeply with the prayer of the tax-collector 'Lord, be merciful to me, a sinner'.

However what they cannot 'disown' is the gift of new life they are now experiencing. It runs counter to their own experience for such couples in a good second marriage or in a life-giving homosexual partnership to be told that they are 'living in sin', or for married couples to be told that their contraceptive-aided love-making is seriously offensive to God. Such people cannot 'disown' as sinful something which they actually experience and 'own' as grace-filled. Far from 'living in sin', they believe they are forgiven sinners living in grace. And they are grateful to God for this gift.

It is sometimes argued that the conduct of these categories of people has to be publicly 'disowned' because it is a living contradiction to the Church's moral witness. In reality, what scandalizes many people outside the Church, as well as within, is the fact that a Church of sinners which professes belief in a God of forgiveness and compassion seems to condemn groups of people for whom most in our society would feel great respect and understanding.

The sinfulness of office-holders in the Church

As Christians our love for the Church inclines us to presume the integrity of office-holders in the Church, especially since, from the nature of the case, they are usually bishops and priests. Hence, while theoretically we recognise the possibility of their sinning, our natural tendency is to deny, or at least play down, sin on the part of office-holders. I am not referring to sin in their personal lives but in the exercise of their duties of office.

There is no lack of criticism of office-holders in the Church. Like all who carry the heavy burden of exercising authority, they are targets for criticism from all quarters. However, we do not tend to speak of 'sin' with regard to the way they exercise their office. Perhaps this reticence betrays a kind of spiritual immaturity. We find our security in the Church. Hence, we do not like to think of those in positions of authority as capable of letting us down by actually sinning in the decisions they make.

Sinful behaviour means acting in a way which violates human dignity, either that of ourselves or of others. Quite literally it is irresponsible behaviour since it is failing to respond adequately to the needs of the human persons with whom we are dealing.

All sin is inhumanity in some form or other. In the past decade there have been an increasing number of allegations of serious inhumanity in the way office-holders at various levels in the Church have exercised of their authority. The criteria used for the appointment of bishops and the actual appointments made in a not inconsiderable number of cases have been regarded as irresponsible and hence inhuman. The same has been alleged with regard to the way some female religious congregations have been treated as they have struggled to reorder their constitutions in response to their original charism and the needs of the present day. Something similar is alleged to have happened to some male congregations wanting to return to the 'non-clerical' vision of their founder. Numerous theologians of acknowledged competence and integrity who represent the breadth of theological thinking in the Church as a whole appear to have been hounded in a most inhuman fashion by a CDF, even to the extent of silencing them and demanding the destruction of their books. If these allegations are true, and I am inclined to think they are, the situation is serious.

However, the core of the inhumanity alleged to be currently operative among some office-holders in the Church, especially in some of the Vatican congregations, lies deeper than these particular instances. They are the symptoms, rather than the root cause.

The root cause is perceived by many people as being a mindset found among some powerful Vatican office-holders which is not open to views which challenge its own position. Any listening that takes place is not for the purpose of learning but only in order to refute. Local Churches struggling to bring about more genuine inculturation of the Gospel or who are trying to interpret the Gospel in the light of the signs of the times as experienced in their part of the world find their efforts emasculated by curial directives or by manipulation on the part of some curial congregations or officials. According to first-hand reports, the curial manipulation of the 1992 meeting of CELAM seems to have been a blatant example of such an irresponsible and inhuman exercise of authority. Issues which, in the Church at large throughout the world are considered to be burning issues of pastoral urgency are not even allowed on the agenda for discussion – optional celibacy for priests, the ordination of women, not forgetting the issues mentioned in the previous section, contraception, remarriage after divorce and homosexuality.

This kind of inhumanity on the part of some office-holders is beginning to drive many in the Church to desperation. It even provoked such a saintly moral theologian as the late Bernard Häring to overcome his natural reluctance to criticise the Vatican publicly. His little book, *My Witness for the Church* (Paulist Press, 1992), was extremely frank and hard-hitting in its criticisms of the mentality of some office-holders in the Vatican. He felt an obligation to 'do all that is humanly possible to encourage a change, a transformation of the structures and mentalities which are not gospel-centred' and even went so far as to say: 'I believe that we have arrived at the point where it can no longer be disputed that we are in a pathological situation' (p. 90).

To believe in a Church of sinners is to recognise that there is a real possibility of sin in the office-holders of the Church. Consequently, a concern for the good of the Church should make us alert to situations where this possibility may seem to be actually realised. This should not be condemned out of hand as a negative, hyper-critical or disloyal attitude towards the Church. Of course, it is possible that some who criticise office-holders in the Church may in reality be dumping on them unresolved problems from their earlier years. However, that is merely a pathological version of what is fundamentally a very positive and healthy love of a Church which is honestly acknowledged to be a Church of sinners. I interpret Bernard Häring's impassioned criticisms as an expression of such a love of the Church.

Granting the real possibility of sin in the office-holders of the Church, such sin, when it occurs, contradicts the public witness of the Church and so needs to be publicly 'owned' and 'disowned'. If this is done by the office-holders themselves, there is no problem. In fact, 1996 and 1997 have seen a break-through in the Church in this regard. The bishops of England Wales issued a public apology to divorced Catholics for any hurt they had suffered as a result of pastoral insensitivity on the part of the Catholic community (cf. *Briefing*, 28 April 1994, p. 8); a group of French bishops owned the shame of the failure of their local Churches during the time of the Nazi occupation (*Origins*, 16 October 1997, pp. 301-305); on 1 November 1997 Pope John Paul II apologised for Chris-tian anti-Jewish prejudice (cf. *The Tablet*, 8 November 1997, p. 1447) and similar sentiments were expressed, with specific reference to the Holocaust, by the new Papal Nuncio to Britain, Archbishop Pablo Puente, in one of his first public ad-dresses to a mainly Jewish audience: 'At the beginning of the third millennium, the Catholic Church is committed to an important examination of conscience, of clarification and of profound self-criticism regarding the past' (cf. *The Tablet*, 6 December 1997, p. 1555). When, on the contrary, Church authorities refuse to 'own' their sin and even insist on denying it, it needs to be named and 'owned' by other members of the Church, so that it can then be publicly 'disowned' for the sake of the public witness of the Church. However, a catch-22 situation arises when the office-holders concerned claim to be judge and jury in their own case. This is really what happens when they claim the right to set the agenda regarding what issues are open for discussion in the Church. The catch-22 situation is intensified when they attempt to make lesser office-holders promise under oath to keep to the restricted agenda they have set. The ultimate irony occurs when they publicly 'disown' the very people who have the prophetic insight and courage to 'own' and 'disown' the Church-injuring sins of these office-holders. Many felt that the enforced retirement of the Australian, Bishop William Morris pf Toowoomba in May 2011 was such a public 'disown-ing' of a prophetic pastor.

Is 'sin' too harsh a word to be using in this context? I do not think so. My intention is not to vilify these office-holders or attribute personal malice to them. Sin is a word with all kinds of positive reverberations for Christians. To speak of sin with regard to office-holders in the Church is to acknowledge their solidarity with the rest of us. Unlike what we say of Christ in the Fourth

Eucharistic Prayer, they are like us in all things, including sin. To make sin a
taboo word in speaking of them is to refuse to face human reality. It also shows
a lack of faith in the power of God's healing spirit active in the Church – and
a lack of faith in the office-holders in question to be open to that spirit.

The Church we believe in – a Church of sinners, but also a holy Church
Although most of this piece has been looking at the sinfulness of the Church, I
would like to end on a much more positive note. God is the one in whom we
believe. To believe in the Church is to believe in God acting in and through the
Church. To borrow a phrase from Rahner, the Holy Spirit is the dynamic element in the Church. That is why it is totally inadequate to counter criticisms
about the sinfulness of the Church by saying that, on balance, there is more
good than evil in the Church. Our belief in the holiness of the Church is not a
judgement of proportionality. It is belief in the living presence and action of
God in the Church. That is why any pessimism or fatalism with regard to the
Church must be 'disowned' as unchristian. It stands in contradiction to belief
in the Church. While we must 'own' the sinfulness of the Church – and each of
us has a special responsibility to 'own' his or her personal contribution to that
sinfulness – we must not be content to settle for that sinfulness and give it whatever house-room it wants in the Church. Our belief in the Holy Spirit, present
and active in the Church, commits us strongly to 'disown' that sinfulness. To
believe in the Church is to have a confident hope that the Church can become
a truer image of the one whose very name it 'owns' by calling itself Christian.
Hence, we must always have the faith and courage to 'disown' whatever is unchristian in the Church. This must be the case even, or rather especially, when
what is deemed to be unchristian is the way office-holders in the Church are
exercising their authority. The words of Cardinal Ratzinger, quoted by
Leonardo Boff in a letter to his Franciscan Provincial (cf. *The Tablet*, 17 October
1992, p. 1309), might provide an appropriate conclusion to this article:

> Is it unconditionally a sign of better times that today's theologians no
> longer dare to speak prophetically? Is it not rather a sign of a feeble love
> which no longer makes the heart burn with holy zeal for God's cause (2
> Cor 12:2)? It is the sign of a love which has become apathetic and which
> no longer dares to make the painful commitment on behalf of and in
> favour of the beloved. The person who does not feel wounded by the
> shortcomings of a friend, who no longer suffers because of them and
> who does not fight to change them, no longer loves. Should this also
> apply to our relationship with the Church?

CHAPTER SEVENTEEN

The Gift of General Absolution

A greatly admired priest and theologian, the late Hugh Lavery, repeatedly used to make the point that the primary form of the Sacrament of Reconciliation was that involving General Confession and Absolution. He argued this on the grounds that sin is predominantly social, rather than something purely individual. We sin precisely as members of the one Body of Christ. Our sins have an impact on the whole body. Since Vatican II, we are much more conscious of the social dimensions of sin. Hence, our reconciliation should be with the whole community. This is brought out much more powerfully in a General Absolution Service.

A beautiful idea! But it will be objected that such General Absolution is forbidden by Church Law. The eminent canon lawyer, Ladislas Orsy SJ, examines this point in a very thorough article he wrote in Theological Studies, 1984, pp. 676-689. He points out that the rules laid down in the Code of Canon Law on integrity and confession of individual sins all start from one fundamental principle, namely, that they only apply to those who are 'conscious of being guilty of mortal sin' (p. 678). That being the case, he implies that for penitents approaching the Sacrament of Reconciliation as a kind of 'growth sacrament' e.g. for deepening our lifelong ongoing conversion at times like Lent and Advent, the law does not forbid the use of General Absolution. It is worth quoting the whole of the passage from which that implication can be legitimately drawn:

> *The Code explicitly states that individual confession and absolution is the only ordinary means of forgiveness for those who know themselves to be guilty of mortal sin. It follows that if there is a group of penitents among whom, for all intent and purposes, no mortal sin can be assumed, there is no prohibition against the general absolution as the ordinary form of the sacrament (p.685).*

John Paul II's Apostolic Letter, Misericordia Dei, (7 April 2002) does not nullify Orsy's conclusion. Misercirdia Dei is not changing the law. It is simply repeating even more forcefully the legal requirement that Orsy has emphasised, i.e. 'The Code explicitly states that individual confession and absolution is the only ordinary means of forgiveness for those who know themselves to be guilty of mortal sin.'

From my own pastoral experience in three different parishes, I am convinced that General Absolution Services fulfil a deep pastoral need felt by many Catholics. Orsy's article has reassured me that my instinct – and that of so many other priests – is sound and that this practice is based on solid pastoral theology and fully in line with the spirit of Vatican II. The following is a short piece I wrote in the Skelmersdale Deanery Newsletter to reassure parishioners that the practice was fully in order.

The people of Skelmersdale are great, but we are not perfect. That is why Lent is an important time for us. We may be trying to be loving and caring to each other – but we all know how often we fail. So we have to be continually looking for new ways of caring and loving. This makes us aware of opportunities we have missed in the past and stirs us on to improve things for the future. We all need to listen to the Lord's personal call to conversion to each of us this Lent. We all need to try to understand what kind of change God is calling for in us and in our way of living. Conversion is an ongoing process of growth out of the influence of sin in our lives.

Although we are not perfect, neither are we so totally self-centred that we have turned away completely from God coming to us in the needs of other people. Probably, in the lives of many of us there may have been occasions in the past, hopefully rare, when we felt we had wandered away radically from the straight and narrow. Yet when we think of most people we know, we would not presume, if their lives are anything to go by, that that is their normal position before God. Most seem to be trying, with more or less success, to be generous and caring. Perhaps quite a few are not regular Church-goers but the Gospel does not suggest that Church attendance is the prime criterion for Christian living. If real love and generosity are active in their lives, God's Spirit is there and it would be untrue to describe them as radically turned away from God – in other words, in a state of mortal sin.

So Lent is a time for growth and most Lenten Confessions are growth experiences rather than *basic conversions* from radical sin. On a very unique occasion (e.g. time of radical personal conversion of life) individuals may find that they need to make a deeply personal confession. That is a very different experience to the regular individual confession. Few in Skelmersdale these days seem to find individual confession a helpful way of celebrating the sacrament. For most folk here a communal service of Reconciliation is the most meaningful way of celebrating the sacrament of God's forgiveness.

Some might complain that this is simply providing people with an easy way out! In a General Absolution Service we communally focus our minds for nearly an hour on the wonder of God's gratuitous and forgiving love of us and the implications of that for our family and social relationships – and beyond. It is far from obvious how that is an 'easy option' in comparison with an anonymous individual confession lasting little more than a few minutes! Others might say that General Absolution provides a get-out from the shame of personal acknowledgement of sin to someone else. In the Gospels a warm welcome and loving acceptance seem to be more central features of experiencing God's forgiveness than the sinner's sense of shame.

Maybe the reason why people come in such numbers to communal services of reconciliation, especially with general absolution, is that they find this a much more helpful way of celebrating and experiencing God loving forgiveness. Perhaps they also find the communal exercise a great stimulus to growth, tuning in with their instinct that sin, though personal, always affects other people.

There is a misconception that General Absolution is forbidden by Church law except in some very rare cases. As the eminent canonist, Ladislas Orsy SJ, has pointed out, the requirement of individual confession applies only to a penitent 'conscious of being guilty of mortal sin' (canon 960). Consequently, the other laws prohibiting General Absolution are to be interpreted as applying only to such penitents. They do not apply to the devotional use of the sacrament.

Sessions of General Absolution are popular with many Catholics as part of their preparation for Christmas and Easter. They find such celebrations very meaningful in the way they foster an awareness of God's gracious and forgiving love which lies at the heart of these two feasts. These celebrations would certainly qualify as devotional celebrations of the sacrament. They are 'growth experiences' rather than occasions of radical conversion from serious sin.

Many of us were brought up thinking that mortal sin was commonplace, almost as though the normal state for most of us was one of rejection of God and by God. Vatican II has called us back to our Gospel roots of a God inviting each of us to share in the life and love of God. That is our vocation, the journey or pilgrimage we are making together. Our personal stories are part of the love story of God's own self. To gather as fellow pilgrims to celebrate the forgiving and healing love of God communally with General Absolution is a very moving and grace-filled experience. Thank God, the law of the Church has the pastoral wisdom not to forbid such celebrations, despite mistaken ideas on this point. Sadly, a law designed to be pastorally helpful in the exceptional case where a person's radical conversion experience needs individual care is often misinterpreted as applying to the more normal situation where people's celebration of the sacrament is about their continuing to grow out of sin and selfishness into a deeper love of God and neighbour.

CHAPTER EIGHTEEN

Pastoral Care of the Divorced and Remarried

The first book I had published after my doctoral dissertation was Divorce and Second Marriage: Facing the Challenge,(Original Edition, Collins, London, 1982; New & Expanded Edition, Geoffrey Chapman, London, 1996). It was the result of considerable theological pastoral research. I wrote to many bishops conferences round the world asking what was their pastoral policy regarding sacraments to the divorced remarried. I made the same enquiry to numerous canon lawyers and moral theologians, including some of their official bodies. In my adult education work at Upholland Northern Institute I also listened to the personal stories of many divorced and remarried Catholics and their priests. This was fully in-line with Cardinal Hume's wise statement that the experience of married people is an important 'theological resource'. That was why the witness of the 1980 National Pastoral Congress made such an impact on me. It also affected deeply my own Archbishop, Derek Worlock. So much so, that a couple of years later he made the following impassioned statement to the 1982 Synod on the Family in Rome:

> *Despite our best efforts, some marriages fail and family unity is destroyed. To these victims of misfortune, not necessarily of personal sin, or of sin which has not been forgiven, the Church, both universal and local, must have a healing ministry of consolation.*
>
> *Moreover, many pastors nowadays are faced with Catholics whose first marriages have perished and who have now a second and more stable (if legally only civil) union in which they seek to bring up a new family. Often such persons, especially in their desire to help their children, long for the restoration of full Eucharistic communion with the Church and its Lord. Is this spirit of repentance and desire for sacramental strength to be forever frustrated? Can they be told only that they must reject their new responsibilities as a necessary condition of forgiveness and restoration to sacramental life?*
>
> *Some pastors argue that the Church's teaching on marital fidelity and contractual indissolubility are here at risk. They fear lest other Catholics would be scandalised and the bond of marriage weakened. Our pre-synodal consultation would question this assertion. Those who vigorously uphold the Church's teaching on indissolubility, also ask for mercy and compassion for the repentant who have suffered irrevocable marital breakdown. There is no easy answer. But our Synod must listen seriously to this voice of experienced priests and laity pleading for consideration of this problem of their less happy brethren. They ask that the Church should provide for the spiritually destitute to the same degree as it strives today to meet the material needs of those physically starving (Briefing, vol.10, no. 32, p. 8).*

The 'pre-Synodal consultation' Archbishop Worlock mentions was the National Pastoral Congress. Referring to the exercise of listening to groups of committed Catholics at parish level all over England Wales, the summary of the Diocesan Reports makes the following observation:

> *Almost every report makes an urgent plea for a re-examination of present policy on this matter (i.e. admission of the divorced-remarried to the sacraments). A new pastoral strategy should come from the bishops, with special consideration of the spiritual needs of divorcees.*
>
> *People cannot understand the rigidity of the Church in this regard. 'Jesus would not refuse to come to them'. The Church forgives anything, even murder, but not remarriage: this feeling is echoed in many reports. (Liverpool 1980, p. 68)*

The short piece that follows is based on the longer book referred to above. It was written at the request of a Polish moral theologian in the hope that it might benefit people in Poland. It is followed by an abbreviated version of a much longer piece written for The Tablet and which many people seem to have found very helpful pastorally.

Civil divorce does not bar a divorcee from receiving the Eucharist.
The problems for those who are divorced arise with the prospect of remarriage. Remarriage in a Catholic Church is only possible if, in the eyes of the Church, the previous marriage is either null or invalid. In all other cases of remarriage official Church teaching forbids reception of the Eucharist.

However, fidelity to official teaching is not the sole criterion. An ancient piece of Church wisdom says: '*Salus animarum suprema lex*'. That means, the overarching criterion is the pastoral good of people. This echoes the words of Jesus, 'The Sabbath is made for the human person, not persons for the Sabbath.' Jesus was confronting those religious leaders who criticised his healing on the Sabbath.

When some of the early Christians found it impossible to live with their Gentile partners, Paul did not see this as violating the teaching of Jesus on life-long fidelity in marriage. Paul's comment was: 'In these circumstances the brother or sister is not tied: God has called you to live a life of peace' (1 Cor 7:15).

In the Eastern Orthodox Church, so revered by John Paul II, a Christian whose first marriage fails is allowed to remarry. This part of the Eastern Church's pastoral approach is based on the compassion of God in the face of our human weakness.

Moreover, while conscience cannot be used as a cover for individualism or relativism, the age-old teaching on the primacy of conscience was proclaimed with renewed emphasis by Vatican II.

People who have suffered the pain of marriage breakdown and seen the impact it can have on children may well be more convinced than most of us of the value of lifelong fidelity in marriage. If they have entered a second marriage, it is their heartfelt prayer that they will be blessed with a home and family where they themselves and any children can find love, peace and security. To believe in lifelong marriage does not mean turning a blind eye to the pain and suffering that occurs when a marriage goes badly wrong. Nor does it mean denying the deeply needed healing and peace that can result from ending of such a destructive relationship through separation and divorce.

The Church sees its current law as defending the stability of marriage. That is important but it is not the only value to be considered. Pastoral care has other priorities to be looked at. It has to bring 'salvation' (healing) to those situations where fidelity to the rigour of the law would deny people the sacramental nourishment needed for their healthy spiritual growth and development. The *salus animarium* (spiritual healing) given by this kind of pastoral care results from what, in traditional theology, is a form of pastoral discernment (*'epikeia'*). It is making sure people do not suffer unjustly from the rigid application of a general law which fails to allow for the particularities of their everyday lives. For Aquinas *'epikeia'* is part of the virtue of justice.

What does this mean in practice?
It means that in certain circumstances someone in a second marriage after divorce could be making a fully responsible decision in presenting themselves for absolution or Holy Communion. The kind of circumstances referred to are:

1. The first marriage is irretrievably broken down and there is no possibility of its being restored again.
2. All obligations in justice towards the other partner and the children of the first marriage are being fulfilled as far as is humanly possible.
3. The second marriage is being lived in good faith. In other words, they genuinely believe that, all things considered, it is the best they can do in the imperfect and ambiguous situation in which they find themselves.
4. The desire for the sacraments is motivated by their faith. The Confessor or minister of the Eucharist should respect such a fully responsible, conscientious decision.

This is my own pastoral approach and I have the impression that it is accepted as legitimate by many moral theologians and very frequently followed in practice by priests and people.

CHAPTER NINETEEN

Can Marriage Breakdown be a Death-Resurrection Experience?

An abbreviated and revised version of an article which appeared originally in The Tablet (3 August 1991, pp. 935-937) under the title, 'Looking beyond Failure: Life after Divorce'. Some of the ideas expressed owe much to two articles in the 1990/5 issue of Concilium on 'Coping with Failure': Dietmar Mieth, The Ethic of Failure and Beginning Again: A forgotten perspective in theological ethics, pp. 45-57; and Elisabeth Bleske, Failure in the Lifelong Project of Fidelity, pp. 105-116.

The death-resurrection paradigm is central to Christian living. Hence, it must colour a Christian approach to morality. Moral theology needs to be sensitive to wherever this death-resurrection paradigm seems to be at work in human life. Moral theology is quite at home, therefore, with our growing understanding that the development of a lasting relationship in marriage seems to follow this death-resurrection paradigm. It arises out of a lot of dying to self on the part of both partners. Our appreciation of what this entails has been heightened since Vatican II encouraged us to think of marriage in personalist rather than contractual terms.

Can moral theology feel equally at home with the suggestion that the death-resurrection paradigm might also be at work in the case of marriage breakdown, with or without subsequent remarriage? It is certainly true that many men and women who have suffered the trauma of marriage breakdown and divorce speak of their experience in terms of dying or bereavement. If this description accurately expresses the experience of marriage breakdown for many couples, there would seem to be something here that moral theology should be paying special attention to. It might be that somewhere in this dying experience of marriage breakdown lies the seed of resurrection and new life. The aim of this article is to offer a few tentative thoughts on this possibility.

What I would like to suggest is that, if marriage breakdown is experienced as a real 'dying', there are grounds for hoping that out of this 'dying' there might break forth real 'resurrection and new life'. I am also suggesting that this might be true not merely at the level of the breakdown of individual marriages. It might also be true at a more general level. The phenomenon of increasing marriage breakdown in our society might have hidden within it the seeds of an emerging new life for loving and faithful sexual partnerships. Moreover, I get the impression that this suggestion seems to ring true in the lives of some divorced people I know and also seems to have some backing in the reading I have done on this topic over many years. I would stress that I am not saying that every marriage breakdown and divorce is part of a death-resurrection experience.

It could be argued that 'no success without failure' is simply another way of stating the 'good news' brought by Jesus. One could even paraphrase one of the well-known sayings of Jesus as: 'I have not come to call the successful, but failures.' After all, Jesus kept open table for people whom the religiously successful dismissed as failures. In fact, these so-called 'failures' flocked to hear Jesus because he brought them the 'good news' that in the eyes of God they were not failures at all.

This 'good news' challenges our normal criteria for success and failure. The story of Jesus is not that of a successful man who dedicated his life to empowering the world's 'failures' to become 'successes' like him. Jesus deliberately chose a path which he knew was doomed to failure. The Passion and death of Jesus was not an accident. Of set purpose Jesus set his face for Jerusalem and even the baffled apostles could see the inevitable outcome of such a decision.

To deliberately opt for failure seems crazy! Either Jesus has taken leave of his senses or else there is something very mysterious going on here. What we view as success is challenged by the freely-willed dishonourable death of Jesus.

The failure referred to in the statement, 'success is impossible without failure', is the same painful and shattering experience humanity has always found failure to be. The 'good news' lies in the realignment of the relationship between failure and success. In this realignment success itself is redefined. This goes back to what Jesus said about the need to lose our lives in order to find them. It also ties in with his realignment of the relationship between death and life. There too death remains something we humanly recoil from, an experience which in itself we find meaningless and absurd.

The realignment is one of direction. Failure, for all its pain, is no longer seen as the end of the road, a cul-de-sac leading nowhere. Death is no longer the final full-stop in the last chapter of life, after which the story is ended and there is no more to be said. What is being suggested is that the losing of self which is involved in accepting these experiences is the route – the only route – to finding our true selves. To find our true selves we must necessarily let go of and lose our false selves. And finding our true selves is the Gospel meaning of success. What does it profit a person to gain the whole world and yet lose one's own true self?

Dorothy Sölle, reflecting on her own experience of marriage breakdown, comments: 'I noticed that all those who believe limp a little' (quoted by Mieth, p. 48). This is a very penetrating remark. For me it throws light on something I have noted from my own very limited experience. It is that the common denominator linking many people whom I would consider men and women of deep personal faith is not the style or frequency of their religious practice.

Rather it is the fact that they have been through some kind of 'rock bottom' experience which has left them feeling weak and powerless, their helplessness totally exposed to themselves and others. Whatever complex array of defence and escape mechanisms they had built up as a mask hiding their real selves from others and, even more so, from themselves had been stripped away. When this 'rock-bottom' experience has been the failure of their marriage it has shattered whatever semblance of self-esteem they may have had. The person who had made an act of faith in them when they pledged their marriage vows is now saying: 'I no longer believe in you. You are not the person I thought you were.' Such an experience of personal rejection leaves them feeling broken into fragments. It is real 'dark night of the soul' stuff. No wonder they describe it in terms of a 'dying' experience!

Stripped naked like this a person encounters self with no possibility of self-deception. In a very real sense such a person is alone before God. Their instinctive cry is: 'I am worthless. Lord, have mercy on me, a sinner.' Out of the heart of this cloud of unknowing comes the voice of God: 'This is my beloved son/daughter in whom I am well pleased.' Paul Tillich describes this experience very powerfully in a celebrated sermon where he speaks of a voice welling up from the depths of a person at such a moment. 'You are accepted', it says. Commenting in more general terms on the same deeply personal experience Mieth says: 'Human beings are worth more before God than they are to themselves' (p. 46). Dorothy Sölle mentions that the Bible passage which brought her light when she was at rock-bottom was the message Paul heard in his time of weakness: 'My grace is enough for you: my power is at its best in weakness.' (2 Cor 12:9) This led Paul himself to comment: 'For it is when I am weak that I am strong' (v. 10).

It is in her account of the beginnings of her resurrection that Sölle makes her remark about the limping characteristic of believers. It is worth quoting this whole passage as given by Mieth:

> I began to an infinitesimal degree to accept that my husband was going another way, his own way. I had come to the end and God had torn up the first plan. He did not comfort me like a psychologist, who would have explained to me that this was foreseeable. He did not offer me the usual social consolations; he threw me face down on the floor. It was not death that I wanted for myself, nor was it life either. It was another death. Later I noticed that all those who believe limp a little, like Jacob after he had struggled with the angel. They have already died once. One cannot wish this on anyone, but one cannot attempt to spare them the lesson either. There is as little substitute for the experience of faith as there is for the experience of love (Mieth, p. 48).

Faith-provoking failures can come in all shapes and sizes. That is only to be expected, since the unreal selves imprisoning us also come in all shapes and sizes. The question facing moral theologians is whether divorce, with or without remarriage, might be one possible shape of faith-provoking failure. This need not be as shocking as it sounds. After all, a 'successful marriage' does not seem to feature in the New Testament among the basic criteria for Christian living. In fact, a 'successful marriage' could be part of that 'whole world' which it would be pointless to gain if it was to be achieved only through the loss of one's true self.

To say that God is the author of marriage does not commit us to believing that God issued some kind of formal decree commanding marriage to come into being. We can assume that men and women, created by God, used their God-given intelligence to reflect on their developing experience of living together.

Learning as they went along from their mistakes our forebears discovered the 'goodness' of being able to depend on each other for life. They found too that there was usually more chance of peace and harmony in the home – and mutual happiness together – when they kept 'making love' as something special to themselves and did not share it with others, even though that did not exclude their loving other people deeply, especially their children. In discovering all this, they were discovering a deep dimension of their own 'goodness' as human beings. In this way, as co-authors with God, they brought 'marriage' into being. They had learned from experience that this was the 'good' way for most men and women to live together. Though it had its difficulties, it brought them happiness and security and provided a home for their children, thus enabling the human family to increase and grow.

To understand marriage as 'God-given' in this sense is to appreciate that the institution of marriage is a living tradition. We are faithful to this tradition to the extent that we are open to discovering how best marriage should be lived today. That means we too must learn from our present-day experience as well as from the knowledge we have which was not available to our ancestors. For instance, nowadays we have a richer knowledge and understanding of human sexuality and the generative processes. We also know how the sexual dimension of our lives has a crucial impact on our growth as persons from our earliest years. We have a better appreciation of the way human relationships develop and the stages through which they need to pass. Moreover, our understanding of history and culture has made us aware that human sexual relationships can be lived out in a variety of ways. Our late-twentieth century, Western, rather romantic approach to marriage with its accompanying 'nuclear family' model is just one possible way among many in which the marriage relationship has been lived and can be lived. It is not necessarily the best way. So we should be open to learn from experience how marriage today can become better adapted to current needs. If we refuse to draw on the full riches of our modern under-standing and insist on imposing on people an earlier model of marriage, we may well find ourselves being unfaithful to the death-resurrection paradigm which is so basic to our Christian faith.

One of the very striking images of the creative work of God is that of the potter, working with his clay, fashioning and refashioning his material, even breaking the vessels in order to reshape them anew. Perhaps that is an image we should keep in mind in our role as co-authors, with God, of the human in-stitution of marriage. Maybe the times we are living in are a very creative mo-ment in the unfolding of God's plan for the way men and women should live together lovingly and responsibly

A theology of marriage and human relationships which is sensitive to the death-resurrection paradigm at work in human affairs should not only be open to the 'signs of the times' at a general level. It should also be able to speak a positive word of hope to men and women who have been through the 'dying' experience of the failure of their marriage relationship. The death-resurrection message that can help to release new life in them is not the deadly reiteration of the 'bad news' that they have failed. To interpret the Gospel in terms of an obligation to remain faithful to a partnership which in reality has ceased to exist is to impose a burden which cannot but dishearten and crush a person since it is impossible of fulfilment in any meaningful sense. It is refusing to face up to the reality so clearly expressed by Dorothy Sölle: 'I began to an infinitesimal degree to accept that my husband was going another way, his own way. I had come to the end and God had torn up the first plan' (Mieth, p. 48).

The death-resurrection message of the Church is not a consolidation of the experience of failure. Rather it offers a positive interpretation of that negative experience. It could perhaps be paraphrased somewhat along the following lines:

> You are shattered by your failure. You may feel worthless. This painful experience might lead you to believe that you are not capable of taking on a commitment to lifelong fidelity and sustaining it. Do not believe all that about yourself. The Lord invites you to believe in him and to believe in yourself. You are not alone. He is with you to strengthen you as you continue your journey through life. Arise! Come forth and live. Leave behind your old self, that half-truth you were living. You have lost that false self and found your true self.
>
> Live your new and true life by loving as I have loved you. Have con-fidence to follow that love wherever it leads you. If your new life turns out to be a life lived in the single state, whether alone or as parent to your children, live it out with complete belief in your own dignity and that of those around you. Live out your singleness as the gift of the richness of

yourself to the present and the future. Refuse to let all the love you can share as a single person be devalued by 'negative' utopian thinking. That would turn it into a life-denying noose placed round your neck by the restraining obligation of a partnership which no longer exists.

If your new life eventually leads you to a new life-giving relationship, accept that with gratitude and live it out in faith – faith in yourself, in your partner and in your God who is entrusting his gift of love to you in this new chapter of your life.

The experience of some who have been through the painful experience of the failure of their marriage would suggest that a crucial act of faith for them can be the moment when they finally commit themselves to leave the false security of a marriage which has been imprisoning and destroying them and take a major step out into the unknown. Elisabeth Bleske writes: 'The way of divorce and remarriage … can in fact be a bold decision to life and further development' (p. 112). When I read that, it reminded me of Rosemary Haughton's reflection, out of her experience of sharing life with mothers forced to flee with their children from a destructive marriage:

We simply cannot go on pretending that we can put back together the pieces of a theology of marriage which has been shattered by experience. For many women the moment of conversion, the true metanoia, has come when they reach the decision to seek a divorce ('The Meaning of Marriage in Women's New Consciousness', in William P. Roberts, edit., *Commitment to Partnership*, p. 149).

CHAPTER TWENTY

Is there a link between Sex Abuse and Systemic God Abuse in the Church?

The issue of clergy sex abuse has rarely been out of the news in recent years whether in Ireland, mainland Europe, the Vatican, worldwide or here in the UK. Only a few minutes before getting to work on the introduction to this chapter, I finished reading a very challenging article by my good friend and fellow moral theologian, Peter Harvey, entitled 'Safeguarding What?'(now published in The Furrow, March 2012, pp. 138-146). This same weekend the Tablet (5 November 2011) carries two pieces on the topic, one related to the jailing of a former Plymouth diocese safeguarding officer and the other on the Vatican investigation into sex abuse at Ealing Abbey. On top of that, the current issue of The Furrow has an article, 'The Politics of Child Abuse', by Andrew McMahon. There is certainly no escaping from this topic. And that is only right, since it is a major scandal today in the life of our 'sinful Church'. The terrible suffering endured by so many at the hands of priests who played on their trust puts the Church to shame, especially when aggravated by the disgraceful way the whole issue has been mishandled by many exercising authority in the Church.

In his article referred to above, Peter Harvey makes a very perceptive comment when he speaks of the Church being 'committed to treating the most horrifying symptoms of what is wrong as if it is itself the disease'. For Peter and for many, myself included, the real disease is 'the clericalist culture whose diseased condition, most experts agree, is at the heart of the ongoing crisis'.

I have been struggling to get my mind round this horrendous issue for some time now. The piece which follows is the result of that long struggle. I have re-edited it many times and I am still far from satisfied with it. I have read widely in preparing it as well as discussing the issue with various people, clerical and lay. In fact, at the moment of writing this introduction I am awaiting delivery of a new major work, Child Sexual Abuse and the Catholic Church, Gender, Power and Organizational Culture (Oxford University Press, 2011) by the eminent Dublin psychotherapist and academic, Marie Keenan, who has worked extensively with victims and perpetrators of sexual abuse.

God Abuse

The Irish moral theologian, Sean Fagan SM, has suggested that the Church sex abuse scandal might well be related to the idea of God nurtured in both people and priests by a guilt-ridden theology of sin. This is a fear-inspiring and punishing God, rather than a loving Father. Consequently, many people's lives have been ruled by a sense of dread and fear, not love. For Fagan this is 'spiritual abuse', stunting people's emotional and spiritual lives (cf. his essay, 'Spiritual Abuse', chapter five in Angela Hanley & David Smith, edits. *Quench not the*

Spirit: Theology and Prophecy for the Church in the Modern World, Columba, Dublin, 2005).

Vatican II broke through the 'fear barrier' in the Catholic Church by presenting God as a God of love. For the most part Catholics have experienced this work of renewal as an outpouring of God's Spirit of love on the Church. No wonder the present Pope, writing as a young theologian shortly after Vatican II, highlighted Paul VI's closing words at the Council saying that, in fact, Vatican II had all been centred on love:

> When a historian would in the future ask what the Catholic Church did in this age, the answer, the pope said, would have to be, 'It loved'. From that final address of December 7, we can perhaps infer that it was this thought that made it possible for the pope to approve texts he had at first viewed with doctrinal reservations. In that final address he again reviewed the objections which not only conservatives but also some of the observers had meanwhile raised against the Council's 'modernism'. Pope Paul found the answer in the formula that 'the religion of this Council was primarily the religion of love'. This, said the pope, was also the answer to the objection that the Council had defected from the gospel. 'The Lord said, "by this shall all know that you are my disciples, that you love one another"(John 13:35)'. The primacy of love overcomes doctrinal doubts. It justifies the Council. Let us add now a word from the pope's speech on September 14, which also shows with how little illusion the pope understood love: 'The art of loving is often converted into the art of suffering. Should the Church abandon its duty to love because it has become too dangerous or too difficult?' (Joseph Ratzinger, *Theological Highlights of Vatican II*, Paulist Press, New York, 1966 p. 139).

Jesus led the way in showing how the art of loving is converted into the art of suffering. He suffered and died at the hands of the religious authorities of his day because his love for 'publicans and sinners' led him to stand up against the way the scribes and Pharisees were abusing such people by labelling them as unclean in the eyes of God. To the disgust and scandal of the self-proclaimed righteous, Jesus ate and drank with publicans and sinners. The hypocrisy of the scribes and Pharisees even aroused Jesus to anger, provoking him to condemn them as 'whited sepulchres and a brood of vipers'. Yet even his anger was driven by an impassioned loving desire to heal them from their destructive blindness. It was the same loving desire to heal that elicited from Jesus his profoundly moving stories of the Prodigal Son and the Good Samaritan.

For Jesus the religious leaders were distorting people's understanding of God and thus poisoning their inner relationship with God. People's ability to feel loved and lovable was being stunted. The very notion of a loving God was being abused. What the people needed was not condemnation but acceptance, healing and liberation. That is why I would suggest that the phrase 'God abuse' might be even more appropriate than Sean Fagan's 'spiritual abuse' to describe the image of God which the scribes and Pharisees tried to impose on the ordinary Jewish faithful. It defamed and violated the image of the God of love revealed in the life and teaching of Jesus. Putting it very bluntly, it constituted an 'abuse' of God.

An abuse of Power and Teaching Authority

The Irish clinical psychologist, Marie Keenan, writes: 'Child sexual abuse is by definition an abuse of power ' (cf. 'The Institution and the Individual – Child Sexual Abuse by Clergy' in *The Furrow*, 2006, p. 7). This ties in with the conviction of many that sex abuse in the Church is connected with the issue of power and control, especially when this is almost exclusively in the hands of celibate males. Moreover, the dysfunctionality of the Church's power structure is sustained by a form of spirituality which indiscriminately claims God as the ultimate source of all authority in the Church. This can lead to an unhealthy respect for the Church's teaching authority. As a moral theologian, I have often said that part of my role in the Church is to encourage people not to take the Church too seriously! It is clearly an abuse of power to claim the authority of God for teaching which may be doubtful, debatable or, at best, second-rate. Christian fidelity to God does not demand unquestioning acceptance of such teaching and the moral directives based on it.

Teaching is a moral activity. Teaching is immoral if it fails to respect the dignity of those being taught, abuses their freedom, imposes the teaching on them, regardless of whether they are able to accept or appreciate its truth and even punishes them for non-acceptance of what is being taught. Such immoral teaching (even when what is taught is true) diminishes and disempowers people – even infantilises them. It stifles healthy critical questioning, inhibits and cripples their creativity, quenches their spirit, and is profoundly anti-Gospel. Such immoral use of teaching authority in the Church is unworthy of the Church. The Vatican II Declaration on Religious Liberty states: 'The truth cannot impose itself except by virtue of its own truth, as it makes its way into the mind at once quietly and with power' (no.1). Part of the renewal of the Church would seem to be moving from an exercise of teaching authority based on domination and control to one based on loving service and empowering leadership.

A whole list of instances of the abuse of power could be given. Examples which are often mentioned are: Papal and curial control over the Synod of bishops, rejection of the report of the consultative committee on Birth Control in the case of *Humanae Vitae*, Benedict XVI's lack of consultation over his 2009 Apostolic Constitution, *Anglicanorum Coetibus*, offering special status to groups of Anglicans entering the Catholic Church corporately. Also worthy of mention are John Paul II's *Ad Tuendam fidem* and its CDF commentary extending the 'Oath of Fidelity' much wider than matters of faith, thus ensuring that office-holders do not cause disruption by dissent or public criticism (cf. Ladislas Orsy, *Receiving the Council*, Collegeville, Liturgical Press, 2009, chapter nine).

All inhumanity on the part of the Church is an abuse of God, since the very meaning and mission of the Church is to be a sacrament and sign of God's love for all humanity. This is also massively the case with regard to the horrendous destructiveness of child sex abuse, especially when perpetrated by priests. It is a heinous betrayal of the trust of young people and can seriously debilitate their capacity to experience love and to express love. To this is added the inhumanity of the cover-up and irresponsible mishandling by many Church authorities and the warped understanding of Church and its mission which this reveals.

Many people have shared with me their disillusionment with the Catholic Church as they experience it at this moment in history. They do not find it inspiring. As an institution it seems to have lost its way. I can sympathise with them and understand why they feel this way. After all, as the psalms remind us, lamentation is a very genuine form of prayer. It makes sure that we are living in the real world and that that is the world in which our relationship with God is played out. Nevertheless, as I have pointed out in an earlier essay in this volume, it is within this sinful Church that we believe and hope. That has been true down through the centuries and remains true today. Our hope is not a subtle kind of despair, hoping against hope. It is true hope, what we call in the Eucharist 'certain hope'. Such hope is expressed by our doing what little we can to build the future we hope for.

I find this form of realistic hope expressed in the following two long excerpts from articles in a special issue of the Irish Redemptorist monthly magazine, *Reality*, following the publication of the Murphy Report on Abuse in Dublin Archdiocese. Both writers, Irish priests, are drawing attention to the systemic inhumanity found in much of the structural and cultural life of the Church. Peter McVerry is a Jesuit whose ministry is deeply immersed in the lives of some of the most marginalised in inner-city Dublin. Brendan Hoban is a Mayo parish priest, renowned for his courageous outspokenness. Though they are writing about the Catholic Church in Ireland, I would suggest that what they say applies to the Catholic Church as a whole. They put their fingers on some of the main issues which have been explored in this article.

Peter McVerry SJ, in Reality, January 2010, pp. 38-39

The Catholic Church in Ireland is in crisis, a crisis of its own making, one that is not going to go away. This crisis goes much deeper than the actions of individual bishops, or even the Vatican. Without root and branch reform, the Church, as it currently exists in Ireland, will die – and I will shed no tears. I believe in the Church; I have received so much from the Church; I believe that the vision of Jesus is vitally important for our time and that the Church is the bearer of that vision – but not in its present form.

The Church is Jesus' legacy to the world, to continue his mission. How people understand God and relate to God, is therefore strongly influenced by how they see the Church. The image the Church projects becomes a reflection of the image of God

What image does the Church project? It is an authoritarian Church that tolerates no criticism, that silences dissent; that stifles discussion of issues which divide the Church, such as married priests, that excludes people who refuse to conform, such as those in second relationships; that defines our relationship with God by observance of laws that are obsessively focussed on sexual relationships, and that condemns those who do not observe those laws. How could anyone want to believe in such a God?

I believe many people are leaving the Church because they no longer find God there. And that pains me. My criticisms arise not from disloyalty, but from a passionate desire that the Church be what it was intended to be, the revelation of God's love for the world ... (The Church's) self-contained clerical structure generates its own clerical culture and clerical mindset, and needs to be demolished.

This is a Church that interprets criticism as disloyalty and, by extension, displeasing to God. Many priests I know will privately voice strong criticism of some of the Church's moral teaching or discipline, but would not dare say it publicly, for fear they would be strongly reprimanded – and for what? They know the Church's authorities will not listen and nothing will change, so why stick your head above the parapet and get it shot off for nothing? And so silence, born of fear, is interpreted as commitment ... a Church that does not witness to the infinite and unconditional love of God, expressed in its love for all, but especially the weak and the sinner, a Church that witnesses instead to a God of judgement, condemnation and exclusion, deserves to die. But after death, there is resurrection to new life.

What McVerry has written seems to me to go to the roots of the abuse scandal in the life and culture of the Catholic Church. Moreover, he is typical of a growing number of writers, lay and clerical, who are making similar points. In fact, it is very striking that there is a common voice coming through most of what is being written on this topic.

For instance, Louise Fuller highlights a very similar group of concerns:

The Ferns, Ryan and Murphy reports leave the Church with some very uncomfortable questions in relation to authority, communication, clerical culture, celibacy, sexuality, its attitude towards the laity and the formation that priests and nuns receive ... while the recent reports are concerned with the issue of abuse on many levels, the implications for the Church go far beyond the abuse issue. They raise deep and fundamental questions about Catholic culture, questions which are not confined to Ireland. They concern issues deeply embedded in Catholic history and theology ('Disturbing the Faithful: Aspects of Catholic Culture Under Review', in *The Dublin/Murphy Report: A Watershed for Irish Catholicism?* Columba, Dublin, 2010, pp. 169-170).

McVerry points to a systemic inhumanity found in much of the structural and cultural life of the Church. Marie Keenan, the Irish clinical psychologist makes some very thought-provoking comments on 'organisational pathology' in a talk she gave to the Irish Theological Association, 'An Organizational Cultural Perspective on Child Sexual Abuse in the Catholic Church' (printed in *Doctrine and Life*, October 2010). She points out that:

Rarely does the senior leadership (in the Catholic Church) see the necessity for a root-and branch review of the man-made aspects of the very institution itself. It has been long established by social scientists and theologians that a review of the Church's governance structures, power-relation and sexual ethics are long overdue.

Her final conclusion is worth quoting at length:

It is not just the content of Catholic sexual ethics that is in need of reform. It is equally the problematic nexus of issues around sexuality, power, relationship, male-domination and the distinctions between the ordained and the non-ordained, all of which are implicated in the current crisis of sexual abuse within the Catholic Church, and all of which need to be analysed comprehensively. What matters here are the power dynamics that are at work in a human institution that will not allow itself to be comprehensively examined even when the calls for such an examination come increasingly from within.

While dealing with the abusers and the cover-up is the responsibility of Church and civil authorities, tackling the systemic inhumanity is something which is the concern of all of us. To face that task we need to explore whether and how far each of us, ordained or not, has colluded in sustaining this inhumanity within our Church. This is particularly true for those of us who are ordained priests.

That is why the clerical sex abuse scandal is a matter of grave concern to me personally. I have been involved in the field of moral theology for more than fifty years. For ten of those years I was engaged in the formation of future priests. Moreover, as a diocesan priest, I have lived my life within the 'clerical culture', something I have become more aware of and increasingly uncomfortable with over the years. I am very conscious, therefore, that in various ways I have colluded in the inhumanity which I can see now has been one of the enabling factors with regard to clergy sexual abuse. I feel a sense of personal shame about that. Accepting my personal share of ownership for the sin of the Church is a necessary part of my own ongoing conversion.

Some writers have noted a tendency to demonise clerical abusers in order to distance them from the rest of the Church (and humanity), thus leaving the 'holiness' of the Church unblemished and ourselves completely blameless. Eugene O'Brien points out that 'Institutions tend to minimise responsibility by blaming such problems on isolated, abusive individuals rather than examining the role that the leadership and culture of the institution played in the abuse' ('The Boat had moved: The Catholic Church, Conflations and the Need for Critique', in John Littleton & Eamon Maher edits., *The Dublin/Murphy Report: A Watershed for Irish Catholicism?*, Columba, Dublin, 2010, p. 104).

In addition, Brendan Callaghan SJ in his entry, 'On Scandal and Scandals' in the UK Jesuit website, *ThinkingFaith* links this with the phenomenon of denial:

> Denial is at the heart of abuse ... we don't like to think about child sexual abuse, and so take what opportunities there are not to think about it ... we maintain as much distance as possible by labelling abusers in ways that make them appear as distant as possible from us and from 'people like us' (p. 2).

Influenced by Girard's work on 'scapegoating', Eamonn Conway stresses that this kind of distancing

> encourages the view that while there may have been one or two 'rotten apples', the barrel itself is sound. The permanent exclusion from active ministry of priests and religious who have been convicted of sexual offences allows us to believe that with it, all clerical problems have been resolved and we can get back to business as usual. The clerical cast, as such, remains intact and deeper questions need not be asked ... we can dismiss as irrelevant questions about the appropriateness of a highly authoritarian exclusively male celibate style of leadership ('The Service of a Different Kingdom – Child Sexual Abuse and the Response of the Church', in *The Furrow*, 1999, p. 457).

I strongly believe that we all have a responsibility to look at these 'deeper questions'.

Brendan Hoban includes among these 'deeper questions' the Church's failure to fully implement the vision of Vatican II. Hence, among his 'top ten' wishes for the Church in Ireland in 2010 he highlights some of the key elements of Vatican II on which Church authorities have been dragging their feet:

A people's Church – That we might put flesh on rather than minimise, explain away or re-interpret – the insights of Vatican II so that we would become what God told us he wanted us to be – a people's Church; and that by listening to the signs of the times and taking our cue from the experiences of our people, we might connect with the world we live in.

Authority – That collegiality and 'co-responsibility' be allowed to stand their ground and reflect the kind of shared leadership that would allow us to recognise the difference between what really matters and what is ultimately unimportant – the pain of the victims of clerical child sexual abuse or the needs of the Church as institution. What a price we have paid for the belief that office constitutes authority, much less wisdom.

Change – That new leaders in our Church might recognise that the very pulse of change is a constant of our time, that yesterday isn't always better than today, that epiphanies of certainty and stability that hug the memory are out of tune with the unreason and inconvenience of the modern age. The old world is dead and trying to resuscitate is it not a credible strategy.

Clericalism – That the clerical club that controls the Church, a secretive, exclusive, male, celibate, hierarchical and authoritative elite – might recognise the high price the Church has paid for this failed and aberrant culture and calmly organise its own demise in the interests of the gospel and for the good of the Church.

New Mass Translation – That the Irish bishops, in the interests of common sense and alert to the danger of further infuriating Irish Catholics might appeal to Pope Benedict to bin the new English translation of the Mass as unfriendly, archaic, obsolete, liturgically unwarranted, pastorally unwise – and example of a deliberate campaign to derail creative efforts to connect the mysteries we celebrate with the ordinariness of the lives we lead.

Sexuality – That the Church recognise that there is an emerging consensus that Catholic sexual morality is deeply flawed, that there is an interior disengagement among practising Catholics from traditional Catholic sexual morality and that without a credible debate on the issue, Church teaching runs the risk of losing touch with the lived experience and assent of our people.

Loyalty – That, in view of our recent and centuries-old history, we might accept as a Church a more discriminating definition of loyalty that respects and appreciates the contribution of those members of the awkward squad who question the status quo.

Hoban's list is not a million miles away from something I have mentioned at various points earlier in this book . I have seriously questioned whether certain elements in the official moral teaching of the Church are truly consistent with respect for the dignity of human persons as embodied in the teaching of Vatican II. For instance, I mentioned the Church's current teaching regarding the faithful love lives of gays and lesbians, its blanket denial of the sacraments to the divorced-remarried, its ban on even discussing the ordination of women, its current teaching on contraception, its negative approach to Eucharistic hospitality in an ecumenical context and its prohibition of general absolution in sacramental celebrations of God's loving forgiveness except in extreme situations. If there is something in what I am saying, this could mean that these might be instances in which human persons are denied the respect due to them. I have even dared to use the expression, 'God abuse', when the authority of God seems to be put forward as the ultimate basis of the Church's position.

Most of these issues affect people in their everyday lives. They experience the Church's teaching as a violation of their personal conscience and an affront to their dignity as human persons. These people have formed their conscience through a listening process, described by GS no. 16 as 'united with all other people in the search for truth and in finding true solutions to the many moral problems which arise in the lives of individuals and in society.' In this multi-dimensional listening process they have tried to show full respect for the living tradition within the Catholic and Christian community – and beyond. They have listened to the guidance offered by the Vatican authorities and the hierarchical magisterium. They have also listened to the wider public debate going on among theologians (ordained and non-ordained, women and men) in the Catholic community and people of other Churches and faiths. And reflecting on that multidimensional listening experience, they have tried to see what makes the best human and Christian sense in the light of their own experience. According to the late Cardinal Hume, such conscience decisions are a 'theological source' (cf. his words at the 1980 Rome Synod on the Family with regard to the experience of married couples).

Moreover, the present Pope, writing not long after Vatican II, also gave his support to such conscience decisions, even when they are not in accord with official teaching:

Over the pope as the expression of the binding claim of ecclesiastical authority, there still stands one's own conscience, which must be obeyed before all else, even if necessary against the requirement of ecclesiastical authority. This emphasis on the individual ... also establishes a principle in opposition to increasing totalitarianism (Joseph Ratzinger, in Herbert Vorgrimler ed., *Commentary on the documents of Vatican II*, vol 5, p. 134).

To counter such a discernment of conscience with an appeal to teaching authority seems open to the charge of 'God abuse'. God is being used as a trump card when the theological arguments of teaching authority are weak or unconvincing. The Jesuit philosopher, Gerard Hughes, makes this point well:

In practice the appeal to tradition and to teaching authority tends to short-circuit the need for proper inquiry and for argument which will withstand criticism in open debate. These are the normal human means to the attainment of truth, which we ignore at our peril ... we cannot confidently lay claim to the guidance of the Spirit, whether as individuals or as a Church, unless we take the normal human means to try to arrive at the truth ('Natural Law Ethics and Moral Theology', in *The Month*, 1987, pp. 102-103).

'Is there a link between Sex Abuse and systemic God Abuse in the Church?' might seem a very negative title for a chapter in a book on fifty years of receiving Vatican II. Yet it articulates a question which needs to be given serious consideration – the abusive and dysfunctional dimension that is part and parcel of the life of our Church. Yet it is only by facing the obstacles in the way of receiving Vatican II that we will be able to put the reception process back on tract. Leonard Cohen's song encourages such a hopeful interpretation: 'There is a crack in everything; that's how the light gets in.'

Receiving Vatican II – a sign of hope
Ned Prendergast, writing in the April 2010 issue of *The Furrow*, encourages us to see the present in all its darkness as a real *'kairos'*, an invitation and opportunity to redeem the past and build a more Kingdom-orientated future:

I have come to the conclusion, and I am not alone in this, that the only proper spiritual response to the Murphy Report begins in gratitude: gratitude for the gift of truth given to us all; gratitude for the gift of credibility given to victims and their families; gratitude for the reminder that no one is exempt from the sinfulness and brokenness of the human condition; gratitude for the profound lessons in humility for anyone who wanted to hear, for what Timothy Radcliffe called the demolition of pretensions to glory and grandeur so that the Church may be a place in which we may encounter God and each other more intimately; gratitude for those crusts of stagnation, unresponsiveness and ecclesial deafness beginning to crack and break; for the renewed chance to build the people of God to put in place the Church dreamed of at Vatican II … gratitude finally for the words of Isaiah 43:19 whose truth is evident before our eyes: 'See, I am doing something new! Now it springs forth, do you not perceive it' (p. 202).

At Vatican II the Holy Spirit made the whole Church aware of a ferment of renewal that had been bubbling below the surface for many years. The rich fruits of the theological research and insights of theologians like Rahner, Congar, Schillebeeckx, Chenu, Lonergan, Courtney Murray and many others were finally accepted as mainstream, despite a hard core of continued opposition. This enabled the Council to move forward on a whole variety of key areas of Catholic faith and life, for example:

- the nature of revelation,
- the relation between sacred scripture and tradition,
- the meaning and mission of the Church,
- the meaning and role of the liturgy in the life of the Christian community.

These are not just theoretical issues. They are truly transformative at a very practical level. They bring new life to the Church. Quite literally, they enkindle the fire of the holy Spirit in the Church.

In addition, at Vatican II the neglected riches of previous ages were re-appropriated, reinvigorated and developed still further in the light of our increased understanding of the human condition and the changing world in which we live. This has given us a renewed and deeper understanding of such issues as:

- the Church as the pilgrim People of God and sacrament of God's all-embracing love of humanity,
- the priesthood of all believers,
- collegiality and its implications for hierarchical authority, collaborative ministry and co-responsibility for the mission of the Church,
- the full and active participation of all in the celebration of the liturgy,
- the human person, unique, interdependent, loving and relational, and focussed on the common good, as the core criterion of Christian morality.

Becoming aware of the historical dimension of all life opened the Council's eyes to tradition as a living reality. Change when needed and appropriate could then be seen as an essential element of fidelity to tradition. The Spirit was certainly at work in Vatican II. Even the inevitable conflicts and compromises could be seen in a positive light. The aim of the Council's 'healing diagnosis' was not to create a new Church but to renew and reinvigorate a Church which had become too set in its ways and out of tune with the modern age.

Vatican II certainly remains such a source of hope for people. It has given us an inspiring vision of the Church. The vision of Vatican II opens our eyes to that 'something new' that God is doing in our time. That is the future Church God's Spirit is urging us to continue building today.

Since I wrote the introduction to this chapter I have read Marie Keenan's major work *Child Sexual Abuse and the Catholic Church: Gender Power and Organisational Culture* (Oxford University Press, 2012). She speaks of 'the contradictions that have been building up within the Catholic Church for a very long time' and goes on to say:

> Anything less than structural reform and a new model of the Church will be seen in the minds of many believers as a missed opportunity. Anything less than structural reform will be seen as a crisis weathered rather than a crisis transformed (p. 167).

Keenan has considerable experience of working with both the abused and abusers. Her research is unique in that it also includes careful listening to a sample of clergy abusers. This has alerted her to the importance of context, leading her to state: 'The institutional Church has yet to address the necessary institutional and structural issues that the sexual abuse crisis has brought to the surface' (p. 157). Kevin Egan, from a similar wide experience in this field, has written a 'rave review' of Keenan's book in the February 2012 issue of *The Furrow*. He encourages priests to read it, even including the new apostolic nuncio to Ireland and those conducting the apostolic visitation of the Irish Church. I particularly warmed to Keenan's comment:

> It appears to me that the seismic moment has arrived for a wider consultative process, in which a different view of Church can be envisioned, orthodoxy can be questioned, and a more representative and accountable Church can emerge from the current crisis (p. 267).

CHAPTER TWENTY-ONE

HIV-Prevention, Women, Condoms:
A Gospel of Life Perspective

For over twenty years I had the great privilege of being a member of the HIV/AIDS Advisory Committee of CAFOD (Catholic Fund for Overseas Development). This was a massive learning experience for me. CAFOD enabled me to visit some remarkable Home-Care projects in Uganda, Zimbabwe and Zambia. I was even invited, along with John Howson, to run two week-long courses on theological and pastoral issues related to HIV/AIDS in Harare and Bulawayo in Zimbabwe. Again, thanks to CAFOD, I was able to participate in theological conferences on HIV/AIDS here in the UK, as well as in Bangkok, New York and Dublin. All this had an enormous impact on me. Clearly, I felt an obligation to share what I had learnt so that people could become more aware of the terrible suffering and devastation being caused, especially in the developing world, by the AIDS pandemic. My eyes were opened to the fact that the rapid spread of HIV/AIDS in the developing world was linked to such fundamental issues as poverty and the second-class status of women in society. In my concluding essay in the ground-breaking work, Catholic Ethicists on HIV/AIDS Prevention, edited by James Keenan and others (Continuum, New York/London, 2000), I pointed out how that point had been made very forcefully by Teresa Okure:

> *An African theologian, Teresa Okure ... startled her hearers by saying that there are at least two other viruses which are even more dangerous than HIV and which are the carriers enabling this virus to spread so rapidly among the most vulnerable in society.*
>
> *One is a virus which affects people's minds and their cultures – almost a form of human madness. It is the virus which makes people look on women as inferior to men – and it affects women as well as men. The other is a virus which is found mainly, though not exclusively, in the developed world. It is the virus of global injustice which is causing such terrible poverty in many parts of the developing world (p. 325).*

Another eye-opening experience I had was to be invited to attend the 2004 International Conference of the Medical Missionaries of Mary (MMM) held in Nairobi. It was a gathering of sixty-two sisters, all medical professionals, including many doctors, who had been working at grass-roots in the caring for people living with HIV/AIDS. Their wealth of experience was mind-blowing. Moreover, as part of the preparation for this conference sisters were invited to contribute to an e-forum based on various practical questions. The question which drew the most impassioned responses was 'What puts fire in your bellies?' I am grateful to the MMM sisters for permission to quote from this e-forum in the article which follows.

I naturally felt obliged to share my experience of HIV/AIDS in my moral theology teaching at both Heythrop College in London and Liverpool Hope University. In addition, sharing my experience was the main motivation behind a number of articles on HIV/AIDS, as well as a major book on HIV/AIDS. Sadly the publishers of my book insisted that it should not be restricted to HIV/AIDS ('people would not be interested in that topic'). Hence, it covered the much wider field of sexual ethics, appearing under the title, New Directions in Sexual Ethics: Moral Theology and the Challenge of AIDS (Geoffrey Chapman, London, 1998).

All who have been directly involved in the field of HIV/AIDS know that, if prevention is to be tackled effectively, it needs a fully comprehensive approach. The provision of condoms can be part of that strategy in some circumstances but its role is often massively exaggerated by the popular media. The article which follows tries to put the issue of condoms into this much wider comprehensive context. Even Benedict XVI recognised this in a very cautious and somewhat ambiguous way in his much-publicised comment in his book, Light of the World (CTS, London, 2010).

I am very grateful to Christine Allen and her Progressio staff for encouraging me to write this article and also to Ann Smith of CAFOD for her advice. Gill Patterson also kindly offered me helpful advice. This article has not been published elsewhere.

Introduction

After a number of AIDS-related visits to Africa and Asia I feel deeply affected by the human tragedy of HIV and AIDS, especially in the developing world and particularly regarding the situation of many women and how they are treated as second-class citizens. In fact, the inferior status of women in Africa was recognised as a major concern at the Second African Synod of Bishops in Rome in October 2009, thanks to the strong and courageous interventions of many of the twenty-five women invited to participate.

One very privileged experience was to be invited as theological consultant to a week's conference in Nairobi in 2004 with Medical Missionary of Mary (MMM) Sisters from across the world, all involved with people living with HIV and AIDS. The sixty-two MMM participants at Nairobi were doctors, nurses, pharmacists and hospital administrators working in the field of HIV and AIDS in Angola, Benin Republic, Brazil, Ethiopia, Honduras, Ireland, Kenya, Malawi, Rwanda, Tanzania, Uganda and USA.

To prepare for the meeting they ran an e-forum to let each sister share her experience of the pandemic and how it had touched her personally. The e-mail replies came pouring in. They were deeply moving and showed how profoundly the sisters shared the pain of those for whom they were helping to care. In answer to the question, 'What puts you fire in your belly?', some replies were very revealing:

I get angry when I see the poverty of the people, especially women and girls. They have to keep working even when they are sick. This leaves them even more vulnerable to infection.

The injustices and fear women face on a daily basis – and little opportunity or 'safe place' to share this and find any support/solace.

Women abandoned, put out of their home and left penniless. Who will speak for them or help them to get their rights? Orphan children struggling on their own – and in the end exploited and abused. Sexual abuse of children. teenagers, orphans and a legal system which fails them. Physical abuse of children – within their own families.

This 'fire in their bellies' prompted some of the sisters to get involved with women who had become sex workers, due to the enormous pressures on them:

The Medical Director asked us to do something about the 700 women in the sex-trade. We contacted them indirectly. It took almost three months before the first women came. Six months later we had 48 registered clients. Today we follow about 300 women 'in distress'. We have a small group of young rape victims who are not in prostitution, another small group of widows who are occasionally in prostitution and about 250 women who are single mothers and engaged in prostitution. Our women are very poor, mostly orphans. 40% have had virtually no education.

The sisters also shared how their faith sustained them. The psalm verse, 'The Lord is close to the broken-hearted' gave them great comfort. They quoted lines from the psalms which gave expression to their cries of anger and desperation to God – almost feeling abandoned – like Jesus on the Cross – 'Jesus falling under the weight of the cross ... he didn't stay down ... gives me courage for myself, a hope and courage I can pass on to others'. A final word from one of the sisters captures the pain they shared: 'Sometimes I feel so angry, so inadequate, so frustrated, I want to scream.'

Being women themselves, the Sisters could see how women bear the brunt of the AIDS pandemic. Many were angered by the Church's attitude to women:

I want the Church to show concern and compassion for the women caught up in the tragedy of AIDS. I would like to feel that the Church understands the powerlessness of women, how they are looked on as 'the guilty ones'. Many women have 'remained faithful', – but now have AIDS and, after the death of their husbands care for their HIV-positive children. The older women care for their grandchildren and suffer deeply from poverty and from the abuse of their families. Can the Church show that it has heard the cry of these women, will stand by them and seek for justice for them?

I saw for myself the tragic reality the sisters are confronting on a daily basis on my various visits to Zambia, Zimbabwe and the huge Kibera slum on the outskirts of Nairobi in Kenya. Many husbands have to live most of the year in very dehumanising work-place dormitory accommodation. Overcome by loneliness, some find that the only way to survive is by setting up a second home (and family) with another woman. Others may forego that but find solace with a woman (lone-parent or widow) who has been forced into the sex industry to feed and support her children. If HIV-infection occurs through these arrangements, the wife at home might eventually find herself HIV-positive despite her being totally faithful to her husband. She might also eventually find herself a widow, after having nursed her husband when he came back home to die. There is also the tragic possibility that she might even have infected her own children. I was told of a whole variety of other dehumanising situations during my various visits – children forced to have sex with their teacher or examiner to get their grades, young girls responsible for child-headed families having no alternative but to seek help from an exploitative 'sugar daddy', widows and orphans reduced to being virtual slaves by the relatives of their deceased husband or father. In recent years, antiretrovirals, when available, have reduced somewhat the number of AIDS-related deaths.

Ann Smith, HIV CAFOD's former Corporate Strategist, echoes the experience and feelings of the sisters very powerfully:

> Too often, behaviour change is viewed through a Western, 'developed' world perspective which assumes that autonomous individuals make informed choices based on in-depth understanding of the facts. One of the erroneous assumptions is that everyone wants to be sexually active from an early age; another is that anyone sexually active outside marriage must be promiscuous. These ignore the fact that for many in the developing world sex is often the only commodity people have to exchange for food, school fees, exam results, employment or survival itself in situations of violence. There are immense social and cultural pressures on men and women to conform to accepted stereotypes; there are economic pressures that result in the break-up of families as migrant workers spend months on end far from their spouse and family support, plunged into unbearably harsh working and living conditions by exploitative local or multi-national employers. Nor is the spread of HIV always linked to promiscuity. Most HIV-women worldwide are infected by the person they considered to be their monogamous, lifelong partner (*The Tablet*, 25 September 2004, pp. 8-9).

Despite the awful inhumanity of this whole scene, the miracle is that so much goodness, self-sacrifice and moral heroism is found in the midst of it all. I constantly felt humbled by the commitment and dedication of most of the people I met, many of them HIV-positive themselves. I am reminded of something I wrote many years ago:

> Moral theology is not meant to condemn the plant emerging from the seed simply because it does not live up to the promise of the idealised picture on the packet. Rather it appreciates the growth that occurs. Sometimes what might look like a puny and undeveloped plant might, in fact, be a miracle of growth, given the adverse conditions under which it has had to struggle (*From a Parish Base*, p. 109).

Writing about the virtue of mercy James Keenan remarks:

> 'Inasmuch as mercy is the willingness to enter into the chaos of another so as to respond to the others, justice thickened by mercy insists on taking into account the chaos of the most marginalized' ('What does Virtue Ethics Bring to Genetics?' in Lisa Sowle Cahill edit., *Genetics, Theology and Ethics*, Herder & Herder, New York, 2005, p. 104).

In the same volume Hasna Begum makes a similar comment:

> 'Mere rational thinking, in the absence of direct experience of situations unique to poor countries, cannot possibly comprehend them in their uniqueness' (*Genetics, Ethics, Theology: A Response from the Developing World* in Cahill, op. cit., p. 182).

I will never forget a young woman I met in the Philippines. Feeling worthless after having been abused by her father, when the responsibility for all the family (including her young siblings) fell on her as eldest, she found that the only way she could cope financially was to sacrifice herself for their sake by supporting them through becoming a sex worker. She was already HIV-positive by the time I met her and was working as a carer in a Church-sponsored HIV-hospice. Despite all the ambiguity in her life, as she shared her experiences with me, I was reminded of the words of Jesus, 'Greater love …'. The following chapter, Maria's Story, gives a fuller account of this remarkable woman.

Not only is it too facile to think in categories of 'the lesser evil' or being 'excused from sin' when talking about people's courageous and self-sacrificing decisions in such dehumanising and freedom-diminishing situations. It can be deeply offensive to them and is lacking in respect for the love which may inspire their decision. In the circumstances their decision may well be awe-inspiring.

Pastoral compassion calls for an appreciation of the complexity of the whole issue of HIV-prevention and of the kind of world in which most people affected by HIV have to live their lives. In another article, James Keenan emphasizes the fact that most people affected by HIV live in 'very unstable environments' (cf. 'Four of the Tasks for Theological Ethics in a Time of HIV/AIDS', in *Concilium*, 2007/3, pp. 64-74). Any comprehensive approach to HIV-prevention will need to look at the root causes of such unstable environments. For the most part these causes lie almost entirely outside the direct control of the individuals affected.

People today are becoming increasingly aware of the interconnectedness of the lives of everyone. The roots of this interconnectedness go so deep that the social, economic and even cultural pressures which can so massively diminish some people's freedom of choice may be linked to the very structures, institutions and assumptions of what people presume to call 'the free world'. One person's freedom can so often entail another's captivity. As mentioned in the introduction to this article, the Nigerian theologian, Teresa Okure, insists that two other 'viruses' play a major role in HIV-infection – the 'prejudice virus' which sees women as inferior to men; and the 'global injustice virus' which is one of the root causes of such dehumanising poverty in many parts of the developing world.

A Comprehensive HIV Prevention Strategy

One of the most fully comprehensive approaches to HIV-prevention was that presented to the 2004 international AIDS Conference at Bangkok by CAFOD's HIV specialist workers. Entitled 'HIV Prevention from the Perspective of a Faith-Based Development Agency', it won widespread approval from delegates.

The CAFOD presentation makes very effective use of the 'problem tree' model for analysing the HIV and AIDS pandemic. The tree's branches and leaves represent the impact of HIV-infection – personal consequences such as sickness, death, trauma, bereavement, stigma, discrimination and increased poverty; and also social consequences such as increased demands on health services, loss of economic productivity, increased burden of care and lost educational opportunities, especially for women and girls. The roots of the tree represent the causes of HIV-infection. These are the factors which lead to people becoming HIV-infected. Some of these roots are more visible – the kinds of activity which put individuals at risk of infection. Other roots lie at a much deeper level and are less visible – factors increasing personal vulnerability (sexual-health ignorance, loneliness, peer pressure, low self-esteem, violence and lack of education) or social vulnerability (poverty and its root causes, armed conflict, cultural and religious traditions which put people at risk or instil discriminatory or judgemental attitudes).

To be truly comprehensive a HIV prevention strategy needs to aim at mitigating the impact, and decreasing the vulnerability, as well as reducing the immediate risks. With regard to reducing the risks from sexual transmission, people need to have full and accurate information on the effectiveness and limitations of all means of reducing risk, so that they can make the choices that are possible in their specific circumstances. Initiatives that promote only a single option – whatever that option – are both ineffective and a denial of people's rights to make fully informed choices.

Stigma is a major factor to be combated in any comprehensive HIV-prevention strategy. Since religious attitudes can be part of the problem, Christian Churches and other faiths have a special responsibility to tackle the roots of such stigma. Gillian Paterson insists on this very forcefully in her pamphlet, 'Stigma in the context of development: A Christian response to the HIV pandemic', *Progressio Comment* 2009.

Theology is about trying to make sense of how the God of faith is God-with-us in human history and fleshly reality. To be faithful to this task, theological reflection on living with HIV and AIDS must always be grounded in an honest and truthful analysis of the key human realities involved. Too often, faith-based discourse on HIV prevention has lacked a sense of HIV literacy; similarly, much criticism of faith-based approaches has lacked a faith-literacy, misunderstanding or misinterpreting the core values and insights which should in fact unite all who strive to halt the spread of HIV and AIDS. During my various visits, I was struck by the importance of faith in many of those living with HIV. Moreover, it seemed to be a major motivating force behind their personal involvement in community-based, home-care HIV and AIDS projects. I found the same to be true among those providing financial support in my own community back in St Basil & All Saints parish.

The Place of Condom usage within a comprehensive HIV Prevention Programme
One of the MMM sisters referred to earlier, a medical doctor, wrote: 'The official teaching of the Church condemns the use of condoms and this is killing our people.'

Her comment represented the feelings of many of the sisters. However, neither she nor her companions were suggesting that condoms were the only or even the main solution to the HIV and AIDS pandemic which was wreaking such havoc in people's lives and thus causing such anguish to the sisters themselves. She was simply putting into words their conviction that an absolute prohibition of condoms ran counter to what they could see was urgently needed in some situations and did not ring true to the compassion of the Christ they loved and served in their AIDS ministry.

The original purpose of the condom was to prevent conception. It was seen as a more or less effective means of contraception. However, with the advent of HIV-infection a totally different purpose for the condom appeared on the scene. This was its ability to act as a barrier to prevent transmission of the HIV-virus. In the days when HIV-infection was virtually a 'death sentence', the condom was seen as a form of life-protection rather than life-prevention. More recently antiretrovirals, where available and in conditions favourable for effective use, have reduced the level of AIDS-related deaths. When antiretrovirals are being used, condoms can still have a health-protection role, even though antiretrovirals themselves can also help in reducing the risk of transmitting the virus.

Obviously, condoms protect health only insofar as they are effective barriers to HIV-infection. Consequently, there are morally significant questions to be faced on this level. As a barrier to HIV-infection, the effectiveness of condoms is open to scientific investigation and will depend on the answer to such questions as: (1) given a good quality condom, how effective is it as a barrier to HIV-infection? (2) what about the additional factor of 'user failure'? (3) how 'user friendly' is it? (4) what safeguards are built in to check the quality of condoms?

The key question of how effective is a condom as a barrier to HIV-infection is tackled in a major US health report published in 2001 – National Institute of Allergy and Infectious Diseases, National Institutes of Health, Department of Health and Human Services, Scientific evidence on condom effectiveness for sexually transmitted disease (STD) prevention, 20 July 2001. In the light of this research, James Keenan SJ has noted that HIV is a very inefficiently transmitted infection compared to other sexually transmitted diseases. For instance, sixty to eighty per cent of women are infected as a result of a single exposure to gonorrhoea, whereas only 0.1-0.2 per cent of women are infected after a single exposure to HIV. In fact, as Keenan noted, using a condom reduces the already low transmission rate of HIV by eighty-five per cent. Consequently, in the light of this largest 2001 analysis of published peer-reviewed studies on condom effectiveness, Keenan is prepared to state very confidently: 'The conclusion is clear: condoms are not perfect, but for those who choose (or are forced into) sexual contact, significant protection is afforded by this method' (James Keenan, 'Four of the Tasks for Theological Ethics in a Time of HIV/AIDS', in *Concilium*, 2007/3, p. 182).

Presuming that the research data given in the above survey takes account of 'user failure' and 'user-friendliness', current research would seem to indicate that, provided adequate quality control is in place, condoms are a highly, though not completely, effective means for reducing the risk of HIV-infection.

Although it is commonly assumed that 'Catholic teaching' does not permit the use of condoms as a method of protection from HIV-infection, there is, in fact, no 'official' teaching on the use of condoms in the context of HIV. In fact, the use of condoms is not actually mentioned by Paul VI in his 1968 encyclical, *Humanae Vitae*. What is forbidden by the Pope is 'any action, which either before, at the moment of, or after sexual intercourse, is specifically intended to prevent procreation – whether as an end or as a means' (no. 14).

Most commentators agree that in the above passage from n.14 the Pope was mainly, though not exclusively, talking about using 'the pill' with the deliberate intention of preventing conception. However, he makes it quite clear that he is not condemning using 'the pill' for a therapeutic purpose even though it might indirectly prevent conception:

> The Church in no way regards as unlawful therapeutic means considered necessary to cure organic diseases, even though they also have a contraceptive effect, and this is foreseen – provided that this contraceptive effect is not directly intended for any motive whatsoever (no.15).

At the time of *Humanae Vitae*, the condom was not seen to have any therapeutic use. Its only purpose seemed to be as a form of contraception; and to intend contraception, either as an end or as a means, was forbidden by Paul VI's encyclical.

The advent of HIV-infection some years after *Humanae Vitae* gave condom-use a new purpose and meaning i.e. its ability to act as a barrier preventing HIV transmission. This new situation means that there can also be a quasi-therapeutic use for the condom i.e. therapeutic in sense of infection-preventing. Although not a curative use, when it is directly intended as a barrier to HIV-transmission, it can truly be described as 'safeguarding health' and even 'saving life'.

Hence, it could be argued that, if *Humanae Vitae* was being written today, the paragraph quoted above could legitimately be interpreted as meaning that the Church in no way regards as unlawful using condoms with the explicit intention of preventing HIV infection – even though condoms also have a contraceptive effect, and this is foreseen – provided that this contraceptive effect is not directly intended for any motive whatsoever.

Some may argue that the condom is not a 'necessary therapeutic means' since there is always the possibility of a couple abstaining from intercourse. Vatican II, more in touch with the reality of people's lives, warns against that line of action: 'When the intimacy of married life is broken off, the value of fidelity can frequently be at risk and the value of children can be undermined' (*Gaudium et Spes*, no. 51). Enforced total abstinence fails to respect the role of sexual intimacy in a couple's loving relationship which the same Vatican II document describes in relational terms as 'mutual self-giving … welling up from the fountain of divine love' (cf. no. 48 and 49). A couple bound together by such love will want to do what they can to avoid their love-making being health-threatening, possibly even life-threatening. To do otherwise would be to go against nature i.e. the nature of their married love. Hence, when one or both of them are already HIV-positive, their natural instinct to safeguard health might lead them to use a condom rather than threaten their love and fidelity by permanent abstinence.

In such situations a number of cardinals and bishops have accepted condom-use for HIV-prevention as a way to protect health and even life itself. To give but one instance, in 2004 Cardinal Danneels stated on Dutch TV:

> For one who does not want or cannot follow this path (of chastity and faithfulness) and who opts to engage in unsafe sexual behaviour, it is morally justifiable to use a condom … Other cardinals and bishops all over the world share this perspective … This comes down to protecting yourself in a preventive manner against a disease or death. It cannot be entirely morally judged in the same manner as a pure method of birth control.

Shortly after this, Cardinal Murphy O'Connor stated his agreement with Cardinal Danneels's position (cf. *The Independent*, 26 July 2004). Benedict XVI's reply to Peter Seewald's question, 'Are you saying, then, that the Catholic Church is actually not opposed in principle to the use of condoms?' hit the headlines, even though its precise meaning was unclear:

> She of course does not regard it as a real or moral solution, but, in this or that case, there can be nonetheless, in the intention of reducing the risk of infection, a first step in a movement toward a different way, a more human way of living sexuality (*Light of the World: Conversation with Peter Seewald*, CTS, London, 2010, p. 119).

In the above analysis of the teaching of *Humanae Vitae*, I have refrained from mentioning that the adequacy of this authoritative but non-infallible teaching on contraception is questioned by many Catholic theologians, myself included. Moreover, very many Catholic couples do not seem to follow it in practice. However, the purpose of this article is not to discuss directly the teaching of *Humanae Vitae* on contraception, but merely to argue that condom use for HIV-protection is not excluded by this teaching.

Moral considerations arising from the wider context
Around the world there are various public health campaigns seeking to tackle health and welfare issues, including HIV. The quality, reach and accessibility of these is variable, but they make up an important social context which needs to be considered. For instance, there are HIV-prevention programmes which actually promote the usage of condoms whenever people at risk are having sex together. As has already been noted, this can happen in a variety of scenarios.

The aim of such programmes is to prevent the spread of HIV-infection. They belong within the field of health promotion. Their objective is HIV-prevention, not birth-prevention. Hence, within such programmes condom use is specifically for a quasi-therapeutic purpose. Contraception is not the issue. Moreover, the intention of those promoting such programmes is presumably to promote 'safe' (i.e. non HIV-infectious) sex. It is not to encourage casual sex which would be socially irresponsible.

Nevertheless, such programmes raise some moral questions. But the questions they pose are not to do with contraception but with public health promotion. There are arguments for and against such programmes.

On the one hand, it is argued that making condoms easily available for young people facilitates immature and irresponsible relationships and so constitutes a threat to the young people themselves as well as to the social health and well-being of the society. The health and well-being of any society depends largely on the stability of families, whether in marriage or other similar long-term relationships. It also depends on the education of young people in social responsibility, including developing a capacity for mature and lasting life-giving relationships.

On the other hand, it is argued that where the environment is so unstable, many people, including those in the younger age group, feel pressurised into sexual activity with all the resultant risks of HIV-infection, and therefore that information and education is important to reduce those risks. The power of these social and environmental pressures is vividly described by Ann Smith (cf. *supra*, pp. 155-156).

A further social dimension also needs to be considered. If society is concerned to do all it can to ensure that parents are sufficiently mature and able to shoulder their child-rearing responsibilities, governments, local authorities and other concerned bodies will naturally be relieved when young people do not become parents before they are fit and able to undertake such a major role. The very instability of the environment makes it difficult or even morally impossible for many young people to enter into or maintain responsible long-term relationships and hinders the process of their maturing in social responsibility. The result of this can be a succession of partners, or multiple partners, all of which leave such young people much more vulnerable to HIV-infection. In the kind of socially unstable situation where HIV and AIDS are usually found, it could be argued that the availability of condoms to avoid HIV-infection might indirectly also prevent young people from becoming parents before they have matured sufficiently for such a role and before they have developed the kind of stable relationship needed for the healthy human upbringing of children. In that way, condoms could be playing an indirect, though important, role in furthering their personal and sexual development. The birth prevention involved here is not the purpose of the condom-use and so is not the deliberately intended contraception Paul VI is referring to. In their context and faced with the wide-spread threat and fear of HIV-infection, the prime concern and, in many cases, perhaps the only concern, of these young people would be to avoid HIV-infection. Likewise, the key motivation of health authorities in promoting condom-use would be HIV-prevention and health promotion.

Faced by such conflicting considerations the most helpful moral tool for resolving the dilemma would seem to be the 'principle of double effect' with its fourfold conditions. The first three conditions all seem to be fulfilled – 1. the act (condom-use) is not evil in itself; 2. the intention (health protection) is good; and 3. the evil effect (weakening of moral standards) is not a means to the good effect (HIV-prevention). Therefore, it would seem to come down to whether there is a proportionate reason for allowing the harm to occur. In other words, on balance does the good achieved outweigh the harm caused? The negative impact on social health through facilitating more casual sex and hindering personal development through its over-individualist focus needs to be weighed against the health-promotion effect in terms of preventing even more widespread HIV-infection.

This is an extremely difficult judgement to make. Society has the unenviable task of judging which policy is likely to bring about the greater good and cause least harm. Christians, Church authorities and NGOs have a responsibility to offer what wisdom and experience they can contribute to this difficult debate. In making their contribution it is important for them to recognise that they are dealing with a prudential judgement. To appeal misguidedly to the prohibition of condom-use as a moral absolute on this matter would be tantamount to short-circuiting the discussion. That would be inexcusable since what is at stake here is the possibility of a serious threat to the health and even life of many, especially women, currently at risk of HIV-infection.

The greater vulnerability of women

Statistical evidence shows that women are more vulnerable to HIV-infection than men. Often use of a condom by the male will be an essential safeguard for the health, even the life, of the woman. Yet mutual agreement on condom use is rare. Many men refuse to use a condom, regarding it as unmanly and diminishing their sexual enjoyment. Because of the inferior status of women in many cultures, it is not within their power to insist on condom use. Even women sex workers, driven by their family's poverty to earn as much as they can, are often forced into unprotected sex for commercial reasons. As long as such widespread inequality continues, any blanket prohibition of condoms consolidates still further the oppression suffered by these women and is hardly in keeping with the liberating message of the Gospel. The heart of the 'The Gospel of Life' (cf. subtitle of this article) speaks a specific challenge to men in the kind of situations envisaged here – 'if you are not going to respect these women sexually, at least respect their lives and do not threaten their health by unprotected sex'.

This highlights an obvious weakness in any approach which is too reliant on condoms. It still leaves men in control. What is needed is a major cultural shift so that men and women recognise each other as equal partners in any sexual exchange. Whether or not a condom (male or female) is used should be a matter of mutual agreement. Such a cultural shift would also involve liberating men from 'macho' stereotypes of masculinity and so empowering them to accept the mutual equality of both sexes.

Obviously, those opposed to condom use policies need to propose some alternative strategy for HIV-prevention. In fact, over many years a number of highly professional self-help educational programmes have been organised. Working on a peer-group principle, these are staffed by deeply motivated young people themselves. Inspirational pioneer work was done in this regard by Sister Miriam Duggan of the Congregation of Franciscan Missionary Sisters of Africa, a renowned surgeon and former Medical Director of St Francis Hospital, Nsambya in Kampala. When I visited Uganda in 1994 I was told that her 'Youth Alive Clubs' had attracted 5,400 young people as members. Their aim is to help young people appreciate the value of abstinence before and fidelity within marriage in terms of respect for themselves and their future partners, as well as its obvious role in HIV-prevention. Such initiatives are admirable and deserve support from Church and State, though a proper evidence-based analysis of the long-term effectiveness of such programmes is still needed to give them greater credibility.

Conclusion

Whatever line one takes on the condom issue, no HIV-prevention programme can afford to turn a blind eye to the enormous pressures coming from the wider environment and with the consequent effect of virtually disempowering many vulnerable individuals and leaving them with a very limited ability to make any kind of 'free' choice. It is impossible to stem the deadly spread of the AIDS pandemic unless the root causes which make people vulnerable in this way are unearthed and tackled. Any specific HIV-prevention programme will only be really effective if it is part of a fully comprehensive strategy. Over and above methods aimed at direct risk reduction, such as using condoms as a barrier to HIV-infection, eradicating root causes such as poverty, gender inequality, sexual violence, stigma and enforced migration are essential elements of any comprehensive HIV-prevention strategy.

On my first AIDS-related visit to Africa I had the privilege of meeting Noerine Kaleeba, a Ugandan woman whose husband had died of AIDS in the early days of the pandemic. Together with some companions who were going through a similar experience, Noerine and her husband, Christopher (while he was still alive), had formed TASO (The AIDS Support Organisation). By the time I met Noerine in 1994 TASO had grown into one of the largest and most effective HIV and AIDS support organisations in sub-Saharan Africa. The TASO group, like Noerine herself, made a deep impression on me. Their attitude was extremely positive. Their slogan was 'Living positively with AIDS'. For them AIDS made people much more aware that each day of one's life was a precious gift to be lived as fully as possible. While completely professional in catering for the multiple needs of people living with HIV / AIDS, they encouraged them to live positively. At a meeting of Asian theologians on HIV and AIDS I attended in Bangkok some years ago, something similar was said by a Thai man who spoke to us. After his life had fallen apart for a time, he seemed to find a new sense of direction when he discovered he was HIV-positive. The words he used to describe his experience were, 'AIDS is my gift'. While none of us could accept that life-threatening AIDS is a gift, his words brought home to us how profoundly it had affected his life.

Any Christian approach must be positive in its outlook and life-promoting in its aims. Jesus says: 'I have come that they may life and life in its fullness' (John 10:10). Certainly, the deepest desire of the MMM sisters mentioned earlier and the desire of all involved with HIV and AIDS is that those who live with, or who are affected by HIV 'should have life, and life in its fullness'. The emphasis must be, and must be seen to be, a 'yes' to life, rather than just a 'no' to condoms. Perhaps what is most prophetic in Paul VI's encyclical, *Humanae Vitae*, is its very title, 'human life'. What is life-preserving and life-enhancing must be the guiding principle of any truly human, and Christian, comprehensive HIV and AIDS programme and must be brought to bear not just on individual relationships but also on the whole variety of social, cultural, political and economic forces which have an impact on the HIV and AIDS scene. It is a 'yes' to authentic human development in the fullest sense. It is interesting that the English title of Benedict XVI's highly praised encyclical on the current economic situation is *'Integral Human Development in Charity and Truth'*.

CHAPTER TWENTY-TWO

Maria's Story and other HIV/AIDS encounters

At the invitation of CAFOD I attended a Consultation of Asian moral theologians on HIV/AIDS 25-28 January 1995 held in Bangkok. This had a deep impact on me, especially the witness of people who were invited to share their experience of living with AIDS. While I was in Asia, I took the opportunity to lengthen my visit to enable me to meet a number of groups in Bangkok and in the Philippines who were working at grass-roots to support people living with HIV/AIDS. A few years previously I had been bowled over on my first visit to Africa by encountering numerous people living with AIDS in Uganda. Their courage and resilience had affected me deeply, as did the commitment and professional competence of all who shared in caring for them. What follows is made up of a few excerpts from some of my diaries. It gives just a tiny flavour of what I experienced from these encounters. It is a revised version of four short articles I wrote in the Liverpool Archdiocesan weekly, The Catholic Pictorial (3 December 1995). Since the whole experience had opened my eyes to a whole new world, I felt obliged to share it as widely as possible. My book, New Directions in Sexual Ethics: Moral Theology and the Challenge of AIDS, London, Geoffrey Chapman, 1998, was another result of what I had experienced in this field. While the situation has changed radically since 1995, especially through the development of retroviral drugs and their greater availability, HIV infection still remains a major health threat in sub-Saharan Africa and other developing countries. Some of the details of what I have written are now out-of-date, yet the underlying causes remain the same.

I was speaking to a saint last week. She was a young Filipino woman called Maria (not her real name) whom I met in Manila.

Maria was raped by her father while still very young. This left her feeling unclean and worthless and fit only for the rubbish dump. In many Asian cultures men expect women to be virgins when they marry, even though the men set a much lower standard for themselves. So Maria felt she was now sub-standard. Moreover, young Asian women are usually expected to shoulder the responsibility for looking after their younger sisters and brothers, as well as providing for their parents. In Maria's case she felt this obligation all the more since she wanted to safeguard her younger sisters from her father.

To get money to support them, Maris tried a variety of jobs but the pay was never enough. Eventually she joined the thousands of other girls who, out of desperation and in order to support their families and parents, are forced into prostitution through sheer poverty. In Maria's case, her decision was a decision she felt obliged to make since it was the only way to earn enough to support her sisters. The way Maria put it to me was that she felt so worthless and unclean she had nothing to lose by becoming a prostitute. It was all she was good for – and it would help to save her sisters. As she was saying this, I could not help thinking of the words of Jesus, 'Greater love has no one than to lay down one's life for one's friends.' It had never dawned on me before that becoming a prostitute might be an act of heroic self-sacrifice. Yet that seems to have been so in Maria's case.

Eventually – almost inevitably – Maria became infected with HIV.

With the help of a Catholic organisation in Manila she was able to give up working as a prostitute and is now involved with them, helping with educational work to prevent the spread of the virus. As she said to me, 'When I was told I was HIV-positive, I prayed to God that I might be the last person this would happen to.' She is also spending a lot of her time helping to nurse men and women in the more advanced stages of full-blown AIDS. Not only does this expose her to the possibility of further infection due to her diminishing immune system. It is also making her face the suffering and physical degradation that almost certainly lies ahead for her. In many cases of full-blown AIDS a person's bodily functions more or less collapse and their condition becomes really terrible. Maria spoke very openly to me about this prospect lying ahead for her, probably in the fairly near future. She said she trusted God absolutely and knew he would be with her through whatever horrors she had to face. I was almost moved to tears as she was speaking by her deep faith and utter trust in God.

We are told to hate the sin and love the sinner. The only trouble with that advice is that it sometimes goes hand in hand with mistaken identity. In Maria's case, we can too easily interpret that advice as meaning that we should hate Maria's sin of becoming a prostitute but love her, the sinner. I think that would be a serious misreading of the situation. One thing that came home to me very forcefully as I listened to Maria and other women with similar stories is that such women should not be branded as sinners. Rather they are victims of sin. They are the victims of the sinful men who abuse them and of the widespread sinful attitude that regards women as inferior to men, a sinful attitude shared by many in our own country and even in our own Church. They are also victims of structural sin of an economic system which has destroyed the livelihood of the farming communities most of these women come from and reduced them and their families to abject poverty. And the roots of that structural sin lie much closer to home than the Philippines. A Good Shepherd sister I met in Thailand who is working with women in a similar plight to Maria insisted that such women should not be called prostitutes. She always refers to them as 'women lacking opportunities'.

Many people would condemn Maria and say that it is her own fault that she has AIDS. It serves her right for engaging in prostitution. God is punishing her for her sin. Those words sound more like the sentiments of the scribes and

Pharisees, than those of Jesus. I am sure Jesus would see behind the circumstances that drove Maria into dehumanising prostitution. He would be able to penetrate the depths of her soul and be moved by her spirit of generous self-sacrifice. 'Greater love has no one ...'

Before I left, Maria asked me to pray for her. I replied by asking her to pray for me. I honestly believe that her prayers will carry greater weight before the Lord than mine. I feel privileged to have a living saint praying for me.

We in Britain generally tend to be rather complacent about HIV/AIDS. There was a tremendous scare some years ago that the HIV infection would sweep across the country. That has not happened. So we breathe a sigh of relief and get back to business as usual.

People in the know consider this to be a very dangerous attitude. We cannot afford to relax our guard. Because of the long latency period of the infection which can be in excess of ten years, far more people may be HIV-positive and passing on the virus than we might suspect. Habits of sexual behaviour in our country are sufficiently permissive to favour a fairly rapid spread of HIV infection, once it is firmly established in the heterosexual population. And we need to remember that, contrary to popular opinion, most men and women infected with HIV are heterosexual.

Although the immediate causes of the spread of HIV/AIDS are mainly multiple-partner sexual activity and intravenous drug use, the underlying factors which are facilitating the rapid spread of AIDS through the world, especially among the heterosexual population in developing countries, are intimately linked to issues of social justice. These underlying factors would seem to be (1) poverty; (2) the inferior status of women in many cultures and societies linked to patriarchal attitudes and male irresponsibility; (3) sex tourism and the sex trade in general; (4) drugs and the drugs trade.

These four underlying causes are very closely interconnected. An example of this interconnection can be seen in the way they affect the lives of women in developing countries. Many women become infected with the HIV virus simply through being faithful to their husbands who either follow a 'double standard' morality or whose employment leads them to be away from home for long periods. Moreover, poverty and their inferior status force many women into prostitution. On top of this, sex tourism is created partly by the poverty of some countries and is made acceptable through the low status accorded to women. Furthermore, the drugs trade is linked to prostitution and drugs crops are often the only means the poor have to earn a meagre living. Then again, poverty affects medical care. For instance, lack of proper testing equipment may result in HIV infected blood being used in transfusions. This poses a particular danger to women since they may have a greater need for transfusions due to frequent pregnancies. Poverty, too, is a seedbed for TB (tuberculosis). The breakdown of the immuno-deficiency system by the HIV virus allows TB to develop. As a consequence of this, a new life-threat is likely to become rampant, posing a special danger to those living in poverty. This is because TB, especially in certain strains, is far more infectious that HIV. Finally, certain cultural practices affecting women (female circumcision, for instance) create 'HIV-friendly' conditions affecting the health of women

The human tragedy behind the HIV / AIDS statistics is not a tragedy without any hope. The best way to show both sides of the coin is to give an excerpt from the diary I kept during a visit to Uganda on behalf of CAFOD in July 1994. I was taken out into the Rakai district of Uganda to see what was being done by the Orphans Project set up Sister Ursula Sharp, an Irish Medical Missionary of Mary. Its numerous workers, drawn from the local community, visit families at home and help to organise local self-help and support schemes. At the time I was there, the Project was caring for a total of 8,700 orphans, 4,300 of them in the Rakai district. In fact, in the Rakai district seventy-five per cent of the children of ten years and under are orphans. Most of what follows is taken directly from my diary.

Our first visit was to an orphan-headed family. The parents had died of AIDS four years ago and the children had been looked after by the mother's sister until she too died of AIDS. The family is headed by a young girl aged twelve, who looks after her two brothers, one aged eleven and the other aged nine. All three are at school, their fees paid for by the Orphans' Project. The project has also built them a tiny little house with a bit of ground around for growing foodstuffs.

Our next visit was to a primary school. There are 475 children in the school (aged from five to sixteen) and 365 of them are orphans. The staff is comprised of twelve teachers, nine of them qualified. This is a high proportion for Uganda. Normally only about three in ten teachers in a school would have any teaching qualification. The orphans' school fees are covered by the Orphans' Project.

We next drove on a terrible road (really just a narrow footpath) through a kind of banana jungle and finally came to a little clearing where another orphan-headed family was living. This was a family of seven children, headed by their sister, aged twenty. Their parents had died of AIDS about three years previously and they had then been looked after by their mother's sister. After she too died of AIDS, the eldest girl, aged twenty-five, looked after them – and had a baby herself during this time. Then she too died of AIDS, so now the next eldest sister is in charge. The Orphans Project are helping the family reclaim some of the banana plantation which has gone wild. This will allow them to generate some income for themselves. They are also paying the eldest girl's fees to train as a teacher.

Our next visit was to another orphan family, this time looked after by their grandmother, aged eighty-four. There were six children, the eldest aged fourteen. Their parents had died in 1990 and 1991. The Project pays the children's school fees. The granny was thrilled with our visit. She insisted on doing a 'welcome' dance inside her little house.

Our next stop was to see an income-generating project. This was to help a widower, aged forty-four, whose wife had died of AIDS and who is in a fairly advanced stage of AIDS himself. He has five children, aged from seven to fourteen. The Project is helping with funds to clear some land for a crop of kasava (a root plant, used for producing a kind of flour). After that we drove to a parish complex. The priest there lives in a very poor little house. The parish consists of twelve sub-parishes and has two priests. Each sub-parish gets Mass once a month. There are 15,000 parishioners, of whom 4,000 are orphans. There are eleven Catholic schools in the parish. The local primary school has five hundred children in it. There is one senior school.

The main purpose of these orphan projects is to help either guardian-headed or orphan-headed families to be able to reach a fair standard of self-reliance, even, if possible, also generating income to cover necessities such as school fees. The financial help given by the Orphans' Project is mainly for (1) school-fees; (2) seeds and plants for cultivation projects; (3) help with reclaiming land or building some kind of little house.

When a young girl is head of an orphan-headed family, she is under great pressure. Poverty means that she has no money to buy things for herself, despite peer pressures from other girls at school. Hence, there is a great danger of their being exploited by men – sexual favours for little practical gifts. This is a further reason why income-generating projects are so important.

A team of six full-time staff are carrying out a programme of counselling and behaviour change with these children and those they live with and their school-fellows. This behaviour change programme is very necessary. A survey of the orphans' sexual behaviour in the diocese found that by the age of twelve, thirty per cent of girls are sexually active, rising to eighty-five per cent by eighteen years of age. For boys, ten per cent are sexually active by the age of fourteen, rising to seventy per cent by the age of eighteen.

The reasons for becoming sexually active are mainly economic need, peer pressure, rape (by strangers, relatives and teachers) and lack of parental supervision. To counteract these, the programme concentrates on such issues as income-generating activities (to combat economic need), group sensitization (against peer pressures) and educational programmes about sexual behaviour and AIDS.

The Orphans' Programme tackles the lack of parental supervision by developing a Guardians' programme. In this way when a parent is dying, careful plans are made as to who will look after the children – generally someone from the extended family. The programme makes sure that these 'guardians' are able to cope by helping with school fees, when necessary. It also enables the guardians to set up their own income-generating programmes – usually growing bananas, nuts, coffee or various fruits or vegetables for sale.

Where appropriate, the Orphans' Programme also helps to support 'orphan-headed' families, where the older brother or sister (sometimes quite young) becomes the head of the family. This is considered preferable to splitting up the family or their being placed in some kind of institution.

The tragedy of the HIV/AIDS pandemic in the developing world has direct links with ourselves in the developed world. Since part of the problem lies with us, part of the solution lies with us too.

Compassion means suffering with. To be compassionate we need to have some feel for the suffering people are enduring. That is equally true of compassion for people living with HIV/AIDS. The purpose of these articles has been to help us towards the beginnings of compassion for our sisters and brothers in the developing countries who are living with HIV/AIDS.

Compassion also leads us to ask the question, what can I do to help? Through funding HIV/AIDS projects in many developing countries, CAFOD is providing one practical answer to that question. CAFOD enables us to help in very concrete and direct ways, as is the case with Sister Ursula Sharp's Orphans Project which is funded by CAFOD.

However, it is becoming clear that HIV/AIDS in the developing world is not just a terrible tragedy which we in the richer countries should respond to with compassion. Those working on the ground are becoming more and more convinced that one of the major underlying causes of the rapid spread of HIV/AIDS in the developing countries is the poverty of so many of their people. And the root cause of this poverty can be traced back to the sinful structure of the world economic system which is geared to serve the interests of the better-off in the developed countries and the minority elites in the developing countries who work in partnership with them. People tend to blame irresponsible sexual behaviour for the spread of HIV/AIDS. While there is some truth in that, it overlooks the question as to who is primarily responsible for this sexual behaviour which is promoting the spread of HIV/AIDS. Is it the poor woman driven into prostitution as the only way to support her family? Is it the young husband forced to spend most of the year in an all-male dormitory away from his wife and family in order to hold down a poorly-paid job on some distant mine, or building site or industrial complex. Force is the key word in market forces. They do exert force. They can be a form of violence. Their supporters may appeal to the notion of freedom and free trade, but in reality the end result tends to be a drastic reduction in the effective freedom of the poorest in our world. The poor of our world, especially in the developing countries, are increasingly paying the cost of the prosperity of the moneyed elite. And at this moment in time, a major item in this cost they are paying is the rapid spread of HIV/AIDS in their midst. So the crucial question is: 'Who is ultimately responsible for the sexual behaviour which is assisting the spread of HIV/AIDS?' Do we find the answer to that question among the poor of the developing countries or among the prosperous elite here in the West?

There is no way the HIV/AIDS pandemic can be tackled effectively without a serious and committed effort to remedy the root causes of the poverty of the developing countries. Although it is false to claim that the HIV/AIDS pandemic is God's punishment for our sinful behaviour, nevertheless, human sin might still lie at the root of this pandemic – the sin of global injustice and the sinful attitude which leads men to treat women as second-class human beings.

A remarkable Ugandan woman, Noerine Kaleeba, has coined the phrase 'living positively with AIDS'. This is the slogan of her TASO organisation. Last July I had the privilege of meeting some wonderful Ugandan women from TASO who were HIV-positive and whose positive attitude to life and the preciousness of the opportunity each day presents would put the rest of us to shame. However, Noerine insists that it is not only those with the virus who must live positively with AIDS. It is a challenge to all of us. For the prosperous West that challenge necessarily involves a commitment to eradicate the human causes of poverty in the developing world and also to rid our world of so much injustice caused by the down-grading of women.

HIV/AIDS is an unmitigated evil. Nevertheless, God can draw good even out of evil. A world living positively with HIV/AIDS would be a very healthy world since it would be a world committed to eradicating economic injustice and promoting sexual equality. I firmly believe that living positively with HIV/AIDS is an essential element of the message of the Gospel for us today.

CHAPTER TWENTY-THREE

Vatican II Moral Theology in Practice:
Part One – Bernard Häring

Bernard Häring, a German Redemptorist priest, is generally acknowledged as one of the founding fathers of post-Vatican II Moral Theology. He played a major role in Vatican II itself. His two major writings in the field of moral theology are his Law of Christ and Free and Faithful in Christ – both comprising three volumes. Of particular interest to readers of this volume might be two books in which he recounts some of his own 'personal odyssey' in receiving Vatican II, Embattled Witness and My Witness to the Church. The latter is referred to in the following text as MWC. The following is the unpublished text of a lecture I was invited to give in Cambridge by the Margaret Beaufort Institute of Theology, a Catholic college for women in Cambridge. It was one of a series they arranged to honour the memory of Bernard Häring.

One point to avoid confusion – In some of my quotations from his writings, Häring refers to the Holy Office or the Doctrinal Congregation. These are pre-Vatican II names for what is now the CDF.

I first met Bernard Häring in the late 1960s. He came to Liverpool to run a three-day workshop on the Sacrament of Reconciliation. I had only recently begun lecturing in moral theology at our archdiocesan seminary in Upholland, Lancashire. The impression left by those three days was of a man who was passionately concerned that we should not give people a false image of God by the way we presented and celebrated the Sacrament of Reconciliation. Those were the days when many Catholics were still going to Confession on a very regular basis, often even once a week. The moral theology taught to priests was designed principally to equip them for dealing with the confessional. The presumption seemed to be that God's main concern was with people's sins and the priest had to help them recognise the gravity or otherwise of their sins, as well as their frequency. Integrity of confession was the object of the exercise and integrity meant that all possible serious sins had to be confessed. The priest had to make sure that that obligation was fulfilled. The image of God that came over was that of a bureaucratic judge, dispensing juridical forgiveness provided the sins confessed by the penitent tallied with those on the Lord's register. There had to be sorrow, of course – and a purpose of amendment. The tragedy was that the sins confessed were often peripheral to the important concerns of real life. So the sorrow felt tended to flow from a kind of devotional piety rather than being linked to any harm caused by sins committed. And the purpose of amendment was often a naked act of will, lacking any real credibility.

Those three days with Bernard Häring made a deep impression on his hearers, most of them priests or teachers. He was concerned about the authenticity of our celebration of the Sacrament of Reconciliation. It has to be true to God and true to ourselves. In other words, it should be grounded on the image of God revealed to us through the whole story of God's saving action in history and pre-eminently in the person, life and teaching of Jesus of Nazareth. It should also be grounded in who we are as human persons in relation to this God and our human family. For Bernard Häring the parable of the Father and his two sons, both deeply loved by him and unaware of how precious they are to him, is one of the major controlling images for our appreciation of this sacrament. Writ large in the life of Bernard Häring, therefore, were God and human persons, as loved by God.

The next time I met Bernard Häring was when he came to Upholland Northern Institute to give a course there. He arrived on a Sunday evening. I have a most vivid memory of concelebrating Mass with him the following morning, along with one or two other priests. We were the only ones with him in this small chapel. I had the impression of sharing in the eucharistic celebration of a saint. He was not pious in any trivial sense. Perhaps I can best express what I felt by saying that the Eucharist that morning seemed to express the wonder of his being. His whole being was eucharistic – deeply appreciative of the goodness of life and people and overflowing with gratitude to God. This experience came back to me later in the week when I was talking to him about his prolific writing. He told me that of all the many books he had written the one he himself liked best was a little book he wrote on the Eucharist.

Clearly, the eucharist was also writ large in the life of Bernard Häring.

The next time I met him was in Rome. By that time, I knew from various things he had written that the Congregation for the Doctrine of the Faith had been on his back. He had also provoked their ire by his stance on *Humanae Vitae* and by his support for Charles Curran. He even accompanied Charles to the Holy Office for his meeting with Cardinal Ratzinger and some other officials. What was eminently clear to me from what he wrote about all this, as well as from my personal knowledge of him, was that he had a very deep love for and commitment to the Church. In no way could he be accused of working out any authority hang-ups of his own in his dealings with the Congregation for the Doctrine of the Faith. Though he had a deep belief in the inherent goodness of people, he was not blind to our propensity to sin and knew that this affected not only personal relationships but also human structures and how they work and are maintained – even within the Church. He had a good understanding of how the inner corridors of power in the Church operated. This came from his long years of teaching in Rome, his involvement with the process of drafting documents prior to and during the Second Vatican Council and also his being a member of the Papal Birth Control Commission. So he had first-hand experience of the human face of structural sin within the Vatican. Consequently, his passionate love for the Church was sometimes expressed in anger when he was convinced that the actions of some officials were an obstacle to the legitimate search for truth or impeded important initiatives in pastoral practice or were motivated by personal advancement or power politics and not by any commitment to a ministry of service.

That time in Rome was my last meeting with him. We were at an international meeting of moral theologians hosted by the Accademia Alfonsiana to celebrate the bi-centenary of St Alphonsus. The Vatican did not approve of this meeting and imposed some additional speakers on the programme. Just before Häring was due to have a public debate with one of these, I was talking with him in the courtyard. I asked him about that particular moral theologian, whether he was a diocesan priest or a member of some religious congregation. Häring replied: 'He belongs to the congregation of careers!' I then asked whether many theologians supported his hard-line views on moral theology. The reply came back: 'The congregation of careers has many members.'

Those words may seem harsh and unkind. However, they vividly express Häring's pain that positions of authority and influence in the Church could be occupied by people whose motivation seems to be their own career rather than the good of the Church and the people it serves. I get the impression that in his later years, because Häring loved the Church so passionately, he became more and more outspoken on this point.

So the Church, too, was writ large in the life of Bernard Häring.

When I was preparing this talk, I jotted down a long list of Häring's concerns as a moral theologian whose principal concern was in the pastoral field. That list had many items on it, but the more I tried to see how they were all linked, the more I began to see that the foursome I have focused on in this introduction seem to be central to his whole approach:

God	loving, compassionate, forgiving, empowering.
Human Persons	loved by God, precious to God, gifted by God, invited into a communion of love with God and with each other.
Eucharist	sacramental celebration of this love of God for persons, a sign and instrument of unity, forgiveness, reconciliation, a table which is inclusive rather than exclusive.
Church	a gathering of people called to be a sign, sacrament, witness of God's all inclusive love.

Four Points of the Compass

Looking for an image to portray these four major points in relation to all the other items on my list, I settled for the image of the four points of the compass, something simple and easy to remember. Obviously, God has to be the north. We take all our bearings from the magnetic north. In other words, when we focus on human persons, or Eucharist, or Church, it is always in relation to God. So if our God-setting is wrong, our other three settings will be thrown out of alignment. So I settled on the following four points: God as North, Human Persons as West, Eucharist as East and Church as South

Let us imagine these four points I have highlighted as the four points on Häring's compass guiding his approach to pastoral issues.

North-West: Häring's commitment to God and human persons

Obviously, getting this alignment right is an essential dimension of pastoral practice. One could give a whole series of lectures on what is implied in this alignment. I would like to touch on just two issues which I believe are a very important interface between moral theology and pastoral practice at the present time:

'Oikonomia' (Economy) or epikeia

An interesting angle on this topic is found in Häring's little book, *No Way Out? Pastoral Care of the Divorced-Remarried*. As an introduction to his discussion of this pastoral issue, he writes first about 'the spirituality and practice of oikonomia'. 'Oikonimia' is a pastoral tradition in the Eastern Churches which is similar to but goes far beyond *'epikeia'* in the West. Both are about humanising apparently inflexible laws by taking into account the more intimate personal situation. Häring speaks of the 'benevolent father of the household' (perhaps a reference to the father and his two sons) and also of 'trust in the good shepherd who knows and calls each and every one by name and when necessary leaves the ninety-nine healthy sheep behind for a while and astonishes them in order to go lovingly after a single lost sheep to rescue it' (p. 40).

Stressing the fact that 'the letter without the spirit can only kill', he goes on to write: 'Economy is a much more broadly understood concept and a spirituality which includes and decodes the best of our Western statements about *'epikeia'* but goes far beyond these' (p. 41). Häring also makes the following comment, drawing together both the Eastern and Roman Catholic tradition: 'Along with virtually the entire tradition of the Eastern Churches and a large part of the Roman Catholic tradition, St Alphonsus Liguori taught that even in questions of the natural law there is room for *epikeia*' (MWC, p. 224).

The issue of *'epikeia'* featured in Bernard Häring's first brush with the Holy Office. It involved the pastoral interpretation of *Humanae Vitae*. To quote Häring's own description of a communication he received from Cardinal Seper:

It is a very clear expression of the firm determination of the Doctrinal Congregation, in regard to the prohibition of artificial contraception, to stand rigidly with absolute inflexibility and absolute exclusion of every kind of application of *'epikeia'* or *'oikonomia'*. No one should be allowed to think that an infringement of the objective scale of values would be permitted (MWC, p. 139).

Häring was deeply disturbed when the John Paul II came out with a particularly hardline statement about *Humanae Vitae*. Among other things, the Pope seemed to suggest that questioning the absoluteness of the teaching of encyclical was calling in question the idea of the holiness of God. Häring felt obliged to write a personal letter to the Pope. In it he wrote:

How can one expect the critically-minded people of today, including devout Christians, to accept the statement that in the interpretation of the norm laid down by *Humanae Vitae* every exception (all *'epikeia'*) must be absolutely excluded, and then put forward the statement: 'In reality, what is called into question by the rejection of this teaching is the very idea of the holiness of God' (MCW, p. 227).

The issue of the flexibility of norms haunted him to the end of his life. In one of the last books he wrote, he reveals his deep feelings very starkly with his very personal comment that, after his 'intimate experience of war, the intimate experience of senseless killing and dying, the personal witnessing of the brutalising of many':

I find it absolutely laughable and at the same time frustrating that at my age I still have to pour out so much energy on questions like flexibility or inflexibility concerning the forbidding of contraception and in the struggle against sexual rigorism (MWC, p. 24).

'Do the best you can in your situation' as a guide for decision-making
With the needle of the Häring compass still pointing north-west, i.e. God and human persons, I would like to touch on a second 'gap' which concerns the interface between moral theology and pastoral practice at the present time.

One of the best articles on moral theology and pastoral practice that I never wrote carried the title, 'On Starting from where people are...!' Incidentally, the Incarnation is the prime example of that. However, that is another story – though not really.

The gap between Church law and practice is not just about the tension between the universal and the particular. It can also be due to different worldviews and theological approaches between some Vatican directives and the convictions of many in the Church, theologians and lay. The pastoral practitioner, therefore, needs to be able to handle this gap without hurting individuals or violating their rights – and yet without destroying people's love and respect for the Church.

Häring managed to achieve this even on those occasions when he was quite open in his disagreement with a particular piece of Church teaching. This was even true when he was expressing his anger at the failure of those responsible for such inadequate teaching. Perhaps they had failed to honour the necessary consultation process needed to ensure that the teaching represented the best current understanding in the Church.

A case in point is his handling of the so-called 'infallible' statement about the non-ordination of women. He devotes the whole of chapter sixteen of *My Hope for the Church*, the last book he wrote, to this issue. Häring makes it perfectly clear that, despite John Paul II's intention to make an infallible decision, he did not observe the criteria for infallibility laid down by Vatican II. Yet, in stating this, he is not trying to score a point. In fact, he presents these built-in safeguards as redounding to the credit of the Church. Their very purpose is to help the Church be true to its teaching mission even in the face of a mistaken use of authority.

There are two levels to all these disagreements about the adequacy of Church teaching on a particular moral issue.

There is the level of theological or ethical argumentation. Some disagreements can be traced back to different ethical or theological presuppositions. It is common knowledge that there are different schools of moral theology in the Roman Catholic Church at present and that decisions emanating from the CDF – or even Pope John Paul II himself – tend to reflect the thinking of only one of these schools.

However, there is a second level which involves the individual person and his or her conscientious decision. Naturally, any well-disposed person will try, as far as possible, to be attentive to the concerns voiced at the first level I have just mentioned. However, that might still leave them dissatisfied. Their decision cannot await the outcome of complex theological-ethical debates. It is something to be faced now. Previously, when lay people were less well-educated and when such issues were debated behind closed doors, most might have resorted to consulting their priest. However, today people are urged to accept their own responsibility for decision-making.

In his book, *Moral Demands and Personal Obligations*, Washington, Georgetown University Press, 1993, the German moral theologian, Josef Fuchs states: 'The distinction is made today between the ethical goodness of the person - morality in the truest sense of the word – and the ethical rightness of action or behaviour' (p. 157). For Fuchs 'the ethical goodness of the person' is 'morality in the truest sense of the word' because it is dealing with the inner integrity of a person. That is why it goes to the heart of a person-centred approach to moral theology.

In the area of practical decision-making what is meant by 'ethical goodness' is that a person tries to honour his or her personal integrity in the reality of everyday life to the best of their ability. They do this if they have with openness and integrity tried their best to discern what course of action in their particular circumstances and taking account of their personal moral capacity is most in keeping with the criterion of the dignity of the human person, integrally and adequately considered – a criterion to which they are fully committed. They realise that their judgement is fallible and so it is possible that they are mistaken. Nevertheless, as long as they have made a serious conscientious judgement according to their best lights, they have clearly demonstrated their commitment to personal integrity.

Within the Roman Catholic Church, for instance, this means that no official teaching on sexual ethics can oblige a Catholic to act against their conscience or to accept as true any ethical ruling of the Church which they conscientiously believe not to be true. It also means that a person is abdicating their moral responsibility as a human person if they decline to follow their own convinced conscience purely because a Church directive on sexual ethics forbids them to do what they know they really should do. This is not saying anything which is contrary to what Roman Catholic moral theology has always taught.

Hence, if a couple are convinced that the Church's official teaching on contraception is erroneous, they are not obliged to accept this teaching as true. In fact, they would be wrong to do so while they remain in their present state of mind. If they go on to decide that the good of their own marriage dictates they should use contraception themselves, they should regard their decision as well taken and so they can rest assured that they remain pleasing to God. Something similar would hold true across the board in the whole field of sexual ethics. So, for instance, it would also apply to similar conscientious decision-making on the part of gay men and lesbian women expressing their love sexually in a committed, faithful relationship or cohabiting heterosexual couples or people entering a second marriage after divorce.

In all of these cases I am assuming that we are dealing with people who are trying to do their best in a moral sense. They do not have a purely self-centred agenda. They are committed to the basic moral criterion of the dignity of the human person. They are also trying to behave responsibly both in the ongoing task of conscience-formation and in how they go about their conscientious decision-making. That being the case, in all these instances people are obliged to follow their conscientious judgement as to what is the right thing to do; and that this remains true, even when their conscientious judgement seems to be at odds with Church teaching. Häring often expressed this by saying: 'What does not come from an honest conviction is a sin' (MWC, pp. 145, 164).

Put very simply, therefore, a person following their conscience in this way can be absolutely certain that, in so doing, they are doing the best they can and God does not ask for more. They are being true to their commitment to be faithful to God's will and are being 'ethically good' as persons, even though it is possible that what they are doing might not be 'ethically right'.

Häring's compass, pointed north-west to God and the human person, can be a great pastoral help to people struggling to do their best in the process of pastoral decision-making.

North East: Häring's commitment to God and the Eucharist
It is remarkable how many day-to-day pastoral problems are linked to the Eucharist, especially within the Roman Catholic community. The cutting edge of the issue of divorce and remarriage is often experienced when it comes to the reception of Communion, especially if couples have young children and want to give them good example and encouragement by themselves receiving Holy Communion at Sunday Mass each week. Funerals would be another time when this is highlighted.

The Eucharist was of tremendous importance to Bernard Häring – not just personally but as the central celebration of the whole community. So he was deeply disturbed when the observance of purely human laws and practices were given priority over the availability of the Eucharist to provide spiritual nourishment. This is why, on the issue of obligatory celibacy for the ordained ministry, he is prepared to state very frankly that 'the present situation in the "Latin" Church (i.e. Western-Roman Church) is in my opinion untenable' (MWC, p. 208). This is because, as he says,

> the right to regular participation in the eucharist comes from the solemn testament, the act of empowerment of Jesus: 'Do this in my memory. Take and eat this, all of you.' On the other hand, the admission of only the unmarried to the priesthood is a purely human tradition. It must be clear that in cases of conflict the divine act of empowerment has to have priority … my main concern is that the Western Church may not violate the right of a regular participation in the eucharist of a large part, indeed, even the majority of the faithful, for the sake of a law of celibacy based on this human tradition and legal structure (MWC, p. 209).

As far as I know, Häring never extended this line of argument to the ordination of women. However, I am sure that, had he lived a little longer, he would certainly have done so. In recent years his position on the ordination of women moved considerably. As mentioned earlier, he discusses that issue in the last book he wrote. Chapter sixteen is entitled, 'The Future of the Church and the Issues of Women'. He is in no doubt that, before long, women will be ordained in the Roman Catholic Church and he goes so far as to say: 'I suspect that the rejection of ordaining women to celebrate the Eucharist is a relic of magical thinking' (MWC, p. 114). He even dares to express the hope that 'it would be splendid if the pope were to realize and humbly acknowledge his error before he leaves us ... It would be a special sign of God's grace to ecumenism' (MWC, p. 118). Häring says these things out of his commitment to the full and equal dignity of women, certainly. In fact, he even writes: 'I consider Rome's "infallible" decision not only inopportune, but also out of touch with the times.'

Perhaps to a greater extent, he is motivated by a concern that the Eucharist should play its full and powerful place in the Church's mission to the world. This comes out in a story which Häring repeats in two of his recent books. In Häring's early days in Rome, the Jesuit, Fr Hurth, had great influence with Pope Pius XI (he was one of the editors of the encyclical, *Casti connubii*). He used to lecture to packed halls. Häring tells of hearing him spend the whole of one lecture discussing whether a priest should be allowed to celebrate Mass twice on a weekday if this was the only way it would be possible for people to attend Mass at least once a year. Hurth's answer was an emphatic 'No'. And the reason he gave was that people have never been obliged to attend Mass on a weekday. Häring expected the whole student body to rise up in protest – but there was not a murmur. Authority had spoken. Häring ends his narrative by saying:

> I took my hat and departed, deeply shaken: So, the Eucharist is only 'a law', not a means of life, not an experience of the community of faith and salvation, not a celebration of grateful remembrance, not life from the New Covenant and for the New Covenant! (MWC, p. 32).

Somehow, Häring seems to be bringing in all four points of his compass here in challenging Hurth's view which is unpastoral in the extreme. Häring sees the Church not in legal categories but as a community of people. For him the Eucharist is the lifeblood of that community. And God is not a trivial God delighting in legal niceties but a dynamic, life-giving God, empowering people, inspiring the Church and giving every eucharistic celebration an inclusive potentiality to be a symbol of the unity of our whole human family.

I have a feeling that, despite all the violence, ethnic cleansing and discrimination of our age, one of the 'signs of the times' of our day is a yearning for inclusivity. I do not mean this in any collectivist or totalitarian sense – no Big Brother state, not even Europe (even though I am a pro-European). Somehow I feel that the Christian Church is called to be the symbol (sign or sacrament or whatever) of this inclusivity. It is not an inclusivity which threatens our uniqueness as human persons. It rejoices in the unique giftedness of each of us but recognises that this is enriched, not diminished, by the celebration of our relatedness and interdependence.

I am amazed at how often the prayers in the Eucharist express a belief that it is through our sharing in this Eucharist that we are drawn together. I was saddened by our Bishops' Pastoral Letter, *One Bread, One Body*. Somehow it gave the impression that the Eucharist is a celebration of an 'in group'. You had to belong to fully participate.

North-South: Häring's commitment to God and the Church

What about the North-South axis on our compass? North-South these days smacks of inequality. That is certainly true when we line up God and the Church together. The Church through the sinfulness of some of its structures can easily obscure the true face of God. Having experienced this in the life of many of his fellow theologians and even in his own life. Häring was even prepared to say that in the Church 'we are in a pathological situation' (MWC, p. 90). However, far from letting this get him down, he saw this as a call from God to which he should respond – a living example of his moral theology of responsibility. He writes very movingly of this period of his life:

> This was the most creative period of my life. The perspective of an imminent death gave me a great inner freedom from every form of external pressure ... Without irony or sarcasm I believe that I can say that my experiences with the Holy Office, and the later Doctrinal Congregation, have had a liberating effect on me ... Whoever loves the Church must also be prepared to suffer in the Church, with the Church, through the Church, and for the Church (MWC, p. 93).

This very moving passage reminds us that what is sometimes presented as rebellious opposition creating confusion and fermenting unrest may, in reality, be deep loyalty to the Church, solid commitment to the truth and a burning pastoral concern for people, struggling with the complexities of everyday life. That was certainly true of Häring. In one of his communications with the Holy Office, he made it clear that the responsibility for confusion in the Church does not lie solely, or even principally, on the shoulders of theologians. The Vatican, by its refusing to accept the legitimacy of pluralism on moral issues, is itself a major cause of any confusion that might exist:

> The faithful certainly know already, or at least have a right to know, that in questions of interpretation there is a pluralism in the Church, which by no means needs to lead to chaos or laxism. My question to the Doctrinal Congregation is precisely this: Must it not lead to a much greater confusion among critical and uncritical faithful if the Doctrinal Congregation takes a position on a very concrete question and authoritatively presents a very specific solution while, at the same time, many learned

theologians and physicians, on the basis of their expert knowledge, experience, long term reflection and discussion, are of another opinion? (MWC, p. 159).

It might be helpful to quote an even longer passage from a document Häring wrote to the Doctrinal Commission of the Holy Office in 1977 when they were challenging his orthodoxy:

> Reformable teachings cannot demand an act of faith nor absolute agreement. All the world know that in the past the Magisterium itself has reformed several doctrines which it had previously presented in emphatic fashion; and that was made possible by the strength of the loyalty and honesty of many theologians.
>
> I will always attempt to honour the Church, the People of God, and its Magisterium through absolute honesty, even if that should bring me a threat. This loyalty and honesty is for me a holy duty, even in all those questions in which after serious reflection and prayer, I have come to the conviction that I cannot accept the all too narrow interpretations of the Doctrinal Congregation. This is especially so when I know myself to be at one with many bishops, with the majority of theologians, and with a large number of laity zealous for the faith. I would not have such great trust in my own insights if I found myself in contradiction to the great majority of theologians or to the sensus fidelium of the Christian people (MWC, p. 153).

Häring did not enjoy this kind of encounter. In fact, in a later letter to Cardinal Seper, the then Prefect of the Congregation, he said that his trial at the hands of the Holy Office 'has transformed my love for the Church into a suffering and critical love' (MWC, p. 155). This makes it clear that, although he did not enjoy it, he saw it as expressing his love for God and God's people through his love for the Church. That is why he is a challenge to theologians. We are failing in our pastoral responsibility if we remain silent when we believe that an instance of Church teaching is either mistaken or misleading to people. Häring puts it well:

> A theologian or group of theologians becomes inauthentic when, rather than suffer for the truth, they allow themselves to be frightened and choose to bury the talents of creative freedom and creative loyalty in favour of 'safe' repetition of old formulas … A theologian can betray the Church and truth when he denies his conviction of the truth 'out of obedience' (MWC, p. 180).

Nevertheless, he warns his fellow theologians against 'struggling for their cause out of resentment and bitterness ... in rebellious disobedience' (op. cit.).

Conclusion

By way of conclusion, I would say that Bernard Häring offers the Church, and moral theologians in particular, a shining example of the immense gifts that can come to the Church through faithfully receiving the teachings and spirit of Vatican II. In particular Bernard Häring was a moral theologian who:

- believed in persons and in the dignity of every human person;
- appreciated that persons live in history and are themselves historical beings, actually making history;
- recognised the theological importance of human experience;
- was aware that each person's call from God is unique and ongoing throughout life;
- understood the creative tension between the universal and the particular;
- was deeply conscious of how human structures are part of the complex web of interdependence between persons;
- knew what terrible harm to the dignity of human persons can be done by unjust structures, themselves a human construct and maintained by the connivance or collusion of fellow human beings;
- believed that his passionate commitment to human persons was an integral part of the love of God poured into his heart by the Holy Spirit, a love revealed in the burning love of Jesus for all persons, but especially for the marginalized and despised;
- experienced how that passionate love was inflamed with anger whenever the dignity of human persons was violated, but especially when this violation was perpetrated in the name of religion;
- had a deep love for the Church and served it faithfully, despite the suffering he experienced at the hands of Church officials.

CHAPTER TWENTY-FOUR

Vatican II Moral Theology in Practice:
Part Two – Charles Curran

Charlie Curran and I have been good friends for many years. Hence my use of the familiar name, Charlie, in what follows. All who know him well are used to calling him 'Charlie'. Even though friends, we have had our disagreements. For instance, I have never been keen on his insistence on using the word 'dissent' with regard to our reaction to erroneous or inadequate official Catholic teachings. I have always preferred to speak of 'disagreement'. To me 'dissent' can sound too confrontational and does not give sufficient status to the alternative view being proposed. I elaborated on that point in two articles in The Tablet articles under the overall heading of 'Obedience and Dissent' (14 & 21 June 1986, pp. 619-629 & pp. 647-649). The article printed below is an unpublished tribute to Curran which I was invited to deliver at the Cincinnati Convention of the Catholic Theological Association, 5-8 June 2003.

I see being a moral theologian as a particular vocation. In this short piece all I intend to do – and all I feel competent to do – is to describe briefly under eight headings how Charles Curran has influenced me through the way he has lived out his vocation as a moral theologian. To me the best way to learn about the 'vocation' of a moral theologian is through the lives of dedicated and outstanding moral theologians like Bernard Häring and Charles Curran. In a sense, this gathering is a living Festschrift to Charlie – we all have our own readings of his life as a moral theologian. a magnificent volume. And since the rest of his life is still to be written by him – and read by us – we are still at the stage of work in progress! Let me move on to my eight headings.

1. Vocation

The title of this session refers to the 'vocation' of the moral theologian. That is a very rich word. I believe that our primary vocation is to be ourselves. And that is true of Charlie. His vocation is to be himself, Charles Curran. Being a Catholic Christian, priest and moral theologian all flow from responding to his personal vocation. Charlie throws his own unique light on the vocation of a moral theologian precisely because he is such a sensitive, loving, warm human person; because his Christian faith reflects so deeply the love, compassion and burning zeal for justice in Christ; because Charlie has such a belief in and commitment to the Catholic Church and its Spirit-inspired mission, despite all its sinfulness and dysfunctionality; and because he is such an outstanding scholar, teacher, practitioner and guide in the field of moral theology.

I think Charlie is showing us that the more integrated we are as persons, the more richly will we be able to follow our vocation as moral theologians.

That does not mean that moral theologians need to be exceptionally well-rounded human persons in every possible way. But it does mean that we need to be able to live with ourselves and other people, as well as with the mystery of our multi-faith world, our divided Christian Church and our beloved but very sin-infected Catholic Church.

2. Ecclesial Vocation

In its 1990 Instruction, the CDF adds the adjective 'ecclesial' to 'vocation' as applied to theologians. Again Charlie's life has helped me to understand much more deeply how a moral theologian's vocation is 'ecclesial'. In 1986 the CDF ruled that Charlie could no longer be recognized as a Catholic theologian. Implicitly it was saying that Charlie had not been true to his ecclesial vocation. I suspect that most people who know Charlie and are familiar with his writings and teaching cannot accept that. I certainly cannot. I believe that in his dispute with the CDF Charlie was being very true to his ecclesial vocation. However, I have never been completely convinced by Charlie's use of the term 'dissent' to describe his position. As he sees it, being true to his vocation as a moral theologian means that he should be prepared to 'dissent' from the non-infallible teaching of the Church when convinced it is not true.

To my mind, the word 'dissent' gives away too much. After all, the 'ecclesial vocation' of the theologian resonates with the deeper tradition of the Church which speaks of the theological magisterium as well as the hierarchical magisterium. Yves Congar reawakened the Church to this rich vein of our tradition. In his dispute with the CDF I believe that Charlie was fulfilling his role as a member of the theological magisterium. To speak of such a positive action in terms of 'dissent' does not, to my mind, do justice to the positive contribution he is making. He is implicitly saying: 'The Catholic Church has much richer teaching to offer than is contained in this official statement. We must not sell people short.'

Sometimes theologians like Charlie are not supported as they should by many of their colleagues, by theological institutions and even by the theological establishment itself. If we do this from a fear of institutional reprisal, it is we, not Charlie, who are not being true to our ecclesial vocation. That is another reason why I do not like the word 'dissent'. 'Not dissenting' can give a respectable aura to not supporting someone like Charlie, when, in fact, we are failing in our corporate responsibility as members of the theological magisterium.

3. Pastoral Vocation

In 1973 Charlie wrote a two-part article, Divorce: Catholic Theory and Practice in the United States, in the *American Ecclesiastical Review*. Not long after reading this article, I moved from teaching in the seminary to establishing a centre for Clergy In-Service Training and Adult Formation in the North of England. This exposed me to the human pain and tragedy of marriage breakdown – and the anguish of priests who felt unable to respond positively to what they saw was clearly the healing power of some second marriages. As a result of this experience I wrote *Divorce and Second Marriage: Facing the Challenge* (London, Collins, 1982) a book which many lay people and priests in the UK seemed to find pastorally helpful. I can honestly say that I would never have written that book, had it not been for the pastoral example and inspiration of Charlie.

On the issue of *Humanae Vitae*, I found Charlie very challenging. Prior to *Humanae Vitae*, I had helped my own Archbishop offer pastoral guidelines to priests based on the assumption that a change of teaching was coming. *Humanae Vitae* was a great shock to me. It was something I had not expected. When it was published, I had to sort out where I stood myself. After a period of prayer and reflection, I argued publicly that we needed time to reflect on its teaching. Perhaps the Holy Spirit was speaking to us through this disconcerting letter from the Pope. With hindsight I feel that I failed people pastorally, not so much through a lack of courage (though that may have played a part) but through a defective ecclesiology. Here again Charlie taught me another important lesson – you cannot be true to your ecclesial vocation as a moral theologian unless you have a sound ecclesiology. I love Bryan Massingdale's comment in the Black Theology workshop: 'We must be the Church we believe in.' Our ecclesial vocation must not hide the real Church, but reveal it.

4. Healing and Growth-Encouraging

I once prepared a talk on Adult Christian Education by simply reflecting on my work as a moral theologian with priests and lay people over many years. That process made me aware that what I had been involved in was a process of remedial Christian Education – for myself as much as for others. Very misguided views of sin were at the root of some of the harmful attitudes needing such remedial treatment. Charlie's early writings on sin were particularly helpful at that stage. He helped me to appreciate more deeply the healing dimension of the vocation of a moral theologian.

Although I never warmed to Charlie's theory of 'compromise', what he wrote on that theme made me more aware that the vocation of the moral theologian involves being sensitive to where people are, their strengths and weaknesses and the difficult and ambiguous situations in which they have to live their lives.

5. Public

I am a naturally shy and retiring person. I dislike media attention and am horrified when it comes my way. So I admire Charlie's willingness to appear on the public stage, when appropriate, and can recognise that it is not motivated by ambition or desire for self-glory. It probably goes against the grain for him as a person. But he sees it as being bound up with his vocation as a moral theologian in this day and age.

Even though I did not realise it at the time, looking back I can see that the way Charlie lived out the public dimension of his vocation as a moral theologian inspired me to write the following passage in one of my books:

If moral theology is to be in tune with the spirit of our modern age, it can no longer confine its discussions behind closed doors or to the privileged pages of some inaccessible theological journal. Moral questions are the constant topic of open debate in the media. Moral theologians today have to make a choice. They can refuse to play any part in this public debate. That might give them a quiet life and avoid any tension with the Vatican or their local hierarchy. However, it would be an evasion of their ministry as moral theologians in the Church and the world.

Or they can involve themselves in the thick of the debate. That means that they must be prepared to say what they honestly believe. Obviously, they can, and usually should, report the authentic teaching of the Church – that is part of the contribution they are expected to make. However, they must also be prepared to be critical of that teaching to the extent that it is open to serious theological questioning. To evade such a critical stance when demanded by sound theological scholarship would be to surrender their credibility in the dialogue. Moreover, it would also harm the credibility of the Church's commitment to truth (*From a Parish Base: Essays in Moral and Pastoral Theology*, DLT, London, 1999, pp. 126-127).

That gives a very true description of how Charlie has lived his vocation as a moral theologian. Bryan Massingdale made the same point in different words earlier in this meeting: 'We have been given a shared obligation to speak the truth.'

Readers might be interested to know that, on my personal odyssey, only on two occasions have I had something published in the UK national press. One of them was a piece in *The Times*, 'Sexual Ethics and the Vatican' (30 August 1986), supporting Charlie when the CDF were conducting their proceedings against him.

6. Ecumenical

I suspect that Charlie, after holding his Professorship in the illustrious Southern Methodist University since 1991, might feel it somewhat unnatural, to return to teaching moral theology in an academic setting which was exclusively Roman Catholic. He is a witness to us all that the vocation of a Roman Catholic moral theologian today must be solidly ecumenical. By ecumenical, I mean recognising our fundamental solidarity with other Christian theologians, respecting the riches of our specific ecclesial traditions and being open to learn from theirs, even to the extent of modifying our Catholic teaching or, in some instances perhaps, acknowledging that we have got it wrong. If we believe that God's Spirit is at work in other Christian Churches, this implies that, when there are particular issues of moral disagreement between the major Christian Churches, the current Catholic teaching should not be presumed to be the definitive Christian position on this topic.

As mentioned in the previous piece, Charlie's close friend, mentor, great admirer and support, Bernard Häring, wrote a book entitled *My Witness for the*

Church. That beautiful title could be applied to Charlie's years at the Southern Methodist University. It was very wrong and sad that Charlie was removed from his post at the Catholic University of America and that other Catholic universities could not see their way to offering him an appropriate post. Nevertheless, I suggest that we should not see those years as a period of exile for Charlie; rather they are his witness to the Church that, in our ecumenical age, perhaps the most appropriate setting for living out one's vocation as a Catholic moral theologian is not one which is an exclusively Catholic setting. As Jill Raite said in her plenary lecture: 'Ecumenism is not a choice, but a necessity.'

7. Conversation

We often apply the term 'conversation' to theology. A friend of Charlie and myself, the late Austin Smith CP, has often pointed out that the words, 'conversation' and 'conversion' have the same root. To be true to our vocation as moral theologians we need a listening spirit, open to be challenged and converted to a richer understanding of the truth. This ties in with Margaret Farley's 'grace of self doubt'. It reminds me of a remark of Jack Mahoney's: 'I would love to hear a pastoral letter beginning with the phrase, "I may be wrong but …!"'

In the seventies I once shared running a Summer School in the UK with Charlie. On every topic he painstakingly laid out the pre-Vatican II Catholic position of the manuals. Then, at the end of each such presentation he very respectfully added what he called 'some critical comments', pointing out its weaknesses in the light of new empirical knowledge, or a deeper understanding of the Church's tradition, or a richer paradigm of interpretation. Looking back, I can see that Charlie was actually engaging in a respectful conversation with the tradition he had inherited. He was modelling for the rest of us the kind of mindset needed to be true to our vocation as moral theologians.

8. Women Sharing in the Vocation of the Moral Theologian

I am told that Charlie played a large part in opening the Catholic Theological Association to women theologians – and he was there on hand to welcome and support the first female members. I do not claim that it was Charlie who broke through the wall of my own sexual prejudice. I have to thank my many women students, friends and colleagues for that ongoing grace of conversion. Since then I have grown more and more convinced that the health and integrated development of Catholic moral theology is largely dependent on Catholic women being given an equal opportunity to pursue the vocation of a moral theologian and on their special contribution being recognized and given its full status and authority in the Church. I have argued that point strongly in a number of my books and I feel affirmed in this by the fine example of Charlie himself. I know that Charlie has left no stone unturned to ensure that women are given full recognition and equal status in the theological enterprise.

CHAPTER TWENTY-FIVE

Dissent or Disagree:
A Debate with Charles Curran

As mentioned in the previous article, I disagree with Charlie over his insistence on using the word 'dissent' with regard to his critical reaction to erroneous or inadequate official Catholic teachings. I prefer to speak of 'disagreement'. Charlie's own view on our difference of opinion is found in his book, Loyal Dissent: Memoir of a Catholic Theologian, (Georgetown University Press, Washington DC, 2006) pp. 67-68. He ends by commenting: "We theologians at the Catholic University of America were obviously aware of the negative connotations of the term (i.e. 'dissent'). Which is why we titled our book, Dissent In and For the Church; the word for was important for us. In my view dissent is a positive force and need not carry negative connotations. In the political realm, this attitude has often been expressed as the highest form of patriotism, which consists in resisting one's country or one's government when it is in the wrong. In the context of the Church, for me, dissent means speaking the truth in love, and that has always been my intention." Clearly we are both in substantial agreement. My own thinking is found in two articles in The Tablet articles, 'Obedience and Dissent' (14 & 21 June 1986, pp. 619-629 & pp. 647-649). Readers will notice that they were written prior to the lamentable decision of the CDF declaring that Curran could no longer be recognised as a 'Catholic Theologian'. What follows is a combination of those articles. I hope readers will find them interesting, not so much for the dissent/disagree debate but for the more general comments on the limits of teaching authority in the Catholic Church.

The Learning Church

The heart of the dispute between the CDF and Fr Charles Curran lies in a question of fundamental importance for Catholic theology. It is the issue of dissent, especially public dissent, from authoritative Church teaching. The CDF's Observations of April, 1983 leave us in no doubt on that point:

> The issue of whether a person who privately dissents from the ordinary magisterium of the Church has the consequent right to dissent publicly is at the basis of the Sacred Congregation for the Doctrine of the Faith's difficulties with Fr Curran.

The case for public dissent can be argued from the very theology which provided the vision of renewal in Vatican II itself. Vatican II enabled the Church to grow out of the restrictive theology which had made theologians limit dissent to respectful silence or, at most, to expressions of dissent limited to the rarefied atmosphere of professional theological debate. The pre-Vatican II model divided the Church into the teachers – the Pope and the bishops – and the learners – the rest of us. The teacher was presumed to possess the truth and his basic role was to pass on that teaching to the learners, whose principal task was to receive it docilely. Learning was interpreted virtually as an exercise of obedience. The emphasis was on acceptance of what was taught. That was why public dissent from the Church's teaching authority, the magisterium, was seen as open rejection of it, and was thus unthinkable. This is far removed from a much earlier understanding of a more widely shared magisterium which is found in the Church's tradition.

When the bishops met for Vatican II, almost the first thing they did was to reject this juridical and hierarchical model of the Church as determinative. Instead they chose to see the Church primarily as the whole people of God. Within this community, the Pope and the bishops fulfil a God-given service. They do not stand over against the Church and they are not above the Church. According to this model the whole Church is both a learning Church and one which shares its teaching mission. And learning comes before teaching. Evangelisation begins with the Church itself.

In each age the Church has to receive and make its own the revelation given in and through Jesus and entrusted to it. This revelation is not a lifeless body of religious information that is passed on from age to age. It is not a timeless deposit. It is a living tradition which is only truly received when it becomes incarnate in the minds and hearts of Christians belonging to a particular age and culture as they try to grapple with contemporary life in the light of the Gospel. Revelation does not truly occur in each age and culture without this process of reception. Before it can be a teaching Church, the Church must first be a learning Church; and to be a learning Church, it must necessarily be a listening Church.

This model of the Church was not thought up out of nothing by the bishops at Vatican II. It had a sound basis in Scripture and tradition. It also flowed from the 'signs of the times' as interpreted by the council. The greater appreciation of the dignity of each individual person and the corresponding values of personal freedom and participation as well as communal responsibility and solidarity were seen as coming from the prompting of the Holy Spirit. These 'signs of the times' obviously had implications for how the Church should understand itself and live its life in this present day and age.

Sharing

It is in the light of this deeper self-understanding of the Church that the issue of public dissent needs to be re-examined. Fr Curran is clearly aware of this when he argues, in his 10 August 1983 response to Cardinal Ratzinger, that the question of public dissent needs to be treated 'in the light of the Church's contemporary teaching on the right to know, the duty to inform, the right to free self-expression, the role of public opinion in the Church and the use of modern means of communication'. The CDF, however, seems unwilling to move beyond the limits imposed on dissent by theologians before Vatican II. Yet the situation now is radically different.

If learning is a primary focus within the Church's life, then the dynamism of the learning process has to be properly respected. That dynamism demands that all the riches of genuine experience, interpretation and understanding available within the Church are shared as widely as possible. Within the learning model a good teacher is one who tries to make sure that all the riches of the individual members of the learning group are shared with the whole group. The teacher's role is one of enabling individuals to share, of empowering the whole group to grow in collective understanding and of occasionally checking out that collective understanding by trying to articulate it in a way that does justice to the level of learning the group feels it has achieved. As a member of the group the teacher will, of course, have his or her own personal contribution to make, but that will be secondary to his or her other main teaching role as outlined above. And in a group with great riches to be shared, the teacher's personal contribution might be quite minimal.

The pope does not need the permission of the Church before he articulates its faith. However, his articulation is binding only because it is the faith of the Church that it articulates. His own personal judgement, if it is not an expression of the faith of the Church, will be listened to with respect, but individuals may well disagree.

I would suggest that one of the greatest examples of teaching in the Church in recent centuries was John XXIII's calling of the Second Vatican Council. Although John XXIII may have contributed little to the council himself, he enabled the tremendous riches with which the Spirit had blessed so many individuals and movements in the Church to be made available to and shared by the Church as a whole. In this way John XXIII was a most effective teacher; he empowered the Church to grow in wisdom and understanding.

Against this kind of background public dissent is seen in an altogether different light. Obviously it will still need to be honest and responsible. By that I mean that the teaching being dissented from has been examined seriously and a real effort made to assess its truth. Also, grounds for dissent must not be trivial but should be based either on personal expertise and competence, or general understanding arrived at either through one's own considered reflection or through dialogue with others whose wisdom and integrity one respects. Granted this kind of dissent, to share this with others and, when appropriate, to voice it publicly would seem to be a form of positive responsible participation in the learning process in the Church.

Need for Dialogue

In fact, unless one has already sufficiently aired one's dissent and one's reasons for it, keeping a respectful silence could be seen as a form of disloyalty to the Church and an evasion of personal responsibility. Karl Rahner states this very clearly in his *Theological Investigations*:

> In the concrete conditions prevailing today in the Church and in public life in the world, the respect which the moral theologian has to pay in his teaching to an authentic but not defined pronouncement of the Church's magisterium can no longer imply that the moral theologian concerned must either defend a doctrinal pronouncement of this kind through thick and thin as absolutely the only opinion which is certain and admissible for all ages or else he must simply be silent. In conformity with what has been said up to now he cannot in honesty adopt the first position, and if he adopted the second he would both be failing in his task as a moral theologian and at the same time doing no service to the Church, to the moral standards of the faithful, and to the Church's teaching authority (vol. XI, pp .283-284).

As Fr Curran pointed out in his 11 March 1986 press statement, other world-acclaimed Roman Catholic theologians such as Yves Congar and Bernard Häring propose the same position. So have many American Catholic Theologians, such as Avery Dulles, Richard McBrien, Richard McCormick, and David Tracy.

Avoidance of scandal is one of the accepted criteria for discerning whether a particular exercise of dissent is legitimate. Scandal means harming others by leading them astray. If we see ourselves as a learning Church and if we see morality as based on truth rather than on authority or law, we might well be guilty of scandal if we remain silent when we believe that the guidance given to people is either not true or else does not do full justice to the truth. Curran puts this very succinctly in his letter of 10 August, 1983: 'One can rightly conclude that at times it would be a scandal if theologians did not dissent publicly.' It seems clear that the CDF is working on entirely different principles. For the CDF public dissent constitutes a challenge and a threat to teaching authority in the Church. 'Suspension of (private) assent does not provide grounds for a so-called right to public dissent, for such public dissent would in effect constitute an alternative magisterium' (cf. *CDF Observations*, April, 1983). This is a long way from the process of dialogue appropriate to the learning model.

Dissent or Disagreement

In their dispute, neither Cardinal Ratzinger nor Fr Curran have done full justice to themselves and to what is really at stake. For they have made dissent the main issue. This is unfortunate.

Dissent is a negative word. It belongs to the same stable as terms like deny, oppose, contradict. There is nothing positive or affirmative about it. Focusing on the issue of dissent, therefore, has two unfortunate consequences. It creates a climate of confrontation and it makes true dialogue virtually impossible. Moreover, it deflects attention from the fundamental question which underlies the whole dispute: the respective roles of the teaching authority, theologians and all believers in the Church's mission of serving and proclaiming the truth.

The Church has to penetrate the truth more deeply and understand its implication for contemporary life. It must discern how humanity can become increasingly true to itself as made in the image of God and bearing responsibility for the stewardship of God's creation. This is a task which is shared by all the members of the Church. As we are more aware since Vatican II, it is shared also by all Christians and, in their own way, by non-Christian religions and even non-believers. It is a common search.

In this task, Christianity has a specific and essential contribution to give: but this does not make the contributions of the other participants any less important. The common search remains a shared human venture. As GS put it (3):

> The Church guards the heritage of God's Word and draws from it religious and moral principles without always having at hand the solution to particular problems. She desires thereby to add the light of revealed truth to humankind's stores of experience.

Seeing the Church as a servant of the truth in this way, it is not surprising that Vatican II laid such a strong emphasis on dialogue as the method most in keeping with this mission (see GS, 43-44, 58, 62, 92; cf. also Paul VI, *Ecclesiam Suam*, *passim*).

Dialogue, according to Vatican II, is not simply the appropriate way for the Church and Christians to engage themselves with society at large. Dialogue is also to be fostered and respected within the Church itself (GS, 92):

> By virtue of her mission to shed on the whole world the radiance of the gospel message, and to unify under one Spirit all people of whatever nation, race or culture, the Church stands forth as a sign of that kinship which allows honest dialogue and invigorates it. Such a mission requires in the first place that we foster within the Church herself mutual esteem, reverence, and harmony through the full recognition of lawful diversity. Thus all who compose the one People of God, both pastors and the general faithful, can engage in dialogue with ever-abounding fruitfulness. For the bonds which unite the faithful are mightier than anything which divides them. Hence, let there be unity in what is necessary, freedom in what is unsettled , and charity in any case.

It is acknowledged that true dialogue demands freedom of inquiry and thought within the area of one's own field of competence and experience. Thus GS recognises that, 'all the faithful, clerical and lay, possess a lawful freedom of inquiry and of thought, and the freedom to express their minds humbly and courageously about those matters in which they enjoy competence,' (62). Real dialogue also implies mutual respect in the face of honest disagreement:

> Solutions proposed on one side or another may be easily confused by many people with the Gospel message. Hence it is necessary for people to remember that no one is allowed in the aforementioned situations to appropriate the Church's authority for their opinion. They should always try to enlighten one another through honest discussion, preserving mutual charity and caring above all for the common Good (43).

Necessary Tension

Dissent does not fit easily into the context of dialogue. It is too much of a conversation-stopper. That is why Fr Curran is not doing himself justice when he describes his stance as one of dissent. The heart of his position is not captured by the statement 'I dissent from the Church's teaching'. More accurate would be something like: *Drawing on the riches of the Church's tradition and in the light of the Church's deeper knowledge of this aspect of human life gained through its dialogue with the human sciences today, I believe that what I and many Christians are saying is a more adequate expression of the richness of our present Christian understanding than is found in the current statement of the Church's teaching.* Although this is manifestly the mind of Curran himself, I feel that his use of the term 'dissent' does not do justice to all that is positive in such a position – respect for tradition, concern for the truth, love of the Church, shared responsibility for the Church's mission in the world. It does not express the respect for teaching authority in the Church which motivates someone adopting this kind of stance.

Teaching authority, when properly exercised, empowers. It helps people to have a better understanding of the truth. The critical stance described above does the same. It seeks to make sure that the truth in all its richness is not sold short by the teaching authority. Understandably this often gives rise to tension, as the International Theological Commission (ITC) has recognised. In its Thesis on the Relationship between the Church's Magisterium and Theology (6 June 1976), the commission acknowledged that the role of theologians in interpreting the teaching of the magisterium 'entails a function which is to some extent critical, while being positive and not destructive' (8, 3). It went on:

> It is not uncommon to find tension in the exercise of the tasks of the magisterium and of theologians. Nor is it surprising. And there is not ground for hoping that this tension will be fully resolved on earth. Wherever there is real life there is tension. And it is not enmity nor opposition but a living force and a stimulus to exercising together by means of dialogue the tasks proper to each.

The purpose of such dialogue, the ITC maintained, 'was to serve the truth'. To be faithful to this purpose, the CDF should spend more time exploring why responsible theologians like Fr Curran are dissatisfied with some of the Church's authoritative teaching. Whether such teaching adequately expresses the richest understanding within the Church should, after all, be of particular concern to a Congregation commissioned to serve 'the doctrine of the faith'.

The ITC stated that 'the whole field of truth' was 'suitable matter for dialogue' between the teaching authority and theologians. But, it warned, 'this truth is not something continually to be sought as if it were uncertain and unknown. It has been truly revealed and given to the Church to be faithfully guarded. Thus the limits of the dialogue are the limits of the truth of the faith' (thesis 11). That there is no question of Fr Curran's intending to go beyond these limits by denying any 'truth of the faith' is clear from the statement in his 11 March 1986 press release: 'Note clearly that I do not disagree with any dogmas or defined truths of the Catholic faith'.

On a few occasions in the long exchange between the Congregation and Fr Curran, I get the impression that real dialogue is beginning to occur. Thus the CDF in its April, 1983 observations asked him a series of penetrating questions designed to draw into clearer focus precisely what he meant by some of his positions:

- his view that the magisterium's general teaching does not bind absolutely in every case;
- his theory of 'compromise decisions' which acknowledge personal and situational limitations;
- his referring to New Testament 'ideals' rather than moral norms;
- whether he considered that the actual number of Christians dissenting had any theological significance for moral teaching;
- what part the physical dimension of our make-up plays in determining human morality; and so on.

These questions elicited from Fr Curran some excellent moral theological writing which many will find extremely helpful. However, the dialogue stopped there. After empowering Fr Curran to express himself even more clearly, the Congregation failed to continue the process. The rest of us are the poorer. It could have been a very fruitful exchange and a positive learning experience for all concerned.

Cardinal Ratzinger's final letter to Fr Curran invited him to 'reconsider and to retract these positions which violate the conditions necessary for a professor to be called a Catholic Theologian'. The Cardinal said that Church teaching had to be 'reflected upon' and also 'interpreted' but 'in complete fidelity'. Indeed! However, this fidelity is first of all to the truth. That is why the critical interpretation mentioned by the ITC must surely qualify as interpretation 'in complete fidelity'.

Cardinal Ratzinger said also that students had a 'right to know what the Church's teaching is and have it properly explained to them'. That, again, is true. But the 'right' of the students in question is not really being respected if the Church's teaching is presented to them uncritically. When some of it is being questioned responsibly by theologians or by the faithful in general, that suggests at least the possibility that it is not presenting adequately or satisfactorily what the Church (the People of God) believes. A 'proper explanation' of the Church's teaching has to take this 'theological fact' fully into account. It would be the death of true theology to insist that budding theologians and prospective pastors should be denied knowledge of such divergent views. That applies also to adult Christian education. Christian adults have a right to know what are the riches of current Christian understanding that responsible theologians believe are lacking in authoritative Church statements. In matters of morality this can have profound implications for their lives.

If the CDF considers Fr Curran's teaching unacceptable, it will want to declare this publicly as part of its role of service in the Church. To express its disagreement publicly, giving all its reasons why it considers his teaching to be unacceptable, would be a helpful contribution to the process of dialogue. Moral theologians and others of a like mind to Fr Curran would then be given the opportunity to evaluate how well grounded are the Congregation's reasons for disagreement. If they found them convincing it would provide a stimulus for them to rethink their own positions. If they found them unconvincing, they would be able to give their reasons for this. However, this does not seem to be the procedure the CDF has chosen to follow.

A Better Way

Very understandably the CDF wants to safeguard teaching authority within the Church. And no Catholic would deny the teaching authority of the Pope and the Bishops within the Church. Yet how precisely should that teaching authority function within the dialogue model? It is not immediately evident. Vatican II's strong emphasis on dialogue as the correct method means that the complementary roles, within the Church's teaching mission, of the teaching authority, theologians and Christians in general need to be re-examined very carefully. Such a re-examination would also need to look at how these roles are affected by Vatican II's teaching that other Christian Churches are partners in this dialogue. The CDF would be performing the empowering function of teaching if it were to promote dialogue on these questions among theologians and in the Church at large. If so, the tension between it and Fr. Curran could yet turn out to be a growth point for theology. At present, however, the signs are not hopeful.

At present one particular school of moral theology – essentialist, historical, deductive, aiming at certain and definitive teaching – seems to be dominating the thinking of the CDF. This is a matter of considerable concern, especially when this school does not represent the mainstream of contemporary Roman Catholic moral theology. In fact, the action threatened against Fr Curran will be seen by many as a condemnation of that mainstream. That in itself is serious. Even more serious, however, are some of the consequences that might follow. If the Congregation takes action against Fr Curran, his own Bishop, Matthew Clark of Rochester, fears that 'theologians may stop exploring the challenging questions of the day in a creative, healthy way because they fear actions which may prematurely end their teaching careers'. Furthermore, the kind of action being threatened against Curran will almost certainly be a serious scandal in the ecumenical field.

Eucharist and Vatican II

CHAPTER TWENTY-SIX

The New Translation of the Roman Missal: Lament for a Flawed Process

This article was originally submitted to The Tablet but remained unpublished for a few months. It was also submitted to The Furrow but again it was not published. Feeling that it was making some important points, on the advice of a friend I sent it to all the bishops of England and Wales. A friend of mine asked if he could circulate it to members of the Catholic Theological Association of Great Britain and I readily gave him permission. From that point onwards, I lost all control of its circulation. It seemed to be turning up on all kinds of websites and blogs. As a result I received an enormous number of e-mails thanking me and supporting the views I was expressing. In fact I did not receive a single e-mail response critical of my position. A few months later The Tablet referred to this article in an Editorial (20 August 2011) and the following week made the full text available on its website. This whole experience has made me much more aware of the tremendous potentiality for communications of the web and social networking.

Since then, I have had to face the introduction of the new Translation. Sharing Mass each day with a community of Notre Dame sisters in Liverpool, I felt our decision had to be a shared one. In its Notebook (10 September 2011) The Tablet quoted the following from a letter I sent to the Editor:

> *After reviewing various possibilities, we decided to open ourselves wholeheartedly to praying the Mass in the new translation for a whole year without any changes. Then we would be in a better position to judge whether it has been a help or an obstacle to our praying the Eucharist. I suspect that the latter will be the case, but I hope I am to be surprised by God.*

Although we are only in the early days of using the new translation, from what some of the Sisters have shared with me and from my own personal experience, I do not get the impression that God will have any surprises up his sleeve!

In 1975 in my role as Director of the Upholland Northern Institute (UNI) I was involved in arranging the very first In-Service Training course for the Bishops' Conference of England and Wales. It was on the theme, 'The Bishop as Teacher' and was held at the UNI. When the bishops arrived, they all had embargoed copies of the CDF's Declaration, *Persona Humana*, on sexual issues which was due to be published during the week. Quite a number of the bishops shared with me their deep unease about the Declaration. They were highly critical of it and made no secret of that to me and to each other. I was given a copy and asked to run a special session on it. When I read it, I could see why they felt so critical. Despite its title, *Persona Humana*, it was based on a theological approach which failed to do justice to Vatican II's person-centred vision of moral theology. In my talk I suggested to the bishops that, if they were to be faithful to their role of teachers, they should be prepared to voice their positive criticism of the Declaration, if they were interviewed by the media. I stressed that we owe it to the truth to be honest and authentic in what we say. Positive criticism is intrinsic to good teaching. As far as I know, none of them followed my suggestion in their subsequent television and radio interviews.

What disturbed me even more was the text of a telegram I found in an issue of *Documentation Catholique* a few months later. It was sent to the CDF from the Bishops' Conference of England and Wales and thanked them for their excellent Declaration, *Persona Humana*. That left a bad taste in my mouth. It suggested a kind of 'double speak', as though there was a dysfunctionality in communications within the Church.

That seems to be relevant at present with regard to the new translation of the Roman Missal. I may be wrong, but I have the impression that at least some, perhaps many, of the bishops share the unhappiness about the new translation which is felt by many priests and lay Catholics. Yet the new translation is being promoted as a precious gift. Let me quote from a suggested insert for parish newsletters sent out by Liverpool Archdiocese. 'The new translation brings with it a deeper and more profound meaning of the mystery we have gathered to celebrate at Mass.' This is because 'we have grown as a Church over the last forty years in terms of understanding how to better translate our Latin texts into the vernacular language of the people'. Consequently, 'the changes also bring us a wonderful opportunity as a Church to delve more deeply into the mystery of Christ Jesus and the praise and thanksgiving we offer to God, our Father, during Mass'. The Joint Pastoral Letter of the Bishops' Conference of England and Wales (29 May 2011) on the new translation goes so far as to say:

> There is a recovery of a vocabulary that enriches our understanding of the mystery we celebrate. All of this requires a unique style of language and expression, one that takes us out of ourselves and draws us into the sacred, the transcendent and the divine. The publication of the new translation of the Missal is a special moment of grace in the English speaking world.

I love the liturgy, I really do. I find it a rich source for my own devotional life. But I find those quotations deeply disturbing, arousing the same feeling of uneasiness I experienced with the Bishops' telegram to the CDF. I simply cannot identify myself with what is being said. It smacks too much of a 'double-speak', not the straightforward 'Yes' and 'No' that Jesus urged us to follow.

On the Sunday following Mubarak's stepping down as President of Egypt, I made the following point in my homily to the Notre Dame Sisters with whom I am privileged to share the Eucharist each day:

Re-reading the first paragraph of Benedict's 2009 social encyclical, *Caritas in Veritate*, has helped me to see beneath the surface of what has been happening in Tahrir Square. Benedict writes: 'Love is an extraordinary force which leads people to opt for courageous and generous engagement in the field of Justice and Peace.' He goes on to stress that this force 'has its origin in God' and is a 'vocation planted by God in the heart and mind of every human person.' The crowd in Tahrir Square were mainly Muslims but also included many secularists and Coptic Christians. They showed 'courageous and generous engagement in the field of justice and peace' in their peaceful demands for a non-violent transition to genuine human freedom and justice. To me Benedict's amazing words applied to them and made me very conscious that what I was seeing on TV was God's Spirit present and active in these people.

I am sure many people felt that the same 'extraordinary force' was tangible in the crowds during the Benedict XVI's UK visit. I certainly felt that at Evensong in Westminster Abbey.

However, I also feel that this 'extraordinary force' is manifesting itself at present in the growing unease about the imposition of the new translation of the Roman Missal. A grass-roots resistance seems to be growing among ordinary Catholics who are deeply concerned at the impact this new translation will have on their Sunday Mass. They had no say in what is happening. They feel disempowered. To my mind, their instinct is right. The imposition of the new translation is one more instance of the abuse of power in our Church. It is just the tip of the iceberg. I sense a growing discontent among many very committed Catholics who have a deep love for the Church. They feel it is losing touch with the Spirit-inspired vision of Vatican II and its hope for the future. They want to mount a protest against this but there seems no appropriate channel for such protest.

Vatican II placed collegiality at the very heart of Church governance. Implied in that teaching is the involvement of all the faithful through collaborative ministry and co-responsibility. The Bishops' Conference of England and Wales made that abundantly clear in *The Sign we Give*, the magnificent 1995 Report from their Working Party on Collaborative Ministry. Sadly, these developments in Church governance, so central to the renewal of the Church, have never been properly implemented. That continues to this very day. Until recently most Catholics have felt they had no choice but to tolerate this abuse of power. Now, however, I suspect that the 'Tahrir Square' syndrome in the Church is a sign that the 'extraordinary force' of the fire of the Holy Spirit is beginning to disturb us from our complacency.

The flagrant misuse of power involved in the new translation of the Roman Missal is not just about its pastorally disastrous choice of language. It is also about the serious disregard for Vatican II's teaching on collegiality in the process leading up to the new translation. The original International Commission for English in the Liturgy (ICEL) was set up after the Council and was a fine example of the implementation of collegiality, since it was answerable to the English-speaking bishops' conferences throughout the world. ICEL's only link with the Congregation of Divine Worship (CDW) was the requirement to obtain a *'recognitio'* (a kind of 'rubber stamp') for its proposed texts and translations. ICEL was also true to Vatican II's ecumenical spirit since it worked with the liturgical agencies of other Christian Churches to ensure that the common texts and the cycle of biblical readings would be shared in common by the different Christian Churches. Moreover, it tried to avoid as far as possible exclusive language which might be offensive to women. These original ICEL texts were carefully vetted and voted upon by all the English-speaking bishops' conferences and have been used up to Advent 2011 throughout the English-speaking world.

However, from the start ICEL had been aware that the need to provide English texts as soon as reasonably possible after the Council inevitably meant that their texts were far from perfect. In fact, Archbishop Denis Hurley, a major figure at Vatican II and first Chair of ICEL, quickly set in motion the work of revising and refining these texts. He gathered together a team of liturgical and literary experts to undertake this task. The guiding principle for their work was based on Vatican II's insistence that the 'full and active participation by all the people is the aim to be considered before all else' (Liturgy Constitution, no. 14) Consequently, this team was commissioned to produce texts which, while not being literal word-for-word translations, should be faithful to the meaning of the original, as well as being simple, dignified and easily understandable. In this they were following the guidance enshrined in the Vatican II-inspired 1969 instruction, *Comme le prevoit*, approved by Paul VI.

By 1998 ICEL's revised version of the Roman Missal was complete and had been examined and approved by all the English-speaking bishops' conferences. It was then sent to the Congregation of Divine Worship (CDW) for its formal *'recognitio'*. This was refused, completely disregarding the key Vatican II principle of collegiality. Moreover, without any consultation, the CDW brought out an entirely new set of guidelines, *Liturgiam Authenticam* (LA) which insisted on a much more literal fidelity in translating and actually warned against any ecumenical involvement in the process. Moreover, though LA mentions the issue of inclusive language, the practical implementation is far from satisfactory.

Archbishop Hurley, by then no longer Chair of ICEL, is reported to have said: 'I find the attitude reflected in the proposed change in translation practice a distressing departure from the spirit of collegiality in favour of authoritative imposition'. He even wrote to a friend: 'At times I find it difficult to understand the attitude of the Roman Curia. It seems to be more concerned with power than with humble service' (both quotations from Paddy Kearney, *Guardian of the Light: Denis Hurley, Renewing the Church, opposing Apartheid*, New York, London, T & T Clark, 2009, pp. 292 & 295).

A radically reconstituted ICEL set out to produce a new translation of the Roman Missal following the new guidelines. In due course this was sent out to the English-speaking bishops' conferences. They could have rejected this new translation but instead chose to approve it. One can only assume that they had given up hope of any genuine collegiality. The earlier translation which all the Bishops' conferences had approved in 1998 was virtually binned, despite being the fruit of years of dedicated expertise and ecumenical cooperation by the commission set up by the original ICEL. A full account of this sad and shameful affair is found in chapters four and five of *It's the Eucharist, Thank God* (Decani Books, Brandon, Suffolk, 2009) by Bishop Maurice Taylor. Bishop Taylor was chair of ICEL during the fateful years of 1997 to 2002.

This new translation has provoked widespread dismay and disquiet, especially among many clergy, fearful of its negative impact on parishioners. For instance, in January 2011 the eminent US liturgical scholar, Anthony Ruff OSB, withdrew from a commission given him by the US bishops to help prepare people for the new translation of the Roman Missal in dioceses across the US. In his letter of withdrawal he wrote:

> My involvement in that process, as well as my observation of the Holy See's handling of the scandal, has gradually opened my eyes to the deep problems in the structures of authority of our Church. The forthcoming missal is but a part of a larger pattern of top-down impositions by a central authority that does not consider itself accountable to the larger Church. When I think of how secretive the translation process was, how little consultation was done with priests or laity, ... how unsatisfactory the final text is, how this text was imposed on national conferences of bishops in violation of their legitimate episcopal authority ... and then when I think of Our Lord's teachings on service and love and unity ... I weep (*America*, 14 February 2011).

Anthony Ruff is not a lone voice. On 3 February 2011 the Irish Association of Catholic Priests (ACP) issued a press release entitled 'New Translation of the Missal Unacceptable'. They described the texts as 'archaic, elitist and obscure and not in keeping with the natural rhythm, cadence and syntax of the English language' and say: 'from the few available samples of the new texts, it is clear that the style of English used throughout the Mass will be so convoluted that it will be difficult to read the prayers in public.' Moreover, they continued: 'It is ironic that this Latinised, stilted English is being imposed on Irish people who are so blessed with world-renowned poets, playwrights, and novelists.'

They asked the bishops to follow the example of the German bishops who objected to similar texts being imposed on them and urged them to defer the Missal's introduction for five years to give them time to 'engage with Irish Catholics with a view to developing a new set of texts that will adequately reflect the literary genius and spiritual needs of our Church community in these modern times'.

Two years earlier, an article appeared in *America* (14 December 2009) entitled 'What If We Said, 'Wait'?' The case for a grass-roots review of the new Roman Missal, by Fr Michael G. Ryan. He spoke out of his experience as Pastor of St James Cathedral, Seattle since 1988 and board member of the national Cathedral Ministry Conference. He tells of the reactions of 'disbelief and indignation' of his friends to some of the translations; and of 'audible laughter in the room' at a diocesan seminar for priests and lay-leaders. One reaction will strike chords with many:

> with all that the Church has on its plate today – global challenges with regard to justice, peace and the environment; nagging scandals; a severe priest shortage; the growing disenchantment of many women; seriously lagging Church attendance – it seems almost ludicrous to push ahead with an agenda that will seem at best trivial and at worst hopelessly out-of-touch.

He also notes that when the new translations were mistakenly introduced ahead of time in South Africa they 'were met almost uniformly with opposition bordering on outrage'. Fr Ryan makes a gentle 'What if?' challenge to his fellow priests:

> What if we, the parish priests of this country who will be charged with the implementation, were to find our voice and tell our bishops that we want to help them avert an almost certain fiasco? What if we told them that we think it unwise to implement these changes until our people have been consulted in an adult manner that truly honors their intelligence and their baptismal birthright? What if we just said, 'Wait, not until our people are ready for the new translations, but until the translations are ready for our people?'

I recommend Ryan's article very highly, especially to priests.

Many Catholics seem to have mixed feelings about the Church at present. At one level they really do love the Church and, in the UK at least, felt boosted by the Pope's visit. Yet they also agree with Tina Beattie's comment that the problems have not gone away. A lot of these problems are related to the way the authority of God is being used to shore up teaching which, at the very least, is open to debate and, in some instances, rejected as inadequate by many theologians and most people in the Church trying to be faithful to the spirit of Vatican II. I am thinking, for instance, of the rich understanding of human sexuality found in current Catholic and Christian theology, revealing to women and men, gays and lesbians, the depth of their God-given dignity and the ultimate foundation for their sense of self-worth. The same is true of developments in liturgical and Eucharistic theology with its emphasis on full participation, so crucial to the spirit of Vatican II. Using authority to close down these legitimate debates paralyses pastoral imagination from exploring new ways of coping with such down-to-earth issues as the sacraments to the divorced/remarried, Eucharistic hospitality in an ecumenical context, general absolution's highlighting the social dimension of sin, as well as stifling the much-needed debate on contraception, the ordination of women, and the presence of God's love in the faithful love lives of gays and lesbians, I have already looked at these issues in various essays in this volume.

It seems to be increasingly recognised that abuse of power is also a key factor lying at the heart of the scandal of clergy sex-abuse and Episcopal cover-up. The eradication of this horrendous abuse of power seems to lie not just in dealing with the actual perpetrators but also in a radical conversion of the organisational pathology of the Church itself. I cannot get out of my mind the telling words of Brendan Callaghan SJ: 'The faces of this tragedy are always the faces of the hurt and betrayed children, and we must somehow find the courage neither to turn away from those faces nor to diminish what they show us of death and destruction.'

For some readers this article might seem too negative and disturbing, especially as coming from a seventy-eight-year-old retired priest and emeritus ('past it') moral theologian. I hope and pray that what I have written is empowered by the same 'extraordinary force' of God's love referred to by Benedict XVI which I mentioned in my opening paragraph. God alone can judge that. Certainly it is what I pray for each morning with the words, 'Come, Holy Spirit, enkindle in us (and in me) the fire of your love'.

At the opening of the Second Session of Vatican II, Paul VI spoke of the Church as 'the Bride of Christ looking upon Christ to discern in him her true likeness' and reminded the bishops that:

If in doing so she were to discover some shadow, some defect, some stain upon her wedding garment, what should be her instinctive, courageous reaction? There can be no doubt that her primary duty would be to reform, correct and set herself aright in conformity with her divine model (Yves Congar, Hans Kung & Daniel O'Hanlon, *Council Speeches of Vatican II*, Sheed & Ward, London, 1964, p. 51).

Paul VI was not encouraging a spirit of negative criticism at the Council. He was inviting the bishops to show their love for the Church by facing up to its need for healing and renewal. Positive criticism should be loving, inspiring and life-giving. I believe, along with many others, that the Church needs this kind of love more than ever at this point in time – not a soft love but a courageous reforming love. Henri DeLubac is reported to have said: 'If we do not learn to love the Church in its sinfulness, we will not love the Church loved by the Lord but, rather, some figment of our romantic imagination' (cf. George B. Wilson SJ, *Clericalism: The Death of Priesthood*, Collegeville, Liturgical Press, 2008 p. x). As members of this sinful Church, each of us, myself included, needs to ask the Spirit to help us discern the extent to which we are part of that sinfulness and ask for forgiveness and healing.

CHAPTER TWENTY-SEVEN

The Eucharist and Unity

This article was first published in The Furrow, 2005, September, pp. 464-471. It is the text of a reflection given during a Eucharistic Adoration evening for the Widnes Pastoral Area.

Pope John Paul II's beautiful and challenging Millennium reflections on a 'spirituality of communion' are an appropriate way to begin this meditation on the Eucharist and Unity (*Novo Millennio Ineunte* – NMI):

> A spirituality of communion indicates above all the heart's contemplation of the mystery of the Trinity dwelling in us, and whose light we must also be able to see shining on the face of the brothers and sisters around us.
>
> A spirituality of communion also means an ability to think of our brothers and sisters in faith within the profound unity of the Mystical Body, and therefore as 'those who are part of me'. This makes us able to share their joys and sufferings, to sense their desires and attend to their needs, to offer them deep and genuine friendship (no. 43).

> If we have truly started out anew from the contemplation of Christ, we must learn to see him especially in the faces of those with whom he himself wished to be identified: 'I was hungry and you gave me food, I was thirsty and you gave me drink, I was a stranger and you welcomed me, I was naked and you clothed me, I was sick and you visited me, I was in prison and you came to me' (Mt 25:35-37). This Gospel text is ... a page of Christology which sheds light on the mystery of Christ. By these words, no less than by the orthodoxy of her doctrine, the Church measures her fidelity as the Bride of Christ. Certainly ... no one can be excluded from our love, since 'through his Incarnation the Son of God has united himself in some fashion with every person' (no. 49).

Christ Himself is the Sacrament of Unity. He came to reconcile us to God and to each other. He gave his followers, the Church, the role of continuing this mission – 'As the Father has sent me, so am I sending you'. Therefore, the Church is a Sacrament of Unity. This is basic to the thinking of Vatican II, thinking which John Paul II described as 'the great grace bestowed on the Church in the twentieth century' (NMI, p. 57). Vatican II repeats frequently that 'the Church, in Christ, is a sacrament, that is a sign and instrument, of communion with God and of the unity of the entire human race' (LG, no. 1). John Paul is his Encyclical on the Eucharist (*Ecclesia de Eucharistia* – EE) describes the Church as 'a "sacrament" for humanity' (no. 22).

As 'source and summit' of the Church's life, the Eucharist itself is essentially a Sacrament of Unity. John Paul says: 'In the sacrament of the Eucharistic bread, the unity of the faithful, who form one body in Christ, is both expressed and brought about' (EE no. 21). It is interesting to note that he sees the Eucharist not just as an 'expression' of unity achieved, but also as a means for 'bringing about' unity. In fact, two paragraphs later he actually speaks of the 'unifying power of sharing in the Eucharist' (EE no. 23).

In a very real sense, celebration of the Eucharist is a continuation of the table-fellowship of Jesus. One writer describes Jesus' table-fellowship as 'communion-making' and 'boundary-breaking' (cf. Pierre Simson, *Do this in memory of me*: 'This man welcomes sinners and eats with them', Dublin, Dominican Publications, 2003, p. 43).

Certainly, it was a table-fellowship which scandalized the religious leaders of Jesus' day. In fact, it was one of the key reasons for their plotting to kill him. It went against their belief in a God of strict boundaries – boundaries defined by the Law and the Sabbath observance and boundaries which Jesus rejected in the name of a God without boundaries: 'The Sabbath is made for man, not man for the Sabbath.' The only true image of the God of Jesus was the human person – and in a special and unique way, Jesus himself, God made flesh. John Paul II is making the same point in his 'Spirituality of Communion' quoted above.

Today, when people speak of the 'Real Presence' they normally mean the sacramental presence of Christ in the Eucharist under the form of bread and wine. And when they speak of the 'Mystical Body', they normally mean the Church. For more than half of the Church's history – that is, until the twelfth century – the very opposite was true.

The 'real' body of Christ was the Church. And the 'mystical' body of Christ was the sacramental bread and wine. We can see this usage in operation in the passage from St John Chrysostom which John Paul quotes in his Encyclical on the Eucharist:

Do you wish to honour the body of Christ? Do not ignore him when he is naked. Do not pay him homage in the temple clad in silk, only then to neglect him outside where he is cold and ill-clad. He who said: 'This is my body' is the same who said: 'You saw me hungry and you gave me no food', and 'Whatever you did to the least of my brothers you did also to me' … What good is it if the Eucharistic table is overloaded with golden chalices when your brother is dying of hunger. Start by satisfying his hunger and then with what is left you may adorn the altar as well. (EE no. 20, footnote 34).

Some unhealthy consequences flowed from this change of language in the twelfth century. As Sarah Beckwith puts it: 'The emphasis was increasingly on watching Christ's body, rather than being incorporated into it' (quoted in William T. Cavanaugh, *Torture & Eucharist*, Oxford, Blackwell, 1998, p. 213). People 'attended' Mass, rather than 'participated' in it. It was something to be 'present at', rather than an 'action to be shared'.

Vatican II's approach to the Liturgy, by drawing renewed inspiration from that older and richer tradition, empowered the Pilgrim Church to move forward so as to be able to face the signs of the times in our modern world. The key principle Vatican II stated to guide all liturgical practice was:

> The full and active participation by all the people is the aim to be considered before all else; for it is the primary and indispensable source from which the faithful are to derive the true Christian spirit (Constitution on the Liturgy, no. 14).

The Mass is not 'my' Mass (i.e. not the priest's) but 'our' Mass. We celebrate together, each participating in our own different ways. The Mass is not a place for spectators or observers.

Whenever I dealt with First Communion children, one key point I liked to make was the richness of their response, 'Amen', when the priest holds up the host and says, 'The Body of Christ'. The child's 'Amen' ('Yes, I believe') is not just saying, 'Yes, I am truly receiving Christ in this host.' It is also saying 'Yes, I am the body of Christ.' And it is saying, 'Yes, we, all of us here sharing in this Eucharist, are the body of Christ'. And it is saying 'Yes, all people, especially those in need, are the body of Christ'. In a sense, in this act of committed faith, the child is 're-membering' the body of Christ, i.e. drawing together into unity the members of Christ's body. Obviously, this rings bells – whole peals of them – with John Paul's words about the 'spirituality of communion'.

Eucharistic Devotion & Adoration

Reservation of the Blessed Sacrament began from the needs of the sick and the housebound. They could not be present at the community's celebration of the Eucharist, so, in a sense, the Eucharist had to come to them. To enable this to happen, the consecrated bread and wine began to be reserved in a sacred place. This eventually gave rise to the practice of Eucharistic devotion outside of the celebration of Mass. It is important to remember that this practice did not initially develop independently of the community's celebration, but more as a kind of extension of that celebration. Its purpose was to enable the sick and housebound to participate in the Eucharist.

The Church today is keen that Eucharistic adoration continues to be rooted in some way to the community's celebration of the Eucharist.

We do not adore a static presence of Christ in the Blessed Sacrament. It is a sacramental presence – under the form of bread and wine. That speaks of a nourishing and, dare one say it, an inebriating presence – giving us strength and vitality and setting our hearts on fire. Christ is our food and drink. The bread and wine also speak of Christ's body broken for us, his blood poured out for us. Some hymns seem to suggest that the presence of Christ is 'hidden' or 'concealed' under the sacramental form. Traditional sacramental theology would say the exact opposite. Under the form of bread and wine the living and life-giving presence of Christ is 'revealed' to us. That is why the actual eating and drinking are so significant sacramentally. Communion under the form of both bread and wine should be taken for granted, rather than be exceptional or occasional.

Some earlier prayers spoke of Jesus as being 'lonely' in the tabernacle. That is sheer heresy. How can Christ be lonely, enfolded as he is within the life and love of his Father and the Holy Spirit? The only loneliness Jesus feels is the loneliness of the lonely people in our midst and in our world. Part of the nourishment he wants to share with us is to empower, encourage and inspire us to bring love and comfort to those who are lonely around us. That is being true to the unifying power of the Eucharist.

The Emmaus disciples recognised Jesus in the breaking of bread, yet earlier their hearts had burned within them as he opened the scriptures to them. There is a unity in each Mass between the Liturgy of the Word and the Liturgy of the Eucharist. We break the word to deepen our faith in celebrating the Eucharist. It is the same Christ communicating with us in each. The Vatican II Constitution on Divine Revelation states this very strikingly:

> The Church has always venerated the divine Scriptures just as she venerates the body of the Lord, since from the table of both the word of God and of the body of Christ she unceasingly receives and offers to the faithful the bread of life (no. 21).

Meditating on the weekday or Sunday readings and praying the scriptures deserves pride of place in our Eucharistic adoration. Eucharistic adoration is often something we do silently – even if together; but also something we may do on our own. Yet there should still be a 'unity' dimension about it, if the Eucharist is a sacrament of unity.

In St Basil's, when it was too cold in Church, I often prayed in my upstairs sitting room. There was a TV there. On one occasion I was sitting in my chair praying, with the TV (the 'box') facing me, when suddenly the thought came to me. Through that 'box' all sorts of people come into my life in one way or another. This was very true over John Paul II's final illness and death; also true during the terrible Tsunami disaster.

When St Basil's Reception Class made their first visit to Church, I would get them to sit and look around and then invite them to ask me about anything they see. Invariably, some child would point to the tabernacle and ask: 'What's that box for?'

Much more profoundly than any TV, the Blessed Sacrament, venerated in that 'box', links us to our sisters and brothers even though they are far away in distance and or in time. Every Eucharist unites us with the adoration of the whole Communion of Saints and reminds us of our unity with our whole human family alive today. It is like a network transcending time and space.

This is also true of the whole of creation. In his encyclical on the Eucharist, *Ecclesia de Eucharista*, John Paul II says he has celebrated Mass in all sorts of places on his travels, yet he is always aware that even in the humblest of settings, Mass is still celebrated 'on the altar of the world' (EE, no. 8). This brings out its 'cosmic character'. He is using the language here of Teilhard de Chardin, who wrote eloquently about evolution as God's ongoing – and still continuing – work of creation. We humans alone have the privilege and honour of being able to praise and thank God in the name of the whole of creation. One of the 1998 ICEL Eucharistic prefaces, so scandalously 'binned' by the CDW (cf. previous essay), expresses this very beautifully:

> In the beginning your Word summoned light;
> night withdrew and creation dawned.
> As ages passed unseen,
> waters gathered on the face of the Earth
> and life appeared.
> When the times had at last grown full
> and the earth had ripened in abundance,
> you created in your image humankind,
> the crown of all creation.
> You gave us breath and speech,
> that all the living might find a voice to sing your praise...

And the words of the 'Holy, Holy' after the Preface take up this theme: 'Heaven and earth are full of your glory.'

Two Questions to ponder

Both of these questions are ones which John Paul II has answered in the negative. However, they are questions which will not go away. I suspect the Pope would not want them to. After all, in his Millennium encyclical (NMI, no. 56) he wrote: 'The Church will never cease asking questions, trusting in the help of the Spirit of truth, whose task it is to guide her 'in all the truth' (Jn 16:13).

Moreover, they are questions many in the Church are asking. Hence, they need to be listened to and pondered. Again, John Paul has advice on this. After saying that Pastors should follow the ancient wise practice of 'listening more widely to the entire people of God', he goes on to quote St Paulinus of Nola: 'Let us listen to what all the faithful say, because in every one of them the Spirit of God breathes' (NMI no. 47).

To re-open these two questions is to suggest that the perhaps the Pope's answer needs to be queried. Can we do that? Again, the Pope seems to encourage us when he writes that any healthy community needs legitimate disagreement. It should both allow such disagreement and allow it to be heard. Actually, John Paul II used stronger language – 'justified opposition', not just 'legitimate disagreement' (cf. *The Acting Person*, London, Reidel, jkm 1979, p. 287).

First question: Does the Church need to revisit the issue of ordaining married men – and ordaining women too?

Without the Eucharist, the Pope says that a Christian community's situation is 'distressing and irregular' (EE no. 32). Incomplete solutions like Eucharistic Services should only be 'temporary'. The Eucharist is essential: 'No Christian community can be built up unless it has its basis and centre in the celebration of the most Holy Eucharist' (EE no. 33). This question is considered again at the end of the following essay.

Second question: Does the Church need to revisit its restrictive law and practice with regard to inter-communion and Eucharistic sharing?

Our current practice of restricting reception of the Eucharist to Catholics (with some apparently grudging exceptions) seems to many to fly in the face of our deepest human instincts.

To invite someone to share our table and encourage him or her to share fully in all the companionship and table-talk and then deny that person any share in the meal itself would seem to be an extraordinary thing to do. All the more so when we are not actually the host at the table. And especially so when the host is notorious for welcoming everyone at his table and has actually caused scandal by the kind of company he keeps.

If the Church claims to be a sacrament of the unity of the human family, perhaps the Eucharist should not be a meal at which the presence of outsiders is tolerated within certain strict limits, but rather a meal at which their presence is treasured and accepted as a gift. Communion will then be more truly Communion. In an article in *The Furrow*, 2005, January, pp. 25-36, ''Eucharist and Violence', I quoted the following challenging words from an unpublished paper by my friend, the late David Morland OSB:

> Perhaps the power and fire the Eucharist contains as the breaking of the Lord's body has to be thrown open to the world and all Christians so that no one is excluded who does not chose to be ... Participation in the Eucharist would be the sowing of the seed of God's presence rather than

the affirmation of orthodox membership of the one, true Church. For Christians it would be the bread of pilgrims searching for unity rather than a celebration by the few of a unity they believe they already possess (p. 35 – cf. p.272 for a fuller version of this quotation).

Conclusion

In his encyclical on the Eucharist (no. 6), the Pope uses the beautiful phrase, 'eucharistic amazement'. At the end of the same paragraph, he links it to the disciples of the Emmaus road and says we can 're-live their experience, when their eyes were opened and they recognized him.'

This brings us full circle – back to the opening sentence of what John Paul II says about the 'spirituality of communion': 'We must also be able to see the light of the Trinity shining on the face of the brothers and sisters around us.'

In his book, *Conjectures of a Guilty Bystander* (London, Sheldon Press, 1977 edition, p. 153), Thomas Merton described an experience in a supermarket where he became aware that all the people around him were loved by God and precious to God. If only we could always see each other through God's eyes, he reflected. He continued: 'I suppose the big problem would be that we would fall down and worship each other!' – Eucharistic amazement! The Eucharist is an eye-opening experience. We begin to see each other, and the whole of life, differently.

At the same time, in the face of so much disunity and division, sharing in the Eucharist, the Sacrament of Unity, can be a scary, risky and disturbing experience. A good friend of mine, a Columban sister, who was living alone in a shanty town in Mindanao in the Philippines, once sent me a Christmas card with the greeting: 'May the peace of Christ disturb you this Christmas.' Maybe the Eucharist should disturb us each time we share in it!

CHAPTER TWENTY-EIGHT

The Eucharist and Violence

This piece was first published in The Furrow, 2005, pp. 25-36. I prepared it originally as a talk given at Liverpool Hope University as part of a series of lectures on the Church and Violence organised by Professor Nicholas Sagovsky. It is followed by my reaction to Mel Gibson's film, The Passion of the Christ, which appeared in The Furrow, 2004, pp. 442-443. That is very relevant to the whole theme of this piece.

Violence and the Eucharist seem to be diametrically opposed. The fact that Archbishop Oscar Romero was shot dead at the altar table in the course of celebrating the Eucharist made his murder seem all the more shocking. There were cries of blasphemy some years ago when one of the US nuclear submarines was named 'Corpus Christi', the Body of Christ.

I would like to suggest that violence and the Eucharist are not as far removed from each other as we might think – that there is, in fact, an inseparable link between the violence to which Jesus was subjected in his Passion and the Eucharist which is the triumph of love over violence and hatred.

Part 1: 'Do this in memory of Me': What is Remembered

'Do this in memory of me' commits the Christian Church and every Christian never to forget a horrendous act of violence against the person of the one whom they claim to be the Son of God. However, it is not the violence itself they are focussing on, but Jesus' response to this violence 'Greater love has no one ...'. It is the violent context which highlights the immensity of his self-giving love.

On the previous night, Jesus commanded his disciples to love each other as he had loved them. 'Do this in memory of me', is implicitly saying, 'Be prepared to lay down your life for others, as I have laid down my life for you – and for all.'

The violent response to the life and preaching of Jesus

In the course of his ministry Jesus increasingly met with opposition from at least some of the leaders of the Jewish establishment and eventually came to be rejected by them. This was because they perceived his life and teaching as a direct threat to their power and authority and to the form of Judaism they stood for. In this they were merely typical of most other forms of establishment before and since. In fact, they represent the 'establishment' side of each of us, the shadow side of our human solidarity. That is why Christians believe that we all share corporate responsibility for the death of Christ.

It could be argued that Jesus himself provoked the course of events which ultimately led to his violent death. In being true to his growing consciousness of himself and his mission from his Father, Jesus saw ever more clearly that the path on which he was embarking upon would inevitably lead to confrontation with the Jewish establishment. Jesus trod the road which could end only on Calvary not because he believed that his Father wanted him to die but because, in fidelity to his mission from his Father, he was committed to witness to a God of totally gratuitous, unconditional and all-embracing love. It was in that ultimate witness of love that his Father's will was to be found, not in any sadistic wish for a violent death. For my own part, I find utterly repugnant and totally unacceptable theologies based on the notion that the violent death of Jesus was demanded by the will of an intransigent Father demanding some kind of retribution or expiation from his Son. The bottom line for me must be that the death of Jesus for us reveals not a violent God but a loving God. That might sound simplistic, but I believe it is fundamental.

At least some of the Jewish establishment found Jesus very threatening. It was not just that he was questioning their basic understanding of God. Rather it was because he was making his challenge in the name of the God of their ancestors, the God revealed in the Law and the Prophets. No wonder they felt that their power and teaching authority over the people were being undermined. Far from rejecting the authentic traditions of Judaism, his whole lifestyle, ministry, preaching and parables developed out of his prayerful reflection on and penetration of these same traditions. It is not surprising that he provoked such strong opposition. Moreover, he did not mince his words. The extreme language of his diatribes against the scribes and Pharisees, as found in chapter twenty-three of Matthew's gospel, must have roused their fury. And his driving the money changers out of the Temple (Matt 21:12), a violent act in itself, was hardly calculated to win him friends. Jesus's violent death was the inevitable outcome of the opposition to his mission and ministry..

Jesus own response to the violence inflicted on him was passionate non-violence
It has been customary down through the ages to speak of the 'Passion' of Jesus. It is very interesting that the word, 'passion', is traditionally used of the sufferings of Jesus. In medieval times the word 'passion' was commonly used in the ethical field. It carried a totally different meaning from the word 'passive' (or 'passivity') which has the same root. While 'passive' suggests lack of movement, 'passion', on the other hand, means actually being moved – often moved intensely, as in the word 'passionate' – but by forces not completely under one's control.

Jesus was moved by an almost unbearable intensity of suffering, both physical and mental. To call such suffering the 'Passion' of Jesus suggests that his response to such intense suffering was far from being passive. Though completely helpless in the hands of his torturers and executioners, his response was one of being prepared to have such violence and suffering inflicted upon him. The 'Passion' of Jesus was the ultimate revelation of God's passionate love in all its unbearable red-hot intensity.

Misunderstood, this could give the impression of a masochistic God, a God whose pleasure lay in experiencing suffering. That is light years away from the truth. In his body and spirit Jesus found such suffering repellent. Jesus did not want to suffer. The agony in the garden brings that out very clearly. Nor did his Father want him to suffer. Those who crucified him were not doing the will of the Father. They were not God's agents. In their blindness ('Father, forgive them') there were actually agents of the forces of evil. They were not performing the will of a masochistic or sadistic God. Rather, they personified evil as it has always manifested itself down through history – as destructive and life-denying.

The suffering of Jesus ended in his death. But in the sense in which I have been using the word, the final act of his 'Passion' lay in his resurrection. The Father raised him from the grave and established him in glory, thus giving an even richer meaning to what I said earlier – 'The "Passion" of Jesus was the ultimate revelation of God's passionate love in all its unbearable red-hot intensity.

'Do this in memory of me' is not just remembering an act of horrendous violence – and the heroic and loving bearing of such violence. 'Do this in memory of me' is also remembering the final act of resurrection. As Christians proclaim: 'Christ has died, Christ is risen.'

Part 2: 'Do this in memory of Me: The Act of Remembering'
Eucharist is not just about past memory but about living presence
In fulfilling the command 'Do this in memory of me' in the Eucharist, Christians remember the violent suffering and death of Jesus not to glory in that violence but to draw life and strength from the spirit of Christ risen and living today. In that spirit is found the ultimate power of non-violence, the victory of love over the very worst that violence can perpetrate. It is the food of that spirit with which Christians believe they are fed at the Eucharistic table. In the power of that spirit, they believe that Christ lives today in and through them. In more corporate language, they believe that they themselves are 'the body of Christ'.

Thomas Cullinan, in his collection of talks, *The Passion of Political Love*, London, Sheed & Ward, 1987, has a chapter entitled, 'Violence Within and Violence Without'. In it he speaks about the need today for a new language to expose and challenge the narrow-mindedness and blinkered vision of the dominant speech of modern society and suggests that this new language may be found in the Eucharist. However, if this new language is to liberate us from that violence 'without', it must do the same for the violence 'within'. This double process will set us on a collision course within and without. Just as there will be violent resistance from the established forces without, there will also be violent resistance from within, as our cherished addictions and enslavements struggle to maintain their stranglehold over us. Cullinan puts it very forcefully, paraphrasing Ghandi, 'We are our first enemy. Don't set up the British as the cause of what you are refusing to face yourself' (p. 24).

If the Eucharist commits Christians to a path which will almost inevitably lead them to face some kind of violent opposition, they can expect to face that opposition as much from within themselves as from outside. As Cullinan puts it very starkly, 'The latent conflict within each of us and public conflicts of our society are in fact locked on one to another' (p. 29). I suspect that what the Gospels portray as Jesus' forty days being tempted in the wilderness was, in fact, his struggling with this violence within, probably including the shadow side of his religious upbringing as a young Jewish man.

If Christians claim to be 'the body of Christ' and true to his spirit, it is to be expected that they will provoke violence too
Cullinan insists that when Christians look at the various dimensions of the present-day cultural, social and ecclesial context in which the Eucharist is celebrated, they need to remember that they themselves do not inhabit some world outside of that context. It is part of who they are, their own human reality. Their celebration of Eucharist must necessarily take place within that context. There is nowhere else they can be. If the Eucharist does not speak to and help interpret that context, it can hardly be said to offer a new language. It could even be seen as meaningless and irrelevant.

Part 3: Celebrating the Eucharist in todays world
I have kept insisting that Jesus could be said to have provoked the violence which was inflicted upon him. Yet, that is an over-simplification. Jesus provoked violence because he himself was provoked by violence. Some people seem to be provocative by nature, almost as though they lack any sense of inner security or peace. Such people can sow dissention rather than peace. Jesus was certainly not provocative in that sense. He was provocative only because he himself was provoked. He was provoked by injustice, and especially injustice perpetrated in the name of God. He was provoked when he saw the poor, the sick, the blind, the disabled and lepers labelled sinners and treated as outcasts. He was provoked when religious leaders portrayed God as being more interested in the Sabbath than in relieving suffering and healing sickness. He whom John called the Word made flesh was provoked by religious hypocrisy in which the hollowness of people's religious words was exposed by their lack of mercy and compassion. He was provoked by the very same things that the prophets said provoked the God of his ancestors.

Using 'passion' once again in the sense of being moved by external factors, it could be said that the Passion of Jesus took place throughout all his active ministry. The way whole categories of people were marginalized and despised provoked the passion which filled his whole life and preaching. Jesus was a very passionate person – revealing an extremely passionate God, a compassionate God. Most of the violence Jesus saw around him was systemic and institutional, bound up with religious and social exclusion. We know now how closely all this violence was linked to economic and political factors. Jesus did not operate in a purely religious world.

I was reminded of all this some time ago as I listened to Julian Filochowski preaching at a Mass on the eve of Romero Day. A personal friend of Romero, Julian made it very clear how strongly Romero was provoked by the horrendous injustice and violence of the El Salvador government and its military and political institutions. The God of Romero was the God of Jesus, that same God about whom Sobrino wrote, 'What is most sacred to God is not himself but human beings'. For Romero, 'Do this in memory of me' was intrinsically bound up with being provoked passionately by such violence. It meant being filled with the spirit of the risen and living Christ, and so responding as the body of Christ to the violence and injustice he saw around him. In his preaching at the Eucharist, Romero felt he could not truly interpret the scriptures for his community without at the same time interpreting in the light of those scriptures the social, political and economic reality he saw all around him. For him the Eucharist was intrinsically and profoundly contextualized in the reality of El Salvador, a reality which could itself only be properly understood within the wider economic and political context. In the second paragraph of this article I comment that 'The fact that Archbishop Oscar Romero was shot dead at the altar table in the course of celebrating the Eucharist made his murder seem all the more shocking.' On the other hand, maybe there was nowhere more appropriate for his martyrdom to take place!

Christians should be 'passionate' in celebrating the Eucharist today in such a provocative context of violence and injustice on a global scale

The language of the Eucharist is the language of communion. If that is truly the language of the Christian community, as they come together to share in the Eucharist, they must surely be provoked by all that is dehumanising, demeaning and destructive of human persons in the current climate in society – the individualism, consumerism and relativism which is in the air we breathe; institutional and social prejudice and discrimination in all forms, whether based on race, ethnicity, sex or sexual orientation; ageism and intolerance of physical or mental disability. Moreover, remembering Cullinan's words about the enemy within, Christians will expect to be challenged on all these counts in their own personal motivation and lifestyle. And surely that is all the more true with regard to so much which is dysfunctional in the internal life of the Church itself.

Part 4: Other issues linked to 'Eucharist and Violence'
Using Eucharist as a form of Violence

In Roman Catholic canon law exclusion from the Eucharist would generally be seen as a 'medicinal' penalty. Its purpose would be to heal, to lead a person to change their ways and so help to be welcomed back into the community. Cavanagh argues the case for such 'medicinal' exclusion as follows:

> As an invitation to reconciliation, then, excommunication done well is an act of hospitality, in which the Church does not expel the sinner, but says to her, 'You are already outside our communion. Here is what you need to do to come back in.' Excommunication does not abandon the sinner to her fate; in fact, precisely the opposite is the case. It is failure to excommunicate the notorious sinner that leaves her to eat and drink her own condemnation (William Cavanagh, *Torture and Eucharist*, London, Blackwells, 1998, p. 243).

We need to remember that Cavanagh was writing of his experience in Chile where he saw the torture inflicted by Christians in Chile on their fellow Christians as a deliberate attempt to isolate them from society and depersonalise them. In Christian terms, it was an attempt to 'dis-member' the body of Christ and reduce its members to isolated individuals.

If refusal of the Eucharist might possibly be justified on grounds of healing or even safeguarding the unity and integrity of the 'body of Christ', what about its refusal for other purposes? For instance, there is a controversy in the US Church at present with regard to one or two bishops who have given instructions that politicians who advocate a pro-abortion stance should be refused communion. It is interesting that the National Catholic Reporter filed this story under the heading, 'When Communion becomes a Weapon'. Clearly, the headline writer sees such a refusal as a violent mean to enforce an ethical position with political implications.

Or again, what about people involved in a second marriage while the previous partner is still living? The official line, taught by the Pope and the Vatican and upheld, at least in public, by most bishops, is that they should be refused the sacraments, despite strong theological arguments in favour of a more open approach. Many Roman Catholics see this ban as a form of violence perpetrated against people whose lives have been shattered by marriage breakdown and whose second marriage is experienced as a gift of God and an occasion of grace.

My friend, David Morland OSB, whom I quoted in the previous article, puts it even more bluntly:

> The idea that a past broken relationship (e.g. divorce-remarriage) should bar a person from the very sacrament whose purpose is to heal wounds

and rebuild life seems as perverse and blind as the criticism of Jesus by the Pharisees of a miracle of healing performed on the Sabbath.

Another instance might be the denial of the sacraments to Catholics living publicly in a committed gay relationship. Is that medicinal? Many would regard it, too, as life-denying and destructive.

Doing Violence to the Eucharist

It has struck me more and more over the years that we Catholics cause ourselves problems by isolating the act of 'receiving Communion' within the whole integrated action of the Eucharist. So we talk about 'refusing Communion' to people, even though we are happy for them to join us in all the other prayers and actions of the Eucharist. 'Receiving Communion' thereby becomes a separate entity in its own right.

This is very strange since it is the community's celebration of the Eucharist as a whole, not some isolated part of it, which constitutes the sacrament of unity and reconciliation. As I mentioned in the previous article, to invite someone to share in the unifying experience round the table and then tell them they cannot share in the community meal seems to be bad manners and totally inhuman. After all, Christ, the host at the table, caused scandal by the kind of the kind of company he shared meals with!

After a recent Saturday Night Mass, a parishioner wanted a word with me – a very down-to-earth and deeply committed Catholic man, with his feet firmly on the ground. In his broad Liverpool accent he said:

> You know how you were talking about Jesus being committed to an open table in face of all the complaints of the religious establishment. Well, our Catholic bishops don't let us keep an open table, do they? I think it is shocking that those who are not Catholic aren't allowed to share at the table. I know people bring up all sorts of reasons why not. Some even say – you never know what awful things they would do with the host. But aren't our bishops already doing something awful with it when they refuse it to those wanting to receive?

This is particularly the case when the discipline prevents married couples from receiving Communion together in so-called 'mixed marriages'. The Anglican bishops highlight the horror of this violence in their trenchant criticism of the discipline of One Bread, One Body on this point: 'The unity in Christ between husband and wife that is created sacramentally or covenantally through marriage, building on baptism, should not be put asunder at the Eucharist' (The Eucharist, sacrament of unity, no. 42).

Oliver McTernan in his book, *Violence in God's Name* (London, Darton, Longman & Todd, 2003), argues that violence in the name of God can be nourished by reading sacred texts as giving the disciple an exclusivist religious identity – God is with me and not with you. Restrictive approaches to the Eucharist could work in that way, strengthening an exclusivist identity among members and creating feelings of unwelcome and rejection among those not allowed to participate.

To accept an 'open table' approach to the Eucharist would mean moving from an attitude of toleration to one of appreciating the gift of difference: If the Church claims to be a sacrament of the unity of the human family, the Eucharist should not be a meal at which the presence of outsiders is tolerated within certain strict limits, but a meal at which their presence is treasured and accepted as a gift. Communion will be more truly Communion. David Morland OSB makes a similar point:

> Perhaps the power and fire the Eucharist contains as the breaking of the Lord's body has to be thrown open to the world and all Christians so that no one is excluded who does not chose to be. The scene of the Last Supper would be transposed into the feeding of the five thousand with no questions asked about faith, merit or moral practice. Participation in the Eucharist would be rather the sowing of the seed of God's presence than the affirmation of orthodox membership of the one, true Church. For Christians it would be the bread of pilgrims searching for unity rather than a celebration by the few of a unity they believe they already possess. Perhaps the destruction of the temple of One Bread, One Body is needed if the real Body of the Lord is to be given shape in the world today.

Another instance of this violence against the Eucharist itself might be in the way in which in many parts of the world, people are effectively deprived of the Eucharist for very long periods due to the Catholic Church's giving higher priority to the ruling on clerical celibacy than to availability of the Eucharist.

Many women – and many men, myself included – regard the so-called theological sign argument that women cannot be ordained priests because the priest acts 'in the person of Christ' as doing violence to the human dignity of women. Those who believe this will also regard this teaching as doing violence to the Eucharist itself. A poem quoted by Elizabeth A. Johnson in her book, *Truly Our Sister: A Theology of Mary in the Communion of Saints* (New York/London, Continuum, 2003) expresses this in a very telling way:

> All the way to Elizabeth
> and in the months afterward,

she wove him, pondering,
"This is my body, my blood."

Beneath the watching eyes
of donkey, ox, and sheep
she rocked him, crooning,
"This is my body, my blood."

In the moonless desert flight
and the Egypt-days of his growing
she nourished him, singing,
"This is my body, my blood."

In the search for her young lost boy
and the foreboding day of his leaving
she let him go, knowing,
"This is my body, my blood."

Under the blood-smeared cross
she rocked his mangled bones,
remembering him, moaning,
"This is my body, my blood."

When darkness, stones, and tomb
bloomed to Easter morning,
she ran to him, shouting,
"This is my body, my blood."

And no one thought to tell her:
"Woman, it is not fitting
for you to say those words.
"You don't resemble him."

CHAPTER TWENTY-NINE

On viewing Mel Gibson's film,
The Passion of the Christ

I found the film very unhelpful in terms of leading me to encounter Christ. All the emphasis was on the violent suffering inflicted upon Christ and on the terrible inhumanity of those who beat and scourged him. It almost gave the impression that what was 'divine' about Jesus was his ability to absorb a superhuman amount of pain and suffering. It gave no indication as to why his Passion should be interpreted as a sign of his love for us. The viewer was almost left to conclude that God wanted Jesus to suffer as much as possible to show his love for us. But what kind of God is that? That probably explains why I felt the film was almost blasphemous in its portrayal of God.

The High Priest and his fellow priests came over as utterly wicked. We were given no idea as to why they should have wanted to get rid of Jesus, what it was about him that made him so threatening to them and their form of religious belief and practice. The soldiers too were totally and mindlessly brutal. There was no suggestion that they were just ordinary soldiers obeying orders and doing their horrendous duty. Hence, there was no way the viewer could feel they might have done the same if they were in their position.

The film read the Gospels as completely historical accounts, rather than as portrayals of a real historical event but with various layers of theological interpretation added on. To make matters worse, it portrayed as historical some events for which there is no historical evidence at all. Moreover, his introduction of the figure of the devil was clearly Mel Gibson's own attempt at theological interpretation. Personally, I did not find it in any way helpful.

After viewing the film I spent about twenty minutes praying in Church. This was not because the film had inspired me to pray. Quite the contrary, I felt a need to pray – almost to purify myself from the experience of watching what I felt was a distortion of something utterly sacred, the most profound sign of God's love for us. Although the Passion of Jesus was most certainly a horrendously violent and inhuman happening, the film gave not the slightest hint that the violence and suffering undergone by Jesus two thousand years ago still continues today.

The Good News is not that Jesus suffered barbarously two thousand years ago but that Jesus in his life and teaching revealed God's utterly unconditional love for us, even at the cost of such barbarous suffering and death. Many of the religious leaders found such unconditional love too hard to swallow. It threatened their authority and way of life. That is precisely why they were determined to get rid of Jesus.

That same unconditional love of God for us remains the Good News today. And we still continue to find it very threatening and disturbing. By virtually collapsing into one the horror of human sin and the horror of Christ's suffering, the film is in danger of confirming our blindness to the fact that the same horror continues today.

Christ continues to suffer here and now, wherever the image of God in his creatures is denied by our inhumanity to each other. And we are all involved in that. Inhumanity today is much more subtle and widespread than that shown in the film. It is the inhumanity which has its roots in systemic and in-stitutional injustice while its effects are felt by many right across the world. The Passion of Christ continues today. Tears shed in the cinema are useless if they only blind our vision still further and prevent us from seeing the suffering of Christ in his brothers and sisters today.

CHAPTER THIRTY

Some Thoughts on the Diminishing Number of Priests

As part of my seven month sabbatical in 1980, I spent two months observing liberation theology in practice in India, the Philippines and Peru. I jotted down these thoughts after what was for me a mind-blowing experience in Peru. Feeling a burning desire to share the experience with others, I wrote it up and it was published in The Clergy Review, 1981, February, pp. 61-63. Although written over thirty years ago, the problem is still with us and what I wrote seems as relevant today as it was back in 1980. In fact, it is even more relevant since here in the UK and in the West in general, there is a very drastic reduction in the number of priests. In my own Liverpool Archdiocese the 2011 Directory lists 149 diocesan priests currently engaged in parish ministry (35 of them also holding other diocesan posts), whereas the 1980 Directory lists over 600 priests in parish ministry serving a catholic population of just over 500,000.

Many say we just have to trust in God. Perhaps God is longing for us to trust in our own initiative and come up with some creative solutions. As I mention in the text below, even if the numbers of full-time priests were to return to what they were, as long as the model of priest to which we are accustomed remains the same, I doubt whether that would be any solution to the problem. Looking around us at an ecumenical level might suggest more imaginative solutions. For instance, when I served in the shared Catholic/Anglican Church in Widnes, the vicar and I used to help with the very thorough training of Anglican men and women on the LOM formation course. LOM means 'Locally Ordained Ministers'. On ordination, LOM priests are licensed for ministry only in their own parishes. It struck me as a form of ministry from which the Catholic Church has much to learn. It might offer one of the 'imaginative solutions' I refer to above.

It does not make sense pastorally (i.e. it is pastoral nonsense) to say that the Eucharist is at the heart of the life of the Christian community and then deny many Christian communities regular access to the Eucharist for the sake of a much lesser (and even questionable) pastoral value, namely that of obligatory celibacy for priests. In many developing countries that is precisely what is happening and apparently on an alarmingly wide scale.

In 1980 I had the privilege of a two-month visit to some developing countries. Admittedly that was a very brief experience but at least it brought me face to face with some undeniable realities. For instance, in the Philippines I visited three dioceses outside of Manila. In Infanta there are approximately 170,000 Catholics and only sixteen priests (including the bishop). In Kidapawan there are roughly 250,000 Catholics and twenty priests (again including the bishop). I did not get the figures for the third diocese, Cagayan de Oro, but from what I saw the situation seemed fairly similar. Moreover, apart from the major cities, I did not get the impression that those figures were exceptional. Furthermore, in these dioceses many of the Catholics are living in tiny villages miles from the nearest road, so that the priest can only get there on horseback or by foot, no mean feat during the monsoon period, as I discovered to my cost!

In Peru I visited Villa el Salvador, one of the shanty towns on the edge of Lima. There again there were a quarter of a million people, this time served by five priests. Some idea of what this means can be gained by imagining my own archdiocese, Liverpool, with this kind of priest-people ratio. At the moment (1980) Liverpool has half a million Catholics and they are served by over 600 priests! According to the Philippine or Peruvian ratio those half-million Liverpool Catholics would be served not by 600 priests but by sixty (Kidapawan and Infanta ratio) or by a mere ten priests (Villa el Salvador ratio). It is virtually impossible for us to imagine what such a situation would mean in practice.

Paradoxically I came back from my short trip abroad with the feeling that one of our problems in England is that we have far too many priests. The little experience I had in the places mentioned forced me to face the disturbing truth that in a strange way a Church with fewer priests seemed to be a Church with a far more active and responsible laity. In the three dioceses I visited great emphasis had been laid on the development of basic Christian communities and the result was that in many of the villages or sectors of the shanty towns there were very active praying, caring and socially involved Christian communities. Many of these communities were seldom able to celebrate the Eucharist (just a few times a year) due to the shortage of priests but they were sufficiently well-formed and organised to undertake their own Sunday para-liturgy and to run their own catechetical and community care programmes. I seemed to detect a quality of Christian community life in these places which I would not associate with the average parish in this country. Not having a priest living in their midst seems to have forced these communities to take on their own responsibilities. However, it should be recognised that the bishops, priests and sisters in these areas have made it a top priority to foster these local communities by training supporting community organisers and local leaders and catechists. In other words, the priests and sisters have taken on the role of providing and co-ordinating apostolic formation for local lay leaders and such work is the main thrust of their full-time ministry. The very positive element in this situation was the faith and vitality of the local lay community. The negative side lay in the fact that for most of the year many local Christian communities were deprived of the Eucharist. This had the additional disadvantage that they could not even celebrate in the context of the Eucharist the key events and feasts of their life as a community.

Maybe we need to say more than that there is a crying pastoral need for priests. Maybe we should also look at the kinds of priests that are needed. I cannot help feeling that it would kill the life of those basic Christian communities suddenly to have thrust upon them a full-time priest (whether a married man or a woman would be irrelevant) whose priestly role was patterned on the style of priesthood to which we are accustomed. As far as I can judge, what those communities need is the recognition or authorisation ('ordination') that one from their midst (man or woman, married or single) can preside at their Eucharist. This would be no more a full-time role than is the present role of leader of the liturgy in their communities. Whether it should be a permanent role for one specific individual or whether it should be a role shared by a number of appropriate members of the community would need further consideration. The book of essays, *Minister? Pastoral? Prophet? Grass roots leadership in the Churches* by Schillebeeckx and others (SCM, London, 1980) is very relevant to this issue.

If this is indeed the form of priesthood needed in these basic Christian communities, it is probable that normally the most suitable people would turn out to be married and employed in the kind of work normal in their community. To make this kind of priestly ministry full-time would be inappropriate and would only result in concentrating in one person the various ministries currently shared by the whole community. That would be a very retrograde step and would be detrimental to the development of the Christian community as such.

However, I can see that there is also a need for a full-time ministry somewhat along the lines of that currently being exercised by the priests and sisters working to promote and sustain the local communities and their leaders. They would probably need some community base themselves and it would be appropriate that they should at least share in the Eucharistic presidency in their local community – and maybe also in the communities they visit on their roving commission. This would surely be true at the level of breaking the word of the scriptures with these communities.

This full-time pastoral ministry would be a different form of priesthood. Such priests would also be more effective in symbolizing the unity of the local community with the wider local Church presided over by the bishop. This fact is another important reason for their being able to exercise Eucharistic presidency in their visits to the local basic communities. Although I would not argue that celibacy is essential for such a full-time ministry, I would certainly say that those who have committed themselves to consecrated apostolic celibacy (men and women) would, other things being equal, be very suitable persons for this ministry.

As regards our own country, it would be foolish to translate uncritically what has proved helpful in a different setting and culture. Nevertheless, I think we have much to learn from the experience of the developing world. One point strikes me very strongly. We would be unwise to assume too easily that a reduction in the number of priests in this country is a pastoral disaster. The experience in parts of the developing world suggests that it might well be a glorious pastoral opportunity for forming a 'Sharing Church' along the lines so beautifully portrayed by the bishops in Part One of The Easter People. If there is any truth in this, we might be committing a major pastoral blunder if we make it a priority to increase the number of full-time priests before undertaking a radical reappraisal of the kind (or kinds) of priesthood needed for such a 'Sharing Church'. Whatever pastoral value might be involved in obligatory clerical celibacy, it certainly should not be allowed to stand in the way of the supreme value of the Eucharist in the life of the local Christian community. To deprive many Christian communities of the Eucharist for long periods of the year for the sake of upholding obligatory celibacy seems to be a policy without any adequate justification theologically or pastorally.

It might be worth quoting some lines from the diary I kept of my visit to Peru. It is referring to the local Church in one of the very remote rural areas linked to the town of Tambogrande:

> The sisters too are affected by the shortage of priests. For a while they had an elderly Peruvian priest in Tambogrande but he has gone. Now they have no resident priest. A retired military chaplain comes for Sunday Mass but he is not very reliable. Consequently, it is very hard for the Sisters since they cannot be sure even of weekly Mass, let alone daily Mass. Despite it all, they remain a very prayerful community, thank God.
>
> One moving experience I had there was to celebrate Sunday Mass in Callejones, a tiny village about three hours drive (by jeep through desert with no roads) from Tambogrande. Sister Therese Hartley SND had prepared a group for their first Communion, mostly teenagers. All the families turned out and filled the little Church which they had built themselves. Sister Therese looked after the first part of the Mass (including the homily) and I took over at the offertory procession. Sister Mary McCallion, another SND Sister there, had taught me enough Spanish to be able to say the Second Eucharistic Prayer but that was as far as I could go! Callejones (and the many villages like it) would only have Mass a couple of times a year. It was a Mass I will never forget. I felt very privileged to be able to share in it. Yet it made me even more convinced that it is a serious pastoral mistake for the Church not to ordain women in such situations. How can we say that the Eucharist is at the heart of our Faith and our Christian life and yet deny such communities the Eucharist for the lack of a priest when there is a sister available – especially when she has as much theology and far more spirituality than most of us priests and is fully accepted in that community as the spiritual leader and the one in charge of the liturgy?

I would not want these remarks to be read as taking away from the tremendous work being done by many very dedicated foreign priests in these countries. For the present many of them are playing an indispensable role in building up these basic Christian communities. But the long-term solution must surely lie with the men and women who make up the local indigenous Church.

CHAPTER THIRTY-ONE

Is 'No' to Female Priests 'Good News' for women?
Letter to The Tablet, 2 December 1995

My burning pastoral concern expressed in the previous piece that the availability of the Eucharist should be a prime concern in the Church has never left me. In fact, it has deepened over the years. It is one of the main reasons why I feel so strongly that the Church needs to reconsider its position on the ordination of women.

However, there is a much more fundamental reason which comes out in the following excerpt from a letter which was published in The Tablet 2 December 1995, p. 1548. The article which follows spells out more fully the position outlined in the letter.

In its reply denying the possibility of women being ordained priests (see *The Tablet*, 25 November 1995), the CDF links this teaching to the deposit of faith. The Vatican congregation seems to be saying that the inadmissibility of women to the ministerial priesthood is an essential part of the Good News of the Gospel which brings joy and freedom to all human persons, women and men.

Could I dare suggest that the inadmissibility of women to the ministerial priesthood should only be presented as belonging to the deposit of faith if it can be shown to be an integral and essential element of the Gospel which has consistently been heard and experienced as 'good news' by women down through the ages? I suspect that the opposite has been the case. Far from being an integral part of the 'good news', it seems more like part of that cultural conditioning down the centuries which John Paul II referred to as 'an obstacle to the progress of women'.

I have been drawn to this conclusion through reading texts from various early Christian writers explaining how they saw women to be different from men. This is the cultural climate which nourished the tradition that women cannot be admitted to the priesthood. It does not make edifying reading today. Augustine, for instance, believed that women are so obviously inferior to men in every other way that the only reason God created them must have been for the sake of procreation. The fourth-century Ambrosiaster, who wrote strongly against the ordination of women, argued his case on the grounds that women were not made in the image of God. They were made in the image of man. Most early Christian writers seem to have believed in the moral inferiority of women and point to Eve's tempting Adam as an example.

Ultimately, the main reason that seems to have been behind the tradition against women's ordination was that women are naturally subordinate to men and so are incapable of exercising authority and leadership over men. This line of thinking seems to have continued right through the tradition. It is found in

Aquinas and even features in the textbook out of which I was taught moral theology in the mid-1950s:

> The reason why a woman cannot receive holy orders is because the cler-
> ical state demands a certain superiority since it involves ruling the faith-
> ful: whereas a woman by her very nature is inferior to man and subject
> to him, even though at a personal level she can excel a man in her natural
> and graced giftedness (Noldin, *Summa Theologiae Moralis*, vol. III, no. 465).

It is difficult to see how the centuries-old tradition against the ordination of
women can be identified with the 'good news' which we call the deposit (or
treasure-house) of faith.

Not long ago, in order to stand up for their basic social, economic and political rights, women had to disregard those who told them that what they were
doing was a sin. Such women come in for great admiration from John Paul II
in his Letter to Women (see *The Tablet*, 15 July 1995). He implies that they were
right to disregard those who told them that what they were doing was sinful.
Could it be that women who today disregard the CDF's statement and continue
believing in and working for the ordination of women will be the object of similar admiration on the part of some future Pope?

CHAPTER THIRTY-TWO

The Inhumanity of excluding Women from the Priesthood
A talk given in 1977

This is part of a talk entitled 'Being human means being sexual' which I gave way back in 1977! It was the first of eight lectures on the theme of 'Love and Marriage'. My original intention was to emphasise the truth that our sexuality is a key dimension of our being human. However, while I was preparing this talk, I was also reading a recently published book, The Ministry of Women in the Early Church, by R. Gryson (Liturgical Press, USA, 1976). It blew my mind. His research seemed to demonstrate very clearly that the basic reason why women were regarded as ineligible for ordination in the early Church was tantamount to denying women the fullness of humanity given by God to men. Men were made in the image of God. Women were not. They were made only in the image of men! That is why they were by nature subservient to men. Authority in the Church was restricted to men since women were considered incapable of exercising authority. The same was true of the ministry of teaching. It would seem that this understanding of women provided the fertile ground in which the Church's tradition of denying ordination to women took root.

It struck me at the time that, if Gryson's research is accurate (and I have not seen it refuted anywhere), then not only could the Church's position on the non-ordination of women be described as 'inhuman', but the Church's approach to sexuality was fundamentally flawed, since women's humanity was considered as inferior to that of their male counterparts!

It is possible that further patristic research has raised questions about the validity of Gryson's position. I must confess that I have not had the opportunity to follow up that line of enquiry. However, I would be surprised if this were the case. Certainly two major reports give no grounds for thinking that there is conclusive New Testament or patristic evidence which would rule out any possibility of discussing women's ordination in the Church today. The Report of the Biblical Commission 'Can Women be Priests' chaired by the CDF Prefect, Cardinal Seper, was inconclusive, as is clear from its final three paragraphs:

It does not seem that the New Testament by itself alone will permit us to settle in a clear way and once for all the problem of the possible accession of women to the presbyterate.

However, some think that in the scriptures there are sufficient indications to exclude this possibility, considering that the sacraments of eucharist and reconciliation have a special link with the person of Christ and therefore with the male hierarchy, as borne out by the New Testament.

Others, on the contrary, wonder if the Church hierarchy, entrusted with the sacramental economy, would be able to entrust the ministries of eucharist and reconciliation to women in the light of circumstances, without going against Christ's original intentions.

The other major work is a 1997 paper commissioned by the Catholic Theological Society of America (CTSA), 'Tradition and the ordination of women'. Much of it is devoted to examining the 1995 CDF's 'Responsum' that John Paul II's Apostolic Letter, Ordinatio Sacedotalis (which states that the Church has no authority to ordain women), belongs to the deposit of faith and is therefore infallible teaching. The CTSA paper examines this claim very carefully and its very clear conclusion was put to the secret vote of the whole assembly :

> There are serious doubts regarding the nature of the authority of this teaching namely, the teaching that the Church's lack of authority to ordain women to the priesthood is a truth that has been infallibly taught and requires the definitive assent of the faithful and its grounds in tradition. There is serious, widespread disagreement on this question not only among theologians but also within the larger community of the Church ... It seems clear that further study, discussion and prayer regarding this question by all the members of the Church in accord with their particular gifts and vocations are necessary if the Church is to be guided by the Spirit in remaining faithful to the authentic Tradition of the Gospel in our day.

Of 248 members present, 216 voted 'Yes', 22 'No' and 10 abstained. The fact that a tradition is constant does not automatically mean that it is part of the core Gospel message. When Benedict XVI was professor at Tubingen, he wrote the following with reference to the Vatican II debate on the Constitution on Divine Revelation:

> Not everything that exists in the Church must for that reason be also a legitimate tradition; in other words, not every tradition that arises in the Church is a true celebration and keeping present of the mystery of Christ. There is a distorting as well as a legitimate tradition. Consequently, tradition must not be considered only affirmatively, but also critically. We have scripture as a criterion for this indispensable criticism of tradition, and tradition must therefore always be related back to it and measured by it ... There is, in fact, no explicit mention (in the Constitution) of the possibility of distorting tradition ... which means that a most important side of the problem of tradition, as shown by the history of the Church, as been overlooked (Joseph Ratzinger, The Transmission of Divine Revelation, in Herbert Vorgrimler, edit. Commentary on the Documents of Vatican II, New York, Herder & Herder, 1969, vol. 3, pp. 184-185, 193).

Karl Rahner applies this point of theology explicitly to women's ordination in the chapter, 'Women and the Priesthood', in vol. 20 of his Theological Investigation. Rahner makes specific reference to the argument from tradition given in the 1976 Vatican Declaration:

> If the Declaration appeals to an uninterrupted tradition, this appeal is not necessarily and justifiably an appeal to an absolutely and definitively binding tradition, an appeal to a tradition which simply presents and transmits a 'divine' revelation in the strict sense, since there is obviously a purely human tradition in the Church which offers no guarantee of truth even if it has long been undisputed and taken for granted. With this Declaration, which has an authentic but not defining character, the fundamental question is whether this appeal is to a 'divine' or a merely human tradition (pp. 37-38).
>
> It does not seem to be proved that the actual behaviour of Jesus and the apostles implies a norm of divine revelation in the strict sense of the term. This practice (of ordaining only men to the priesthood) even if it existed for a long time and without being questioned, can certainly be understood as a 'human' tradition like other traditions in the Church which were once unquestioned, had existed for a long time and nevertheless became obsolete as a result of sociological and cultural change (p. 45).

Another key Vatican II theologian, Bernard Häring, has stated very forthrightly that the Pope's alleged 'infallible' decision on this issue does not satisfy the criteria needed for an infallible statement. Firstly, there was no 'determining through ecumenical councils or investigating the conviction of the Church dispersed all over the earth', as required by the constitution, Pastor Aeternus of Vatican I. Nor has it found a 'reception' in the entire Church. This leads Häring to conclude: 'Both lines of thought complete and confirm one another on the ordination of women. They back the conviction that despite the Pope's undeniable intention of proclaiming an infallible doctrine, no such thing took place' (Bernard Häring, My Hope for the Church, p. 116). Readers will remember what I wrote earlier in this volume in my specific piece on Häring:

> In the last book Häring wrote, chapter sixteen is entitled, The Future of the Church and the Issues of Women. He is in no doubt that, before long, women will be ordained in the Roman Catholic Church and he goes so far as to say: 'I suspect that the rejection of ordaining women to celebrate the Eucharist is a relic of magical thinking' (MWC, 114). He even dares to express the hope that "it would be splendid if the pope were to realize and humbly acknowledge his error before he leaves us … It would be a special sign of God's grace to ecumenism' (MWC, p. 118). Häring says these things out of his commitment to the full and equal dignity of women, certainly. In fact, he even writes: 'I consider Rome's "infallible" decision not only inopportune, but also out of touch with the times.'

As I have repeatedly said throughout this volume, I do not consider myself to be an original theologian. I believe deeply in the Church, sinful and dysfunctional though it may be. I am fearful lest my position on the ordination of women might be construed as a denial of the infallible teaching of the Church. I have laboured the above points to make it clear that my position is solidly within the Church, even though not held by all in the Church. The reception process for a truth takes time. It cannot be steamrollered, but neither should it be outlawed. My 1977 talk follows:

Being Human means being a Man or being a Woman

We all recognise the fundamental equality of men and women, as human persons. This is a key element in the Church's teaching. *Gaudium et Spes* is very strong in its condemnation of sex discrimination. It states that all discrimination must be "overcome and wiped out as contrary to God's will" and then it continues:

> It must still be regretted that fundamental personal rights are not yet being universally honoured. Such is the case of a woman who is denied the right and freedom to choose a husband, to embrace a state of life, or to acquire an education or cultural benefits equal to those recognized for men (No. 29).

That is a very clear statement and it is one which we would all endorse. As Christians we are all opposed to sex discrimination. But are we?

Discrimination is usually based on prejudice and prejudice is often unconscious. It influences the way we act and feel and react and relate – but we are not aware that we are being influenced by it. That is why discrimination not only denies the rights of those being discriminated against – it also means that those oppressing them are similarly captive. They are slaves to their own prejudices. They are blind to what they are doing and why they are doing it.

During the international women's year, 1975, Pope Paul VI referred to the emerging consciousness of women about their full dignity as human persons and spoke of this as one of the 'signs of the times'. This emerging consciousness involves becoming aware of the subtle ways in which the full dignity of women as human persons is not given due recognition (either by themselves or by others).

If we accept that this emerging consciousness of women about their full dignity as human persons is one of the signs of the times, then we need to try to tune into this emerging consciousness. And when I say 'we' I mean all of us. I am not just referring to men. All of us, both men and women, need to tune into this emerging consciousness. The very phrase 'emerging consciousness' implies that we are coming out of a state of human sub-consciousness in which it was not fully accepted either in theory or in practice that being a woman is as full a way of being a human person as being a man. In fact, it seems to me that one of the consequences of this unconsciousness has been the impoverishment of the full human reality of being a man. After all, if our human sexuality highlights the truth that as human persons we are relational beings – i.e. we grow and enrich ourselves and others through interpersonal communication and relationships – it would seem obvious that man also is under-developed as long as he relates to woman as superior to inferior, rather than as equal human persons, each with special riches to share with the other.

The Second Vatican Council called us to an examination of consciousness not just as individuals but also as a Church. At the end of the first post-Vatican II meeting of the Bishops' Synod in Rome in 1971, it issued a powerful document on 'Justice in the World'. Its Introduction is as inspirational today as it was in 1971. The way its final sentence has been received and quoted so repeatedly in all kinds of official Church documents gives it an authenticity and authority all of its own:

> Action on behalf of justice and participation in the transformation of the world fully appear to us as a constitutive dimension of the preaching of the Gospel, or, in other words, of the Church's mission for the redemption of the human race and its liberation from every oppressive situation.

To be credible in carrying out this mission we, the Church, have to make sure that freedom and equality are being fully respected within our own community. More specifically, we need to look at whether in the Church women are truly free to be themselves as human persons – or whether there is sex discrimination within the Church with the result that all of us, men and women, are less than the human persons God is calling us to be. To make this examination very concrete, I would like to focus on a controversial issue which is very much to the fore these days.

Can women be ordained Priests?

There are a variety of reactions to that question. Some people say: 'The day that happens, I am leaving the Church'. Others have no objection and cannot see the force of the arguments against the ordination of women. Some women actually feel a call to be a priest. Others say they would never go near a woman priest.

Why should I be discussing the question of women priests in a course entitled 'love and marriage'? It is because I believe that the attitude which gets unearthed when we discuss the ordination of women is part and parcel of a wider attitude underlying all those other areas of life in which only now is a new and deeper consciousness of personal worth beginning to emerge among women.

In what follows I am doing no more than offering my own considered opinion, an opinion formed from reading, study, reflection and listening to women in whom this new consciousness is emerging. What I want to suggest is that the issue of the ordination of women priests can be looked on as a symbol of the status of women in the Church. As long as we cannot accept the ordination of women, we as a Church are communicating through symbol that women are not fully human persons, sharing equal dignity with men. I would even dare to suggest that this attitude is a cancerous growth within the basically healthy body of Christian tradition.

Delving into the memory of the Church.
In order to face this issue squarely, we need to go back into history. This is not unlike the process in psychoanalysis in which a person thinks back to early childhood in order to discover the origin of certain attitudes which may be preventing or impeding full personal development. History is the memory of the Church, a memory which affects us much more deeply than we realise. With respect to the full and complete acceptance of women in the Church there is urgent need for a profound healing of memories, and many women are in need of this healing as much as men.

What could there be about women which would exclude them from being ordained priests? One recent writer, after a very extensive survey of the major writings in the first six centuries of the Church, concludes that the writings of the early Church considered women to be 'weak, fickle, light-headed, of mediocre intelligence' (R. Gryson, *The Ministry of Women in the Early Church*, Liturgical Press, USA 1976, p. 113). Naturally all the writers were men – Bishops, Priests, Canonists and Theologians. I would dare to say that even today not a few Bishops, Priests, Canonists and Theologians still have this attitude, although they would not admit it publicly and might not even be aware of it themselves.

However, that is not the deepest scar in the memory of the Church. After all, even some ardent feminists today might be prepared to admit that there could have been an element of factual truth in some of those descriptions at that time; but that would have had nothing to do with the reality of being a woman. It would have been due to the dehumanising effects of a cultural, social and educational system which denied women the possibility of full personal development.

There is a much deeper scar in the Church's memory. Evidence of this is found in Ambrosiaster's commentary on First Corinthians. This was a very influential fourth-century document:

'Women should keep silence in the Church'. In an earlier passage Paul has ordered that women should be veiled in Church. Now he explains that unless they are quiet and reserved, there is no purpose in their being veiled. For if the image of God is man, and not woman, and if she is subject to man on account of natural law, how much more in Church should she be submissive ... What does the law say? 'Your desire shall be for your husband, and he shall rule over you'. This law is for the whole species. Therefore, Sarah called her husband, Abraham, her 'Lord' ... Although woman is one flesh with man, there are two reasons why she is, nevertheless, ordered to be submissive: first, because she originated from man; and secondly, because through her sin entered the world (Gryson, pp. 92-93).

In his commentary on 1 Tim 2:11-14, Ambrosiaster further expands these two reasons and spells out their implications:

> Women must not only dress modestly; but Paul also prescribes that she be refused authority and that she be subject to man, so that as well by her dress as by obedience she be under the power of man from whom she draws her origin ... Since man was created first, Paul places him before woman; it was not man that the devil deceived, but the woman, and man was duped by her intervening; therefore, no concessions should be made to her audacity, but instead, since through her death entered the world, she ought to remain in submission (Gryson, p. 9).

What is happening here? The writer is not just attributing to women certain weaknesses which could easily be accounted for by lack of educational opportunities due to cultural and social factors. No, he is going much further than that. He is making a number of statements of much greater seriousness.

First of all, he is saying that only man is made in the image of God. Woman is not made in the image of God. She is only made in the image of man. That is clear in the first passage quoted – 'the image of God is man, not woman'. This is not just a temporary lapse since we find Ambrosiaster making the same point even more forcefully in other parts of his writings. In one of them he examines the question head on and comes up with a very firm negative answer that woman is not made in the image of God.

> Man is the image of God; for it is written 'God created man in his own image, in the image of God he created him'. For this reason Paul says: 'A man ought not to cover his head, since he is the image and glory of God'. On the other hand, he says: 'Let a woman wear a veil'. Why? Because she is not the image of God. For this reason, Paul repeats: 'I permit no woman to teach or to have authority over men' (Gryson, p. 94).

In fact, later in the same work Ambrosiaster argues against a false basis for saying that man is the image of God. That false basis would be man's mandate from God to have dominion over all the animals. That cannot be the basic reason why man is in the image of God since it is also true of women. Yet, as Ambrosiaster comments: 'It is obvious that woman is not the image of God'. Making the same point a few lines later he even goes so far as to say:

> If it is true that man possesses the image of God in his domineering power, then woman would have to be recognised as the image of God, which is absurd. When it is clear that she is subject to the power of man and she has no authority whatever, how can we say then that woman is the image of God? (Gryson, p. 95).

A second point that Ambrosiaster makes is that the order of nature, or natural law, demands that woman should be submissive to man since she is naturally inferior to man. This means that woman should not exercise authority over man. It also means that woman should not exercise a teaching role in the Church when this involves exercising teaching authority over men. A further point he makes is that this natural inferiority of woman comes out clearly in the story of the Fall. It is woman who brings sin into the world through her weakness and her fickleness.

Am I making too much of this one writer? I leave specialists in Patristics to judge that. However, the reading I have done, though limited, suggests that Ambrosiaster is fairly representative of the thinking in the first six centuries of the Church in both East and West. He comes from the West but it is worth quoting a similar work from the East, the fourth century Apostolic Constitutions. This has been described as the largest canonical and liturgical collection of antiquity. In one section the writer is dealing with the possibility of women administering the Sacrament of Baptism:

> Now as to women's baptising, we let you know that there is no small peril to those that undertake it ... it is dangerous, or rather wicked and impious. For if the 'man be the head of the woman', and he be originally ordained for the priesthood, it is not just to abrogate the order of creation ... For the woman is the body of the man, taken from his side, and subject to him (Gryson, pp. 56-67).

The writer then goes on to stress that for a woman to baptise would be 'contrary to nature'. He also says that if this had not been so, Jesus would have been baptised by his Mother, rather than by John the Baptist. But Jesus did not let this happen since 'he knew the order of nature ... being the Creator of nature'.

Another Greek writer, Didymus the Blind, writes: 'Paul does not permit a woman to write books impudently, on her own authority, nor to teach in the assemblies, because, by doing so, she offends her head, man; for 'the head of woman is man, and the head of man is Christ' (Cor, 11:3). The reason for this silence imposed on women is obvious to Didymus, since it was women's teaching in the beginning that caused such havoc to the human race. As Didymus puts it: 'For the Apostle writes: 'It is not the man who was deceived, but the woman' (Gryson, p. 77).

Having written to the Galatians that 'there are no more distinctions between Jew and Greek, slave and free, male and female, but all of you are one in Christ Jesus', St Paul himself would never have believed that women are not made in the image of God. Nevertheless, there are some passages in Paul which might have led later commentators to their deeply prejudiced conclusions: e.g. 1 Cor 14:34-35, 1 Tim 2:11-15 and 1 Cor 11:2-16.

The attitude in the early Church, therefore, seems to have been that, though women were accepted as human persons, they were not regarded as being fully human in the way men were. In fact, this view even affected the way they understood the process of generation. Under the influence of Aristotle, such a major figure in Christian tradition as Thomas Aquinas actually looked on woman as a defective man. He admitted that woman was created by God but this was precisely because she was needed for human procreation. So the reason for her specific existence was purely functional!

Despite his deep reverence for his mother and his faithful relationship with the mother of his son over many year, Augustine seems to have shared the same functional view of women many years earlier:

If woman has not been made for helping man by bearing children, what other kind of help can she give? Not manual labour, since another man is much better help than a woman. Not for the sake of company if a man is feeling lonely because another man is much better company and you can have a much more worthwhile conversation with a man than with a woman.

Not even for the sake of having people in society who are by nature submissive to men and who will obey orders – men have shown that they can do that just as well as woman if order in society demands it. So honestly, I do not know what the point is of God making woman if it is not for the sake of bearing children (Cf. St Augustine on his *Comm. on Gen* (*De Gen*. ad litt, IX no. 5 CSEL, XXXV111 [1]).

I have concentrated mainly on the early centuries of the Church but there would be no difficulty in tracing the effects of this trend through the long centuries of the Church's life right up to the present day.

Until very recently, it was customary for women to be excluded from any form of liturgical ministry. Altar girls were unheard of and even women readers began their existence outside the sanctuary. In the ordering of new ministries in the Church, women are expressly excluded, even from the ministries of reader and acolyte. Officially, their exercise of these ministries is only tolerated on an 'extraordinary' basis.

It is not surprising that similar anti-feminine attitudes have coloured Church law down through the centuries and were still in the 1917 Code of Canon Law (replaced only in 1983). In 1976 a statement issued by an official symposium of the Canon Law Society of America acknowledged this and pinpointed numerous areas of Church life in which Canon Law subordinates women to men (either on protective or on paternalistic grounds), and also in which it actually discriminates against women. For instance, women are excluded from jurisdiction and also from administrative and judicial posts.

The same discriminatory approach is found in the 1976 Declaration on the Question of the Admission of Women to the Ministerial Priesthood which continues to maintain that women are ineligible for the priesthood. It bases this position on the fact that Christ did not make women priests even though he defied his own culture by having women among his close followers and that this has been the constant tradition in the Church, one which the Church has no power to alter.

Part of its argumentation is that the priest acts 'in the person of Christ'. Therefore, it is essential that the priest be a man, since the sign value would not work if a woman were a priest (There is a misleading reference to Aquinas as supporting this argument). This raises a fundamental Christological question. Is the difference between man and woman of such deep significance that a woman cannot act in the person of Christ? To answer 'yes' would seem to lay such an emphasis on the maleness of Christ as to have serious repercussions for the basic good news of the Gospel. The Good News is not that the Word became male, but that the Word became Flesh. This 'sign' argument would seem to locate the Incarnation in the maleness of Christ, rather than in his Humanity.

It is true that St Thomas stresses the sign-value of the sacrament and concludes from this that a woman cannot be a priest – but the sign value he is referring to is based on man's superiority over woman. Since by nature woman is in a state of subjection to man, she cannot be the symbol of pre-eminence which is involved in the priesthood. The authors of the Vatican Declaration would hardly accept that argument since they are prepared to admit that 'modern thought would have difficulty in admitting or would even rightly reject' some of the earlier arguments.

We all know from our own personal experience that the reasons we give for our beliefs are not always the real reasons which influence us. Unknowingly at times we try to maintain a position by using arguments which are not the

real reason for our stand. The earlier male superiority argument against the ordination of women might be so deeply embedded in the Church's memory, we
would be naïve if we were to presume it has lost all its influence. For instance,
I can still remember the reason given in Noldin's manual of moral theology
against the ordination of women, other than the Pauline texts:

> The reason why a woman cannot receive Holy Orders is because the cler-
> ical state demands a certain superiority since it involves ruling the faith-
> ful; whereas, a woman by her very nature is inferior to man and subject
> to him (III, no. 465).

Noldin was honest enough to admit that an individual woman might in fact
be more talented than a man. Noldin's manual was the text book from which I
first studied moral theology and was in use in many, if not most, seminaries
throughout the world until the mid-1960s.

There is one thing we can say for certain: Christ did not consider women to
be inferior to men and less human than men. If we accept that, we are accepting
as true that there is nothing about women which makes them incapable of exercising both priestly ministry and jurisdictional authority in the Church.

The Church's 'tradition' on the ordination of women down the centuries
has been too closely linked with an underlying attitude towards women which,
as part of today's 'emerging consciousness', is increasingly being recognised
as inhuman and therefore un-Christian.

This brings us back to the sign issue. Signs matter. That is precisely why
this question of the ordination of women as something important in the
Church. We have seen that one of the 'signs of the times' is the emerging consciousness among women of their full dignity as human persons. And we are
living in a time of growing acceptance of this among men. I would suggest
that the continuation of the Church's stand that women are excluded from
being priests is going to be more and more a counter sign. In today's world
with its modern critical thought it cannot but be seen as one of the remaining
vestiges of sex-discrimination. The more women become educated and conscious of their full personal dignity, the more they will be forced into an intol-
erable position. Either they will repress that dignity in the sphere of religion –
yet how can this be done since Christianity is about personal dignity – or they
will increasingly regard the Church as irrelevant to the realities of human life
in the modern world.

That would be my answer to those who might object – why the hurry?
Why not let the role of women in the Church develop gradually? The subor-
dination of women to men in the Church is so deeply embedded in the
Church's memory that it needs radical surgery to heal it. In the present form
of Church life, as long as women are barred from ordination to priesthood,

they are also excluded from any real share in authority and effective decision-making in the Church. That is keeping the Church itself at a serious level of human under-development.

Being human means being sexual. As long as we do not exorcise the demon of sex discrimination from the Christian consciousness by some radical step like accepting the ordination of women, it seems to me that the Church will not be fully human since she will not be fully sexual. And such a Church will never be able to understand and share the full implications and riches of its teaching on love and marriage. As long as authority and ordained ministry remain a totally male preserve in the Church, there is a danger that the Church herself will not be fully alive. A fully alive Church must be a fully human Church, sharing the complementary riches of men and women at all levels of Christian life and mission.

CHAPTER THIRTY-THREE

Celebrating the Eucharist in the Spirit of Vatican II

On 2 March 2004, the CDW issued an Instruction entitled, 'On certain matters to be observed or to be avoided regarding the Most Holy Eucharist'. Its Latin title was 'Redemptionis Sacramentum'. When I read it, fresh in my mind were two inspired pieces of writing which I had just been reading: 'Vatican II: A Matter of Style' by Professor John O'Malley SJ, the 2003 President's Letter of the Weston Jesuit School of Theology; and an unpublished talk by Timothy Radcliffe to Catholic Peers and MPs given in 2004. What follows is a slightly revised version of my article which appeared in The Furrow, 2004, pp. 397-400 under the title, 'A Eucharistic Dis-Service – a personal reading of Redemptionis Sacramentum'. I wanted to share with readers my personal impression that this Instruction was actually 'untrue' to the Spirit of Vatican II. As will be obvious from the text, I was still parish priest in the shared RC/CE Church of St Basil and All Saints in Widnes when I wrote this piece.

John O'Malley SJ, a distinguished Church historian who has written extensively on Vatican II, pinpoints five essential features of the 'spirit of the Council'. He focuses on 'how' questions rather than 'what' questions. How is the Church to be – 'what kind of procedures does it use, what kind of relationships does it foster among its members, what is its style as an institution.' His five essentials are:

(1) *horizontal* – 'the Council called the Church from what had been an almost exclusively vertical, top down style of behaviour to one that took more account of the horizontal traditions in Catholicism.' He highlights such horizontal words as cooperation, partnership, collaboration and especially collegiality;
(2) *serving* – the Council's style and mentality is 'more consonant with serving than with controlling';
(3) *changing* – though Vatican II never used the word 'change', its use of words like 'development', 'progress' and even 'evolution' were precisely about change and implied that its own provisions were 'somewhat open ended';
(4) *inclusive* – a move from 'exclusion' to 'inclusion' marked by 'friendship words like sisters and brothers, and men and women of good will' and extending this friendship far beyond fellow Christians to 'anybody wanting to work for a better world';
(5) *participative* – a move from 'passive acceptance' to one of 'active participation and engagement' – not just in the liturgy but actually as 'a norm for the way we behave, that is constitutive of our style as Church'.

Timothy Radcliffe reminds politicians how the 'truthfulness of our talking' plays a major part in the 'quality of political life'. He develops a 'spirituality of truth', stressing that 'telling the truth is our human vocation'. Rather than being reduced to mere exactitude, telling the truth is about giving life to people and helping them become free. As he puts it: 'Our words can give life to another or they can kill. We can share in speaking God's word, which builds people up, and makes them strong and alive. Or we can squash people like flies.'

He insists that there are ways of speaking which belittle or denigrate:

> If we talk about human beings as if we are above all consumers, then we unmake the children of God. If we talk about schools and hospitals as if they were profit-making businesses, then we undermine civilization; if we talk about killing civilians as 'collateral damage' then we rubbish our victims.

Truth telling is also about building community. Our society is threatened by a 'crisis of suspicion' which thrives on accusation and creates mistrust and insecurity. Radcliffe insists: 'For a Christian, we never see the truth of another person unless one has first seen a glimpse of their goodness'. It means seeing people through God's eyes, eyes of mercy and love. 'It means having a prejudice in their favour.' He ends his talk with Paul's words in Eph 4:29: 'Do not use harmful words in talking. Use only helpful words, the kind that build up and provide what is needed, so that what you say will do good to those who hear you.'

All this was in my mind as I began reading the Instruction of the Congregation for Divine Worship. I must confess that my heart sank and I was deeply saddened by what I read. It seems far from the 'spirit of the Council'. There is little 'horizontal' about it, no empathy with those in parish ministry struggling to make the liturgy an inspiring and life-giving experience for people. Its emphasis seems more on control than on 'service', on uniformity rather than on healthy evolutionary 'change'. Its tone is hardly friendly, tending more to the exclusive rather than the 'inclusive'. Though it uses the Council language of 'participation' at times, its heart does not seem to be in it and there is little enthusiasm for 'full and active participation' as a distinguishing feature of Church life today.

In terms of Timothy Radcliffe's talk, it does not come over to me as a life-giving document in line with his criterion for truth telling. Some of its ways of speaking are denigrating. For instance, terms like 'abuse' and 'reprobated practices' run like refrains through the text with little appreciation that some deviations from the letter of the law might possibly be obedient and faithful responses to God's call coming through the particular needs of specific groups or situations. The tension between liturgical prescription and pastoral theology is a creative tension and can provide the spark for new life. To try to extinguish this spark by dictate from above is hardly 'sharing in God's work of creation',

which is how Radcliffe speaks of telling the truth. As for today's crisis of suspicion, the Instruction actually ends by encouraging people to make accusa-
tions of 'liturgical abuses' to their bishops or even to the Holy See, a sure recipe
for mistrust and insecurity.

I am a fairly typical parish priest, struggling to be faithful to the spirit of
Vatican II at a time when, rightly or wrongly, many people are feeling alienated
from formal institutions, including the Church. Against the odds I try to do
what little I can so that our parish Masses are prayerful and participative celebrations involving all the basic ingredients of adoration, wonder, instruction
and reflection. Like most other priests I do not find this easy. It involves a lot
of work in terms of preparation, reflection and prayer. Yet it is also a wonderful
privilege and can be a very grace-filled experience. In my preaching, inadequate though it is, I try to be open to God speaking to us in the readings and in
our personal and social lives, as well as in current events, both positive and
negative. I read the Instruction carefully but, in all honesty, found little in it
which gave me any positive help in my priestly ministry. It failed to answer
my need for encouragement and inspiration. It seemed to be inspired by a different spirit from what O'Malley portrays as the 'spirit of the Council'.

What authority has this Instruction? It carries the necessary signatures to
give it 'external' authority. However, to me it is lacking in 'internal authority'. It
does not seem to carry the signature of the Spirit according to the mind of Vatican II. It lacks the authority of truth in the sense outlined by Timothy Radcliffe.

I was very struck by the fact that the Instruction has 295 footnotes! These
refer to Church documents from various levels of authority. That suggests that
this Instruction is simply repeating things that have been said before. It is not
saying anything new. At least that should be a comfort to those of us involved
in parish ministry, including priests and bishops. If we have already been using
the principles and insights of pastoral theology to ensure that we are true to
the spirit of the law rather than over-subservient to its letter, there is no reason
why this new Instruction should alter our practice in any way. Our priority
must always be the full and active participation of the people of God in a life-
giving celebration of the Eucharist.

Since composing this personal reflection, I have read in a Catholic News
Service report (10 May 2004) that the topic for the October 2005 Synod of Bishops is the Eucharist. I hope and pray that the bishops attending the Synod will
be as open to the Spirit as were the world's bishops at Vatican II. That openness
led them to take the momentous step of breaking free from the very limited
and limiting vision of the preparatory curial draft documents. It is possible that
the Synod bishops might face a similar challenge since, according to the
Catholic News Service report, the preparatory 'lineamenta' for the Synod seem
to reflect the style and spirit of 'Redemptionis Sacramentum' rather than Vatican
II itself.

Going back to O'Malley's article, I found myself wondering what an Instruction would look like which is written according to the spirit of the Council. I suspect it would be one which is based on a lot of listening. It might offer us a whole variety of examples of best practice which have been tested on the drawing board of experience at local level. It might also encourage us and our congregations to be prudently creative in our patterns of worship. It could even ask us to share our experience with the Congregation so that we and others might benefit from such a sharing of best practice. As well as being truer to the spirit of the Council, such an instruction would better respond to our shared vocation of telling the truth in a life-giving way.

CHAPTER THIRTY-FOUR

'Mind the Gap': Person-centred Liturgy

In this chapter, originally published as chapter four of my From a Parish Base, I have combined a working paper for the 1996 National Conference of Priests with part of a short written reflection requested as possible background reading for a study session for members of the Bishops' Conference of England and Wales.

As in Jesus' day, the life-giving wisdom of good laws continues to be at the service of pastoral ministry today. However, even good laws need to be handled well. What better law than the Sabbath – yet even that was open to abuse. Much of the art of pastoral ministry lies in interpreting good laws in such a way that they are life-giving for those for whom they are made. That is where the virtue of pastoral sensitivity comes in. Pastoral sensitivity is a mindset rather than a set of rules of practice. The good pastoral minster is rather like the good artist. He or she needs to know the basic skills of the trade and the rules of thumb to be followed. However, more than that is needed. Like Jesus, the Good Pastor, a pastoral minister's main concern must be the needs of those to whom he or she ministers. Each of these people is a unique human person, situated at this unrepeatable moment in his or her personal story. What is good pastoral care for one person need not necessarily be so for another. Something similar is also true for communities. Each Christian community has its own distinct character.

A resolution passed by the 1995 National Conference of Priests spoke of 'the growing gap between the official regulations of the Church and the demands of pastoral practice.' Such a gap is almost inevitable. After all, the philosophy of law embraced by the Church down through the centuries has always recognised that laws, because of their universality, have at best only general validity (*'ut in pluribus'*, as Aquinas puts it, following Aristotle). That means that pastoral ministers need to develop the ability to discern when the good purposes of any law would be vitiated by keeping to the strict letter of the law in a particular instance. The traditional name for this is *'epikeia'*. Aquinas insists that it is a virtue. It is part of the general virtue of justice. It is not an anarchic way of evading the law. In fact, its aim is to make sure that the deepest purpose of the law is achieved. This deepest purpose will always be the pastoral good of persons in some form or other. That explains the wise dictum taught to priests in the seminary, *'salus animarum suprema lex'* (the salvation of souls is the law to trump all laws). In the light of the National Conference of Priests' resolution *'epikeia'* could perhaps be called 'the gap virtue'. It is a virtue which is particularly important for all engaged in pastoral ministry. Moreover, it becomes increasingly important, the greater the gap grows between the official regulations of the Church and the legitimate demands of wise pastoral practice.

It is sometimes suggested that, for the sake of the common good, laws should always be strictly observed. In fact, our tradition says the very opposite. The good of individual persons is an essential component of the common good. Hence, it is the common good itself which calls for the virtue of *'epikeia'*. Perhaps Jesus was making a similar point in his pastoral story about the shepherd leaving the ninety nine and going to search for the lost sheep.

This gap virtue is needed right across the board in pastoral ministry. To explore what it might mean in practice, it might be helpful to look at one specific sphere of pastoral ministry, namely liturgy. Like all other Church laws, liturgical laws and rubrics need to be interpreted in a way which is pastorally beneficial to the people of God.

According to Vatican II 'the full and active participation by all the people is the aim to be considered before all else; for it is the primary and indispensable source from which the faithful are to derive the true Christian spirit' (Constitution on the Sacred Liturgy, no. 14). That is where the common good lies in the area of liturgy. The Liturgy Constitution and subsequent documents lay down liturgical regulations spelling out how this is to be achieved in practice. However, these regulations remain subservient to this fundamental principle spelt out in no. 14. That is even true of the Constitution's general norm no. 22, $3: 'Absolutely no other person, not even a priest, may add, remove, or change anything in the liturgy on his own authority.' That is a wise and important regulation. Priests, badly instructed in the liturgy, can cause havoc, hindering the full and active participation of a congregation. Wisely, only a few lines after stating its basic principle, the Constitution insists that it is 'vitally necessary' that a high priority should be given to the liturgical instruction of the clergy. This is because a major part of the pastoral ministry of priests is to foster the full and active participation of the congregation in the liturgy.

However, liturgical instruction is essential but not sufficient. Complying with liturgical regulations does not guarantee good liturgy. Participation must not be simply a matter of ensuring that people are given the opportunity to take on active roles in a liturgical celebration. People must feel that liturgy touches their down-to-earth everyday experience at its inner core and gives expression to its deepest meaning. If, at times, this can only or best be achieved through creative and imaginative adaptation within the overall structure of the liturgy, that kind of flexibility is completely faithful to the fundamental principle of good liturgy. Priests who take such steps to facilitate the possibility of that depth of participation are merely exercising the gap virtue in their liturgical ministry. Of course, this would be impossible without a feel for the life-situations of the people in the congregation. That means that those responsible for the liturgy need to be closely in touch with the everyday lives of people. Elite liturgical teams, however well-intentioned and liturgically literate, can wreck havoc in a parish if they are not in tune with the reality of the lives of people in the congregation. It goes without saying that what is needed to achieve full and active participation will vary according to people's pastoral needs.

It might help to offer some specific examples from my own earlier pastoral ministry in inner-city Liverpool. Life in Vauxhall is hard for most people. The negative effects of multiple deprivation over many generations are all too obvious. That is why pastoral practice has to take people where they are. Only in this way could it help them believe they are loved by God precisely 'where they are'. In the eyes of God they are precious people, not just statistics in a table of social deprivation. It is belief in their own dignity which provides the springboard for further growth. This belief in themselves is strengthened by their experience of being able to improve some of the social conditions affecting their lives. Sound pastoral practice must consolidate that experience. Therefore, the main thrust of pastoral ministry in such a situation is to help people feel that everything that they experience as good in their lives is accepted, affirmed and celebrated in the presence of God.

The priests in the area are not in the business of judgement and condemnation. Where their people are at is different from a middle-class parish. Though most of them are not regular churchgoers, in no way should they be labelled as 'non-practising Catholics'. They really do 'practise' their faith in the Gospel sense of struggling to do their best to live lives of justice and love, often in situations where the odds can seem stacked against them. It would be appalling pastoral practice for a priest to contradict or undermine this belief and pride in their Catholic identity. Hence, the message they hear in the liturgy should not be a disheartening 'no' condemning them where they are presently at in their lives. Rather it needs to be a resounding 'yes', accepting them where they are at but also encouraging them to believe that they are capable of even greater things. They need to be empowered to hear the Gospel as 'Good News' in their lives. If the liturgy is, as the Liturgy Constitution insists, a 'primary and indispensable source' from which they derive the true Christian spirit of this Good News, then doing whatever is needed to help them to participate fully and actively in the Eucharist is a serious responsibility on those who serve as pastoral ministers in the community.

Against that background, I believe that my fellow priests and I were exercising the gap virtue (and, at the same time, respecting the fundamental principle of liturgy) when we held general absolution services in Advent and Lent or incorporated a short penitential rite with general absolution in any Funeral Mass where there was a fair number of 'non-regular churchgoers' from the local community in the congregation. Sometimes we used our own Eucharistic prayers which fitted in with the Sunday readings or the particular feast being celebrated or special occasions in the lives of those sharing in the Eucharist.

With couples cohabiting, or in a second marriage after divorce, or who habitually missed Sunday Mass, we normally raised no objections to their having their children baptised. And when, in the strange ways of God's providence, they were drawn to come to the Eucharist we were happy if they felt at peace in their conscience to come forward to receive Communion.

These are not offered as examples of recommended pastoral practice which others ought to adopt. Different local situations require different pastoral solutions. For some these examples may be very unacceptable. In fact, whether any or all of these practices can be adequately justified in pastoral theology is not the point. The point is that 'the demands of pastoral practice' must always come first if we are to minister pastorally after the model of Christ himself. The old dictum, *salus animarum supreme lex*, could be translated as 'where there is a gap between the official regulations of the Church and the demands of pastoral care, the latter must always take priority.'

Of course, obedience has a place in pastoral ministry. Pastoral ministers are not commissioned 'to do their own thing'. But obedience (*ob-audire*) is about listening. Listening to people's deepest needs and discerning how best to respond to them is one of the main ways a pastoral minister hears and obeys the voice of God. Whatever else the call to holiness in pastoral ministry is about, it is certainly about that. Holiness and pastoral life cannot be put in separate compartments.

How does this kind of pastoral practice fit in with a pastoral minister's duty to live in communion with the local bishop and with the wider Church? Is it not bound to provoke a reaction from the bishop? The impression is sometimes given that the 'communion' bishops should be concerned about is a 'trouble-free' kind of communion, namely, making sure that nothing is done to rock the boat or provoke criticism from the Vatican. Wanting to be sympathetic towards the kind of 'divergent' pastoral practices mentioned above, a bishop who feels constrained by his concern for that 'trouble-free' kind of communion might feel that the best support he could give would be to turn a blind eye to what is happening at parish level. Clearly, that kind of 'I would rather not know what you are doing' stance is far preferable to outright prohibition. Nevertheless, it is not entirely satisfactory from the point of view of pastoral theology.

After all, the pastoral practices mentioned above and those similar to them are actually about living and deepening communion at local level. It is that positive communion of life that a bishop, as pastor, is primarily called to serve. Provided the practices in question are solidly based in sound pastoral theology (and that assessment would need a sensitive appreciation of the locality and its people), they are precisely the kind of thing bishops should be encouraging in their role as servants of communion. The main focus of a bishop as servant of communion should not be on seeing that the letter of the law is observed. It should be on seeing that the deepest Gospel values (of which laws are servants, not masters) are being honoured in pastoral practice.

CHAPTER THIRTY-FIVE

Samples of Eucharistic Prayers

A priest friend of mine who is a liturgical specialist once told me that one of the criteria for being chosen as bishop in the early Church was the ability to improvise Eucharistic Prayers. Some priests whom I have greatly admired have, on occasion, either written their own Eucharistic Prayers or used alternative ones from other sources. These priests are not liturgical mavericks. They are good, devoted and holy pastors of their people or are Religious who have a wide experience of people's needs. As mentioned in the previous article, this has encouraged me occasionally, when appropriate, to use Eucharistic Prayers I have composed or adapted myself. I have tried to be faithful to the basic pattern of the Eucharistic Prayers authorised by the Church.

1 Justice and Peace

Father, we praise and thank you in the name of our whole human family, especially all struggling to make your kingdom come in our world. We bring before you the deep longing for justice and peace of so many of our sisters and brothers through the world, as we join the hymn of all the angels and saints: HOLY, HOLY, HOLY …

Father, your son, Jesus, has opened our eyes to the presence of your Spirit within us, between us and among us, a Spirit which empowers us to love and respect each other, especially those in greatest need and trapped in deadly poverty.

May that same Spirit come down on these gifts that they may become for us the body and blood of your Son, Jesus Christ, our Lord.

WORDS OF INSTITUTION

Father in heaven, we celebrate the memory of Christ, your Son. By his suffering, death and resurrection he has brought hope to our world.

God of history, in the face of all the violence of our world, may your Spirit help the leaders and governments of nations to respond to the terrible poverty and injustice in our world. Heal our blindness and give us wisdom and courage to remedy all the damage we are doing to the wonderful creation you have entrusted to our care. Free us and all people from any addiction to consumerism that we may be more truly disciples of your Son, committed to justice and peace in our world. Empower nations suffering corrupt government to be freed from their slavery.

May all who believe in you, of whatever faith or creed, be led by your Spirit into a closer communion with each other. Together with our Muslim sisters and brothers and all men and women of good will, may we build your kingdom of justice and peace in our world today. Give us all a desire to live simply, sustainably and in solidarity.

Heal any blindness holding our Church back from seeking true justice. Bless BENEDICT, Bishop of Rome, our own bishop, PATRICK, the whole college of bishops and all Church leaders.

May all our dead, especially those who have given their lives for justice and peace, in communion with Mary and all the saints, be sharing with your risen Son, Jesus, the joy and happiness of your own life and love. THROUGH HIM …

2 Christian Unity

God of love, we thank you for the longing to live together in unity and peace you have planted deep in our hearts. Your Son, Jesus, revealed that this longing is your own Spirit of unity and love poured out into our hearts. In the power of that spirit and with all your spirit-filled family down through the ages, we give you thanks and praise on behalf of all creation as we say: HOLY, HOLY, HOLY …

God of love, we thank you for the longing for unity and peace you have planted deep within us. Your Son, Jesus, revealed that this longing is your own Spirit of unity and love poured out into our hearts.

Through the power of that same Spirit may these gifts become for us the body and blood of Jesus, our brother and our Lord.

WORDS OF INSTITUTION

Let us proclaim the mystery of faith …

Father, we celebrate the memory of Christ, your Son. Having shared our suffering and death, through his resurrection he has brought hope and meaning to our world. May we become one body, one spirit in him.

Renew in us the gifts of your Spirit. Heal the memories of past cruelties and intolerance which have made fellow Christians view each other with fear and suspicion.

May your Spirit lead our Christian Churches to a unity which is open to the rich gifts of our different traditions. May we be a more effective sign and instrument of the unity of our whole human family.

Bless BENEDICT, Bishop of Rome. May your Spirit guide him in his special ministry of unity and love. Bless, too, the whole college of bishops, along with ROWAN, Archbishop of Canterbury. Be with our Merseyside church leaders as they continue to walk in faith towards the unity your Son prayed for, especially our own bishops, PATRICK and JAMES.

We commend to you all our dead. In the fullness of time, may we be one with them in your kingdom, sharing the peace and unity of your Son, Jesus, in communion with his mother Mary, and all your spirit-filled family down through the ages. THROUGH HIM …

3 Creation

Blessed are you, Creator God. In the beginning you called forth life out of nothingness and order and beauty out of chaos. Down through the ages, by your creative power, life in all its richness has gradually evolved. When you deemed the time right, like a potter lovingly shaping his clay, you fashioned women and men and made us in your own image and likeness. You opened our eyes to the grandeur of the work of your hands. Like you, we were able to say: 'Yes, it is good, very good'. And so, in the name of all your creatures we give you glory as we say: HOLY, HOLY, HOLY …

Creator God, in the fullness of time you sent Jesus to be your 'Yes' to all goodness and beauty, all love and compassion, all healing and forgiveness in our world. He used the everyday things of your creation to open our eyes to the goodness and beauty you have given us – bread and wine, seeds and vines and trees, water and storms and wind, sparrows and the birds of the air, fish, pearls and precious stones. He spoke to us amid the beauty of natural scenery, by the lakeside, in the fields, on top of the mountain.

Sharing the faith and vision of Jesus, we are gathered here in the power of your life-giving spirit to celebrate once again this sacred meal which feeds our faith and nourishes us on our journey through life.

May that same spirit of love which filled the heart of Jesus brood over this bread and wine, produced from the womb of Mother Earth. May they become for us the body and blood of Jesus, your Son.

WORDS OF INSTITUTION

Father, as we remember the Passion and death of Christ, your Son, we rejoice that he is risen from the dead, the first fruits of all creation.

Fill us with your life-giving Spirit. May our hearts be in tune with the love and energy which animates all creation. May our ears and eyes be open to your revelation in our world today. May our thoughts and prayers be at one with all our sisters and brothers of every faith and none who are striving to live by the truth.

Bless BENEDICT, Bishop of Rome, our own bishop, PATRICK and the whole college of bishops. May our own Catholic Christian community proclaim by word and example the dignity of the human person in our world today and promote whatever is true, good and beautiful in life. .

We commend to you all our dead, each in his or her own way a unique image of your love and goodness. May we one day share with them in communion with Mary and all the saints, the joy and peace of the King-dom of your Son, Jesus. THROUGH HIM...

4 Humility

Father, the gift of your Holy Spirit enables us to see ourselves and each other through your eyes, precious and lovable despite our weakness and sinfulness. And so, grateful for your gift of being who we are, we join in the hymn of thanksgiving of all women and men down through the ages, as we sing: HOLY, HOLY, HOLY …

Father, giver of all gifts, we thank you for your Son, Jesus, the greatest of all your gifts. He is your own love made visible in our midst. We thank you, too, for the gift of all the people who are part of our lives, our par-ents, our families, our friends and neighbours. Through them you have gifted our lives with warmth, joy and laughter; through them you have given us comfort and support in times of grief and hardship. Through them your Holy Spirit is present and active among us, inspiring all the love, kindness, forgiveness, generosity, self-sacrifice and faithful perse-verance we experience all around us.

May that same Holy Spirit come down upon these gifts of bread and wine that they may become for us the body and blood of Jesus Christ, our Lord.

WORDS OF INSTITUTION

Father, we give thanks for the self-giving love of your Son, Jesus, crucified, buried and risen from the dead. Your word made flesh, he speaks the 'Yes' of your love to us for all time. He has poured into our hearts of the gift of your Holy Spirit.

May that same Holy Spirit fill our hearts with your love – so that we may all be generous with the gifts you have given us; and recognise and value each other's gifts. May your Spirit brood over us and our world, healing the blindness which makes people of different faiths view each other with fear and suspicion. May those who are divided live together in peace. May your Spirit free us from selfishness and enable us to bring the gift of your compassion and comfort to all troubled in mind and heart or finding life cruel or difficult. May your Spirit give wisdom and understanding to all our leaders, in Church and State.

Bless BENEDICT, Bishop of Rome, our own bishop, PATRICK and the whole college of bishops. May your Church accept in all humility its mission to be a sign of unity in the midst of our divided and violent world.

We return to you the gift of our dear ones who have died. Together with Mary and all the saints, may they be gifted with the fullness of life and love in the kingdom of your Son, where there will be no death, no more mourning and sadness. THROUGH HIM …

5 The Gift of Diversity

Father, we thank you in the name of our sisters and brothers from all the races and nations of your human family. Young and old, women and men, we praise you for the richness of your image revealed in our diversity. We may differ in the colour of our skin and the shape of our faces, in our languages and our customs, in the way we dress and the food we eat, but we are all your family and belong to each other. So together we join in praising you: HOLY …

Father, we bring before you the joys and hopes, the sorrows and fears of your whole human family. Through your Son, Jesus, you revealed to us that our human family is your family and that you want us to live to-gether in peace and love, reflecting your own inner life of unity in diver-sity. Jesus has opened our eyes to the presence of your Spirit within us and among us.

May your Holy Spirit of love come down upon these gifts of bread and wine that they may become for us the body and blood of Jesus Christ, our Lord.

WORDS OF INSTITUTION

Father, your Son, Jesus, died for us and is now risen in glory.

May his gift of the Holy Spirit inspire all races and nations to live to-gether in peace and harmony. May we rejoice in our differences. Help us believe that we really do belong to each other. May we love and rever-ence as our own sisters and brothers all excluded through poverty and injustice.

Bless BENEDICT, Bishop of Rome, our own bishop, PATRICK, the whole college of bishops and all Church leaders. May your Church bear witness to the presence of your Spirit in other faiths; and may Christians and non-Christians work together for justice and peace in our world. Heal the wounds of division between Christian Churches so that we may love and respect each other as members of the one body of Christ.

We remember our brothers and sisters from all races and nations who have died. In communion with Mary and all the saints, may they expe-rience the joy of being fully one with each other in the Kingdom of your Son, Jesus. THROUGH HIM …

CHAPTER THIRTY-SIX

We are Church, We are Eucharist, We are Theology: A Feast of Thanksgiving

In March 2007 under the auspices of Liverpool Hope University and with the help of a group of moral theologians, parishioners and friends, Gerard Mannion, assisted by Philomena Cullen, organised a three-day 'Festschrift Tribute and Celebration' for me. The whole thing was kept secret from me with the result that I had no inkling of it until Gerard and Philomena told me in the course of a meal twenty-four hours before-hand. Gerard mentioned all the participants he had invited and that there would be a simultaneous Eucharist on the Saturday evening, followed by an Irish Ceilidh in the school with refreshments provided by the parishioners. I felt totally overwhelmed by what he was saying. But there was more to come. When Chris Lappine, who acted as my chauffeur for the weekend, showed me the full programme, I found that my name featured in the titles of most of the talks and presentations on the Friday and the whole of Sunday morning was to be a long series of tributes to me! I was also told that Liverpool Hope University were going to award me with an Honorary Doctorate and that Gerard Mannion, Julie Clague and Bernard Hoose were editing a Festschrift in my honour, Moral Theology for the Twenty-First Century *(Continuum, London, 2008). I was completely thrown by the prospect of being the centre of attention over three whole days. What follows is part of a little piece I wrote afterwards in which I attempt to reflect on the whole experience and try to make sense of the grace-filled experience it turned out to be for everyone.*

Following this reflection I am also including my response to the Award of my Honorary Degree in Liverpool Metropolitan Cathedral. Both themes are related.

As soon as my eyes were opened to what lay in store for me, I knew I had no choice but to throw myself into enjoying every minute of it. What a gift I was being given – a lovely coming together of so many people who were precious to me and who had all influenced my life so much! As with any celebration, it was something we were all invited to enjoy together. To have refused to enjoy it would have been churlish of me. And the whole atmosphere was so positive that the enjoyment was shared by everyone. It was a real celebration from beginning to end. In fact, I found it to be a profoundly grace-filled experience.

There is something deep in me and in all of us that longs to be loved and enjoys being loved. That is a profoundly God-like dimension of all of us. God loves to be loved. In fact, the very inner life of God is about loving and being loved. God is a communion of love. We are made in God's image. God has loved each and all of us into existence and invited us to love each other as he has loved us. That is surely why all of us long to be loved and enjoy being loved.

However, I know there is also something deep in me which resists being loved, a kind of inner voice which tells me that I am not really lovable. It cuts me a-sunder from other people – and 'sunder' is the root of the word 'sin'. This resistance to being loved separates us from each other – and so from God – and ultimately from our true selves. That is why it is truly something demonic. It is a refusal of communion.

I felt the urge of that demonic impulse in me from time to time over the weekend. When people kept saying something like, 'You are loved by a lot of people' or 'How wonderful that so many people think so highly of you', my demon kept trying to pop up to stop me appreciating and being grateful for such love.

That prompted a different train of thought in me. In Baptism we are given the family name of the Trinity, the communion of love within God. This name-giving does not separate us (sunder us) from those not baptised. Rather it opens our eyes to who we are – and who they are too. It reveals that, precisely as human beings, we are called to be 'communion people'. Enda McDonagh put that beautifully in his amazing and inspiring talk when he spoke of God as the host, inviting us all as guests to share in the delights of the Garden of life, but also to be hosts to our fellow guests. That rang a bell with something I say at the baptism of a baby. After focussing on the baby as a unique image of God, I always go on to say that the baptismal promises remind us that the fashioning and shaping of this unique image of God is largely the work of human hands – principally its parents and family, but also including all who will have a positive influence on the child as it grows and journeys through life.

I suddenly became aware that what I was experiencing during our celebration was the amazing reality of this relational and interdependent dimension of who I am (and who we all are) as human persons, images of the communion of love within the Godhead. The gathering was representative of all the people who had played a role in shaping me into the person I have become. I am sure people were able to see where my moral theology had come from as they listened to many of my former colleagues describe the situations we had shared and how we had helped each other respond to the new challenges we faced.

In my closing words on Sunday morning, I read out a short passage from my friend and moral theologian colleague, Peter Harvey:

I am either one with all creation, linked indivisibly with everyone and everything else, or I am nothing but illusion. It is not that I exist only in relationship, it is that I am relationship from the beginning. At no point can I stand outside the web, for there is nowhere to stand (*The Morals of Jesus*, Darton, Longman & Todd, 1991, p. 61).

It dawned on me that the love ('God saw that it was good') I was experiencing was all within the one web of relationships of love to which we all belong – brought out in the 'one body of Christ' image and even more widely in the 'cosmic Christ' image.

Everyone had remarked on the warmness of the atmosphere throughout the whole conference and celebration. Although a few had jokingly described it as a 'Kevin-fest', it struck me that it was much more a 'We-fest', a celebration of the communion of love of which we are all part, a kind of foretaste and glimpse of the joy promised us in the Kingdom. We experienced this 'joyful communion' very tangibly in a whole variety of ways throughout the weekend, not least in the beautiful simultaneous shared Eucharist and in the Ceilidh immediately after, all prepared with such care and commitment by the parish community. What a striking interpenetration between both parts of that unforgettable evening, a dazzling homily in the Eucharist by Fr Charlie Curran and some magnificent and hilarious words of appreciation by Keith Austin, the Anglican Reader, along with the communion-building energy of music and movement and, of course, sharing as guests (and co-hosts) at the Lord's table both in Church and at the fabulous banquet prepared and hosted by parishioners and the school. The School Head, Win Douglas, played a God-like role in enabling this truly 'educational' experience to take place. An extra-special gift for me was the wonderful turnout of my own family and the hilarious *This is Your Life* presentation by my nephew, Steve.

I believe that what we were experiencing together was the Spirit of loving communion breathing in and through us ('inspiring us'). The inspired word was: 'Enjoy the wonder of each other. In doing so you will appreciate just how lovable you all are and you will drive away the demon which tries to cut you asunder from each other.' That is why a 'We-fest' is the only appropriate to describe the whole weekend.

The more I've thought about the weekend, the more I feel that it has helped me confront another demon, another inclination trying to 'sunder' me. It is the demon which tempts me, and all of us, to feel pride in the gifts people are praising in us. If we are all members of one body, all interlocking strands in the one web Peter Harvey refers to, the gifts of each of us are given for the service of the whole.

I may have been stupid enough not to cotton on to what was happening. I hope I am wise enough to recognise that we could have had an alternative event highlighting the weaknesses of Kevin Kelly as a moral theologian, his shadow side as a Christian and his failings as a priest and pastor. But that is another story. I am happy to leave God, the co-author of all our stories, to cope with that part of my story – and all our stories.

A sad postscript

On Sunday evening, the eight remaining moral theologians gathered in the presbytery with me and one of the parishioners, Chris Lappine, for a home-delivery pizza meal. Our conversation included a rich flow of memories of the celebration. However, the joy of the evening was marred by a telephone call informing us that it seemed certain that sometime in the next few weeks the CDF would issue a condemnation of what Jon Sobrino had written about the person of Christ. Jon is a Latin American theologian who lives with painful but glorious memories. He was a member of the Jesuit community in El Salvador who were all murdered, along with their housekeeper and her daughter, because of the stand they were taking to defend the poor in their country from massive injustice. They are truly worthy of being venerated as martyrs. Jon was away on a lecture tour when their martyrdom took place. He now interprets faithfulness to the Gospel of Christ as demanding that he continue their mission and keep their memory alive.

A better use of the teaching authority of the CDF would be to arrange a Festschrift in honour of Jon Sobrino (and his martyr companions) and call together a group of theologians and biblical scholars who have explored the theme of justice in the bible, tradition and the Church's teaching and practice, and including Christians who have committed themselves to the struggle for justice in the world. Women should obviously be given their rightful place at such a meeting. Hopefully, the gathering would be ecumenical, even interfaith. I suspect such a meeting would more truly honour Christ and be a more credible witness of discipleship than what the CDF seem to have in mind.

CHAPTER THIRTY-SEVEN

We are God's Gift to Each Other:
So to Honour One is to Honour All

This is the text of my Acceptance Speech for the Honorary Doctorate in Divinity, Liverpool Hope University, conferred by the Chancellor, Baroness Cox at Liverpool Metropolitan Cathedral.

In his Hope lecture in this Cathedral a few weeks ago, Archbishop Desmond Tutu reminded us that we are interdependent to the very core of our being. The one God in whose image we are made is not a solitary, isolated being but a God whose inner life is a communion of love. When we honour each other, we honour that one God – just as when we dishonour each other, we dishonour God, as you reminded us so powerfully last night, Chancellor.

Today is the first full independent Graduation Day of Liverpool Hope University. There is something very beautiful and deeply symbolic about the fact that the first Degree given today is in Divinity.

In a sense, this honorary Doctorate is for all of us – it reminds us of who we are. Divinity is our calling and our destiny. The love at the heart of our one God has brought us into being so that we can share God's divinity by reflecting that love between us. All the other degrees conferred today are in recognition of hard work, intense study and high achievement over the past two, three or four years – I congratulate all who are being so justly rewarded.

My honorary Doctorate in Divinity, on the other hand, is pure gift. As such it can remind us of the totally gratuitous gift God gives to each of us – and our whole human family – a sharing in God's own divinity.

Some years ago Dr John Ashton, then Director of Public Health for Liverpool, wrote a very imaginative health strategy paper in the form of a walk through the city – half reality, half dream. He envisaged Liverpool as an Open Universe City – long before it was chosen as City of Culture.

We are gathered here together in this Open Universe City of Liverpool within this beautiful Cathedral. This is truly a holy place – not so much because of the building but because of who we are. This is my second graduation ceremony today – I have come from a school leavers' Mass at St Basil's Primary School. I promised the children I'd tell you all the message of their final song; 'Tell everybody I'm on my way'. Very appropriate words for all graduating today.

Like those children, we too are on our way to the fulfilment of our divinity. Our interdependence links together the web of each of our lives, forming a rich tapestry in the eyes of God – in my case, including my family, those in the parishes I have served in and the wonderful people of a HIV-AIDS healthcare team closely linked to our shared parish.

The divinity we share is a challenge to each of us to be true to who we are. It is also a challenge to Liverpool Hope University to be true to its Christian, ecumenical mission – working for justice, reconciliation and peace in its own structures and in the wider world.

Conclusion

CHAPTER THIRTY-EIGHT

Learning from a 1980 'Exposure Experience' in the Philippines

As mentioned earlier, when I finished as Director of the UNI and Archbishop Vincent Nichols took over from me, I had a seven-month sabbatical. I used two of those months trying to get a feel for liberation theology and inculturation at grass roots in some pastorally challenging places in the Philippines, India and Peru. Being keen that others should also benefit from my experience, I kept an extensive diary throughout. The three diary entries which follow are all from my Filipino experience which took up half of the two months.

Throughout this book I have constantly emphasised the Vatican II vision of the presence of God's Kingdom in real life. My unforgettable, though brief, experience of the Church in Bishop Labayan's diocese of Infanta opened my eyes to how challenging that vision is. It is not a model that could be duplicated in the UK, as it stood. However, it has never ceased to inspire and challenge me throughout my pastoral ministry.

My time spent with the Columban Sister, Breda Noonan, in Cagayan de Oro was equally inspiring but also deeply disturbing. Her simple but very demanding style of 'living with the poor' brought alive for me gospel challenges which I have failed miserably to embody in my own life. Fr Austin Smith has had a similar impact on me. As a theological writer and preacher, I have found it comes more naturally to share words than give them flesh in my daily life. Breda once sent me a Christmas card from the Philippines with the greeting 'May the Peace of Christ disturb you this Christmas.' It still disturbs me!

The experience at Kidopawan consolidated the impact of both the above experiences. The generosity of the little community blew my mind, especially when the families themselves had so little to live on. Reality is so hard for so many people, yet their ability to cope with that reality gives them a dignity which has left me deeply humbled.

Many of the articles in this collection have dealt with Church structures and the institution itself. Yet in the end, it is people who are the Church. I think that is one of the basic insights of the vision of Vatican II. The three grass-roots experiences which follow brought that home to me at a very profound level. They have truly 'received' the spirit of Vatican II, even though I suspect many of them may never have heard of the Council itself.

Filipino Diary Entry One
Bishop Labayan and the mission of the Church in Infanta

Bishop Labayan rang to say he would pick me up at 6.00 p.m. That is a pity as it means that most of the journey will be in the dark and I had been looking forward to seeing the countryside. Apparently, the road over is appallingly bad and goes through the mountains, where the guerrillas are.

Bishop Labayan arrived in due course with his housekeeper. They must have been doing their shopping as the back of the car, an estate model was packed with calor gas cylinders, boxes and plants of all sizes and descriptions. We drove for about two hours along a series of good and not so good roads. Then we stopped at a little wayside café. The Bishop produced three hamburgers and a packet of cold chips which he had brought with him. The café supplied us with beer and bananas. Then after we had driven a little further, the Bishop informed me that we were now starting the bad roads.

The next three hours featured the most incredible driving I've ever experienced, especially in an ordinary car. We literally drove over two ranges of mountains on a road which in England would be declared impassable. It was a matter of spotting the rock protuberances in the middle of the road, skirting round all the huge potholes, going slowly through the mini rivers – and all this in the dark, though there was a lovely moon that evening. Most of the time we seemed to be driving through jungle, though at times you could see a steep drop on one side or the other. Often along the way we would pass little clusters of straw or bamboo huts with a little fire or candle burning inside, occasionally groups of children playing in the road. We had to go over a few bridges, which in the dark seemed rather like driving onto the ramp in a garage, i.e. two planks that you had to centre on. Eventually we emerged out of the mountains onto the shore of the Pacific. It looked beautiful with the moon glinting on the water and palm and coconut trees going right down to the water with the occasional light of a fishing boat bobbing on the sea. There was still another three-quarters of an hour's driving and the road was hardly any better!

Eventually we arrived at Infanta which seems a very tiny town with the Cathedral in the main square and the Bishop's bamboo house beside it. After a little meal (including a piece of five-year-old cake!), I went with Fr Francis over to the Priests' house and so to bed, ignoring a couple of giant cockroaches staring at me from a couple of corners in my room.

Saturday 27 September
From 5.00 a.m. I could hear the youngsters outside playing basketball and volleyball. I got up about 6.00 a.m. and enjoyed a nice cold shower. At breakfast I had a very interesting talk with a young priest, Fr Nono, who for the past six

years has been in charge of training lay leaders in the province. That is one of their major priorities in the prelature. He works on two basic principles:

1. Help people to realise their dignity and they will become conscious of what they must do, socially and politically – so it is an indicative/imperative approach. Prayer is obviously integral to this.
2. Formation only occurs in the course of action. Therefore lay leaders are only formed through their involvement in the formation and development of basic Christian communities.

After breakfast I attended a double wedding during Mass – not too different from at home except that the families seem to be more involved during the actual wedding ceremony itself. The entry procession consisted of two boys and two girls carrying what seemed to be bouquets – they turned out to be the wedding rings all tied up in a decorative posy.

After Mass a rather stockily built young lad of about eighteen came up to me and said (as I thought), 'Father, I'm Ephraim. I've come to bring you my gun.' I was puzzled by that but he kept repeating it, so I went with him to the Priest's house-cum-radio station. It turned out that he was saying 'I've come to bring you to Maigang', which is a little village about five miles away. It was explained to me that the community there was holding a three-day seminar so I was invited to go and see what was going on, staying overnight so that I could have a full day with them.

The journey itself was very interesting. First of all we got into what is called a 'tricycle' – that is a motorbike with a little covered sidecar attached. It looked as though it would be a matter of the driver and then the two of us in the sidecar. But not a bit of it. We were directed to one which already had four people in the sidecar (three adults and a girl) and two on the pillion behind the driver. I had to squeeze into the sidecar while Ephraim squashed onto the pillion. Then we started off on their usual bumpy dirt tracks. After a few miles we reached a wide, swiftly-flowing river. Then we got into a long narrow canoe-style boat with two side bars to balance it. An old man rowed us across. Then we walked on a tiny footpath for about twenty minutes, going in and out of the coconut trees with the rice fields running for a few hundred yards and then the mountains beginning. Eventually we reached a house with the sound of singing coming from it. This was our destination and it turned out that they had just started Mass. They knew we were coming through the local radio.

A young priest Fr Francis Clemente (ordained with one and a half years) was saying the Mass. He looks after a number of the surrounding 'barrios'. In the country here, a 'barrio' means all the houses scattered over a particular area, a kind of spread out village. There were also two sisters at the Mass, Sister Clo (dressed in jeans and T-shirt) and Sister Flo (also in lay dress), a middle-aged woman who is Superior of their house in Manila and who had joined the seminar to get some 'exposure'. The group was made up of about thirty adults, along with their babies and young children. I got quite used to the experience of one of the mothers beside me suddenly starting feeding her baby at her breast. They were a very poor, open, welcoming and extremely committed Christian group. Their poverty was evident in the food they ate. I was with them for three meals and each time it was rice and some kind of fish – and not big fish but dried up hard kind of sardines. Apparently, only rarely can they afford meat. It was always water to drink, except at breakfast when we had a kind of sweet coffee made from black rice. They have no gas, electricity or sewerage and the only way to get to them is the way we came – across the river by boat and then walk on little paths. Consequently they have no such things as cars or motorbikes. They don't get beyond a transistor radio.

Yet, they are very well educated at their own level. The seminar itself was ample evidence of that. Apparently this group of families meets together on a weekly basis for prayer, bible study and to discuss their problems. They are helped in this by Nanding, a young man of twenty-six who was a remarkable person (he reminded me of my nephew Chris). He used to work with the Forestry Commission but was persuaded by Fr Nono to give up his work and become a Voluntary Community Organiser. That meant coming to live in this 'barrio' and devoting himself to helping them take more control of their lives by becoming a community caring for each other and refusing to be exploited by outside interests. He is not paid for this work but gets an allowance to cover living expenses. He has been there for a year and a half but will soon be moving to another 'barrio' where he will start all over again. I have rarely met a more committed, self-sacrificing young man who seemed to have no thought for his own comfort or advantage.

The community had decided for itself to hold this three-day seminar on health education and they had invited Sr Clo, who is a trained nurse now working full time in the barrios. By 'Seminar' they meant living together for three days, eating and praying together and following a very demanding work schedule. After lunch, for instance, when all the washing up had been done round the pump, they got together to work out their schedule for the first day and a half. It ran: session from 2.00 p.m. until 4.00 p.m.; then a ten minute break for a bit of some root vegetable which is like a kind of sweet potato. Then back to work again after supper until 9.30 p.m. when they were to have night prayers and then to bed. All this was decided by their talked out and shared discussion, as was the programme for next morning: 6.30 a.m. morning prayers; 7.00 a.m. breakfast; 8.00 a.m. Mass, 9.30 a.m. 1st session. And they had agreed that none of them would work on Monday so that they could continue the seminar all that day too!

The method of working was full participation throughout. For instance, after deciding on their schedule, they next discussed whether to work in groups or as a general body. They decided to go into groups to share their expectations of the seminar but then to come together to pool these and to stay together for the rest of the day. They were concentrating on health education because they had had a lot of trouble with sickness and in the whole area comprising 17,000 people there was only one doctor, three midwives and no nurses! They ended their session by reminding themselves that curing the sick and helping each other in illness was one of the hallmarks of a Christian community.

During the whole afternoon they analysed why the provisions for health were so bad for them and it became clear to them that of all the money spent by the Government on health, virtually none of it benefited the rural people, the poor, even though they formed the majority in the Philippines. Most of the doctors and nurses who were given training ended up going abroad. And most of the money spent on drugs and medicines went into the hands of the multi-national drug companies, even though the components of most of the drugs came from the Philippines and were sold as cheap raw materials abroad only to be bought back at exorbitant costs.

All this was aimed at helping them to realise that even healthcare was influenced by political, social and economic factors. It made them more convinced that they were victims of unjust oppression because of a system which contradicted what the Gospel stood for: concern for others and special love of the poor. The more practical side of the seminar was to make them more self reliant in medical care through better understanding and improved hygiene (though they were all very clean and obviously very careful about hygiene). One thrust of the programme was a better understanding of herbal medicine, i.e. making maximum use of the medicinal qualities of local plants, since the whole area is very luxuriant with every kind of plant life.

When it got dark, a gas lantern was lit. After night prayers, a little group of them carried the lantern to escort me across the paddy fields. You walk on a little ridge about six inches wide with water-filled paddy fields on both sides. It was about a quarter of an hour's walk to the house of Venan, whom they nicknamed 'the Bishop'. He is a young man of thirty with three young children. His wife and the children were sleeping where the meeting was being held. His house was a wooden house built on stilts with a wooden staircase going up to the living level. When we stepped on this I noticed a pig asleep under the stairs with a batch of tiny piglets. The house itself was all wood and, inside, very sparsely furnished but scrupulously clean. Venan laid out a straw mat for me on the floor and fixed up a mosquito net for which I was most grateful, since I was expecting a night exposed to the mosquitoes. After a drink of homemade lemon juice, I went to bed and had a mediocre night on the floor – certainly no harder than the normal Filipino bed and more comfortable than the ultra hard bed in the Priests' house in Infanta. Next morning I washed in the irrigation stream – very clean and cool.

Sunday 28 September

I 'presided' at the Mass but in fact the Community did most of the ceremony. Through an interpreter (only a couple of the people could speak English) I preached a little homily on the Gospel of the Sunday which, providentially, was Dives and Lazarus (Lk 10:19-31). I had my photo taken with Venan and his family and he gave me a present of a lovely calendar in carved ebony (the wood is local).

I got back to the Priests' house in Infanta (still escorted by Ephraim) to find the Radio Station in full swing. I forgot to mention that the Church in Infanta runs a local radio station, which is just as professional as Radio Merseyside or Radio City; though its premises are less imposing yet very well equipped. Fr Francis is in charge of it, though he has a good professional staff working with him. Linda, the Programme Manager, trained at Hatch End in the UK. They broadcast about eighteen hours a day, much of it music but also Bible classes. Every Sunday at 7.00 a.m. the Bishop's Mass is broadcast. Once again it is very community-based.

When I got back from Maigang they were in the middle of the quarter-finals of a children's singing competition. The recording studio (just a large room with a little stage) was jammed tight with children and two compères were organising the contestants. The show was live and the children singing were a scream, they were so serious and professional in their acts. Some must have been only about six or seven years old but they stood on the stage clutching the mike and sang and danced away to the audience. It would have made top-rating TV.

Later in the afternoon Fr Nono took me on the pillion of his motorbike (an essential for all the priests) down to the beach and I had my first swim in the Pacific. It was quite calm and the water was beautiful – warm by our standards so you could stay in as long as you wanted. It was a nice scene with coconut trees all along the edge of the beach and then the mountains rising up about two miles away. Fr Nono had brought a couple of bottles of beer – which we drank in the water. Then we went further along the beach to a little hut where Bishop Labayan was running a day of recollection for about forty lay leaders.

When I got back I sat in the studio while Linda and Fr 'Boots' ran their Bible School on the air. Actually it goes on later in the week but they were recording in advance. It has been going on for a number of years now. Lots of little groups meet all over the Diocese (Prelature) to study the coming Sunday's Gospel and to discuss its implications for their personal and social lives. They get a diploma for following the whole year's course. The group leaders are given additional training. Linda showed me a copy of the history of their radio station (it was virtually a history of Infanta Prelature). It was most interesting and never before have I realised so clearly the importance of the Church's taking the media seriously, especially at local level. Fortunately there were a few copies available so I managed to buy one for myself.

At about 10 p.m. I went to the town square in front of the Cathedral where a big basketball match was beginning. It was the Radio Station (and other Church leaders – including Fr Francis) versus the local bank – complete with floodlights, a commentary over the loudspeakers and most of the town out to watch. There are no televisions in Infanta so there are many more community activities and involvement.

Monday 29 September
Next morning at 7.00 a.m. I left with Bishop Labayan and three other passengers for the return trip to Manila – the bumpy mountain road again, but in daylight this time. I had a most interesting talk with the Bishop en route. His pastoral policy is very carefully integrated and is based around the notion of local communities developing their own life with the assistance of voluntary and some full-time trained lay leaders. There are 170,000 people in his diocese and a total of sixteen priests (including himself). It is clear why lay leaders and radio apostolate are so important. He is also very strong on the importance of social analysis – looking closely at the real situation in the locality and the underlying reason why things are as they are. The Marxist analysis can be helpful in this, although his commitment is to a socially conscious Christianity, not to Marxism. That is why he puts so much emphasis on the centrality of prayer. As a symbol of this he has invited the Carmelite sisters to found a monastery in Infanta but he has insisted that all the sisters who will make up the new foundation must live with the ordinary poor people in the area for three months. This will enable them to understand the situation to which they are dedicating their apostolate of prayer and it will also help the local people to feel that the Carmelites truly belong to their community. Bishop Labayan himself is a Carmelite.

He talked about the need for people to have a very positive vision, based in Christian faith and prayer but also making sense in their everyday lives. He explained to me that he always talked to ordinary men and women (most of them parents) not in terms of the Kingdom of God but in terms of 'the Father's dream.' He would ask them what dreams they have and he says they invariably answer that they dream about a happy future for their children, living in love, peace and prosperity. Then he asks them whether they think that God, their Father, has any dreams. Rather hesitantly they say, 'He probably has'. When asked what the Father's dream might be about, they reply: 'about his children, which means us and all men and women'. Then he asks them to look at the situation in which they are living and asks is this the Father's dream for them. 'No', they answer. So what does the Father expect of them – to make his dream come true? This gives their social and political involvement a deeply spiritual basis since it is Jesus himself who assures us that the Father's dream is our good and happiness.

Besides this most interesting conversation, the drive back was also enjoyable because of the beautiful scenery over the mountains. First of all, mainly banana trees with some lovely flowering shrubs at low level – then giving way to more banana trees. We stopped to visit the elderly mother of one of the priests. She gave us lanzotes to eat, a delicious fruit. It looks like a small yellow plum but you squeeze it open and eat the inside (except for the pips) which is very juicy and tastes rather like a very sweet grape.

On our way back from Infanta we called to see the priest at Real, a little village about ten miles from Infanta. Apparently, the First Lady, Imelda Marcos, plans to turn it into a major international port and to build a highway through the mountains (the 'Marcos Highway') to link it to Manila. It would then be Manila's direct link with the Pacific. Such a plan would drastically alter the whole area and would destroy forever its natural beauty. The priest wasn't in but I saw the tiny little wooden hut in which he lives. One room serves a dual purpose as his oratory (with the Blessed Sacrament reserved) and his bedroom. The Bishop told me that he encourages all the priests to have an oratory like that in their house. It helps them to keep prayer very central in their lives. The Church itself was a very poor structure – a roof without any walls. However, there are signs of a new building around it.

Tuesday 30 September

I've just been reading a most helpful little article 'The Price He paid' by an Indian Jesuit, Samuel Rayan (reprinted in *Loyola Papers* No. 5, pp. 56-60). He is asking why Jesus died as he did and rejects the theories based on God's justice demanding satisfaction for man's sin ('No wonder such a God died in due time and was disowned by men'). But he still links the death of Jesus with the Father's will:

The wholeness and well-being of human persons in community is the centre of God's concern as revealed in the Bible and in Jesus Christ. But there are anti-human forces on earth, which are also, on that account, anti-God. (Note – this reminds me of Tony Lambino's often repeated remark: Communism is against God's will not because it is atheistic but because ultimately it is anti-human and therefore implicitly denies the image of God in us). The effort to be human and the attempt to help others be human are seen to clash with these forces. Loyalty to humanity and God will involve a conflict and may entail the necessity of a struggle to death (Thought – we tend to wear the Cross as a Christian ornament or badge. Perhaps we should wear it as a pledge that we are prepared to engage in the struggle right to death if necessary!). Violence and tragedy are part of our concrete historical situation. They are a historical necessity, not a divine one. They are part of God's plan only to the extent that they are unavoidable in the struggle for human wholeness which is what God wants and wills. They are taken over by the Son of God in his assumption of the human condition as part of the struggle for our humanity.

It seems clear that the death of Jesus was a historical necessity called for by the new and non-conformist path he chose to tread in obedience to the Father's plan to redeem mankind from every brokenness, humiliation and captivity. Part of Jesus' greatness consists in the fact that he stood for the greatness of people before God and within God's love, and readily paid the price for the stand he took. And the price was his life, so young and full of promise. Those who made little of people and of their dignity, freedom and possibilities, and much, perhaps, of riches and power and 'religion', took him and tortured and killed him when they found that he could not be manipulated or cajoled or threatened into conformity to their standards and values.

The struggle still continues. Jesus is still on the battlefield ... He upholds the worth of persons above banks, production systems, parliaments and the politics of the clever few ... The price is being paid today with the tortured students and hanged priests in Brazil ... Jesus lives with and in these people. He is still in our midst as a subversive force and a disturber of the sheriff's peace ... any Church which follows him without glancing furtively to Right or Left will participate with all its power in his mission of bringing the gospel to the poor and liberation to the imprisoned. The more she is thus involved in his mission, the deeper will she get caught up in his destiny and become a Church under the Cross. She will not worship the Cross as such but hold it up as a sign of elected poverty and protest, and as a sign of the affirmation of human persons and our world, whom God loves. The Church of Jesus will be misunderstood, oppressed and persecuted ... Suffering is a 'note' or mark, of the Church (Mk 10:30) but it is suffering for the Kingdom, in Jesus' name, and for the people for whom he lived and gave his life.

This passage from Rayan beautifully sums up the impact that this Philippine experience has been making on me. Somehow the important issue is not the technical discussion of the validity of Liberation Theology as a theological methodology. It is the much debated issue of the intimate connection between our Faith and our social and political involvement in the process of full human growth and development. Somehow it makes Incarnation Theology much more realistic since it situates it in the setting of human sin and selfishness. A theology of human development which ignores the reality of sin is completely idealistic and non-historical. And the Christian faith is nothing if it is not historical.

Filipino Diary Entry Two
Sister Breda Noonan in Cagayan de Oro, Mindanao

Next I went with Sr Breda to her 'convent'. She has chosen to live among the urban slum squatters in the shanty town, Macabalan, on the edge of the harbour. At first sight the area looks appalling – very makeshift houses, some from odd bits of wood or cardboard, no streets, most of the houses are on stilts and many of them have foul looking water underneath. These swampy parts are gradually being filled, which does improve the situation somewhat since they are building open drains at the same time; but unfortunately some of the improvement is directed towards clearing the site for dock development and many of the people are simply being evicted.

Breda's 'convent' (she is the only sister there) is shared with a group of young leaders (early twenties) who are dedicated to trying to help the people in this 'barrio' to develop as a human and Christian community. They are wonderfully dedicated youngsters, four boys and one girl with a few others helping them on a more temporary basis. They have all had a short initial training but most of their learning is done on the job. One of the girls generally sleeps in the convent too – the boys do sometimes when it fits in with what they are doing. They are all from the barrio itself.

The 'convent' is just like any of the houses in the barrio. From the outside it looks very poor and as though a breath of wind would blow it down. Inside, however, it is surprisingly roomy. You enter by going up a kind of ladder staircase on the outside. That brings you into a kind of porch. To the left you go up a step in the biggest room which is completely bare except for some mats and some curtains which can divide it off into sections. This is used for sleeping at night (on the floor of course) but is also used for meetings in the day. The wooden floor is well polished so it is a case of shoes off when you enter. In front of you in the porch is a door into another room, very small with a tiny desk, chair and bookcase. In the far corner of this room is a little staircase going down to a lower level dining room cum kitchen which is a very plain, simple and bare basics room. A little door lets you into an outside toilet.

We sat and talked for a while. Then Breda took me for a tour around the 'Barrio'. We called into a few houses on our way round. Breda is obviously well accepted among them all. They all made us very welcome. Some of the houses are actually on the edge of the sea, the people being fisher folk. They told us that fishing is very poor at the moment. All they have to eat is rice and salt. Though the people were very, very poor, all the houses we visited were extremely clean and most of the people were tidily dressed. One or two of the houses, though very poor and drab on the outside, were very good inside and amazingly well-furnished with an originality all of their own. Some of the men were working at 'Inport' which seems to be the dock unloading firm. They work in gangs and are only paid for the work done. Hence if there are no ships in, they go without pay. Their rate is P1.120 per hour (which is about 7p an hour!) Moreover, five per cent of their wages are deducted for union dues, even though the union is government controlled and in no way represents the men's interests. Strikes are forbidden by law. I got much of this information from a group of men and women who met that evening in a tiny one-room house by the shore. Breda acted as interpreter. The women were far more vocal than the men; Breda said that the women are always the strong ones in these areas. They have to make the going when there is no pay coming in.

Their answer to one of Breda's questions really amazed me. She asked them what were their dreams for the future. I expected them to say that they would like to be away from the terrible place in which they were living. Not a bit of it. They all had the same dream – to be able to live where they were in security and with a steady wage coming in. Apparently, many of them who have built their little shacks there in the past few years are under threat of eviction as the government plans to develop the area as a site for some large factories – Japanese owned. If that happens their homes will just be pulled down and they will be left completely homeless. In fact, the next day I visited another part of the barrio where this eviction was actually in operation. Some of the families had banded together and were refusing to leave unless they were offered alternative accommodation.

This is one of the major tragedies in the Philippines. On the surface development is taking place at a very quick rate. But when you understand what is happening, you discover that the poor who form the vast bulk of the population do not benefit from this development. In fact, it only succeeds in making their situation even more desperate. This is true both in the cities and in the rural areas. It is a crying shame since the Philippines is a very rich country agriculturally and in natural resources. The area around Cagaya de Oro was prolific in all kinds of fruits and vegetables and yet here were people subsisting on rice and salt.

Breda had electricity in her little house (though no running water) so that evening we had a couple of slide shows. One was about the Chico dam, a government project which would involve the virtual extinction of one of the old Filipino tribes and their famous rice terraces. Bishop Claver is a member of this tribe and wrote a famous plea to President Marcos entitled 'A letter from my Father's House'. The tribe are refusing to leave their lands and at present things are at a stalemate even though recently the military shot their leader in cold blood. The other slide show was entitled 'Who owns the land?' and was produced by Billy, one of the young leaders who works with Breda. I was amazed at its high quality and immediately ordered a set, even though it is not yet available commercially. In both these shows the commentary is in English. I must confess that I had never before realised the great potential of slide-cassette presentations.

Saturday 4 October

Next morning Domingo, one of Breda's young leaders, came to collect me and we went on an hour's ride to Tagoloan to meet leaders of the strike at the Vicmar logging factory. We first went to the house of Tony, a Community Organiser in the area. There I met Meindert Kik, a Dutchman in his early thirties, who was working among the young adults in the area. On the surface he was teaching them basic radio technology but at a deeper level he seemed more concerned with helping them appreciate a structural analysis of this situation. I noticed that one of the young people there was carrying a rifle so I presumed I was in guerrilla territory.

When we eventually got to the Vicmar logging factory, I discovered that there was an important meeting in session between the strike leaders and the management. The local Minister for Labour was acting as the "impartial" negotiator. Domingo and I stayed outside the factory gates wondering what we should do. Suddenly the two strike leaders (whom I had met two days previously at the Archbishop's House) appeared and they hauled me along to their meeting.

I was seated in the inner negotiating circle and immediately the Minister for Labour started questioning me. Who told me that the meeting was taking place? I played innocent. Where was I staying? Why had I come to the meeting? After a lot of 'playing innocent' answers from me the meeting continued, partly in English and partly in their local language, Visayan. It was most fascinating to watch the process. It was obvious that the Minister of Labour was on the side of management, yet he made a great pretence of impartial negotiation. However, the strike leaders easily saw through him. He kept saying that a basic principle was 'No work, no pay' (I was dying to say that the opposite was equally true 'No pay, no work'). The basic cause of the strike was that the workers (six hundred of them) had not been paid for more than six weeks (they should be paid every fortnight). The management were claiming problems of cash flow and the need for time to get things ratified with Manila. However, the strikers stayed firm on their position. They gave the management three days to produce their pay, otherwise the strike would continue. I was lost in admiration for the strike leaders since they were in open opposition to the law and by their action they were laying themselves open to the possibility of later arrest. We had to leave after about two and a half hours but I had the impression that the strikers would not give up on their claims.

We got back and had lunch with Breda and her young leaders. Then we had a walk around another part of the 'barrio' with a few visits to various families, followed by an informal Mass with her group and a few neighbours. After that Breda and I went back to the Columban Fathers' house and joined them for supper. One of them told us of a horrific incident of bombing in the area recently. In most of these incidents it seems a debatable point whether the grenades are thrown by the local Moslem guerrillas or by the military (in order to keep up a public image of disorder and so justify the continuation of Martial Law).

I went to sleep on my soft (for a change!) bed in my air-conditioned room. However, I was rudely awakened during the night by my door being opened and a torch being shone in my room. I woke up and asked who was there, presuming it is one of the Columban priests. However, the light disappeared so I got up to see what was happening. There was no sign of anyone around so I felt a bit suspicious and woke up the Superior, Fr Charlie Maher. He soon discovered that one of the windows had been opened and it must have been a burglar in the house. Thank God I must have disturbed him before he took anything. Charlie told me the comforting tale that in a similar incident in a nearby house, the burglar shot the person who disturbed him! I'm glad I didn't know that beforehand!

Filipino Diary Entry Three
Kidapawan and Luz Village

We drove for about three miles and then Gles, three of the women and I got out and began the most extraordinary walk I've ever been involved in. As soon as we left the road we were on to narrow reddish-clay footpaths through the fields. That would not have been too bad except for the fact that we had only been walking for about five minutes when the heavens opened and it just poured rain. The deluge continued for the next three hours of our walk, along with periods of very heavy thunder and lightning. It wasn't long before the paths turned into thick, thick mud. The others were in their bare feet but I was still in my shoes and socks and it was very difficult walking. Soon we came to a river which we had to wade through, so I was forced to take off my shoes and continue in my bare feet. I must say it was easier than sliding around in my shoes. So the next two and a half hours was barefoot walking through forests, up and down hills, across rice fields, in and out of rivers, and across bridges which were just a single tree trunk. After a little while I actually began to enjoy it in a strange kind of way. The women had umbrellas, I had an anorak and Gles made his own umbrella out of the huge leaf of a banana tree. Needless to say I managed to slip in the mud twice and got my jeans filthy; then I half fell into one of the rivers!

Eventually we arrived at a little wooden house in a clearing in the woods. It was one of those houses built on stilts with the animals living underneath. However the cooking and the eating were also done underneath in a kind of open space under the house. As I was covered with mud, I had to strip off and have a wash from a tap in the rain tub in the open air. It was getting dark by then but of course they had no electricity so they brought out their own home-made oil-lamps – a little can with a wick sticking out. I think they must have laid on a special meal for me (even though I think my arrival was completely unexpected to them). They produced rice and tinned salmon and some cooked vegetable. After supper some of the neighbours came in (the rain had stopped by this time) and we drank 'tuba' which is juice tapped from the coconut trees and is a kind of wine. Apparently it ferments at a phenomenal rate. They get a good volume of it every day from their trees. Gles acted as interpreter for me, though Bonaventura, the father of the family where I was staying, was able to speak a little English.

These 'barrios' form their own Christian communities and each has its own chapel. They only have Mass a few times a year but every Sunday they gather and have a paraliturgical service which is very similar to the Mass, but without the Consecration. The one from the community who is elected deacon keeps the Blessed Sacrament in his home so that they are able to have Holy Communion at their service each Sunday. Of course, their existence as a basic Christian community goes beyond the level of prayer. They support each other health-wise and farming-wise. The barrio which I was staying in was called Luz village. Apparently, some big family in Manila had tried to drive them off their land in order to turn it into a big rubber plantation but the people had banded together and refused to leave. The police came in to support the Manila family and some of the villagers were killed. However, they refused to give in and they are still fighting their case in the courts. So a basic Christian community is an integrated community.

When it was time for bed we all climbed the outside staircase and it became obvious to me that Bonaventura and his wife had given up the one bed in the house for me. Actually, upstairs there was virtually no furniture – just a table in one room, a couple of benches and one solid wooden bed. I was given the latter with Gles sleeping on the floor beside me.

Tuesday 7 October

Next morning we were given a very substantial breakfast, rice, chicken, salmon and some more 'tuba'. Both last night and this morning we were also given a big glass of hot sweet milk. It was very nourishing. After breakfast I was informed that the local community was holding a special Bible Service to give me some idea of how they ran things. We walked over to the little chapel which they themselves had built. Before we left Bonaventura's house the deacon had come to join us and also the leader of the liturgy. So a little group of about eight of us set off for the chapel. I thought that would be our total number but not a bit of it. En route we called at their little school and all the children joined the procession. Then we passed a little store and everyone there joined us. I felt a bit like the Pied Piper! Eventually we gathered a group of about a hundred – men, women and children. Three of the men officiated at the altar and led the prayers; two of the women did the readings and the homily was shared among all who wanted to join in.

We got a Jeepney back to new Rizal when we eventually reached the highway. There Fr Edwin gave me a breakdown of how they organised things in the different 'barrios' to form their basic communities. Then I was put on a Jeepney bound for Kidapawan. Hardly had we started when the heavens opened up again. All the way along the route children were coming home from school and they were just soaked to the skin. I couldn't help thinking what a hard life these people live. For instance, the Luz villagers have to walk for three hours before they even reach a road. The older children have a two hour walk to high school every day – and during the monsoon period that walk is through muddy fields and often in pouring rain. Yet they are wonderful people and really have time for each other.

After supper I called over to Bishop Escaler to say 'goodbye'. He is a most wonderful man, a Jesuit, very courageous, clear-minded and a deeply spiritual person. Then to bed and I had a really good sleep even though I had been told that the house was infested by very large rats.

CHAPTER THIRTY-NINE

Retirement in Post-Vatican II Theology

This was originally published in Linda Hogan and Barbara Fitzgerald (edits), Between Poetry and Politics (Columba Press, Dublin 2003); a 'Festschrift' to honour the outstanding Irish moral theologian Enda McDonagh. The original article bore the title, 'It's Great to be Alive'. It was also published in The Furrow. The version which follows is abbreviated from the original. In writing the original article I was greatly helped by two recorded talks by Patrick Purnell SJ and Mannes Tidmarsh and by the latter's excellent pamphlet, Vocation to Retirement (Christian Council on Ageing, Occasional Paper No. 6). Above all, I would like to acknowledge that some of the key ideas in this article have been greatly influenced by the thinking of my good friend, the late Austin Smith CP. I had the great honour of editing a collection of his thoughts, mainly on the theme of ageing, Mersey Vespers: Reflections of a Priest and Poet (Kevin Mayhew, Stowmarket, 2010) which was published shortly before his death.

Life after retirement – stagnation or growth?

It is sometimes said that when we retire we can do what we always wanted to do. That is hardly flattering about the way we have exercised our freedom up to this point in life. A good friend of mine, Austin Smith CP, always insisted that all through life he had tried to do what he wanted to do. And he suggested that is true of most people. A mother sitting by the hospital bedside of her desperately ill child is doing what she wants to do. At that moment, in that particular situation, there is nowhere else she would want to be. Admittedly, when her daughter is back home and better again, that hospital bedside is the last place that mother would want to be. Loving exposes us to a lot of pain and makes us very vulnerable. Yet loving is what we have chosen to do. In that context, disengagement for more radical engagement suggests that we become more focused in our loving. Perhaps, in that sense, it might be true to say that retirement offers us the opportunity to do what we have always wanted to do. Our changed circumstances, though they may be more limiting in some respects, enable us to concentrate on what we regard as the most important priorities in our lives. That is why retirement can be a very enriching time of life. We do not retire from life; we retire deeper into life. In fact, Austin Smith used to describe retirement as 'disengaging to re-engage'. In other words, it is a process of disengagement for more radical engagement, a time for refining one's priorities.

A lot of things change in the life of a person who retires. Though some of these changes may be very welcome, at least in the early years of retirement, others will be experienced as losses which touch a person quite deeply. For

instance, many losses are linked in some way or other with leaving one's normal occupation, whether this be the workplace, school, hospital, university or
even parish. A loss of personal self-esteem and even identity may be felt when
one leaves a position where one's competence is recognised and most of one's
social contacts are located and which has provided the basis for one's financial
security. One may even feel the loss of an ordered structure to one's daily life
when one loses the discipline of a daily timetable and the creative stress born
of the expectations of others.

If retirement is to be a time of personal growth, it is essential that these losses
be acknowledged, properly grieved over and in this way laid peacefully to rest.
Where these losses leave some important human needs unfulfilled, as far as
possible they need to be compensated for. Denial that there are any losses involved could be a recipe for disaster.

Christians are familiar with the gospel image of the seed falling in the
ground and dying so that new life and growth can emerge. Maybe that image
can throw light on the process of retirement. Disengaging to re-engage involves
a reordering of priorities. No longer are we tempted to dance to the tune of the
expectations of others. We can look more deeply into the meaning of life and
thus focus on the things we see to be most important. In a sense, retirement can
spark off a further stage of growth in our more authentic self. In a society which
bases personal worth on such indices as economic achievement and capacity
as a consumer, facing up to retirement can help us to be more aware that we
are more than what we do and what we own. Our self-identity goes much
deeper than our activity and our possessions.

Many retired people say how much they appreciate the freedom of their
new situation in life. Maybe that is a sign they have past beyond the grief of
their loss of work and all that entails and laid it peacefully to rest. However,
greater freedom is about more than having ample free time and the ability to
set one's own agenda. It is not just about freedom from external constraints. It
offers the opportunity for a deeper level of freedom, a freedom for the more
important things in life. This can take various forms. For some it may leave
them free for prophetic risk-taking. Seeing more to the heart of things, they can
challenge laws, procedures and rituals which have lost or come adrift from
their meaning. In that sense, retired people can be powerful advocates for
change. They have a sufficiently rich treasury of memories to avoid being imprisoned by the rigidities of a past which has forgotten its roots in a changing
history. Like the ageing Simeon and Anna, they can interpret the past as a
seedbed of hope and promise. So they are able to read the signs of the times
and believe in a future which is in God's gift but in which God has called us to
share as his artisans in building.

The Jesuit, Patrick Purnell, prefers the expression, 'Sabbath People', to the
more politically correct 'Senior Citizens'. He is not suggesting that retirement

is a time for rest, in the sense of sitting back and doing nothing. Although the Bible pronounces the Sabbath holy precisely because God rested on that day, God's rest was not a long lie-in but consisted of enjoying the goodness and beauty of his creation. Our consumer culture is a restless culture. Advertisers are so busy trying to create new 'wants' with which to whet our appetites for the latest gadgets or computers, people have little time or inclination to sit back and simply enjoy the wonder, beauty and simplicity of life.

Another expression for the retired is 'Ulysses People'. This highlights another essential ingredient of a happy retirement, namely, to continue our life-long voyage of discovery by having a searching mind and heart. People also stress the importance of the mind-body interaction and insist that a healthy lifestyle with exercise appropriate to one's age holds the key to maintaining mental alertness throughout the ageing process. Maybe, unconsciously the 'Ulysses People' name had a bearing on why I included the theme of 'Odyssey' in the title of this book!

As human persons we are essentially social beings. Eugene C. Bianchi, in his article, 'Living with Elder Wisdom', in the April 1996 special issue of *The Way* on ageing (pp. 93-102), writes that 'creative elders oppose the ageing stereotype of withdrawal from social involvements' and quotes some inspiring examples, including one lady who insisted, 'My aches and pains are less important than my agenda' (p. 98). All stress that inspiring social contacts and strong social support groups come high on the agenda for making retirement a continuing growth experience. For some, these groups will offer motivational inspiration and help people to maintain their social commitments. For others, they can help to compensate for the loss of former friends. New friendships can also offer a further stimulus for personal growth in retirement. A retired person's increasing dependence on others can in some cases result in the blossoming of new and very profound friendships.

Retiring 'Grace-fully': Towards a Spirituality of Retirement

I am always a little suspicious of spirituality language. I well remember being at a meeting with Enda McDonagh in which someone remarked that the key to spirituality lay in discovering one's inner self. Enda commented: 'When I look within myself, I can never find any inner self. All I can find is a cluster of relationships.'

Made in the image of a Trinitarian God, we are essentially relational beings. If spiritual growth has any meaning, it must be about growth in the way we live out the truth of all the relationships, human and divine, which lie at the core of our being human persons. That growth needs to continue all through life, including the years of retirement. A whole variety of factors specific to the retirement and ageing process will affect the way we grow during these years. In that sense it is possible to speak in terms of a spirituality of retirement.

However, what we are ultimately talking about is how we grow as human persons during the retirement process.

Retirement can be a time for contemplation, looking at life with eyes of wonder and enjoying its goodness. In a sense, prayer and contemplation are retirement activities. In fact, it could even be argued that retirement offers a very privileged opportunity for experiencing in an even deeper way the mind-blowing truth that we are made in the image of God. It can give us the opportunity to grow as Sabbath People, that is, people who are thankful for the giftedness of life and for the gift of other people – and ourselves. Appreciation of such giftedness lies at the heart of contemplative prayer. All is sheer gift and God is all-giving. Human growth in the period of retirement will often take the form of a deepening of prayer-life into contemplative prayer, though it will probably not be recognised as such. The contemplative prayer-life of some may be gleaned in the way they talk about the great pleasure they get from gardening and how it brings them closer to nature. For others who take up painting or poetry in retirement, it might be seen in the way these creative activities take them out of themselves. For others who are grandparents, their experience of contemplative prayer might be found in the wonder of the gift of their grandchildren and the love they awaken in their grandparents. For others it might be in the way they experience a deeper dimension of life on a long walk, or whilst listening to a piece of music, or reading a good book. Contemplative prayer enables people to see beneath the surface of life.

And it is not only the beauty and wonder of life that they face; they become more aware of the suffering and tragedy that seems so much a part of life. This 'God's-eye view' can make them more tolerant of situations of ambiguity. Similarly, seeing beneath the surface of life can help people to appreciate the goodness of diversity, whether in cultures, or lifestyle, or even in religions. This can even lead to a change in their image of God or the divine. A God of laws and institutions can give way to a more compassionate God whose being is shrouded in mystery rather than enunciated in the precision in dogmatic formulae.

Although initially retirement usually offers a person greater independence, factors such as diminishing strength, mobility, eyesight and hearing along with the greater likelihood of sickness and hospitalisation may eventually increase the level of a retired person's dependence on others. Active acceptance of dependence need not be seen as giving up the ghost or entering into a period of second childhood. Active acceptance of dependence can be a very important human characteristic, provided it is then matched by the dependability of those on whom one is depending. Throughout the whole of our lives, we live in a state of interdependence with each other. That is why dependability (reliability, faithfulness) is such a central Christian virtue. God is the utterly dependable one, the faithful one. A powerfully moving expression of this comes from Pedro Arrupe, the former General of the Jesuits. Towards the end of his life, when severely disabled by a stroke and hardly able to speak, he said in a message to his brother Jesuits:

> More than ever, I now find myself in the hands of God. This is what I have wanted all my life, from my youth. And this is still the one thing I want. But now there is a difference: the initiative is entirely with God. It is indeed a profound spiritual experience to know and feel myself so totally in his hands (*Documents of the 33rd General Congregation of the Society of Jesus*, St Louis; Institute of Jesuit Sources, 1984, p. 93).

Mary Elizabeth Kenel, in her article, 'Preparing for Retirement, in Human Development' (Vol. 23, Summer 2002, pp. 13-18) draws attention to this phenomenon:

> encouraging others to demonstrate an appropriate level of care toward us and to do so in such a way that the very act of accepting care is in itself an act of caring. Caring behaviour does not denote a one-sided dependency. Instead, it is a complex interchange that defines an enduring relationship between persons. Accepting care and resources from another does not transform the recipient into a needy, passive burden. As we prepare to enter the retirement phase of life, let us ask ourselves whom we allow to grace us with the gift of caring (p. 17).

Retirement and Theology

Is there a theology of retirement? That is a question I was tempted to explore in this article – and it is certainly worth looking at. However, the more I got in touch with the real-life experience of retirement, whether through conversation or reading or personal reflection, the more I came to see that it would be much more interesting to explore retirement as a source of theology. To be even more specific, I began to suspect that, for many theologians, embarking on the process of retirement seems to have had a significant impact on their theology. It is almost as though experiencing the human process of retirement is itself a theological source. Maybe this should not be surprising. After all, if theology is more an activity ('theologising') than a finished product (e.g. books or an article), then it is only natural that a major human experience such as the retirement process should strongly influence a theologian in his or her doing theology. In these days when the subject tends to be seen as centre-stage, that is only to be expected.

'Retirement theology', if I may coin a phrase to describe this phenomenon, is likely to reflect a number of those features which we have seen to be associated with the retirement process itself. I would suggest that 'retirement theology' might exhibit some of the following characteristics:

- more focused – in line with 'disengaging to re-engage', it is likely to be a theology which is not interested in peripheral matters and goes straight to the fundamental issues to be faced;
- a greater sense of the preciousness of time ('*kairos*') – a theology which is not afraid to recognize the need for change in life as part of the on-going process of liberation from oppression; and so a theology with a definite sense of urgency, prepared to seize the present opportunity;
- more experience-based – a theology with a greater awareness of and trust in the action of God's spirit in the lives of people;
- more pastoral – a theology which is deeply concerned about the pastoral dimensions of theological issues, acknowledging that, in the final analysis, theology is not about abstractions but about living relationships, human and divine;
- ready to take risks – a theology which is prepared to think creatively and imaginatively, rather than be held back by an over-cautious fear of possible consequences – and so a theology with a greater faith in the future;
- more tolerant of diversity – a theology nourished by a long and rich experience of life, and so one which is more open to the positive salvific role of other faiths and more likely to emphasise that our primary encounter with God lies in the reality of everyday life rather than in liturgy;
- more open to ambiguity – a theology which is prepared to start from where people are and which is more aware of the growth process in life, with all its ups and downs, light and shade; so a theology more prepared to accept 'en-route pastoral solutions' despite their being tinged by compromise and ambiguity;
- more contemplative – a theology which goes below the surface of things and interprets life in a deeper context; hence, a theology which accepts the giftedness of reality as something to be responded to in terms of Gospel values rather than legal and administrative technicalities;
- sabbatical – a Sabbath theology linked to the contemplative dimension of retirement; a theology flowing from the experience of wonder before the incomprehensibility of God and our own sheer 'giftedness' as creatures; the very activity of theologizing itself being our sharing in the divine activity of 'seeing that it is good' and thus at the heart of our being made in the image of God;
- a more humble theology – one which recognises that ultimately we are in the hands of God and that, in its fullness, God's Kingdom is a pure gift of God and not some human making.

Conclusion

The retirement activity of disengagement for re-engagement in a more focused way sounds rather like a description of the process of conversion and renewal. If that is so, perhaps retirement is not just a passing phenomenon in the Church due to the increasing numbers of ageing priests and religious. Maybe the life-giving potential inherent in the retirement process is actually a sign of the times for the Church in our day. It could be that God's spirit is calling the Church into a new phase of its continued growth rather akin to the retirement process. Perhaps there has to be a lot of letting go in the Church in all sorts of ways, especially as regards power and structures and even traditional styles of liturgy and Church-life. If this is true, such losses will need to be named and owned and even grieved over, if we are to let go of them in a life-giving way.

CHAPTER FORTY

Are we ready for Vatican III?

The question, 'Are we ready for Vatican III?' provides food for thought. Is the Church today open to the inspiration of the Holy Spirit in the way the bishops at Vatican II were? The bishops at Vatican II were open to the Spirit speaking to them from outside the Episcopal and Papal Magisterium. They listened very attentively – and humbly – to the expertise and experience of the many Spirit-inspired theologians they had invited as their *'periti'* to join them at the Council. They also listened, especially many of the Latin American bishops, to the experience of the marginalised who were struggling to live the Gospel in situations of desperate injustice, poverty and oppression. In other words, they listened to the 'cry of the poor' mediated through the rich vein of liberation theology. Would such listening take place if a Vatican III was to take place in the Church as it stands at present? Only the Holy Spirit can answer that question. Maybe the presence of laypeople, especially women, would help along the process, provided they are elected by their own constituencies, rather than by the Vatican.

Perhaps the inspired words of Ladislas Orsy, which I quoted in the Introduction to this book, point the way forward. He drew our attention to the resounding cry *'Adsumus'* ('We are present and attentive to the Spirit') of the Vatican II Bishops at the beginning of each day's deliberations during the four years of Vatican II. And he ended with the following proposal:

> Whereas the years from 2012 through 2015 will be the fiftieth anniversaries of the Council, they should be solemnly declared the years of the Council – when the entire people, 'from the bishops to the last of the faithful' (LG, 2, quoting St Augustine), recalls the memory of the 'Sacred Council', studies its determinations, and exposes itself to the transforming light and force of the Spirit – as the Council Fathers did. Over four years again, let the cry *Adsumus*, 'we are present and attentive', resound – not within the walls of St Peter's Basilica but throughout the face of the earth. The Spirit of God will not fail to respond (p. 152).

Maybe the only way we can move towards being 'ready for Vatican III' is by receiving in all its fullness the tremendous gift which God's Spirit has given us in Vatican II. How can we start talking about Vatican III when we still have so much to receive from Vatican II? Rather than distract ourselves by talking about Vatican III, we would do better to devote ourselves whole-heartedly to receiving Vatican II.

Index